Education, Culture and Values

Volume VI

The six volumes that comprise the *Education, Culture and Values* series bring together contributions from experts around the world to form, for the first time, a comprehensive treatment of the current concern with values in education. The series seeks to address this concern in the context of cultural and values diversity.

The first three volumes provide a wide-ranging consideration of the diversity of values in education at all levels, and thus represent a framework for the second three volumes which focus more specifically on values education (moral, religious, spiritual and political) *per se*. The six volumes, therefore, bring the fundamental domain of values together with the important issue of pluralism to generate new, fruitful and progressive reflection and exemplars of good practice.

The series will be of huge benefit and interest to educators, policy makers, parents, academics, researchers and student teachers. The six volumes contain:

- diverse and challenging opinions about current educational concerns and reforms in values education
- chapters from more than 120 contributors of international repute from 23 different countries
- conceptual clarification and theoretical analysis
- empirical studies, reports of practical projects and guidance for good practice.

Volumes I–III: Values Diversity in Education

Volume I – Systems of Education: Theories, Policies and Implicit Values is concerned with the theoretical and conceptual framework for reflecting about values, culture and education and thus provides an introduction to the series as a whole. It is concerned with state and policy level analysis across the world.

Volume II – Institutional Issues: Pupils, Schools and Teacher Education considers values and culture at the institutional level. What constitutes a good 'whole school' approach in a particular area? There are discussions of key issues and reports of whole-school initiatives from around the world. Several chapters focus on the vital issue of teacher education.

Volume III – Classroom Issues: Practice, Pedagogy and Curriculum focuses on the classroom: pedagogy, curriculum and pupil experience. Areas of curriculum development include the relatively neglected domains of mathematics and technology, as well as the more familiar literature and drama. There is a useful section on aesthetic education.

Volumes IV–VI: Values Education in Diversity

Volume IV – Moral Education and Pluralism is focused on moral education and development in the context of cultural pluralism. There are highly theoretical discussions of difficult philosophical issues about moral relativism as well as practical ideas about good practice.

Volume V – Spiritual and Religious Education distinguishes religious and spiritual education and takes a multifaith approach to pedagogic, curricular and resource issues. The important issue of collective worship is also addressed.

Volume VI – Politics, Education and Citizenship is concerned with political education and citizenship. Again chapters from several countries lend an international perspective to currently influential concerns and developments, including democratic education, human rights, national identity and education for citizenship.

Education, Culture and Values

Volume VI

Politics, Education and Citizenship

Edited by
Mal Leicester, Celia Modgil
and Sohan Modgil

FALMER PRESS
Taylor & Francis Group

London and New York

First published 2000 by Falmer Press
11 New Fetter Lane, London EC4P 4EE

Simultaneously published in the USA and Canada
by Falmer Press, 19 Union Square West, New York, NY 10003

Falmer Press is an imprint of the Taylor & Francis Group

© 2000 Selection and editorial material, Mal Leicester, Celia
Modgil, Sohan Modgil; individual chapters, the contributors

Typeset in Galliard by RefineCatch Limited, Bungay, Suffolk
Printed and bound in Great Britain by
TJ International Ltd, Padstow, Cornwall

British Library Cataloguing in Publication Data
A catalogue record for this book is available from the British
Library

Library of Congress Cataloging in Publication Data
A catalog record for this book has been requested

ISBN 0–7507–1018–7 (6-volume set)
      0–7507–1002–0 (volume I)
      0–7507–1003–9 (volume II)
      0–7507–1004–7 (volume III)
      0–7507–1005–5 (volume IV)
      0–7507–1006–3 (volume V)
      0–7507–1007–1 (volume VI)

Contents

Contributors

Helena Araújo Associate Professor of the Faculdade de Psicologia e de Ciências da Educação, Universidade, de Porto Portugal

Madeleine Arnot University Lecturer in Education, School of Education, University of Cambridge, UK

David Aspin Professor of Philosophy of Education, Monash University, Australia

María Julia Bertomeu Professor of Ethics at Universidad Nacional de La Plata, Argentina and co-editor of the journal *Revista Latinoamericana de Filosofía*, Buenos Aires, Argentina

Donald Biggs Professor of Education and Director of Urban Education, University at Albany, Albany, New York, USA

Bruce Carrington Professor of Education, Department of Education, University of Newcastle-on-Tyne, UK

Judith Chapman Professor and Dean of the Faculty of Education, Australian Catholic University, Australia

Robert Colesante Assistant Professor of Education, Seina College, Loudonville, New York, USA

María Victoria Costa Assistant Professor of Philosophy at Universidad Nacional de La Plata, Argentina

Patrick J. M. Costello Reader in Education and Director of the Centre for Applied Educational Research at the North East Wales Institute of Higher Education, Wrexham, UK

Dov Darom The late Dov Darom was formerly Senior Lecturer in Education, Oranim, School of Education of The Kibbutz Movement, Haifa University, Israel

Ian Davies Senior Lecturer, Department of Educational Studies, University of York, UK

Kiki Deliyanni-Kouimtzis Associate Professor, Department of Psychology, Aristotle University of Thessaloniki, Greece

Janet Edwards Deputy Director of The Centre for Citizenship Studies in Education, University of Leicester, UK

Penny Enslin Professor of Education, Department of Education, University of the Witwatersrand, South Africa

Karen Evans Professor of Post-Compulsory Education, School of Educational Studies, University of Surrey, UK

Ken Fogelman Professor of Education and Director of The Centre for Citizenship Studies in Education, University of Leicester, UK

Gary Hook On the staff of New York State Office of Children and Family Services, Albany, New York, USA

Gabrielle Ivinson Research Fellow in the School of Education at the Open University, UK

Mal Leicester Senior Lecturer in Continuing Education, Warwick University, UK

Simon Lichman Director of the Traditional Creativity in Schools Project in Jerusalem, Israel

Tom Lovett Emeritus Professor of Adult

Education, University of Ulster, Jordanstown, Northern Ireland

Celia Modgil Senior Lecturer in Education, Goldsmiths College, London University, UK

Sohan Modgil Reader in Educational Research and Development, University of Brighton, UK

Fernand Ouellet Full Professor, Faculty of Theology, Ethics and Philosophy, University of Sherbrooke, Canada

Leonard A. Parkyn Head of "Cherry Trees", Further Education Centre, Brighton and Hove, UK

Don Rowe Director of Curriculum Resources, The Citizenship Foundation, London, UK

Linda Seger International lecturer in the field of screenwriting, a script consultant and author of six books on screenwriting and film-making

Geoffrey Short Reader in Educational Research, School of Humanities and Education, University of Hertfordshire, UK

Joshua Smith On the staff of The Office of the

Advisement Services Center, University at Albany, Albany, New York, USA

Ben Spiecker Professor of Education, Department of Education, Free University, Amsterdam, The Netherlands

Jan Steutel Professor of Education, Department of Education, Free University, Amsterdam, The Netherlands

Keith Sullivan Director of Postgraduate Studies and a Senior Lecturer in Education at Victoria University of Wellington, New Zealand

Marsha L. Thicksten Assistant Professor, School of Education, Chapman University, California, USA

Amparo Tomé University Lecturer and Research Coordinator in the Institut de Ciencias de L'Educacio, Universitat Autonoma de Barcelona, Spain

Tom C. Wilson Associate Professor in Education, School of Education, Chapman University, California, USA

Editors' Foreword

This is one volume in a series of six, each concerned with education, culture and values. Educators have long recognized that 'education' is necessarily value laden and, therefore, that value issues are inescapable and fundamental, both in our conceptions of education and in our practice of it. These issues are particularly complex in the context of cultural pluralism. In a sense the collection is a recognition, writ large, of this complexity and of our belief that since values are necessarily part of education, we should be explicit about what they are, and about why we choose those we do and who the 'we' is in relation to the particular conception and practices in question.

The first three volumes in the series deal with values diversity in education – the broader issues of what values ought to inform education in and for a plural society. The second three focus more narrowly on values education as such – what is the nature and scope of moral education, of religious and political education and of political and citizenship education in and for such a society? Thus collectively they consider both **values diversity in education** and **values education in diversity**. Individually they each have a particular level. Thus volumes 1–3 cover the levels of system, institution and classroom. Volumes 4–6 focus respectively on moral education, religious and spiritual education, politics and citizenship education. This structure is intended to ensure that the six volumes in the series are individually discrete but complementary.

Given the complexity of the value domain and the sheer diversity of values in culturally plural societies it becomes clear why 120 chapters from 23 countries merely begin to address the wealth of issues relating to 'Education, Culture and Values'.

Mal Leicester, Celia Modgil
and Sohan Modgil

Part One

Politics and Education

1 Holocaust Education and Citizenship: A View from the United Kingdom

GEOFFREY SHORT

Introduction

The Holocaust has been taught as part of the National Curriculum in England and Wales since 1990. It was introduced as a component of Key Stage 4, but following a decision by the Secretary of State in 1993 to make history an option for this age group, rather than a requirement, it became a part of Key Stage 3. A recent survey indicates that the subject is now most likely to be taught at the end of Year 9 to students aged between 13 and 15 (Short 1995).

The Holocaust's inclusion in the curriculum can be justified on two counts, the first revolving around what it means to be educated. As one of the watershed events of the twentieth century, the Holocaust not only enables us to construe earlier events in a different light, but helps to shape our perception of seminal developments in our own time. Its value lies in transforming the way we see the world, and in this sense its study can be viewed as educationally worthwhile (Peters 1966). But on such grounds alone, the Holocaust, despite its cataclysmic quality, has no more claim to space on the curriculum than has any other historical landmark. To press such a claim, it is necessary to consider a second justification, one that focuses on the unique contribution that a knowledge of the Holocaust can make to citizenship education. According to Ronnie Landau (1989: 20), if the attempted annihilation of European Jewry is taught properly, it 'can civilise and humanise our students and, perhaps more effectively than any other subject, has the power to sensitise them to the dangers of indifference, intolerance, racism and the dehumanisation of others.' Similar sentiments have been expressed by others, most notably perhaps by Auschwitz survivor and Nobel Laureate, Primo Levi. In *If This is a Man/The Truce*, Levi wrote: 'We cannot understand [the Holocaust] but we can and must understand from where it springs and we must be on our guard. If understanding is impossible, knowing is imperative, because what happened could happen again' (Levi 1987: 396).

The Holocaust's potential as a vehicle for teaching about citizenship deserves serious consideration at the present time, not least because of mounting criticism in England and Wales over the role played by citizenship education within the National Curriculum. Introduced in 1990 as one of the five cross-curricular themes, it was intended to permeate each of the core and foundation subjects of the curriculum, but research has cast doubt on the extent to which this has happened. Certainly at secondary level, citizenship appears to be widely ignored, with just one school in four having a written policy by 1992 (Witty et al. 1992). A low take-up rate, however, is only part of the problem, for disquiet has also been voiced over the content of the guidance given to schools. For example, Helen Haste has recently condemned the entire citizenship programme as supportive of the status quo (*Times Educational Supplement*, 12 July 1996) and in a similar vein, Wilf Carr (1991) has described it as 'depoliticized'. According to the document *Education for Citizenship* (National Curriculum Council [NCC] 1990), issues that might be broached under the rubric of 'A Pluralist Society' include the following:

1 Britain as a multi-cultural, multi-ethnic, multi-faith and multi-lingual society
2 the diversity of cultures in other societies
3 the origins and effects of racial prejudice within British and other societies
4 a study of history and culture from different perspectives.

Additional topics, clearly germane to promoting a pluralist society, are to be found elsewhere in the document. For instance, in the section entitled 'Being a Citizen' it is suggested that students might learn about different kinds of rights and how these can be exercised, protected, and in some cases threatened (p. 7).

These recommendations appear to have divided the anti-racist community. While some (e.g. Taylor 1992) have seen them as unexceptionable, even worthy, others, such as Gillborn (1995), have derided them as 'narrow and assimilationist'. He writes that:

> Prejudice and discrimination are defined in terms of a reaction to *difference* while racism, as a persistent feature that reflects and recreates the unequal distribution of *power* in society, is conspicuously absent. Despite its liberal facade, therefore, the guidance on citizenship is at best weak and superficial, at worst, a recipe for new racist analyses of cultural difference that place the 'blame' for racism on the alien 'newcomers'. (Gillborn 1995: 136) [Original emphasis]

While I share Gillborn's concern at the omission of any reference to racial equality, I reject his pessimism at the prospect of schools doing useful work in the area of prejudice and discrimination. It seems to me that students could well benefit from an 'awareness of . . . some of the tensions and conflicts that occur between groups which perceive each other to be socially, racially, ethnically or culturally different' (NCC 1990: 6). Indeed, I have argued elsewhere that an analysis of cultural differences, especially one that involves probing children's misconceptions, is an essential prerequisite of effective anti-racist education (Short 1994, Short and Carrington 1996). In this respect there is undoubtedly scope within *Education for Citizenship* for useful initiatives. However, it should not be thought that I am uncritical of the NCC's proposals. On the contrary, in my view they allow individual teachers too much latitude to establish and indulge their own priorities. There are particular areas of knowledge and understanding that I believe have to be addressed directly if we are to secure the future against further violations of human rights on grounds of 'race', religion or ethnicity. Such teaching ought not to be left to chance. Students should know that racism can lead to mass murder; that any ethnic group, if relatively powerless, is potentially at risk and that socio-economic or psychological trauma can transform an undercurrent of racism into state-sponsored genocide. They should also know that racism cannot be circumscribed either geographically or historically. Teachers should apprise their students of critical concepts such as stereotyping and scapegoating; discuss with them the complicity of bystanders and have them rethink their definition of heroism so as to embrace acts of non-conformity regardless of personal cost. Finally, I would urge teachers to encourage their students to reflect upon some of the imperfections of democracy and to consider in particular whether constraints of any kind need to be placed on freedom of speech.

Each of these issues is either integral to the Holocaust or can be broached in ways that are in no sense contrived. The subject also lends itself to developing in students a global perspective in respect of human rights, reinforcing, in this case, one of the crucial dimensions of citizenship that is referred to directly by the NCC. But while an expanded knowledge of racism may be a necessary condition of active citizenship, it is clearly not sufficient. Students must address ways of combating it and to this end it may prove beneficial to raise with them matters such as the deterrent value of punishment for war crimes committed long ago. Discussions of this kind are a natural accompaniment to lessons on the Holocaust. Moreover, recent research suggests that 'the real key to political consciousness and a sense of civic place, is informed but informal discussion with . . . teachers' (see *Times Educational Supplement*, 7 June 1996).

While there can be little doubt that citizenship education in the United Kingdom is in need of urgent reform, it should not be thought that teaching the Holocaust will prove a panacea. It is not known what, if anything, students learn about citizenship in general, and racism in particular, when they engage with the Holocaust as history. More important, it is not known what aspects of their learning they retain over the longer term. It was in order to find out that I undertook the small-scale investigation that forms the empirical core of this chapter.

The research

The sample

The sample was an opportunist one comprising forty-three mixed ability Year 10 students aged between 14 and 16. All were volunteers and came from six randomly selected maintained secondary schools in South East England. There were twenty-two female students and twenty-one male with just over half belonging to 'visible' minorities. The latter included seventeen South Asians and two Afro-Caribbeans. All the students had studied the Holocaust about a year before participating in the research and had opted to take history at GCSE level.

Procedure

Semi-structured interviews were conducted on an individual basis. Each student was presented with a series of set questions that explored the following four areas of knowledge and understanding.

1 Knowledge of the Holocaust
- Tell me what you know about the Holocaust? Were Jews the only group singled out by the Nazis for persecution?[1]
- Why did it happen?
- Could it have been prevented?
- Why was the rest of the world reluctant to take Jewish refugees in large numbers from Germany?
- In respect of the Holocaust, are there any heroes?

2 Preventing a repetition
- Should racist political parties be allowed to stand in general elections?
- Should people of your age learn about the Holocaust? People everywhere or just in those countries directly affected?

3 Racism and the Holocaust: making connections
- What is a racial stereotype? What was the Nazi stereotype of the Jew?
- What is a scapegoat? Who were the scapegoats in Nazi Germany? What were they blamed for?
- What does the Holocaust teach us about racism?
- Could there be a Holocaust (not necessarily of Jews) in England? If 'yes', what would have to happen to bring it about? If 'no', why not?

4 Personal impact of learning about the Holocaust
- Has studying the Holocaust changed you in any way? If so, how?

- What has the Holocaust taught you about being a good citizen?
- What does the Holocaust teach us generally – about life and about people?

Students were informed that they did not have to answer any question they did not wish to and were free to terminate the interview at any time of their choosing. In the event, there were no refusals. However, due to lapses of concentration on the part of the interviewer, some questions were occasionally overlooked.

The findings

1 Knowledge of the Holocaust

The students were initially invited to say what they knew about the Holocaust. The open-ended nature of the request was deliberate, for while the intention was partly to give the participants confidence in their ability to answer the follow-up questions, it also functioned as a means of checking the accuracy of their knowledge.

From the standpoint of accuracy, the most striking aspect of the comments (either made spontaneously or in response to a subsidiary question) was the variation in the number of victims. While the majority (18 out of 29) answered correctly, giving a figure in the region of six million, others were very wide of the mark ranging in their estimates from 'a thousand' and 'six to ten thousand' at one extreme through to 'thirty million', 'forty million' and even 'hundreds of millions' at the other. One student was not sure whether it was 'six million or six thousand'; another did not know whether it was two or twenty million and a third was not prepared to venture a guess. The very low estimates are particularly troubling, for if one of our priorities in teaching the Holocaust is to demonstrate where racism can lead, we must ensure that we do not inadvertently reinforce the credibility of those like Jean-Marie Le Pen (leader of the Front Nationale in France) who attempt to trivialize the Holocaust by referring to it as 'a footnote in history'.

Next the students were asked if Jews were the only group persecuted by the Nazis. The question was posed because of the opportunity the Holocaust provides to deepen young people's knowledge of racism and, specifically, to make them aware that racism does not necessarily have the same targets or the same rationale as is presently the case in the United Kingdom. The responses (given by 37 students) are detailed in Table 1.1.

Table 1.1   Did the Nazis persecute groups other than Jews?

Group	Number of References
Yes	
Blacks	11
Non-Aryans	9
Gypsies	7
Disabled	7
Communists	7
Non-Germans	5
Homosexuals	3
Other religions	3
Arabs/Muslims	2
Slavs	2
Russians	2
Mentally ill	2
Other	2
No	
Just Jews	4
Don't know	1

In view of the reason behind the question, it is disturbing to note so few references to either Gypsies or Slavs. Moreover, four students thought that Jews were the only victims and one was unable to answer. Although a matter of concern, this finding is not altogether surprising, for the majority of textbooks currently in use in schools tend to dismiss the Nazis' non-Jewish victims in no more than a sentence or two (Supple 1992, Short 1995).

As pointed out, one of the things it is important to teach adolescents in the UK about racism is that it affects minorities other than those of African or South Asian origin. In this context, we ought not to gloss over the large number of references to 'blacks' in response to the question. It is, of course, quite true that the Nazis regarded Africans as lower down on the evolutionary scale than Aryans, and this fact should be made known to students, but in no sense can the Nazi treatment of Africans, or those of African descent, be compared with their treatment of Jews or Gypsies.

Table 1.2 shows the responses (of the entire sample) to the question, 'Why did the Holocaust happen?'

Arguably one of the most important things that needs to be learnt about racism of any kind is that it is historically embedded. It is not, as implied by a

Table 1.2   Why did the Holocaust happen?

Reason	Number of References
Hitler wanted an Aryan race/believed Jews were an inferior race	12
Envy (of Jewish success)	10
Jews responsible for Germany losing the war	9
Not sure/don't know	9
Hitler was intolerant of difference	5
Hitler disliked Judaism	3
Jews responsible for economic problems	2
Jew were of different appearance/dark skinned	2
Other	11
(*e.g. The Germans wanted to make their land just their land.* *Hitler thought the Jews would be a threat to him.*)	

number of responses to the question, a natural by-product of envy; nor is it an automatic accompaniment to crisis in the domestic economy or to defeat on the battlefield. And it is not something either that can be summoned up at will in support of the genocidal fantasies of a deranged tyrant. The students reacted with a serious lack of historical consciousness in failing to realize the significance of the rich vein of anti-Semitism that has coursed through European culture for centuries. None of them, for example, mentioned the role of the Church in fomenting a psychological climate that would help to ignite and nourish an anti-Semitic campaign. Such failings are consistent with the survey of teachers' attitudes and practices referred to earlier. For what emerged from that survey was that more than half the teachers questioned 'either made no reference to the historical background (when dealing with anti-Semitism) or covered it quite inadequately' (Short, op. cit.: 177).

I recognize that there is no simple or straightforward answer to the question of why the Holocaust happened. Even so, I was concerned that so few students alluded to either the economic depression or the twin psychological blows of Germany losing the war and having to endure the humiliation of Versailles. The basis of my concern is that an essential element of citizenship education must be an understanding of the threat posed to democratic pluralist societies by industrial collapse and the puncturing of national pride. The following 'explanations' of the Holocaust show how, in many cases, this understanding was lacking.

The Nazis didn't like the Jews because of their religion, their appearance – they weren't Aryan – and because they didn't have a homeland.

Because Hitler thought that the Germans were the only pure race so he wanted to get rid of all the others.
Any other reason?
No

Hitler wanted to start the master race – blond-haired blue-eyed intelligent people. He felt that Jews, Gypsies and the mentally ill were inferior. He just wanted to eliminate them from the human race.

Hitler wanted Germany to be the best and he wanted to get rid of anybody who would get in his way. That included people with disabilities, but mainly the Jews.

These comments also reflect the universal view among the students that Hitler and the Nazis were in a critical sense acting alone. None of the respondents showed an awareness that Nazi ideology appealed to a diverse range of interest groups within Germany, all of whom supported Hitler in his quest for power. In areas such as commerce and the professions, there were obvious benefits to be derived from eliminating Jewish competition, an important point to get across to adolescents in the UK in view of the success achieved in precisely these spheres by sections of the country's minority population.

The next question, 'Could the Holocaust have been prevented?' was included for two main reasons. The first was to test the students' awareness of sources of opposition to government policy – both internal and external. The second was to probe their thinking about potential abuses of democracy, particularly in respect of freedom of speech. This question was addressed to the entire sample and it can be seen (in Table 1.3) that over a third referred to the role of other nations. One student spoke about refugee policy between 1933 and 1941; the rest had in mind military action by the Allies. The actual feasibility of rescue, once the war had begun, is an issue that has divided historians – see, for example, the debate between Lucy Dawidowicz (1992) and David Wyman (1984) – but from the standpoint of education for citizenship, cognizance of the issue serves a valuable purpose. It indicates that students' attention has been drawn to the consequences, in terms of human rights abuses,

Table 1.3   Could the Holocaust have been prevented?

Verdict	Number of References
Yes if:	
Other countries had acted	15
The Germans had not voted Hitler into power	8
The country had not been in such a bad economic/psychological state	4
People in Germany and outside had known what was going on	3
The Jews had fought back	1
The Catholic Church had intervened	1
No because:	
Hitler had a lot of power	4
No reason given	2
Jews powerless to fight back	1
Hitler was mad/determined	1
Other	5

that may flow from adopting a parochial attitude to what goes on beyond one's own national borders. With its advice that teachers examine with their pupils 'the major conventions on human rights', the NCC implicitly recognizes that the notion of responsible citizenship must embrace global as well as local concerns.

Only eight students acknowledged that the Holocaust could have been prevented had the German people not voted for the Nazi party. Perhaps others considered this point too obvious to make. It is, however, essential that students appreciate the dangers as well as the virtues immanent in democratic government. In particular, they must be made aware of the prospect of a badly-educated electorate falling prey to seductive but spurious demagoguery. This was recognized by a few students who noted that the German public was manipulated and rendered incapable of thinking for itself. One girl, for example, said 'They were brainwashed basically and their support was the only way it happened; he couldn't have done it by himself. If the people of Germany had a mind of their own, it could have been prevented.'

When learning about the Holocaust it is essential that young people do not end up blaming the victims for their plight. On the contrary, if anti-racist objectives are to be realized it is vital that students identify with the victims. They may be less inclined to do so, however, if they see them in an unheroic light, as the one student who blamed the Jews for not fighting back is likely to have done. It would serve the interests of anti-racism well if teachers were to inform their pupils not just about the utter powerlessness of the Jews, but about the uprisings in the ghettos – especially in Warsaw in 1943 – and in the death camps of Sobibor and Treblinka.

In other respects, the students' responses to the question reinforce points that have already been made. The fact that only one of them thought to mention the lamentable failure of the Church (and specifically Pope Pius XII) to condemn what was going on is consistent with the earlier finding that showed no student indicting the Church for its complicity in preparing the ideological backdrop to the Holocaust. The tendency for most of the participants to disregard the significance of Germany losing the war and suffering an economic depression is again evident. But on a more positive note, there is clear evidence that some students, at least, appreciate the danger in granting too much power to the executive branch of government. Four of them claimed that the Holocaust could not have been prevented 'because Hitler had too much power'.

Following Hitler's accession to power in 1933, Jews began leaving Germany in search of a more secure future. They tried to do so in ever-growing numbers as the decade wore on but found it increasingly difficult as one country after another tightened its immigration procedures. The students were asked to speculate on the reasons why the rest of the world was reluctant to accept German Jews in large numbers. This question was put to the whole group and, as Table 1.4 shows, a high proportion (25 out of 43) revealed their ignorance of Hitler's original policy towards Germany's Jews which was one of *encouraging* emigration. Receiving countries were therefore in no danger of a German reprisal for providing a sanctuary.

Table 1.4 Why was the rest of the world reluctant to take Jewish refugees in large numbers from Germany?

Reason	Number of References
Fear of German retribution	25
They were racist	11
Don't know	6
Economic reasons/couldn't afford it	3
Didn't believe the stories coming out of Germany	2
Other	1

In posing the question, I was particularly interested to see if the students would offer an explanation in terms of anti-Semitism, thereby demonstrating their awareness of its prevalence and influence throughout the Western world. I was also interested in their awareness of how high levels of unemployment in a country can force that country's government to adopt policies that override humanitarian considerations.

Just over a quarter of the sample thought that the international community's unsympathetic response could have been motivated by anti-Semitism. Their comments included the following:

> They might have felt that their jobs and economies would have been taken over by the Jews if they came in large numbers.

> They were also afraid that if the Jews came into their country, the same thing would happen – the Jews would get the power and the wealth.

> Deep down they must have been scared that Hitler believed the Jews were responsible for ruining the economy and it was because of them that they lost the war and many countries wouldn't want to take the gamble just (in case) he was right and then suffer the consequences.

> If people weren't racist they would freely of accepted Jews coming to their country. In every country there's a minority of racism in everybody.

Two responses to the question were in terms of what would now be referred to as the 'new racism' (Barker 1981), with its emphasis on culture, rather than traditional anti-Semitism.

> If you take in a very large number of refugees of a certain kind, it can have a quite a significant effect on the culture of that country.

> I think everyone has some sort of hostility towards people who aren't the same and they didn't want to be overrun.

Just three students attributed the restrictive immigration policies to domestic economic considerations. As one of them put it: 'Other countries also had their own problems – feeding their own people. There has to be more work for them.'

If anti-racist education is to be successful it has to do more than just teach about the nature of racism, for there is no *a priori* reason to believe that such knowledge will automatically translate into action should the need arise. The specific problem anti-racist educators face is that of teaching pupils to overcome peer group pressure when that pressure would otherwise inhibit action against racism. In other words, the need is to teach appropriate non-conformity. One way of doing this may be to reconceptualize, or at least to broaden, our concept of a hero so as to include those individuals who have stood out against their peers, or against social norms, in order to do what they knew to be right. The history of the Holocaust is replete with such individuals whose moral courage should feature prominently in any Holocaust education programme. In the light of this imperative, the group was asked to cogitate on the following: 'When you think about the Holocaust, are there any heroes?' (see Table 1.5).

Table 1.5   When you think about the Holocaust, are there any heroes?

No:	19
Yes:	
Rescuers	10
The Jews	9
Protectors of Jews	3
Jews who fought back	2

Almost half of those questioned did not see any heroes in the Holocaust. Of those who did, the majority failed to conceptualize heroism in ways that had anything to do with non-conformity. Students who saw Jews as heroic were impressed merely by the fact that they had survived. While roughly the same number hailed the efforts of rescuers, often mentioning Oscar Schindler by name, there were just three students who thought of heroism in terms of a preparedness to pay the ultimate price for defying convention.

The following transcript is illustrative:

In respect of the Holocaust, are there any heroes?
Yes all the people who protected the Jews.
What makes them heroic?
If they'd been found out, they would have been killed. They're risking their lives for what they think is right.

2 *Preventing a repetition*

If, as the NCC (1990: 1) states, 'schools must lay the foundations for positive, participative, citizenship', we have to examine not just students' knowledge of the Holocaust, but how, if at all, this knowledge is likely to affect their behaviour. Assuming a causal relationship of some kind between behaviour and attitudes, I consider in this section of the chapter the attitudes expressed towards different means of preventing a recurrence of the Holocaust. I begin by analysing the students' views on whether racist political parties such as the National Front and the British National Party should be allowed to contest elections. Of the forty-two who were asked, thirty were opposed to the idea. In thirteen cases, some of which are cited below, they justified their opposition in terms of what had happened in Nazi Germany.

If they got elected it would cause a lot of trouble for victims of their racist views like Hitler and the Jews.

If that party gets power, it would be like Hitler coming into power again. Maybe another Holocaust might happen.

It could be like Hitler again, not with the Jews this time, but with minorities from Arab, African and Asian countries.

Of the remaining students who opposed the participation of racist parties in elections, most did so either because of the perceived unfairness of discriminatory politics or the stupidity of elevating racial considerations above all others.

I looked next at whether the group felt sufficiently strongly about Holocaust education to campaign on its behalf should its future ever be put in jeopardy. They were asked if people their own age ought to learn about it. Almost the entire sample were in favour with over 50 per cent (23 out of 41) highlighting its role in preventing a recurrence.

Definitely, to prevent it happening in the future. If people know the causes and the reasons why it happened, what should have been done and what could have been done, then in the future, if anything like this happens, we will be able to step in.

It's important that we learn about the Holocaust because we don't want to get into a situation like that again. Before the Holocaust people were worrying about what was happening in Germany but they didn't do anything to stop it. Because of the Holocaust we've learnt that maybe if you want to deal with things like this you ought to deal with them before they get blown up into big things.

Yes because if people learnt about the Holocaust and about prejudice, we would grow up in a better society.

The remainder of the group made no reference to the future. On the contrary, they saw the value of engaging with the Holocaust solely in terms of becoming more aware of the past. But however they construed its benefits, students supporting the idea of their own age group having to learn about the Holocaust were subsequently asked if this should apply throughout the world or only in those countries directly affected. Nearly all of them favoured the universal option. Some did so because they recognized the potential for racism within every society; others because they wished to teach people everywhere about their global responsibilities.

Everyone should know, to prevent it happening in other countries as well.

It becomes a world situation when it happens because the world has to step in.

3 Racism and the Holocaust: making connections

I turn now to examine what the students learnt about racism from their work on the Holocaust. I will focus initially on the concept of a stereotype, for one of the advantages of Holocaust education is the ease with which it can reinforce and broaden a knowledge of stereotyping by showing that it does not always take the same form or have the same provenance. The students were asked, 'What is a stereotype?' and (following an explanation, if necessary) 'What was the Nazi stereotype of the Jew?'.

It is a matter of some concern that less than half the sample (21 out of 43) claimed to be *au fait* with the notion of a stereotype. Moreover, when the students were later questioned about the image of the Jew in Nazi ideology, around 20 per cent said they did not know or had forgotten. The most frequent response, as can be seen in Table 1.6, was that Jews were seen as evil. However, when asked to elaborate, the responses invariably displayed no real understanding. For example: '[Jews] were bad

Table 1.6 The Nazi stereotype of the Jew

Quality	Number of References
Evil	12
Inferior	7
Caused Germany to lose war	5
Cause of economic ruin	4
Wealthy	3
Others – related to Nazi ideology (*e.g. They want to destroy the Aryan race by putting their blood with the Aryans*)	6
Others – unrelated to Nazi ideology (*e.g. They're thieves*)	8
Don't know/can't remember	8

because they weren't Aryan' or, 'They were horrible to people'. One girl, though, did strike at the core of the stereotype when she stated, 'They are trying to take control'.

If it is important to demonstrate to students that stereotypes can assume forms other than those with which they may be familiar, we should not ignore some of the responses to this question. The fact that a couple of individuals said Jews were 'stingy' and another referred to them as money-lenders, suggests the application of old knowledge to new situations rather than the learning of anything new. The same applies to another respondent who may have had Afro-Caribbeans and Asians in mind when she said 'They were taking the [Germans'] jobs and homes'.

Having dealt with stereotyping I moved on to examine the students' knowledge of creating scapegoats. They were presented with three questions: 'What is a scapegoat?', 'Who were the scapegoats in Nazi Germany?' and 'What were they blamed for?'. Just over half (of the 33 who were asked) were familiar with the concept. The rest either admitted that they did not know or gave an 'example' which confirmed that they did not know. When its meaning was explained, they and the rest of the sample were asked to identify the scapegoats in Nazi Germany. Six were unable to do so, suggesting, in their case, that a vital link between Holocaust education and citizenship had passed them by. In fact, the situation is rather more serious, for when those who knew it was the Jews who had been made scapegoats were pressed to say what they were blamed for, four were unable to answer and a further six proffered quite bizarre answers.

These included 'the way Hitler ruled Germany', 'not being what Hitler wanted them to be', and 'being more successful than the Germans'.

The question, 'What does the Holocaust teach us about racism?' was addressed to every student. Apart from those who said that it teaches us 'that racism is wrong', the largest number of responses (11 in all) were concerned with where racism can lead. Thus:

> It teaches us that we shouldn't be racist because it just gets larger and larger, from one person to a group and it starts getting more violent and you start killing people.

> How it can get out of control and end up in mass killing. It's not just calling names and having a fight.

> It shows how evil racism can end up to be. It might start with calling names but it gets bigger and bigger.

> It has to be stopped before it escalates into something worse. If Hitler had not been allowed to go so far in the beginning, the Holocaust wouldn't have happened.

Other members of the group had learned different, but nonetheless important lessons.

> It teaches us that if a lot of people see racism as a way out and a way to enhance their own lifestyle then a lot of people will go for it. Also, you can get a lot of supporters by telling people what they want to hear.

> People who hold racist views shouldn't be allowed freedom of speech.

> Racism can come from greed.
> *What do you mean?*
> Hitler wanted power and used the persecution of the Jews to give himself power. It also teaches us that racism can come from lack of knowledge and that people have to be taught to stop it from happening again.

There were a few students who did not know or were not sure what the Holocaust had taught them about racism. It also emerged that around half a dozen students had acquired (or, at any rate, had not been disabused of) a fundamental misconception, namely that the Jews suffered because of their religious beliefs.

The question, 'Could there be a Holocaust in England?', was the last one that looked at links between racism and the Holocaust. As might have been expected, the group was divided on the issue with twenty-three thinking it could happen, seventeen thinking it could not and three who were unsure. Those who considered it a possibility were asked what would have to happen to bring it about. Consistent with an earlier finding, there were just five who referred either to economic collapse or to psychological trauma as potential catalysts. This overlay a number of tautological responses suggesting much uncertainty. As can be seen below, responses to this question provide further evidence that some students believe the Holocaust to have been the work of a lone psychopath.

> *Could there be a Holocaust in England?*
> Yes
> *What would have to happen to bring it about?*
> Hitler changed German people's view of the Jews so say if someone over here was in power they'd have to change British people's opinion about a certain group.
> *But what would have to happen for us to elect someone like Hitler into power?*
> We'd have to believe in what they believed in.

> *Could there be a Holocaust in England?*
> Yes
> *What would have to happen to bring it about?*
> Where someone totally brainwashes the majority of England into believing that another group of people was stopping England from becoming more powerful.

> *Could there be a Holocaust in England?*
> If one man came to power in this country, it could happen say against Irish people.
> *What would have to happen to bring it about?*
> The people elected would have to be racist groups and they'd have to influence people in England.

In contrast to those who offered tautological explanations, some argued that a racist party could assume office as a result of some malpractice on the part of a minority.

> *Could there be a Holocaust in England?*
> Yes, if a party like the NF got in.
> *What would have to happen to bring a party like the NF into power?*
> Crime level from black people might rise

> *Could there be a Holocaust in England?*
> Yes

What would have to happen to bring it about?
A racist party would get elected into government.
What would have to happen to bring that about?
An Asian or a black would have to do something wrong and it might get out of hand.

Those who thought a Holocaust could not happen in England did so for reasons which some might regard as a dangerous cocktail of naivety and complacency. The first related to lessons learnt from Nazi Germany.

Could there be a Holocaust in England?
I don't think so because after the Holocaust people's views have changed so much it won't happen.

No, because a lot of people have lessons about what could happen so that would probably prevent it.

No, because people know what happened in the Holocaust, nobody would give it enough support.

No, because the Holocaust is taught and people actually know about it. In this day and age, people can see the warning signs.

A further reason given for thinking that a Holocaust could not happen in England was that powerful, external forces would somehow prevent it. One boy said, 'If black people were attacked in England, other countries would come to their help.' A second boy agreed, saying: 'We've got the United Nations helping us.'

The possibility of a Holocaust was also dismissed on the grounds that racism is not sufficiently entrenched in England to act as a viable launching pad. The comments below represent this point of view.

There's not enough craziness in the country to do it. If someone came to power and said 'go and do this', most people would just say no.

There doesn't seem to be racism on a large scale.

I think people are more open-minded now and there aren't as many racist people around. People get on a lot better now no matter what colour they are.

4 Personal impact of learning about the Holocaust

The first of the three questions in this category

asked the group to consider how, if at all, studying the Holocaust had changed them. Of the forty-one who were asked, fifteen claimed not to have been changed in any way, some adding that the subject had merely broadened their general knowledge. Of those who said they had been changed, seven referred specifically to having been made to think more deeply about the nature of racism:

- It's made me think about racism a lot more.
- It's made me more aware of racism.
- I didn't realise that racism could go that far and that one man could have that much power and ruin so many lives.
- Before I did the Holocaust I didn't know how bad racism was. I think it has made me a lot more thoughtful. You want to know why.

Cited below are some of the comments made by a further nine students who intimated that learning about the Holocaust either had influenced, or would influence, their behaviour.

It's probably changed me in the way that I treat people who aren't the same as me, like people who are a different religion. It's not fair to start picking on them if they haven't done anything to me because that's like what happened then. It's what Hitler did – just picking on easy prey.

It's given me more knowledge about what happened to the Jews and how we should respect other people and not pre-judge them.

It's made me realise that you don't class people as a race; you take them as they come.

It's helped me to think more about life. How precious life is. We shouldn't be so quick to stereotype people; we should maybe take a second to think.

It's strengthened my views on what I believe is right and wrong. I didn't know about the Holocaust before I studied it. I was shocked when I found out this had happened in the twentieth century. Also, it's taught me to stand up for what I believe in.

Two students who claimed to have been affected by their work on the Holocaust expressed views that are especially noteworthy. The first comment is from a boy whose background is both Arab and Muslim. He said:

When I was small, watching the news and seeing what the Jews do in Israel I hated them. After I studied the Holocaust I remembered what happened to them, how they got into Palestine, so it changed me a lot to think of them as normal people and they didn't deserve what they got. They're human and they have the right to live in the country.

Although it should be no part of Holocaust education to foster sympathy for Zionism, it is essential, as has been noted, to cultivate among the young an interest in citizenship and human rights that extends beyond their own national borders. There is, however, no virtue in an ill-informed interest and to the extent that knowledge of the Holocaust is able to dispel some of the myths about the Arab–Israeli dispute, it serves a useful purpose.

The second comment that deserves to be singled out came from an Asian girl who said of her encounter with the Holocaust: 'It's made me more against the Germans'. Although she was the only student in the sample to articulate an anti-German sentiment, her experience clearly points up a potential irony in studying the subject; namely, its ability to intensify prejudice as well as diminish it.

The penultimate question addressed to the group asked them to reflect on what they had learnt about good citizenship as a result of studying the Holocaust. For the most part, the responses were variations on the twin themes of not judging a book by its cover and ensuring that everyone is treated with equality, respect and fairness. A handful of students, however, chose to focus on the importance of taking personal responsibility for their actions. For them, the Holocaust teaches that:

You have to make up your own mind. You don't just follow someone who may bring you something you want but who's going to do something that you don't agree with.

[You should] not just listen to what one person says but listen to what everyone says and then think it all over and think the most logical way to overcome the situation.

[I should not] accept what everyone else thinks is right – to have my own opinion and also to speak out for those who are being affected. If I can prevent it, to prevent it.

You've got to make sure you vote for someone who's not racist and has got good policies.

[You shouldn't] listen to others. Judge people by

what they are not what other people think of them. The German people thought about Jews the same as Hitler, so they were bad to the Jews.
What should the German people have done then?
They should have judged the Jewish people by themselves.

To give the students a final opportunity to consider the relevance of the Holocaust for citizenship education they were asked, 'What does the Holocaust teach us generally – about life and about people?' Not surprisingly, the responses were diverse and, to a considerable extent, reiterated points made earlier. Some, however, were made for the first time and they are reproduced below. The opening comment, for example, was the only time in the entire project when reference was made to the role of bystanders.

It shows how cruel humans can be to one another and that people just turn a blind eye to it.

It tells us that people should have equal rights, but how at some times in history, people didn't have those rights and how not having those rights affected their lives.

That there are evil geniuses like Hitler. If the Holocaust had never happened, we would have thought that something that terrible could never happen. It teaches us that it can.

It teaches us how evil man can be and how men and women strive for power and that we have to overcome [the lust for power] if we want to carry on living.

There are some people who will use their power to do evil and they can't be stopped in a lot of cases unless action is taken very early.

Conclusion

This chapter set out to explore what a group of 14- and 15-year-olds learnt about citizenship as a result of studying the Holocaust as history. Specifically, the data analysis was undertaken in order to gauge both their knowledge of the Holocaust and the impact of that knowledge on their understanding of racism. Bearing in mind the ability range of the participants, it was predictable that they would vary widely in their recollection of important detail and in their grasp of the common threads linking the Holocaust with racism in their own society. In summarizing the findings, I have chosen to concentrate on aspects of the teaching that can be said to have failed in respect of education for citizenship for, as in all things, it is areas in need of improvement that must dictate policy implications.

One of my principal concerns derives from the tendency on the part of many students to interpret the Holocaust as the work of a lone individual. This way of thinking is, perhaps, an extreme example, of the 'rotten apple' theory of racism (Henriques 1984) according to which racism is nothing more than an aberration based on personal inadequacy. To help counter such a view, teachers of the Holocaust must make their pupils aware of the different interest groups that stood to gain from a Nazi takeover in Germany and show how these various groups contributed to Hitler's success. No less essential is the need to stress the nature and significance of the deeply-ingrained tradition of anti-Semitism in the country and this will necessarily entail making reference to its roots in Christian theology. The need for such input is indicated by the fact that not a single respondent alluded to the importance of an anti-Semitic culture when discussing the origins of the Holocaust and only one referred to the non-intervention of the Church when asked if the Holocaust could have been prevented. Highlighting the critical role of anti-Semitism has the additional advantage of enabling students to place the economic depression, the military defeat and its humiliating aftermath in perspective, seeing them as catalysts rather than as direct causes of the Holocaust.

Before leaving the subject of anti-Semitism, it is worth noting that none of those interviewed appeared to know that until 1941 Jews were allowed to leave Germany and many were unaware that anti-Semitism *in other countries* was a major obstacle to their emigration. It is imperative that this fact be made known when teaching the Holocaust in order that Germans are not stereotyped as singularly lacking in humanitarianism and uniquely evil in respect of racism and anti-Semitism. It will be recalled that one student said spontaneously of her experience of studying the Holocaust, 'It's made me more against the Germans'. Others may have expressed similar sentiments had they been asked directly.

The small number of students who demonstrated an understanding of the plight of Gypsies and Slavs during the war has also been noted. Teaching about the fate of these ethnic groups is not just a matter of setting the historical record straight (Cornwell 1996), nor is it simply a means of illustrating the vulnerability of powerless minorities. For the treatment meted out to both Gypsies and Slavs provides teachers with an opportunity to help their pupils understand more about the process of stereotyping. Such work would seem to be an urgent priority bearing in mind that less than half the sample had any real understanding of this critical concept. It will be recalled that similar levels of ignorance were observed in relation to the concept of scapegoats.

Another concern that I have commented upon involves the role of rescuers for, as Table 1.5 shows, less than a third of the sample identified rescuers or 'protectors of Jews' as heroes. Obviously, it would be quite wrong to teach the Holocaust in such a way as to give the impression that the number of rescuers was anything other than a tiny proportion of those who preferred to turn a blind eye. Celebrating their bravery and defiance, however, is another matter. For if citizenship education does not encourage young people to stand up for what they believe to be right, regardless of circumstance, it becomes nothing more than an academic exercise.

Promoting racism or anti-Semitism, even unintentionally, is, of course, totally at variance with any notion of education for citizenship in a democracy. Yet precisely this possibility is inherent in teaching about the Holocaust, and some students, as we have seen, may be tempted to explain the event, partly at least, in terms of Jewish control of the economy. The danger arises from the undeniable fact that in the Weimar Republic, Jews were over-represented in certain professions, notably in law and medicine. They also owned a number of department stores and were particularly prominent in the clothing trade. If these facts are openly taught, as they should be, along with all other relevant facts, they may well reinforce the stereotype of the Jew as necessarily wealthy and, in the process, tilt the balance of sympathy towards their persecutors. Teachers of the Holocaust cannot be expected, *qua* history teachers, to discuss at length with their pupils the nature of stereotyping. They can, however, deal effectively with this one by drawing their pupils' attention to the *Ostjuden* (Jews from Eastern Europe) who constituted around 20 per cent of Germany's Jewish population and who 'frequently fell victim to unemployment and economic distress' (Landau 1992: 92).

They should also make a point of stressing the impoverished state of the Jewish masses in Russia, Poland and elsewhere in the East who were to perish in their millions before the Nazi onslaught.

Despite the risks of accepting at face value students' comments on sensitive issues, I believe that the majority of those who participated in this research learnt much about responsible citizenship through their study of the Holocaust. If history teachers were to incorporate the changes that have been suggested, it is likely that future generations of students will derive even greater benefit. Teachers may well have a chance to ring the changes in view of the moves currently afoot to enable more time to be spent on the study of world history in GCSE syllabuses (*The Times*, 17 July 1996). However, the recent Dearing Report (1994), aimed at slimming down the curriculum, suggested that teachers could choose to tackle some subjects in depth and others in outline. If they opt for the latter in respect of the Holocaust, there is little doubt that a valuable opportunity for furthering the development of a pluralist society will have been lost.

Note

1 Although not directly relevant to the Holocaust, it was felt necessary to ask this question on the assumption that students will be less likely to learn about the vulnerability of all ethnic minorities to persecution if they are led to believe that Jews were the only group dehumanized by the Nazis.

References

Barker, M. (1981) *The New Racism*. London: Junction Books.

Carr, W. (1991) Education for citizenship. *British Journal of Educational Studies*, 39: 373–85.

Cornwell, T. (1996) Massacre denied a page in history. *Times Higher Education Supplement*, 12 July.

Dawidowicz, L. (1992) *What's the Use of Jewish History?* New York: Schocken Books.

Dearing, R. (1994) *The National Curriculum and its Assessment*. Final Report. London: School Curriculum and Assessment Authority.

Gillborn, D. (1995) *Racism and Antiracism in Real Schools*. Buckingham: Open University Press.

Henriques, J. (1984) Social psychology and the politics of racism. In J. Henriques, W. Holloway, C. Urwin, C. Venn and V. Walkerdine (eds) *Changing the Subject: Psychology, Social Regulation and Subjectivity*. London: Methuen.

Landau, R. (1989) No Nazi war in British history. *Jewish Chronicle*, 25 August.

Landau, R. (1992) *The Nazi Holocaust*. London: I. B. Taurus.

Levi, P. (1987) *If This is a Man/The Truce*. London: Abacus.

National Curriculum Council (1990) *Education for Citizenship*. York: National Curriculum Council.

Peters, R. S. (1966) *Ethics and Education*. George Allen and Unwin: London.

Short, G. (1994) Retain, relinquish or revise: the future for multicultural education. *Journal of Multilingual and Multicultural Development*, 15 (4): 329–44.

Short, G. (1995) The Holocaust in the National Curriculum: a survey of teachers' attitudes and practices. *Journal of Holocaust Education*, 4 (2): 167–88.

Short, G. and Carrington, B. (1996) Antiracist education, multiculturalism and the new racism. *Educational Review*, 48 (1): 65–77.

Supple, C. (1992) The Teaching of the Nazi Holocaust in North Tyneside, Newcastle and Northumberland Secondary schools. Unpublished manuscript. Newcastle-upon-Tyne: School of Education, University of Newcastle-upon-Tyne.

Taylor, M. J. (1992) *Multicultural Antiracist Education after ERA: Concerns, Constraints and Challenges*. Slough: National Foundation for Educational Research.

Troyna, B. and Carrington, B. (1990) *Education, Racism and Reform*. London: Routledge.

Witty, G., Aggleton, P. and Rowe, P. (1992) *Cross Curricular Work in Secondary Schools: Summary of Results of a Survey Carried Out in 1992*. Report to Participating Schools. London: Institute of Education.

Wyman, D. (1984) *The Abandonment of the Jews: America and the Holocaust, 1941–1945*. New York: Pantheon Books.

2 Humanistic Values Education
Personal, Interpersonal, Social and Political Dimensions

DOV DAROM

Introduction

Humanistic education and values education have often been considered antagonistic to each other. Humanistic education stresses personal growth, 'Freedom to Learn' (Rogers 1983), self-actualization (Maslow 1954); it focuses on the individual whose growth and development, needs and aspirations are considered paramount in all educational processes. Values education, on the other hand, emphasizes involvement with others – individuals, communities, society – commitment and social action. One of the major challenges in modern educational thought and practice is building bridges connecting self and others, the individual and society, freedom and commitment. This chapter will be devoted to the feasibility of such an integrative approach, of anchoring values education in the philosophy of personal freedom and autonomy, of rejecting the view of the inherent antagonism in favour of seeing the two 'opposites' as complementing each other. Let me state at this point that I regard education that is not guided by these principles as barren and dysfunctional – to the individual as well as to society. On the threshold of the new millennium, integration of personal freedom and societal commitment is probably more valid than ever before.

Dichotomy and polarity

The field of education is full of antagonistic and conflictual situations. To whom am I, as an educator, committed – to the values of school and society or to the needs of my individual students? What is the right approach to my students – to provide challenges, to promote change, to say to them, 'You can do better! Try harder! With some more effort you are sure to succeed!' or to radiate acceptance and empathy and say to them, 'I accept you as you are – your strengths as well as your weaknesses; I have no desire to change you; only in a non-threatening climate will you be able to grow and develop'? Should values education be aimed at adopting the basic values of our society or should it stress fullest freedom for individuals to crystallize their own personal values system, even if this may entail rejection of and revolt against some traditional societal values?

All these dilemmas are phrased as either/or contradictions. If one is right then the other is wrong. The more we compromise towards 'A', the more we neglect 'B'. This is typical dichotomous thinking, which probably is a major factor in perpetuating conflicts instead of resolving them.

Dichotomic thinking modes should be restricted to conflicts between two values, one of which belongs to my values system while the other is opposed to it. There can be no integration between freedom and slavery or between democracy and dictatorship. All the dilemmas mentioned above, however, entail two values, both of which have their rightful place in my value system. For these, integration is preferable to antagonism, polarity to dichotomy, 'both . . . and' thinking to 'either . . . or' approaches.

Polarity is well known in physical phenomena. A magnetic field, for example, is defined by north and south magnetic poles. There is no doubt that the two poles are opposite to each other, that they contradict each other. On the other hand, only the coexistence of the two 'contradictory' poles determines the very existence of the magnetic field. This paradoxical phenomenon of two entities, which simultaneously oppose and complement each other is 'polarity'. This integration of opposites is a far more effective way of dealing with antagonistic situations.

Polarity is also anchored in philosophical thought. Hegel's dialectics – dealing with conflicts on the basis of thesis, antithesis and synthesis – illuminate the issues with which we are dealing from an additional angle.

If we go back to the previously mentioned dilemmas, polaric thinking will guide our search for solutions in the direction of combining challenge with support, and building educational partnerships based on the needs of school and society, as well as those of the individual students. To these can be added any number of educational dilemmas, such as emphasis on process as well as outcome, fully living in the 'here and now' as well as being linked to past and future, consistency as well as flexibility. To all of these, polaric integrations are surely more applicable than dichotomic either/or antagonisms.

Polarity is one of the cornerstones of my approach to education. Integrating personal freedom with societal commitment is – to my mind – the essence of humanistic values education. This chapter will be devoted mainly to this issue.

Humanistic education

Let us look more closely at some of the basic principles and values of humanistic education. Its underlying theme is that the human being is the focus of all educational processes. The individual's needs and aspirations determine educational theory and practice. Outside factors, such as institutions, schools, curricula, external value systems, even religion, are there to serve human beings' spiritual and material well-being – not to dominate them. The trouble with many of our schools is that curricula, examinations and grades, laws and rules dominate the system at the expense of students' growth and development according to their own individual needs and pace.

As I mentioned at the beginning of this chapter, humanistic education stresses first and foremost **personal growth**, **self-actualization** and **individual freedom**. All other considerations are subservient to these.

Humanistic education is **holistic**. As opposed to traditional schooling, devoted almost entirely to intellectual and cognitive learning, it addresses the person as a whole. It views educational processes as integrating four different aspects – the cognitive-intellectual, the affective-experiential, values and behaviour. These four are closely linked – as will be considered in greater detail later – so that meaningful learning activities address the learner in all four domains.

It is worth noting that the school of thought of 'Confluent Education' (Brown 1971) combines cognition and affect and views these two, not as a dichotomy of warring opposites but as a polarity of mutually complementary entities. Together – and only together – they complement each other to a holistic and meaningful totality. I find it important to add two more entities – values and behaviour – thus creating a more comprehensive whole, in which all four domains are valued equally.

Humanistic education is based on **dialogue**. This is the I and Thou type of dialogue (Martin Buber) whose essence is learned as well as practised. True dialogue can take place only among equals (Freire 1973). Looking at this issue superficially, one may conclude that there can be no equality between teachers and pupils. Their knowledge and life-experiences are truly not equal. In their basic humanity, however, in their need to be heard, respected, accepted, never humiliated, there is a large degree of equality. As human beings they are fully equal; their personal needs, aspirations, dreams and hopes, strengths and weaknesses are valued equally. If we can address our pupils in this frame of mind, we create the foundation for meaningful educational dialogue.

Dialogue requires skills of interpersonal communication. These have to be learned, experienced and practised. The primary skill is listening to one another, with true empathic, non-judgemental listening to the words, meanings, body language and feelings. An additional skill is giving and receiving feedback, sharing our thoughts and feelings about the subject on which the feedback is given without judgements and injunctions.

Humanistic education involves **interpersonal caring** too. Each partner in the educational dialogue has the right to be treated with respect, support and trust, without any kind of manipulation, humiliation or violence.

It is **experiential**. Learning experiences focus not only on knowledge and understanding of subject matter, but also touch the learner at the emotional level, have a social dimension, are directed at all possible 'gates of absorption' – the intellectual, emotional, visual, audile, tactile and aesthetic.

Humanistic education is **relevant** to the real questions in the life of the learner. Many problems such as lack of motivation, lack of discipline, misbehaviour and drop-out would be less destructive, if what is going on in the classroom were more relevant to the pupils' lives and addressed itself to the many questions they are trying to cope with.

It furthers **autonomy** of pupils and teachers alike. Teachers are no longer mere officials of centrally-directed educational authorities; pupils cease to be mere objects in the learning process and become active, participatory, responsible subjects.

Humanistic education is **process orientated**, valuing the quality of educational processes no less than the quality of results and outcomes.

It is **democratic**. Traditional schools expect obedience and docility from their pupils rather than initiative and critical thinking. School leadership should be more participative, show more respect to human (pupils') rights and be more conducive to preparing future citizens to function – actively and responsibly – in our democratic society. This can only be done by 'learning democracy' not only on the cognitive level but also on the affective, values and experiential levels.

The values of humanistic education, which are enumerated here – probably too concisely – may sound like a recipe for Utopia. They are, of course, never fully realized. They should be considered as a compass guiding us in the direction of humanistic climates in education, so different from those prevailing in most of our schools. Humanistic climates are described in greater detail by Rogers (1983), Combs (1974), Brown (1971), Darom (1989) and others.

Values education in humanistic climates

Values education has often been considered a 'stepchild' in humanistic education. Let me give some examples. Humanistic education is concerned with values such as personal freedom and autonomy, personal growth and self-actualization. There can be no doubt that these are necessary conditions for meaningful education. But are they sufficient? Rogers (1983) wrote:

> Never in our history have we been faced with so

many serious and complex decisions . . . What action should be taken in regard to the polluting of air and water in our community? What steps should be taken to deal with excessive drug use? How much of our personal and governmental income can we afford for health and care? Who should provide sex education for the young? What are we to do about the crisis in our Social Security system that provides for the elderly? Shall a nuclear plant be erected in our area? How far do we want to go with building up our military system and nuclear bombs? The questions go on and on. It is absolutely essential that young people learn early in life to consider complex problems, to recognise the pros and cons of each solution, and to choose the stand they will take on an issue.

This is a strong social and political statement. But it is the only one of its kind in his book *Freedom to Learn for the 80s*. Most of the book is devoted to people's personal values, such as their responsibility to their own lives. The only connection between personal and societal values is expressed in the somewhat naive belief that a person 'who can truly be himself' will automatically take a stand on social issues.

Even in the context of 'Values Clarification' (see Raths et al. 1966), which advocates active values education in the humanistic classroom, the only concern is with the process of valuing, whereas with regard to the contents of the values considered, the facilitator is expected to be completely neutral. There is no preference for democracy over dictatorship, for freedom over slavery, for anti-racism and anti-violence over racism and violence. Elsewhere I wrote:

> Even the method of Values Clarification which involves students so effectively in a deep exploration of their own values stresses teachers' neutrality on some of the major values issues of today. When listing the values on which the method is based Kirschenbaum (1977) focused on thinking critically, considering consequences and choosing freely. These values are inherent in the method and are indeed vital personal values. Kirschenbaum wrote nothing however about group-belonging, community or society. Moreover, when he claimed that Values Clarification would lead automatically to the development of values such as rationality, equality, justice, autonomy and freedom, the reader is left wondering whether this claim is based on fact or the author's wishful thinking. (Darom 1988)

I believe that aiming for the fullest integration of

personal freedom and societal commitment puts additional demands on educators. Humanistic educators can no longer limit themselves to acting in the field of individuals, stressing only personal values, and ignoring the whole field of a person's responsibility to society. They can no longer relegate these spheres to others. A society lacking a serious core of people who struggle actively for the implementation of the values of freedom and equality, respect for human rights and interpersonal caring in their communities is in danger of deteriorating into a society furthering values antagonistic to these. Moreover, in such a setting it will become more and more impossible to realize these values, even on the personal level. Recent history of certain political right-wing movements and their influence on education all over the world provide ample evidence of such dangers.

Free and autonomous individuals cannot successfully function in a society negating freedom and autonomy. On the other hand, societies conducive to personal freedom and autonomy cannot grow and develop unless more and more individuals commit themselves to furthering these goals by social action and social change. These are quite frequently inseparable from political action and political change.

Holistic values education

I have already mentioned the interdependence of four different domains in education generally, and in values education in particular – cognitive, affective, values and behaviour. I shall now dwell on these in greater detail.

On the cognitive level, values are understood, their context explored, philosophical and psychological implications are studied, their relevance in all spheres of life and in all fields of study are emphasized. On this level, values of critical thinking, rationality and viewing ideas analytically as well as synthetically are of special importance. Needless to say, all this can be experienced in the context of striving for as deep as possible knowledge and understanding of major trends in human cultural, intellectual and scientific endeavours.

The affective domain is the source of endless human energy. It is the world of emotional experiences, enthusiasm, humour, aesthetics, friendship, love and support, as well as 'negative' emotions, such as rejection, alienation, frustration and hatred.

In-depth educators have always understood the influence of emotions on learning processes, and have considered cognition and affect as the 'Siamese twins' of education.

To these two domains, we now add the field of values. A person's values system is like a compass showing the directions to his attitudes, preferences, goals, decisions and actions. It can be likened to an individual's moral backbone, preferably stable enough not to be bent by every blowing wind but flexible enough, so as not to break in strong storms. A person's manifold experiences undergo filtering, digestion and personal processing in order to create a structure more or less stable for continued periods in this person's life – his or her value system. In ecological terms, this is similar to a forest: each and every tree is a world in itself as well as part and parcel of the ecological totality, the forest as a whole.

The fourth domain is that of behaviour. Educational processes – in the cognitive, affective and values domains – cannot be evaluated apart from the field of behaviour. To what extent are our students' behaviour and actions influenced by their moral reasoning? How do they translate their Kohlbergian stages of moral judgement in day-to-day behaviour? How can people succeed in bridging the gap between understanding, feeling and believing and doing, acting and realizing?

For many years, Kohlberg's Moral Dilemma deliberations completely excluded the dimension of behaviour. He concentrated entirely on rational judgement. In 1978, however, he totally revised this approach and wrote as follows:

> The moral educator deals with concrete morality in a school world, in which value content as well as structure, behaviour as well as reasoning, must be dealt with. In this context the educator must be a socialiser, teaching value content and behaviour, not merely a Socratic facilitator of development.

Kohlberg's revisions bear witness to the barrenness of any form of values education in which behavioural dimensions do not play a paramount part.

Education can thus be considered a system having four sub-systems, every one of which plays an equally decisive part in the system as a whole. If any one of them is neglected, the whole educational process is incomplete. If affective experiences are over-emphasized, at the expense of the other sub-systems, the gates to demagogical influences are opened wide. If all activity centres round cognitive processes, and there is no place for expressing emotions in the classroom, people will become more and more like cold and alienated computers. If the values domain is not considered a highly significant part of educational practice, this field will be entirely dominated by the street, the media, unscrupulous politicians and other public opinion moulders. If education does not relate seriously to the behaviour of individuals and groups, it will be just another factor deepening the abyss between words and actions, preaching and practising, moralizing and real-life behaviour.

It is by striving for the fullest possible integration of these four domains, that education has a chance of truly touching young people, of sowing seeds of intellectual and moral honesty and personal commitment. Needless to say, we cannot expect such integrative processes to be harmonious; they will always be characterized – as is life as a whole – by tensions and struggles.

Three components of values education

An individual's value system has three components in close interaction. It encompasses personal, interpersonal and social values. These three are an indivisible whole; a structure whose stability – whose very existence – depends on their more or less successful blending.

Personal values include independence of thought, personal responsibility, moral thinking and acting, and a work ethic. Interpersonal values encompass cooperation, non-manipulation, non-violence, caring, equality of rights, acceptance of others different from oneself. These are closely connected with skills of empathic listening, giving and receiving feedback, conflict resolution – without winners and losers – and creating open and supportive paths of communication. Our social values may involve respect for human rights, non-racism, ecological caring, peace, democracy, active participation in struggles of oppressed minorities for non-exploitation and independence.

When I stress the equal value ascribed to each of these categories, I have in mind certain types of people who do not achieve such integration. Who has not met the great social reformer and leader of masses, who devotes his whole life to worthy social and political goals, but prefers the company of yes-men because he has no idea of the meaning of

interpersonal cooperation and team work? We all know people who propound personal and interpersonal values, but refrain from social action, so as not to be contaminated by politics. In reality, their reluctance to involve themselves in the political arena opens it wide to far less moral forces, which have a destructive influence on our society. There are also people who serve their communities day and night, but in whose personal life there is a void that they have never learned to fill.

Two dangers: indoctrination and values neutrality

At the beginning of this chapter, I dwelled on the fullest possible integration of personal freedom with societal commitment. Are these two cornerstones of education really compatible in values education?

The 'personal freedom' pole may be thought to imply that one should refrain from exerting any kind of influence – explicit, as well as implicit – on our students. This may even mean not stating our own views and values, so as to ensure that young people can crystallize their own value systems as freely as possible. The 'societal commitment' pole, on the other hand, may be thought to warrant exerting maximum influence on our students to adopt those values that are desirable to the society we live in.

'Imparting values' means that society will do all in its power to perpetuate its values, that values education's success is measured by how well young people adapt to society's traditional values. As we have already seen, this is really quite immoral; it robs individuals of their natural right to freedom to choose independently between various alternatives. Moreover, this precludes creating new values, encourages conformism and blind obedience that leaves no place for social change.

The moment we reject indoctrination, preaching and laying down the law as to what values the individual 'should' adopt; the moment we state our belief – and act accordingly – that values education implies free choice for every individual, we are faced with a new question: 'Is the educator entitled to voice explicitly his own values and those of his community?' This is a question of major significance, both morally and practically.

Teachers tend to ask the following questions, which touch on one of the most problematic issues of values education: 'Should controversial social and political issues be dealt with in the classroom? If so, should I express my own views, attitudes and values? And if so, how can this be done without falling into the trap of indoctrination?'

My answer to the first question is an unqualified 'yes'. If we want our schools to be relevant to real life – both of individuals and of society – we cannot possibly exclude issues that may have political implications and arouse controversy. There is no point in trying to make our classrooms sterile so as not to be 'contaminated' by such matters. It is absolutely essential, even if not always easy, to get this message across to parents and educational authorities. Moreover, social and political involvement should actually become a goal in educational practice. It is educationally dysfunctional to let our students be influenced by demagogic politicians, by hidden persuaders, by the media and the street without providing them with tools of rational critical thinking on social and political matters.

The second question, too, deserves a positive answer. Refraining from openly expressing views and values tends to restrict the educational dialogue between pupils and teachers. If education is considered to be first and foremost an interpersonal encounter – a dialogue as open as possible – then enlarging or restricting the dialogue's scope will decisively affect its quality. If we value social involvement and action, the teacher cannot be anything but a behavioural model. And again, the belief that if teachers refrain from openly stating their own values, their pupils will be free to develop their own value systems is a fallacy. There is no vacuum in education – it will soon be filled by value messages of the lowest common denominator. This was strongly expressed in Kohlberg's (1978) statement, in which he revised his previously held position that facilitators of moral dilemma deliberations should refrain from dealing with content and behaviour, and strongly advocated their full involvement in the contents of the dilemma.

So, we come to the third question. This is of paramount importance. The answer to it will determine whether teachers' value statements will not, under any circumstances, limit pupils' freedom of choice or turn into an act of indoctrination. In a classroom, in which controversial issues are raised, and I feel free to express my own views and values, I want to draw a distinct dividing line between political education and political propaganda.

- I shall facilitate the classroom experience so that it dwells on questions of principles and values, rather than on day-to-day party politics.
- I shall apply the principle of pluralism and expose my pupils to a number of conflicting views, not only my own.
- I shall encourage independent critical thinking as regards the various points of view presented, and shall especially submit my own views to my pupils' critical consideration.
- I shall try to create a climate characterized by free and open communication, interpersonal listening and empathy, accepting those who hold different and even opposite views.
- I myself shall try as hard as I can to be accepting to those who do not share my views. This is the real test of the quality of my values education – to distinguish between views and actions with which I disagree and the person behind these views and actions, whom I respect and value.

I believe that if teachers make all possible efforts to realize these guidelines in practice, they are not only entitled to express their views, they are actually obliged to do so. I know of no other way that enables us to steer clear of the pitfalls both of indoctrination and of values neutrality.

The Israeli scene

Values education in a polarized society

Many of the concepts so far dealt with may sound somehow Utopian. Integrating freedom and commitment, addressing the 'whole person' in his or her full humanness, clearly expressing educators' values as well as refraining from indoctrination, open dialogue in which pupils and teachers are equal partners, humanistic climates in schools – all these may lead the reader to ask whether they belong to the world of dreams or are anchored in any way in reality. What is more, can such principles be applied in a multi-cultural and politically polarized setting that characterizes so many of our schools and communities?

Let me give some examples from my own country – Israel. Israeli society is divided by a number of schisms, with the opposing camps warring with each other socially, culturally and politically. First and foremost, there is the national division between Jews and Arabs. Although the Arab minority in

Israel formally enjoys full civil rights, and has – through the years – shown a high degree of loyalty to the state of Israel, there is also a close kinship between them and Palestinians outside Israel, as well as neighbouring Arab states, who have for many decades been waging a bloody war against Israel. Israeli Arabs describe themselves as both members of the Palestinian people as well as citizens of the state of Israel. This cannot but create a situation of contradictions and conflicts.

The rifts among the Jews themselves are manifold: political – those advocating 'returning territories in return for peace' and those who refuse to withdraw from any part of the historic 'Land of Israel'; ethnic – Ashkenazi Jews of European background and Sephardi Jews of oriental background; cultural – orthodox religious Jews (themselves subdivided into various sects, not always at peace with each other) as opposed to liberal and secular Jews. Quite often, the struggles between the various factions inside the Jewish population become violent – frequently even more so than the Jewish–Arab struggle. Only a short time ago our Prime Minister Yitzchak Rabin – a man who translated his vision of reconcilement and peace into real peace treaties with the Palestinians and Jordan – was murdered by a fanatic right-wing, religious Jew. I continue to mourn him deeply.

The Israeli educational system is divided into separate Arab and Jewish schools, the latter – into separate religious and secular schools. Much effort is devoted – not always with great success – to integrating Sephardi and Ashkenazi populations in our schools, so that politically and ethnically most of our schools are multi-cultural.

The political rift is extremely severe. The 'left' pursues an active peace process, and is prepared to withdraw from territories held by Israel (conquered in the 1967 war, but never formally annexed) . The 'right' claims that historically, the Jews are the rightful owners of the 'Land of Israel' and will not give up any part of it. What is more, they intend to continue to fill these controversial territories with Jewish settlers and settlements.

With this background, is it at all feasible to apply my proposal

- to deal with these controversies in the classroom?
- to encourage educators to state their own views?
- to make sure that the process steers clear of indoctrination?

Elsewhere (Darom 1994), I have outlined some guidelines to facilitators of classroom discussions on such matters:

1   I shall attempt to deal with issues of this kind in a multi-directional manner. Our main task is problem-solving. A creative process of problem-solving, in political as well as other spheres, involves in-depth consideration of a number of diverse alternatives.

2   Considering different alternatives involves the classification of the advantages and disadvantages of each one of them. Even the most desirable solution to a problem has its price.

3   Such complex issues always involve values conflicts. These exist not only between two groups but also inside each individual called upon to make a decision. Personally, I feel a deep attachment to all parts of the historic 'Land of Israel', the cradle of my people's history and culture. It is painful to me to hand them over to foreign rule. But the value of peace is much higher in my hierarchy of values, so that I willingly pay the price of withdrawing from territories for the sake of achieving peace and an end to killing.

4   I shall try to relate empathically to those whose views are opposed to mine. I shall firmly oppose all sorts of demonization of the political opponent, which is so common in day-to-day political polemics.

5   Above all, I shall state in no uncertain terms my commitment to democracy and my conviction that all of us must respect majority decisions, even in moments of extreme controversy and pain.

This is by no means a recipe for harmonious conflict resolution. These are a number of guidelines for political education in a multi-cultural society.

Peace education: encounter and dialogue

Among the most enlightening examples of humanistic principles applied to values education are the various projects in Israel promoting encounter and dialogue between Jewish and Arab young people. One of these programmes – CTC or 'Children Teaching Children', coordinated by the 'Jewish–Arab Centre for Peace' at the Kibbutz movement's campus at Givat Haviva – promotes a 2-year-long programme, two lessons a week, in which two parallel classes, one from an Arab school and one from a Jewish school, meet on a regular basis. The binational meetings alternate with uninational meetings in the original homerooms, in which the experiences of the encounter are processed and in which each group explores its own national and cultural identity.

I have described the humanistic character of this programme (Darom 1996):

- The very emphasis on encounter and dialogue stresses that personal and interpersonal processes are no less decisive in peace-making than historical and political aspects of the ongoing conflict.
- The youngsters are given an opportunity to engage in processes such as interpersonal acquaintance, exploring the two different group identities, examining and understanding the meaning of stereotypic thinking, conflict resolution, sharing fears and anxieties on personal and group levels.
- Values dilemmas involving interpersonal empathy, acceptance, pluralism and democracy are confronted in an atmosphere of developing trust.
- Personal, interpersonal and socio-political issues are integrated as fully as possible. So are cognitive, affective, values and behavioural dimensions.
- The teachers and coordinators hold their own fortnightly meetings, planning the oncoming pupils' encounter according to the problems, needs and emotions aroused in the previous meeting. This ongoing planning is based not on a pre-determined curriculum, but on the joint creation of a curriculum, based on here-and-now needs of the participants. The teachers create a team – not shying away from their own difficulties and misunderstandings – and model team work and cooperation.

At the end of the 2-year programme, both sides report an increase in interpersonal acquaintance and in knowledge and awareness of relevant issues, a decrease in feelings of mutual strangeness and alienation, a more realistic understanding of the conflict in its complexity, a growing legitimation that each side grants to the national aspirations of the other, a significant drop in feelings of personal and group hatred towards the other national group, and a rise in feelings of optimism that a solution is feasible.

In addition to this list of research findings, it is enlightening to note some of the individual answers of youngsters aged 14–15, who participated in the CTC programme, when asked 'What did you learn?'

- Not to reach hasty conclusions before examining all aspects of a problem.
- To be open to different points of view.
- To reject stigmas on others.
- Not only Jews suffer pain inflicted on them by Arabs, but Jews also inflict pain on Arabs.
- All in all, they are quite similar to us.
- Not to hate human beings.
- They are eager for good relations with us, just as we are.
- They have fears just like us.

To me personally, this programme and its outcomes are most encouraging. I wonder if such projects could be applicable in other warring areas on our troubled globe.

Values education in teacher training

Most teachers consider themselves unqualified to engage in values education in their classrooms. Their training did not effectively equip them – and did not even attempt to equip them – to deal with values issues with their pupils. Some accept this situation as 'natural', claiming that values education should be the concern of parents and religion, but not of schools. Others may sincerely wish to engage actively in values education, but simply do not know how this is done.

I believe that values education is the very heart of educational theory and practice, today more so than ever before. Teachers training colleges, as well as schools of education in the universities, can no longer refrain from including this field in teacher education. I shall illustrate this point by describing how we approach this task in Oranim, the School of Education of the Kibbutz Movement in Israel.

Our students participate in an annual workshop bearing the title 'Values Education in a Democratic Society'. Its goal is to enable teachers to facilitate processes, in which their future pupils can learn to deal with significant values issues and, in the process, explore and build up their own individual values system. This process is individual, but takes place in a social setting. Values are considered in a climate of open interpersonal dialogue. Values education, as an individual as well as social process, is another polarity, the importance of which cannot be sufficiently stressed.

The workshop on values education is held in the setting of a humanistic climate, which characterizes our whole teacher training programme. This stresses holistic and experiential study of issues such as classroom climate, interpersonal communication, group processes, democracy in schools, education and community, group facilitation as well as the more conventional fields of study in teacher training. The workshops are presented in both pre-service and in-service settings.

Values education is explored on five different levels:

1 **Cognitive-Theoretical**: includes many of the issues presented in this chapter such as, freedom and commitment, Kohlberg's cognitive-developmental approach, other models of values education.
2 **Didactic**: the students undergo Values Clarification activities as well as Kohlbergian Moral Dilemmas deliberations. Needless to say, humanistic education stresses the need for personal experience of clarification about their own value systems, before they can facilitate such processes with others.
3 **Personal**: participants are encouraged to raise personal values dilemmas in their lives and process these with their colleagues in the supportive atmosphere of the workshop. It is this personal involvement of the participants that lends the workshop its depth.
4 **Educational**: students prepare short learning units on any values-loaded issue of their choice, present this to their colleagues, receive their feedback, teach the unit in their classrooms, and evaluate the whole activity in the workshop.
5 **Socio-Political**: participants prepare and present issues of current affairs in an innovative and creative manner – followed by feedback from the group. Education's influence on social and political reality are examined – on the general level of how to create a positive culture of controversy and dialogue as well as on the level of specific Israeli problems.

This multi-directional approach has a significant impact on the students. Time and time again, we witness how they harness their own personal experience in the workshop to engage successfully in meaningful values education with their pupils.

Hidden messages

The quality of values education depends on three factors. One is the character of the 'open messages' – the value statements explicitly expressed – that reach the individual student. The second is the world of 'hidden messages', all those behaviours, norms, incongruence between words and actions, that are never explicitly stated but exert considerable influence. The third is the 'educational climate', that complex system of interpersonal and group processes in the school that determines general feelings of belonging or alienation, trust or distrust, self concept and well-being.

I have already dealt with explicit messages in values education, as well as with the nature of educational climates. I shall conclude this chapter with a consideration of hidden messages and their impact on the learner.

Hidden messages derive from a number of sources – the individual teacher, the norms of the school's and society's value system. Teachers' behaviour is often quite incongruent with their verbal messages. They may pay eloquent lip-service to the ideals of democracy, but, at the same time, exploit their authority for oppressing views that deviate from their own. Others may expound universal values of justice and equality, but in practice act unfairly towards certain individual pupils. Pupils experiencing such treatment may react with confusion or anger, and frequently with cynicism and a growing lack of trust. By no means do I believe that these teachers have any evil intentions; they are simply not aware of the confusions they transmit and their destructive influence.

School systems as a whole also transmit some highly confusing messages. Aspy (1986), after observing some 200,000 lessons in all kinds of schools all over the United States, lists a number of injunctions to pupils that dominate the interactions but are never made explicit:

> **Don't feel!** because no one will respond to your feelings.
> **Don't think!** because teachers are interested only in your memorizing what they teach.
> **Don't talk!** because schools are not interested in student initiatives.
> **Line up!** because teaching is organized in rows and aisles.
> **Don't get involved!** because school expects you to be bland and bored rather than to experience the intensity of learning.

Jackson (1968) relates to the 'Hidden Curriculum', which he defines as 'the norms and values that are implicitly, but effectively, taught in schools, and that are not usually talked about in teachers' statements of ends or goals.' This hidden curriculum is loaded with value messages; students 'inhale' them in their twelve years of schooling – and many of them for a number of additional years of higher education. The major message is 'Be obedient to authority!' The fruits of this message are harvested not only in school, but also in places of work, political systems and the family.

Society – including schools – relates negatively to social conflicts. This is a truly paradoxical situation. In countries all over the world, such as the US, France, Latin America, China, Israel, widespread celebrations are devoted to the heroes of their struggle for independence, who, during their lifetimes, were considered rebels against formal and legal authority. The revolutionary of the past is now granted full legitimation, but, in our own times, conservative society rejects all forms of social conflict or revolutionary thinking. This absurdity is well anchored in society, school curricula following suit in echoing this rejection of social conflict.

As regards the issue of schools' approach to social conflicts, I should like to quote Apple (1975). Writing about 'two tacit assumptions in teaching and curricular materials', he adds: 'The first centers about a negative position on the nature and uses of conflict. The second focuses on man as a recipient of values and institutions, not on man as a creator and recreator of values and institutions'.

I have no illusions that educational processes can be truly harmonious, or that it is practically possible to bridge entirely the gap between open and hidden messages. Nevertheless it is highly important to sharpen our awareness to the overwhelming influence of hidden messages. Meaningful values education must include developing skills to expose hidden messages, to make the implicit explicit, and to assist our students to 'immunize' themselves against their destructive influence.

Conclusion

Let me conclude, as I have begun, with polarity, with the integration of apparent opposites. We have considered the merger of freedom with commitment, of open messages with hidden ones, of

statements with actions, of personal and interpersonal values on the micro level with the macro level of social and political values. These integrations are inherent in humanistic values education.

There is, however, an additional field of integration. Educators (and not only educators) are usually either theorists or practicians, and there is very little contact, flow of information, even trust, between the two. There is frequently an implicit refusal to be influenced by 'the other side'. This is surely the height of absurdity of dichotomic either/or thinking.

Let us strive for fullest possible integration of these two poles, which are, after all, the two sides of the same coin. Strengthening the mutual influence – and the mutual benefit – of theory and practice, bridging the gap that is so detrimental to good practice, as well as to good theory, is a major challenge to education in general and to values education in particular. I should like to express my hope that processes of integrating 'opposite' poles, which is part and parcel of humanistic education as a whole, will enable our community of values educators to make some significant advances in the sphere of theory and practice.

References

Apple, M. (1975) The hidden curriculum and the nature of conflict. In W. F. Pinar (ed.) *Curriculum Theorising*. Berkely, Ca: McSutchan.

Aspy, D. N. (1986) *This is School! Sit Down and Listen!* Amherst, Mass: Human Research and Development Press.

Brown, G. I. (1971) *Human Teaching for Human Learning – An Introduction to Confluent Education*. New York: Viking.

Combs, A. W. (1974) *Humanistic Teacher Education*. Fort Collins: Shields.

Darom, D. (1988) Freedom and commitment – values issues in humanistic education. *Journal of Humanistic Education and Development*, **26**: 98–108.

Darom, D. (1989) *Climate for Growth – Freedom and Commitment in Education*. Tel Aviv: Sifriat Poalim. (In Hebrew)

Darom, D. (1994) Am I entitled to express my political views in the classroom? *Chinuch Acher*, **10**. (In Hebrew)

Darom, D. (1996) Peace education in Israel – encounter and dialogue. Paper delivered at the 25th Anniversary Conference of the Journal for Moral Education 'Morals for the Millenium'. Lancaster, 15–19 July 1996.

Freire, P. (1973) *Pedagogy of the Oppressed*. New York: Seabury Press.

Jackson, P. (1968) *Life in Classrooms.* London: Holt, Rinehart and Winston.

Kirschenbaum, H. (1977) *Advanced Value Clarification.* La Jolla, Ca: University Associated Press.

Kohlberg, L. (1978) Revisions in the theory and practice of moral development. In W. Damon (ed.) *Moral Development.* San Francisco: Jossey Bass.

Maslow, A. (1954) *Motivation and Personality.* New York: Harper and Row.

Raths, L., Harmin, M. and Simon, S. B. (1966) *Values and Teaching.* Columbus, Ohio: Merril.

Rogers, C. (1983) *Freedom to Learn for the 80s.* Columbus, Ohio: Merril (Bell and Howell).

3

Political Learning and Values Education: Problems and Possibilities[1]

IAN DAVIES

Introduction

This chapter draws attention to some of the challenges and opportunities associated with the development of education for citizenship in England and Wales. There are four main sections:

1 The status of political learning in schools.
2 The goals that have been suggested for education for citizenship and their relationship with values education. Comments are made in three sections: the evidence for values commonly and currently held in a number of European countries; issues arising from conceptual disagreements about the nature of values and values education; and the different types of political learning that have been suggested in recent decades.
3 The nature and extent of the current implementation of values education and political learning.
4 Finally, a number of ways forward are suggested. This is not done in a simplistic and dogmatic manner. Rather, there is an attempt only to focus on some general areas and a limited number of specific initiatives that could be explored further.

The status of political learning and values education

Of course, given the wide ranging title used for this section, only rather general issues can be tackled. It is clear, though, that there have been recent efforts 'to re-emphasise the moral element in the concept and status of citizenship' (Oliver and Heater 1994: 130). There is a growing awareness that there is a 'need to recognise that learning about and through values will create the effective citizen' (McGettrick

1991). Values education is said to touch 'on some of the central questions facing contemporary British education' (Ofsted 1994: 4) and this is reflected in other European countries (Barr 1991). The Parliamentary Assembly of the Council of Europe has recently adopted a Recommendation on a European strategy for children which is obviously relevant to values education. Osler and Starkey (1996: 69) quote Jeleff when referring to this resolution:

> Children are citizens of the society of today and tomorrow. Society has a long term responsibility to support children and has to acknowledge the rights of the family in the interests of the child. Responding to children's rights, interests and needs must be a political priority. The Assembly is convinced that respect for children's rights and greater equality between children and adults will help preserve the pact between generations and will contribute towards democracy.

Debates in North America also show the widespread concern with the political aspects of values and education both in a general way (e.g. Hughes 1993) and also in relation to the development of character education by organizations such as the Association for Supervision and Curriculum Development (Virginia, USA).

When work that relates generally to values education (rather than just that which emerges from an explicit connection with political learning) is considered, it is clear that there is something of a revival of interest in the area (Tomlinson and Quinton 1986, Cummings et al. 1988, Bottery 1990, White 1990, Robb 1991a, Robb 1991b, Carr 1993, Rowe 1994, Halstead and Taylor 1996). It seems that a search for the meaning of a pluralist society is occurring.

This rise in status, however, is not always

unproblematically positive. Enhanced status for this area has meant in the past that there is a perceived sense of crisis in society. Stradling (1987) refers to a greater interest in political learning in 1918, 1930 and 1939–45. Entwistle (1971), Derricott (1979) and Marshall (1988) make the same point. In the first half of this century, voices that were heard at times of crisis, such as Gollancz and Somervell (1914), Stewart (1938) and Cole (1942), have been seen at times of relative stability as cries in the wilderness. The perceived crisis can be seen in more recent times: a need to fight the growth of political extremism in the 1970s; attempts to overcome economic inefficiency (as the New Right strove to introduce economic diversity and an entrepreneurial spirit within a substantive moral framework) in the 1980s; and demands to tackle moral decline, fragmented communities and rising crime, particularly among young people, in the 1990s. A recent example of a call for action in a climate of crisis can be seen in some documents of the Council of Europe (1996: 21) which refer to the 'climate of intolerance, aggressive nationalism and ethnocentrism which expresses itself in violence against migrants, people of immigrant origin and minorities such as gypsies'.

Of course, there will be debates about the extent to which these crises have been real or imagined (e.g. following a survey of over 22,000 young people, there is some evidence of the average adolescent being rather conservative, Garner 1997). But in the 1990s there does seem to be an urgent need for action to be taken. High profile cases and the interpretations that emerge from them are contributing strongly to the need for something to be done. Within England and Wales appallingly tragic events, such as the murders of the toddler James Bulger and the London head teacher Philip Lawrence, have led directly and indirectly to an increased concern with values and citizenship. The Home Office is now promoting the Philip Lawrence citizenship awards. The National Forum on Values is at work. The increasingly diverse nature of modern society has given rise to multifarious if not pluralistic cultural groupings; technological advances that have made the information explosion possible have made society aware of this increased diversity; and academic thinking and research calls increasing attention to aspects of society's values and how they do and could impact upon the development of political culture, and how it can be learned and influenced. The interrelationships between values education and political learning seem vitally significant. There will be huge difficulties to achieve pluralistic consensus at a time when intellectual and political fragmentation seems very evident.

The goals for political learning and values education

The goals for political learning and values education must be discussed, first, within an understanding of the nature of those values that are currently and commonly held. A full consideration of the nature of social integration that would allow for an expression of citizenship would involve a study of the long term processes of political, social and economic convergence at three levels: the structural make-up of societies; their institutions and organizations; and the patterns of orientation of their citizens (Sobisch and Immerfall 1997). Ester et al. (1993) have noted that there is as much evidence for value divergence as for convergence, and have written of the development of individuation as opposed to a common approach to anything, including individualism. There seems some doubt as to whether there is as yet a common European society. Within England and Wales there is some evidence of a diversity of views which is perhaps too broad (Roberts and Sachdev 1996). Dahl's (1982, 1985) questions of how wide is the pluralist spectrum and who should control the pluralist society are, as always, very relevant.

Given the above, it is of little surprise that there are many different positions on what should constitute the essential nature of political learning that takes appropriate account of values education. At times this is an essential element of the debates that must occur within a healthy, politically-aware, pluralist, democratic society. This sort of debate can encompass both different views between people and shifting positions of individuals. However, at worst, there are either competing coherent views that are so divergent as to mean that a way forward would never be found or, alternatively, simple confusion within and between the various perspectives. One way to demonstrate this unsatisfactory position is to refer to the fundamental issue of the nature of procedural or substantive values.

For Bloom (1987), it is important to promote substantive values. These are never clearly defined but, he argues, there should be some greater commitment to a more traditional approach and there is an appeal to discontinue the efforts of promoting relativism. Mendus, however, (quoted by Jonathan 1993: 171) develops a very different argument: 'we should understand education as a means of developing reflective consciousness in students, and that will require fragmentation and the immanent conflict of traditions rather than a background of agreed values'.

In contrast to the positions offered by both Bloom and Mendus, an increasing number of authors argue that there must be some middle way steered between substantive and procedural values. For Jonathan (1993: 172) education must be thought of as 'a social process with social goals, which require but are not solely constituted by the intellectual emancipation of the individual'. Some of these differences seem insurmountable. And, of course, a full range of perspectives has not been considered here. Perhaps most obviously, the postmodern perspectives (that are opposed so strongly by some e.g. Osler and Starkey 1996; and supported by others such as Huckle 1996) are not discussed. In my view, many of the perspectives associated with postmodernism do not assist the development of a valid form of education for citizenship or values education. As not all would agree with me, I am aware of the difficulties in establishing an overarching framework for education for citizenship which would be supported by all. Citizenship is (to use W. B. Gallie's phrase) essentially contested. There is probably some sense in searching for a form of broad consensus but it is also necessary to accept that complete agreement by all will never be achieved. In a democratic society it is wise not to seek adherence by all to one narrowly-defined framework.

Significant differences can also be seen in the various models of citizenship that have been proposed. Fouts (1997) has discussed the work of Heater (1990), McLaughlin (1992) and Rauner (1997) to show the different perspectives that are encapsulated, respectively, by the notions of multiple citizenships; maximal and minimal citizenships; and post national citizenship.

When these debates are taken one step closer to the classroom, but not necessarily in such a way as to have an impact with teachers and pupils, the differences and difficulties become even more apparent. It is true that some (e.g. Rowe 1994) have attempted to give some reference to a teaching

programme related to the development of values for citizenship, but many are silent on this theme. Unfortunately, documentation has tended to present only 'pious vacuities and conceptual confusions' (Carr 1993: 193). Crick (1978: 72) advised waiting 'until we discover far more from teachers, students and surveys about what happens in practice and what works best'.

When one sees Crick's own efforts in this field, one is tempted almost to agree with him. The work on values education provided by the Programme for Political Education was on the whole uninspiring (Davies 1996a). The confusion among those centrally involved in the programme itself is clear. Harber (1987), for example, argued that the emphasis given to procedural values kept the Programme for Political Education version of political literacy distinct from conservative or radical perspectives. For others however, 'It is in the area of attitudes that there seems to be the greatest overlap between political education (of the PPE variety) and Peace Education' (Lister 1980: 71). Given that there has been perceived to be some justification for suspecting the value messages of Peace Studies (Lister 1984), there is obviously some difficulty. While the gross use of values that one might find in certain publications are avoided (e.g. Ministry of Education 1949, O'Neil 1979, Milson 1980, Apple 1981, 1986), it is not at all clear that Crick was able to establish an overwhelmingly coherent argument for procedural values.

Finally in this section, it is necessary to draw attention to the more general difficulties associated with characterizing the areas of political learning and values education. As has been argued above, it is not the case (and should not be) that one can always see consistency. Models shift over time. But the difficulty for those engaged in teaching and learning politics is to know what is happening at any particular point and what is appropriate. There are many debates or models within values education that will not be discussed here. Twists and turns in the debates about political learning have followed a pattern which has been described elsewhere (Davies 1994a). Briefly, prior to the 1960s, there was very little explicit political education in schools. Heater (1977: 62) has cited four key factors to explain its neglect:

1 a lack of tradition;
2 few teachers who were professionally committed to political education;

3   a belief that politics was solely an adult domain;
4   a fear of indoctrination.

This attitude led to political education being taught, if done in any explicit sense, as information based civics with substantive values being promoted (Osborne 1980).

From the 1960s the situation changed. In very general terms, three types of political learning have been significant during the last three decades: political literacy (from the 1970s), global education (from the 1980s) and citizenship education (from the 1990s).

Drawing from the ideas of Ian Lister, an overview of the meaning of those three types would see political literacy being concerned with skills, issues and action appropriate to the operation of democratic politics; global education being characterized by affective learning and holistic approaches to world issues; and citizenship education focusing on voluntary service in a society where obligations are perhaps more important than rights. Each of the models has been variously described and supported but, generally, two simple points can be made: political learning has not been characterized, at least for the last two to three decades (and, possibly, never) by common agreement; and that no form of *explicit* political learning has ever been implemented widely in England. Whether or not the current revival of interest in political learning in the form of education for citizenship will lead to a change in this rather pessimistic position cannot be known at this point.

The implementation of values education and political learning

A brief discussion of the nature and extent of efforts to implement such work also reveals significant difficulties. The National Curriculum for England and Wales currently gives little, if any, explicit emphasis to social and political knowledge. While it is asserted that certain traditional subjects such as history can be a 'priceless preparation for citizenship' (DES 1990), in reality there are some concerns about the potential of history teachers to meet this challenge alone (Davies 1996b). The cross-curricular themes are largely ineffective (Whitty et al. 1994), and the NCC document specifically on education for citizenship was unsatisfactory in many ways (Davies 1994a).

This rather pessimistic perspective is not developed in order to blame teachers. Often they do a difficult job with enthusiasm and commitment. But they are not trained for their work; they normally work in modular structures that do not allow them to get to know their pupils well; and they have to work with colleagues from a diverse range of backgrounds who, at times, are selected for this work due to the spaces on a timetable after allocations for specialist subjects have been catered for. Above all, the amount of timetable space given over to the explicit preparation of young people for democratic capability is slight. Unfortunately, three 40 minute lessons each year is about the best that can be expected in many schools (Davies 1993). The way in which the hidden curriculum works in schools does not suggest, whatever headteachers have said in questionnaire based research about the significance of school ethos for this work, that this pessimistic picture can be altered easily (Davies 1994b).

Ways forward

The need for the development of a broad consensus on a framework to explore education for citizenship

Given the nature of the intellectual difficulties discussed above, and the long term neglect of education for citizenship, it is not possible to provide simple quick fix solutions. In an attempt to be positive and constructive there may be some hope for cutting through some of the conceptual difficulties by referring to the work of Carr and Freeman. Carr (1993: 205) argues that we need:

> people who have themselves strong and definite value commitments on the basis of reasonably mature moral reflection, but who are yet also prepared, in a spirit of proper openness to moral improvement, to welcome and honestly address the challenges that others may be prepared to offer to what they hold dear.

Freeman explores the ways in which it is possible to avoid relativism and still hold fast to universal traditions and agreements. He argues that while it would not be possible to argue that universal declarations relating to education may offer either a complete moral theory, or a detailed course of action for all specific cases that could be imagined, there are, nevertheless, principles that can be encapsulated in social and political contexts that may be professionally promoted by educators (Freeman 1994). There are frameworks that deliberately explore ways forward in this manner. Intercultural education is one that could be mentioned (see the *European Journal of Intercultural Education* for many useful examples of the ideas and practices). The efforts to investigate what we can learn from each other within a coherent and clear framework are important.

The work of Micheline Rey is important in understanding intercultural education (see Rey 1997, Davies and Rey 1998). Using the word 'intercultural' means putting the whole weight on the prefix 'inter': interaction, exchange, opening up. It also means giving proper emphasis to the word 'culture': recognition of cultures, lifestyles and symbolic representations. This form of education emphasizes both time and space. Simultaneously it recognizes the reality of interdependence, and provides a perspective for action. Of course, there are dilemmas and many questions relating to how to take action. But intercultural education aims to provide ambitious strategies, the most important of which aim to do the following:

- to question our convictions whether they are egocentric, sociocentric or ethnocentric;
- to transform the representations through which we make judgements and take action;
- to modify the value given to different abilities, norms and cultures (which may or may not be present in the local community);
- to transform and diversify the existing power structure and give equal rights to groups that have been depreciated as to their cultural referents, their skills and their means of expression;
- to break down isolation and acknowledge the complexity of the relationships existing between cultures, social classes, institutions, education, school subjects and scientific subjects as well as between human beings whatever their origins;
- to develop communication and negotiation between individuals, groups and communities that are positive and enriching for all parties involved.

It may not be possible to arrive at an agreed framework immediately. The characterization of an intercultural approach given above is only one way forward. But, at the very least, a mechanism to facilitate discussion to this end is essential. Academics and teachers need to be brought together in a new or revised forum to allow for discussion of these issues. The 'coalition for citizenship' (a loose network of organizations such as the Citizenship Foundation, the Centre for Studies in Citizenship Education and the Council for Education in World Citizenship) need to find a way to come together more often and with greater impact.

The need to understand more about teachers' conceptions of education for citizenship so that in-service work and appropriate school programmes may develop

It is very important to ensure that work promoted in schools builds on what we currently know (and there should be opportunities for us to know more) about how teachers characterize citizenship and moral values. A start has been made on this (e.g. Bousted and Davies 1996) and work is continuing (Davies, Gregory and Riley 1997). Some recent work has shown that there are 'social concern characteristics' which teachers associate with good citizenship. In other words, being a good citizen is overwhelmingly characterized by teachers in terms of the recognizing, and being prepared to act upon that recognition, of the responsibilities we owe to others as fellow members of the (normally local) community. The ways in which these views are expressed seem to suggest that the ethical/moral dimension to being a good citizen is inextricably part of the teacher conception of good citizenship. There are also important knowledge characteristics in these conceptions. Teachers, particularly those from secondary schools, are often ready to discuss the political dimension of issues of citizenship, and all teachers want to develop the disposition and ability to question and to recognize and accept the fact of opinions other than one's own. Finally, although there is no evidence of crude conservatism or patriotism in the guise of narrow nationalism, teachers will cite their own characteristic obedience to laws as evidence of being good citizens. Although some draw a distinction between law and justice, most feel 'that in 99 per cent of cases they really do come down to the same thing where the law in most practical cases [does coincide with the] ordinary basic moral values assumed by the community' (cit. in Davies, Gregory and Riley 1999).

No citizenship education programme is likely to work in schools unless it builds obviously from teachers' thinking. However, it is also important to ensure that existing teacher views are not accepted as all that can be achieved. Still not enough is known about how and what teachers think about pluralist democracy. The limits of their values and any consequent actions are not known clearly. Furthermore, it was noticeable in the study that generated these findings that teachers were unaware of key writings in this field and that their views do not sit at all easily with the work of theorists. This should not be taken as necessary criticism of either the teachers or the theorists, but it does suggest that there may be a need for in-service education so that these tensions can be explored. It would, obviously, be completely unacceptable if teachers of traditional academic subjects, such as history or English, declared themselves unfamiliar with current debates in their specialist field; and it would be worrying if those academic debates did not relate in an obvious way to the contexts which give rise to the analyses.

Furthermore, it is vital not to make simplistic assumptions about the nature of good practice in schools in light of the views shown above. The teachers have declared that participation in the community is important. As one said:

> I mean hopefully its playing an active and positive role in putting something back . . . so that not only are you sort of good spirited but you actually act in such a way that the community is benefited in some way.   (cit. in Davies, Gregory and Riley 1999)

This does not necessarily mean, of course, that we should adhere to the 'voluntary obligations' (Hurd 1989) that some have recommended. The way in which the report of the Commission on Citizenship (1990) became identified in many people's minds almost entirely with the 'fourth dimension' of volunteering was most unsatisfactory. It is important not to assume simplistically that the voluntary principle is always the best (see Warren 1986, Wringe 1992). It may be important to explore more critical and constructive social engagement which others have begun to develop (e.g. NYA 1997, Willow 1997). But, again the limits of the pluralist spectrum need to be explored with teachers and by teachers with school students.

The need to know more about the ways in which young people make sense of values

Some of the above discussion makes it clear that there has already been some work undertaken with

adults on value positions. There is little work that has been done with young people (a rare exception is Roberts and Sachdev 1996). An important recent piece of work based on extensive research suggests that three value orientations have a high influence in modelling images of democratic citizenship: social solidarity; socio-political cosmopolitanism; and political autonomy (IBE 1997). It would not do to interpret these results simplistically, but it is necessary to consider the proposition that if pupils hold certain values they are likely to react more positively to key features such as feelings of political efficacy. This may provide both a starting point for educational work in the form of important contextual considerations, and perhaps also will help determine important preferred outcomes.

It is vitally important to know more about how young people react to education for citizenship. Far too much is currently asserted and not explained. A parallel can be drawn with the ways in which the political socialization literature has normally dealt with young people. It has not been uncommon for young people to be seen as being subject to initiatives in a rather simplistic manner. Even the very valuable pioneering work of authors such as Greenstein (1965) can be seen in this light. We need to know how different pupils will react to – and interact with – particular programmes and people. A recent piece of work which evaluated a whole school series of events and activities under the title of 'Democracy Day' (Davies, Gray and Stephens 1998) noted important differences between pupils. Girls always reacted more positively than boys to the activities. Whether this is another example of boys' relatively weaker adherence to school life in general or a reaction against particular teaching methods cannot be known at this stage. Another difference was associated with age. Simply, reactions became more negative as the age of the pupils increased. However, it does seem that certain activities are regarded more positively by older pupils. A mock election, for example, led to older pupils saying that it 'made me think about our political government in a different way'; while younger pupils said that there should have been 'shorter speeches' and that 'it could have been easier to understand'. Of course, all teachers will take great care in ensuring that in their specialist teaching areas work is appropriately differentiated. The point here is simply that this professional skill should be exercised when education for citizenship within a pluralist democracy is being targeted.

The need to promote cooperative work between teachers

The difficulties of establishing cooperation between teachers or even in encouraging teachers to look beyond the boundaries of their own specialist areas are well known (e.g. Lortie 1975, Hargreaves 1991, Bousted and Davies 1993). In a recent piece of work investigating the ways in which RE (religious education) and history departments choose to teach about the Holocaust, it was somewhat disconcerting to find that there was a lack of knowledge about what other colleagues were doing, which meant that in some cases the same resources were being employed (Brown and Davies 1997). Perceptions of the status of departments, and the nature of events as being more appropriately cast within one particular framework meant that instead of the occurrence of valuably differentiated and more extensive work there was only fragmentation and repetition. The points made here are not meant to contradict those above about the need for specialist understanding. Rather, there is an additional need for teachers to at least be aware of the different approaches of their colleagues and to make allowance for cooperation when appropriate. This is particularly important in an area such as education for citizenship, which can potentially relate to so many areas of the curriculum and without some explicitly focused attention will be subject to the *rhetoric* that all are involved and the *reality* of little and/or inconsistent coverage.

The need for rigour

Too often, work on values education and education for citizenship has been characterized by vaguely-felt good intentions. There is a pressing need to avoid 'the mish mash that in many schools passes for personal and social education' (Rowe 1997). This is essential and in many ways reinforces the proper link between education for values and rigorous political learning: 'Adequate reasoning in political, moral and other valuational contexts, *presupposes* [emphasis in the original] an adequate grasp of values. Value-education, in any sphere, is thus the foundation of reason in that sphere, not its product' (Dunlop 1996: 77).

Guidance on what is needed to supply this rigour is already available; Newmann (1990a and 1990b) has identified six minimal criteria for the effective promotion of higher order thinking:

1 Sustained examination of a few topics rather than superficial coverage of many.
2 Substantive coherence between and within lessons.
3 Students given an appropriate time to think and respond.
4 Teacher asks challenging questions or structures challenging tasks.
5 Teacher is a 'model of thoughtfulness'.
6 Students offer explanations and reasons for their conclusions.

Newmann has also identified certain activities that may promote higher order thinking:

1 Scrutinizing arguments for logical consistency.
2 Searching for counter examples.
3 Distinguishing between relevant and irrelevant information.
4 Distinguishing between factual claims and value judgements.
5 Rhetorical strategies such as stipulation of disputable claims to let an argument proceed.
6 Using metaphors and analogies to represent problems and solutions.
7 Discussion strategies such as asking for clarification, pressing people to stay with an issue, summarizing the progress of the conversation.

It is important to note that the above factors are broad enough to be applied to a range of concepts, and to be used with a number of different teaching styles. A debate about teaching methods that focuses on the supposed polar opposites of 'traditional' and 'progressive' is not being used here. There must also be ways to take proper account of the relationships between the cognitive and the affective, with a mutually exclusive approach being inadequate. There are more explicit and specific discussions about the sort of classroom work that could take place. Attention needs to be paid to content, ensuring that appropriate material is covered to allow for understanding of the key aspects of citizenship; access must be considered in that the school must make opportunities for openness to exist in terms of who studies these key issues (the approach of encouraging one or more groups of pupils only to study citizenship with the parameters still in some schools being set by ability is completely unacceptable); and the process of study by school students ensuring that there are opportunities for cooperation with people in other schools and in the wider community and that a critical engagement with knowledge is developed.

One example of a classroom exercise has been described by Davies and Rey (1998) which meets some of these criteria. In this work the focus is on interpretations of invented contemporary political traditions. After some background work which alerts students to the existence of invented traditions (Hobsbawn and Ranger 1987), a contemporary example is given (the use by John Major of the phrase 'a thousand years of British history' could be relevant). The nature of British history is then explored in outline, with some questions being developed about the nature of interpretations arising from advice provided by government agencies (SCAA undated). The 'story' of recent European integration is considered to provide some context and to allow students to consider the possibility of the existence of invented traditions in the European scene. A particular common account is likely to be identified from existing textbooks and alternative interpretations are to be noted by their exclusion. Symbols with a European theme used in Britain could be investigated to help students consider the ways in which identities have and are being established. Place names (e.g. Waterloo or Trafalgar), days for celebration (for instance, St. George's day), parades and other mass gatherings (e.g. 11 November), monuments (such as Admiralty Arch) may suggest particular interpretations associated with England and not Britain; war not peace; the nation and not Europe or the world. A similar list can be devised for the development of European traditions with the following currently providing important signposts to identity: the flag of the EU; the new passport for British citizens; the celebration of 9 May as Europe day; the use of Beethoven's *Ode to Joy* as an anthem. It is possible to consider the flag with only fifteen stars, the passport with the British emblem emphasizing the nation so prominently, the choice of 9 May with a special emphasis on France and Germany (the date of the Schumann Declaration) and the use of a particular sort of music can all be discussed. It would then be interesting if pupils could discuss the different symbols that could be used if one were to emphasize a geographical Europe, or an economic Europe, a cultural Europe, a political Europe, a Europe within the world or whatever. Students' understandings of

the struggle for the limits of pluralism can possibly be developed in this way.

The above is only an example of what could be done in a classroom. It would not be expensive. It could lead from, and into, other work that explored the notions of citizenship and values in very active and interactive ways. It does not expect simple socialization (Slater 1989). It seeks to establish work in a manner that has rigour and builds on and from the traditions associated with academic thinking; political and moral frameworks within which we live; and the cognitive and affective continua that shape educational work. It is not suggested as some sort of panacea. Ultimately, professional teachers will find other, and better, ways forward. But what must be clear is that it is not possible for the current situation to continue. We must break from the trumpeting of high-minded but vague and often contradictory ambitions; especially when the means to implement even some of these notions are not provided. It is vital, and this is really a very simple and obvious point, that high expectations combined with weak aims and inadequate implementation strategies will lead to failure. Success depends on clearly conceptualizing the ends and willing the means. While simplistic links are best avoided, it does seem not unreasonable to suggest that if a genuinely pluralistic democracy is to mean anything in the present and future it is necessary not to leave this educational work to chance.

Note

1 This chapter was written before the publication of the Crick Report (1998).

References

Apple, M. (1981) *Ideology and Curriculum*. London: Routledge and Kegan Paul.
Apple, M. (1986) *Teachers and Texts: A Political Economy of Class and Gender Relations in Education*. London: Routledge and Kegan Paul.
Barr, I. (1991) The role of the SCCC in values education. In W. Robb (ed.) *Values Education: Some Recent Developments in Scotland*. Aberdeen: Gordon Cook Foundation.
Bloom, A. (1987) *The Closing of the American Mind*. New York: Simon and Schuster.
Bottery, M. (1990) *The Morality of the School*. London: Cassell.
Bousted, M. and Davies, I. (1993) Bridge that gap! Are there opportunities for History and English teachers to

work together? *Teaching History,* 71: 10–15.

Bousted, M. and Davies, I. (1996) Teachers' perceptions of models of political learning. *Curriculum,* 17 (1): 12–23.

Brown, M. and Davies, I. (1997) Teaching and learning about the Holocaust in England: history, religion and human rights. Paper presented at the symposium on *Teaching the Holocaust* held at the Haus der Wannsee Konferenz, September 1997.

Carr, D. (1993) Moral values and the teacher: beyond the paternal and permissive. *Journal of Philosophy of Education,* 27 (2): 193–207.

Cole, M. (1942) *Education for Democracy.* London: Allen and Unwin.

Commission on Citizenship (1990) *Encouraging Citizenship.* London: HMSO.

Council of Europe (1996) *History Teaching and the Promotion of Democratic Values and Tolerance: A Handbook for Teachers.* Strasbourg: Council of Europe.

Crick, B. (1978) Procedural Values. In B. Crick and A. Porter (eds) *Political Education and Political Literacy.* London: Longman.

Cummings, W. K., Gopinathan, S. and Tomoda, Y. (1988) *The Revival of Values Education in Asia and the West.* Oxford: Pergamon Press.

Dahl, R. (1982) *Dilemmas of Pluralist Democracy.* New Haven: Yale University Press.

Dahl, R. (1985) *A Preface to Economic Democracy.* Cambridge: Polity Press.

Davies, I. (1993) Teaching political understanding in secondary schools. *Curriculum,* 14 (3): 163–77.

Davies, I. (1994a) Whatever happened to political education? *Educational Review,* 46 (1): 29–38.

Davies, I. (1994b) Education for citizenship. *Curriculum,* 15 (2): 67–76.

Davies, I. (1996a) Values and the teaching and learning of European history: a focal point for education for European citizenship. *Children's Social and Economics Education,* 1 (1): 51–60.

Davies, I. (1996b) The teaching of history and education for European citizenship. *The European Legacy,* 1 (3): 872–7.

Davies, I., Gray, G. and Stephens, P. (1998) Education for citizenship: a case study of 'democracy day' at a comprehensive school. *Educational Review,* 50 (1): 15–27.

Davies, I., Gregory, I. and Riley, S. (1997) Concepts of citizenship: results of research on teacher perceptions in England. Paper presented at the British Educational Research Association conference held at the University of York, September 1997.

Davies, I., Gregory, I. and Riley, S. C. (1999) *Good Citizenship and Educational Provision.* London: Falmer Press.

Davies, I. and Rey, M. (1998) Intercultural approaches to education: issues for teachers and children in the exploration of identities and citizenships. In N. Clough and C. Holden (eds) *Children as Citizens.* London: Jessica Kingsley Publishers.

Derricott, R. (1979) Social studies in England: perspectives, problems and reconsideration. *International Journal of Political Education,* 2: 231–3.

DES (1990) *History for Ages 5 to 16.* London: HMSO.

Dunlop, F. (1996) Democratic values and the foundations of political education. In J. M. Halstead and M. J. Taylor (eds) *Values in Education and Education in Values.* London: Falmer Press.

Entwistle, H. (1971) *Political Education in a Democracy.* London: Routledge and Kegan Paul.

Ester, P., Holman, L. and de Moor, R. (1993) *The Individualising Society: Value Change in Europe and North America.* Tilburg, NL: Tilburg University Press.

Fouts, J. (1997) Models of citizenship. Paper presented at the British Educational Research Association conference held at the University of York, September 1997.

Freeman, R. (1994) Are human rights universal? Lecture at the University of York.

Garner, C. (1997) Drugs and cigarettes? We're the generation who like to say no. *The Independent,* 28 July, p. 3.

Gollancz, V. and Somervell, D. (1914) *Political Education at a Public School.* London: Collins.

Greenstein, F. (1965) *Children and Politics.* New Haven and London: Yale University Press.

Halstead, J. M. and Taylor, M. (eds) (1996) *Values in Education and Education in Values.* London: Falmer Press.

Harber, C. (1987) Political education and peace education. In C. Brown, C. Harber and J. Strivens (eds) *Social Education: Principles and Practice.* Lewes: Falmer Press.

Hargreaves, A. (1991) Contrived collegiality: micropolitics of teacher collaboration. In J. Blase (ed.) *The Politics of Life in Schools.* London: Sage.

Heater, D. (1977) A burgeoning of interest: political education in Britain. In B. Crick and D. Heater (eds) *Essays on Political Education.* Lewes: Falmer Press.

Heater, D. (1990) *Citizenship: The Civic Ideal in World History, Politics and Education.* London: Longman.

Hobsbawn, E. and Ranger, T. (1987) *The Invention of Tradition.* Cambridge: Cambridge University Press.

Huckle, J. (1996) Globalisation, postmodernity and citizenship. In M. Steiner (ed.) *Developing the Global Teacher: Theory and Practice in Initial Teacher Education.* Stoke on Trent: Trentham Books in association with the World Studies Trust.

Hughes, R. (1993) *The Culture of Complaint.* Oxford: Oxford University Press.

Hurd, D. (1989) Freedom will flourish where citizens accept responsibility. *The Independent,* 13 February.

International Bureau of Education (IBE) (1997) What education for what citizenship? *Educational Innovation and Information.* Geneva: International Bureau of Education.

Jonathan, R. (1993) Education, philosophy of education and the fragmentation of value. *Journal of Philosophy of Education,* 27 (2): 171–8.

Lister, I. (1980) The problems of peace studies. Paper available from the Department of Educational Studies, University of York, England.

Lister, I. (1984) Peace education and political education. In C. Reid (ed.) *Issues in Peace Education.* Published for the United World College of the Atlantic. Wales: D. Brown and Sons Ltd.

Lortie, D. (1975) *School Teacher: A Sociological Study.* Chicago: Chicago University Press.

McGettrick, B. (1991) Values education and the Gordon Cook Foundation: towards a policy for funding within an educational plan. In W. Robb (ed.) *Values Education: Some Ways Forward.* Aberdeen: Gordon Cook Foundation.

McLaughlin, T. H. (1992) Citizenship, diversity and education: a philosophical perspective. *Journal of Moral Education,* **21** (3): 235–50.

Marshall, S. (1988) The origins and development of political education. *Teaching Politics,* **17** (1): 3–10.

Milson, F. (1980) *Political Education: A Practical Guide for Christian Youth Workers.* Exeter: The Paternoster Press.

Ministry of Education (1949) *Citizens Growing Up.* Pamphlet number 16. London: HMSO.

National Youth Agency (NYA) (1997) *Volunteer Action: Young People Making a Difference in their Communities.* Leicester: National Youth Agency.

National Curriculum Council (NCC) (1990) *Education for Citizenship.* York: National Curriculum Council.

Newmann, F. W. (1990a) Higher order thinking in teaching social studies: a rationale for the assessment of classroom thoughtfulness. *Journal of Curriculum Studies,* **22** (1): 41–56.

Newmann, F. W. (1990b) Qualities of thoughtful social studies classes. *Journal of Curriculum Studies,* **22** (3): 253–75.

Ofsted (1994) *Spiritual, Moral, Social and Cultural Development.* London: Ofsted.

Oliver, D. and Heater, D. (1994) *The Foundations of Citizenship.* London: Harvester Wheatsheaf.

O'Neil, D. (1979) Politics and Catholicism. *International Journal of Political Education,* **2**: 205–12.

Osborne, K. (1980) Civics, citizenship or politics. What should we teach? *Contact,* **46**. Ontario: Canada Studies Foundation.

Osler, A. and Starkey, H. (1996) *Teacher Education and Human Rights.* London: David Fulton Publishers.

Rauner, M. (1997) Citizenship in the curriculum: the globalization of civics education in anglophone Africa 1955–95. In C. McNeely (ed.) *Public Rights, Public Rules: Constituting Citizens in the World Polity and National Policy.* New York: Garland Publishing.

Rey, M. (1997) Human rights education and intercultural relations: lessons for development educators. In J. Lynch, C. Mogdil and S. Mogdil (eds) *Education and Development: Tradition and Innovation* (Volume 1: Concepts, Approaches and Assumptions). London: Cassell: 173–83.

Robb, W. (ed.) (1991a) *Values Education: Some Ways Forward.* Aberdeen: Gordon Cook Foundation.

Robb, W. (1991b) *Values Education in Scotland: Some Recent Developments in Scotland.* Aberdeen: Gordon Cook Foundation.

Roberts, H. and Sachdev, D. (eds) (1996) *Young People's Social Attitudes – Having Their Say: The Views of 12–19 Year Olds.* Ilford: Barnados.

Rowe, D. (1994) *Moral Values and Citizenship: The Development of a New Programme for Primary Schools.* London: The Citizenship Foundation.

Rowe, D. (1997) Citizenship must not be overlooked. *Times Educational Supplement,* 18 July.

SCAA (undated) *The Assessment of Interpretations and Representations and the Use of Sources in GCSE History Examinations.* London: SCAA.

Slater, J. (1989) *The Politics of History Teaching.* London Institute of Education: University of London Press.

Sobisch, A. and Immerfall, S. (1997) The social basis of European citizenship. In I. Davies and A. Sobisch (eds) *Developing European Citizens.* Sheffield: SHU Press.

Stewart, M. (1938) *Bias and Education for Democracy.* Oxford: Oxford University Press.

Stradling, R. (1987) Political education and politicization in Britain: a ten year retrospective. Paper presented at the International Round Table Conference of the Research Committee on Political Education of the International Political Science. Ostkolleg der Bundeszentrale für Politische Bildung, Koln, March 9–13, 1987.

Tomlinson, P. and Quinton, M. (eds) (1986) *Values Across The Curriculum.* Lewes: Falmer Press.

Warren, A. (1986) Sir Robert Baden-Powell, the Scout movement and citizen training in Great Britain 1900–1920. *English Historical Review,* **101** (399): 376–98.

White, J. (1990) *Education and The Good Life.* London: Routledge.

Whitty, G., Rowe, G. and Appleton, P. (1994) Subjects and themes in the secondary school curriculum. *Research Papers in Education,* **9** (2): 159–81.

Willow, C. (1997) *Hear! Hear! Promoting Children and Young People's Democratic Participation in Local Government.* London: Local Government Information Unit.

Wringe, C. (1992) The ambiguities of education for active citizenship. *Journal of Philosophy of Education,* **26** (1): 29–38.

4   Teachers' Idealized Identity and Immigrant Education

MARSHA L. THICKSTEN

> Actually, we were raised that everyone was equal.
>
> (Brindley, teacher narrative)

Introduction

This chapter examines the nature of teacher acceptance and resistance to the education of immigrants and bilingual education in relationship to questions of idealized national identity. Teacher narratives were collected that revealed concerns about the changing of schools and values in the United States of America. The narratives also revealed how teachers accept or resist immigrant realities, English usage and bilingual education.

Bilingual education has created intense conflict and heightened divisiveness. This in turn has made education more conflictual and problematic. The purpose of this effort is to uncover the complexity of this conflict. It is an attempt to understand teachers working with and within this conflictual situation: who they are, what they experience, and how they feel about bilingual education and the education of immigrant students. Their clear recommendations are stated in their expectations of students, parents and the school districts. Their stories about their family values and how these were passed on to them gives a glimpse of why they teach and feel as they do. Further dialogue and communication, along with participation in a democratic forum of teachers, community members including parents, administrators and teacher educators is needed. All students have a right to education. The perceived conflict between teacher values and immigrant values requires a commitment to understanding one another and freedom of choice in decisions about what is the good and moral life.

Values and high morals

Understanding sentiments about immigration and language in order to describe the values that contribute to our ideal of the United States of America as a country that is democratic, fair, and just, may be one of the most crucial functions necessary in our society today. Values and high morals are two themes that seem to reoccur in the narratives of teachers as being important in the lives of grandparents, parents, children and the sample teachers' own lives in America. These are also what seem to be threatened – certain values – when some sample teachers express alarm about how immigrants and their children chose to live their life in America.

My goal is similar to Varenne's in *Americans Together* (1977), when he endeavors to discover what he can about Americans. Brindley, a teacher for twenty years, says it a different way by describing teachers as "real people." Other than her immediate family, her only outside contact as a youth was through teachers at the grade school across from her home. When she went to school to help the teachers, she learned early on that those teachers were real people. When she walked into her first classroom as a new teacher, who did her young students see? When small children looked in at her through the windows of the small black neighborhood school (a segregated black school closed in the 1960s, then converted much later into an integrated school) that December day she began her first teaching job, who did they see? The small children saw a real person, who happened to be their teacher. They saw a person who had to prove to that black, small town community that she cared, even though she had freckles and was white. This, then, is about people who happen to be teachers and how teachers perceive the world from their experience and life.

Brindley

Brindley is a family person. She spends most of her time interacting with her children, relatives and husband. She lives a modest life. Her family looks forward to home cooked meals and time together. They take walks on the beach together. Activities for their teenagers are chaperoned until they reach age 16 and then monitored closely and decided upon as a group. Brindley's family helps people who need help, but they do it not through money but through talking and providing a bed or a meal. They help others on a one-to-one basis, in an individualistic way. Most of their time and energy is directed toward their children and their needs. Brindley and her husband want their children to have values like theirs. Brindley wants her students to have those values too. What are the values? They are being kind to others and trying to understand how others feel; following through on the work that you say you will do; allowing others to accomplish what they want to accomplish without disruption; consideration; lack of selfishness; cleanliness and order. These are values that Brindley's family also cherished when she was a youth. There are differences however. Her children will visit and date whomever they choose. Race, language, or religion does not affect her opinion of a person. She is concerned with how people treat people.

This does not mean that she wants to learn Spanish and teach in Spanish. After teaching for almost twenty years, she just does not have the will nor time to devote to that kind of endeavor at this point in her life. She teaches children, all children, but she does so by using her strengths, expertise and talents that she has developed over the years, rather than by using a language that she does not speak. She advises that we do not use the resources of the bilingual community surrounding so many of our schools.

Janet

Janet is the most vocal of the five sample teachers about what immigrant education should be. Much of her identity is derived from being a teacher and, so, her feelings run deep. Hard work, preparation for life, academic discipline and English only would be her recommendations for what is taught in school. She believes that other staff should teach English Language Development skills, and that her time should be spent teaching students in intellectual and academic areas. She believes strongly that immigrants should assimilate if they plan to stay in the country and become Americans. Janet speaks of her parents' dreams that did not come true. She is dedicated, as is her husband, to supporting the programs in their son's education. They attend every parent meeting related to special education; they contribute time and energy, and they attend presentations that his school offers for parents. They are engaged and involved in his education as parents. Janet has specific expectations of herself in her role as parent regarding how to honor education and her son's teachers. Janet expects that same support from immigrant parents. Janet is frustrated with her district and with the bilingual program, as she has experienced it.

Kay

Kay describes herself and her family:

> Now that my husband and I are our own family, we have adopted the positive aspects of both of our families' values. In addition, we view of the utmost importance the unconditional love and respect and acceptance for others and ourselves, no matter what similarities or differences exist, positive communication within our family and outside our family, the health of our marital relationship as a priority, in order that we may be a positive and stable element in our children's lives and a positive element in the lives of those with whom we come in contact, a strong commitment to our faith, equality, appreciating the diversity of ourselves and others, being involved in our world, rather than passivity, constant self evaluation (keeping our actions and motives in check), and taking time to enjoy life and those in it.

Kay is presently learning Spanish. But she is not doing it through a state sponsored class or through a university program. She is learning her Spanish just as she did a few years ago – by asking students in her classroom how to say things in Spanish. She is young, and she has a facility for language. Teaching, modeling consideration and community-building are critical to her. She would like less tattling and more helping. She believes that bilingual education is one way to do this. She wants her own children to speak at least two languages, and she wants to be part of an effort to create a more multi-lingual world.

Madeline

On our last visit, after much talk about her involuntary transfer from a school with predominantly Spanish speaking students because she was not "fluent Spanish speaking," I asked Madeline to tell me more about herself and asked, "Who are you?". She replied,

> I'm still a very Midwestern mental-ied person, if that's a word. I try to follow rules, and I resent people who don't. I'm not a person who believes in taking moods out on other people. I've tried very hard to be a good wife and mother. I expend a great deal of energy in the work place, in the classroom, as well as energy [in] getting along with colleagues. Looking forward to retirements (which is something a little bit new). I bend over backwards to be a good daughter [to mom].
>
> I went to visit my mother in the Midwest and took the battery cables off of her car, because she had let the battery run down, only to find that the brakes did not work (old age), so we spent a solid week together not going anywhere. As she would repeat the same story over again, I realized that I had matured. Rather than get irritated like I used to do, I would try to repeat it word for word to myself to see if I could remember it. Our culture does not appreciate the old people in it. I am trying to work on it because someday I'll be there. The Oriental, they appreciate the older people and family members. It's like the old Oriental woman, she kept breaking her daughter's dishes, and pretty soon the daughter sent her son out to buy a wooden bowl so that her mother would not be able to break it. And the son came back with two wooden bowls. When his mother reminded him that one was all she asked for, he replied, 'Yes, but I thought I should get two because, soon, you will be there." She thought and agreed. Well, that's where I am. We live in a country that doesn't value the old, so I try to value my mother because someday I will be there.

The five sample teachers all have a rich heritage of what they would call American values, which contributes to a view that there is one way to live the "good life" that represents what it means to be American. Using the data from the five sample teacher narratives to summarize, these values are: usefulness, small town values, cleanliness, strictness, being a good worker, having Christian virtues such as being a good mother, not working on Sundays, being thrifty or frugal, using resources wisely, honesty, thinking about economic security and valuing education as a means to success, valuing people's privacy and individualism, not taking freedom for granted, following rules, no plundering or lying, speaking and acting like an American, feeling that "success" is important, freedom of choice, no sexual misconduct, timeliness, church attendance, no dancing, being practical and pragmatic, able to make decisions, and to be strong, fit into appropriate roles, work ethic, and doing one's best.

This notion of the good life as an American seems to be something that must be earned by immigrants. According to the majority of the narratives, newcomers to America have certain rites of passage they must achieve before they deserve the American good life.

These teachers have very specific standards for immigrant students and families. While the five sample teachers are willing to teach immigrant students, certain criteria are important to them:

1 Regular attendance.
2 Parental support.
3 Learning English.
4 Assimilation to the American way of life.
5 Student attitude toward school.
6 Academic success.

Though the teachers do not all agree that these standards are a result of their own heritage and culture, these standards have much to do with how Americans think about who they are and how they live and what prevalent belief systems have been and are becoming.

Teacher concerns

The five sample teachers share certain values. They also share common concerns about bilingual education as it exists in California public schools. The greatest concern expressed by the five sample teachers was the issue of inconsistency in the implementation of bilingual education in schools with large quantities of immigrant and bilingual students. This inconsistency exhibits itself in many ways:

1 District to district variations in interpretation of the state mandated policy and procedures.

2 Within district school site level, variations in interpretation of state mandated policy and procedures.

3 Lack of teacher training or appropriate programs at the university level over the past twenty years in working with immigrant students, bilingual classrooms, and students of ethnic diversity.

4 Lack of district support staff and expertise in teaching immigrant and bilingual students.

5 Lack of academic and administrative leadership in school principals which is fair, equitable, and consistent for students, teachers, family members, and community in the area of immigrant education and bilingual education.

6 Lack of checks and balances to assure that districts and schools will have continuity from one school to another, as students, teachers, and principals transfer within a single district and beyond.

7 Equitable resources and materials for all students do not exist.

   • Spanish and English speaking students do not have equitable materials such as workbooks, reading books and content area materials.
   • Students do not have access to qualified personnel.
   • Time and space resources are not evaluated and fairly distributed.

8 Lack of teacher participation in the policy, planning, and implementation of bilingual education and immigrant education.

9 Lack of state and administrative policy that is explicitly defined with regards to teacher expectations and rights about teaching in a bilingual classroom.

   • Policy for tenured teachers about learning a second language.
   • Policy for new teachers and teachers new to districts and state about learning a second language.
   • Policy and procedure about teacher job security in reference to needs of immigrant and bilingual students.

10 Lack of thorough and ongoing staff development in the area of cultural sensitivity at all educational levels.

11 In practice, lack of parent participation in decision-making about immigrant student and bilingual student language choices.

12 Insensitivity to the enormous burden that bilingual teachers experience due to shortage of qualified staff.

13 Piecemeal programs to prepare instructional assistants for the task of supporting existing non-bilingual teachers in bilingual classrooms, as well as those bilingual teachers in bilingual classrooms.

14 Minimal resources and personnel at university, state, county, and local school district level to examine and create a forum for constructive dialogue, leading to change where necessary and to improvement of practice as needed, to assure the highest quality of education for all students including immigrant and bilingual students.

15 Lack of structures that moderate rapid change and stability both functionally and psychosocially for all staff and students and families in the community.

16 Lack of examination into why teachers are not as actively engaged in the teaching and (learning) of immigrant students and bilingual students.

17 A lack of arena that includes both time and space for elementary school teachers to prepare, dialogue, and reflect on their practice, individually and collectively, in all areas including the moral dilemmas of educating in a diverse society.

Teacher beliefs and voices

Former Secretary of Education, William Bennett, believes that "the vast majority of Americans share a respect for certain fundamental traits of character: honesty, compassion, courage, and perseverance. These are virtues. But because children are not born with this knowledge, they need to learn what these virtues are." He believes further that we should

> help anchor our children in their culture, its history and traditions. Moorings and anchors come in handy in life; moral anchors and moorings have never been more necessary . . . in teaching these stories we engage in an act of renewal. We welcome our children to a common world, a world of shared ideals, to the community of moral persons. In that

common world we invite them to a continuing task of preserving the principles, the ideals, and the notions of goodness and greatness we hold dear. (Bennett, 1993)

Evidence from these teacher narratives reveals that teacher values and expectations of students, as well as what the teachers are supposed to teach, are based upon values like those that Bennett describes. However, the narratives reveal a high level of intolerance and fear as well. Three teachers chose to include stories of racism. They infer that race was somehow related to the issue of bilingual education and immigrant students. Use of language was the controversial issue that seemed to extend to the issue of race directly. In the interviews, people and students of color were referred to in terms that were sometimes racist, which points to a continued, though not new, concern about the issue of racism in education and in educators.

The mislabeling of prejudice

Shauna: My grandmother is a type of different personality. She is very strict, high morals . . . can . . . you know, you just . . . there would never be any interracial marriage in the family, that kind of thing. I remember an incident where we had black people come to our house to work, and my grandmother was very good to them and she gave them water, but as soon as they left she boiled the glasses.
Me: Boiled?
Shauna: Boiled the glasses because, of course, we did not want to catch anything from . . . from these black people. And, you know, I remember that so well because it seems that, even as a child, there seemed to be something a little unusual about that and [I] did not really understand it until I left my home there, became more exposed to the world, I understood it was just a case of prejudice, that is what it really was. But, you know, it was her upbringing too, you know. You did not associate with black people and they called black people "niggers" but not in a derogatory manner – that is their names. That is what they were raised with and they don't call them. When they call a black person a nigger it is not intended as a bad thing. That's their name, it is just like if you say "Caucasian".

Racism and prejudice involved color of skin, language usage, and immigrant status.

Values at home and school

In her narrative, Brindley talks about how she learned to do her best, and that by junior high school, "It became a natural way that we behaved." The efficient and thorough completion of family chores was valued in her home as a child. Brindley sees the family as the key teacher of values. She also is a disciplinarian in her classroom and believes that teachers teach certain values such as taking care of property, keeping desks and materials clean and orderly, and she wants her students to be polite. Brindley's parents and family valued the effort grade more than the academic letter grade. In Brindley's teaching, she too, values effort and attitude toward school, property and others.

Shauna's grandmother taught her not to lie or plunder. Shauna learned the value of thriftiness and working hard for food and shelter. Her grandmother was strong; her family was expected to be strong too. Being practical was a virtue. Honesty was expected. In Shauna's classroom, she expects the same values to be held and enacted. These ways of being help us make sense of our life, too, and define what we see as the "good society." Kay, in her early twenties and a second year teacher at the conclusion of the two years of interviews, selected her parents' faith system and their caring and concern for their children as her values. She discarded other values that seemed too controlling to her. Madeline, after over twenty-eight years of teaching, still holds in high esteem "small town values," and prefers her present community because of those "small town values." As a child, her mother and grandmother did perpetuate the expectations of the town, as shown by the example of Madeline being admonished for raking leaves on Sunday in a community where Sunday was seen as a day of rest. Janet's family believed that it was important to respect a teacher's judgment in all matters. They believed that their children should be in school every day and that the word of the teacher was "the word." Janet wants her immigrant students and their families to believe the same. Familial belief systems do impact the practice of the sample teachers.

Teachers' view of immigration

Janet is concerned that the immigrants of today not only don't want to be in school, but don't want to be in America. She said,

I think the biggest difference with the immigration that we are seeing now is that the people who immigrated here from the 1920s and 1930s, people came here with the idea of becoming American, that was their goal, which did not mean totally obliterating [their] cultural heritage. We still have little Italys, and I think that's a real richness. However, the overall umbrella is to be American, and to assimilate and to be successful in this country. Also, I think they came here with the idea that they were severing their ties. They came here to be Americans. I think with the current ways of immigration that we are seeing, that is not the goal. I think that they are coming for economic reasons, and there is nothing wrong with that if, along with that, you are planning to assimilate as much as you can, and inculcate yourself to fit in to at least some degree . . . But I think now we are seeing some come with a real chip on their shoulder, I think that is part of the reason why there is such an anti-immigration sweep right going to California. It's not just me. I see it in the newspaper. I hear it talking to other teachers. I know very few teachers who are happy about what's happening. I hear teachers talking about leaving teaching, except they have so many years teaching it would not be wise to leave at this point, a lot of people bailing out of southern California because of this, and so, getting back to bilingual education, I don't see this as any gift we are doing for these children. In fact, I think we are condemning them to second class citizenship when we don't promote their English skills and have them realize that's the way they go. I tell my students, 'You will be employed; you will have a job; you won't be on the streets; you'll have a decent home; you'll be able to raise a nice family, but if you don't have English skills you are not going to be able to have it, that's just an economic fact of life.' I started off very idealistic, that I was going to teach all these wonderful things and that children were going to be beyond grade level . . . but from that year on, I noticed each year more and more limited English students in the classroom, and consequently the levels of the entire classes abilities kept on going down and down.

Madeline said,

I like very much working with immigrant students. I much prefer that cross section in a classroom than middle or upper income children because they come in so needy of everything that they appreciate anything and every thing that you do for them. They are not jaded children. I long for values that existed in America. Also, the parents, in general, are very accepting and respectful. I would still do this if I had it to do over again. I would still work with immigrant students.

The thing I think that we have become, rather than a melting pot, I think it comes, although I think the Vietnamese people are doing this to a certain extent, you know these kids have these gangs, and gangs have always been around, but I think that the language barrier divides them even more, and, quite frankly, I think the added emphasis on their culture sets them apart too, rather than melting into. I think that every culture has their traditions and their holidays, and on a personal level they celebrate them. And so a couple of years ago we started having Cinco de Mayo, and there is nothing wrong with doing that except that we have a lot of other cultures in our school too. You know that old song, well they need to be proud of who they are and where they came from, that should be coming from the home. When it comes to school they should be being proud because they are Americans, and I think it does divide the cultures. And all these people, you know when they have that, the bit hoohaw at, where the high school students marched? You know, because they wanted a Mexican study program. My reply is, 'If you care that much, check some books out of the library and educate yourself.'

I think Americans in general, I can say, I think we're a complete and total melting pot, and I think that's made us what we are, and that's why it bothers me so much that this one particular group is being separated and treated differently; that isn't what America is all about. I don't know about your friends, but any time I bring up bilingual education and all of the different things that we have to do, they are aghast. They cannot believe in America, in California, in our schools, that this kind of thing is going on. And I tell them, you're the ones that should be doing something about it, because it's hard for us as teachers to stand up and do a whole lot without leaving ourselves out in the open.

And, back to my education and everything. As I said, there was no bilingual education back then, so you certainly were not given any courses. I would like to bet a lot of money in Kansas . . .

Bilingual education

There are wide variations in what bilingual education means academically, let alone public opinion and idiosyncratic perceptions about bilingual education. Madeline, Shauna, and Kay modeled the state required bilingual education in all classroom lessons that I observed. Of all of these teachers, Kay is most aware of the numerous programs and definitions and how these impact upon policy, planning and practice. James Crawford (1989) notes that the United States Department of Education, under the direction of Terrel Bell in 1975, defined bilingual education thus: "Bilingual education is . . . an education program in which two languages or mediums of instruction are used for any part of or all of the school curriculum."

The premise in the district where Shauna teaches is that teachers who use dittos (papers with fill-in-the-blanks questions) and workbooks are bad teachers. However, because many teachers are not bilingual or do not speak even limited Spanish, the district decided that Spanish speaking children could use workbooks, since the teachers are unable to teach these children directly. When districts make arbitrary rules such as these, it appears that Spanish students are receiving special treatment. Meanwhile, the premise behind such a decision is never discussed with teachers nor is it ever refuted out loud in staff meetings.

English monolingual teachers can give English speaking students creative, challenging, academic assignments without a "cookbook" (workbook) approach because they can speak the English language and spend time with the students. However, the premise continues that an English monolingual teacher cannot give the same attention to Spanish speaking students. Therefore, at least giving the Spanish speaking students a workbook (in Spanish, with the Spanish speaking, non-college educated, instructional assistant), for their seat work when they are finished with an assignment means they can have something to do – a type of busy work while the teacher works with the English speaking students.

The entire premise that Spanish speaking students can have workbooks was based upon an assumption of differentiated curriculum for Spanish speaking students and English speaking students. It was a deficit model assuming that the teacher was not literate in Spanish and, therefore, could not give accurate spelling, grammar, and content questions. It assumed that instructional assistants were limited in ability and academic acumen, therefore giving workbooks would take care of inaccuracies and the incompetence of both the teacher and aide.

Many English speaking monolingual teachers had the opposite view that, in the 1980s and before, Spanish speaking students had no materials. Ten years later, Spanish speaking students received all the materials and workbooks in the school, following the state mandates. This sentiment that the Spanish students were getting all the benefits of public education, but that the English students were being relegated to the sidelines, has contributed to a grave misunderstanding by resistant teachers. This sentiment was further sparked by the misconceptions of public opinion from parents whose students are in those classrooms and from parents who refuse to allow their children in those classrooms.

To an extent, what appears to be the case could be construed to be true, depending upon how a school is managed. If a school does not include teachers in decision-making about budget decisions then, indeed, such sentiments can form. If, on the other hand, teachers and parents are more involved in budgetary decisions, then deliberation over funding, policy, planning and practice is decided publicly and democratically. If there are issues that are state directed and funding with federal strings attached, then this same public forum can bring attention to these and solicit democratic methods to deliberate at state and federal levels to meet the expectations of a democratic society.

Kay describes a situation where teachers and parents went to the school board with concerns about having bilingual/limited English speaking students at their school. Given a choice of GATE (Gifted And Talented Education) students ("intelligent students" according to certain school districts) or bilingual students, the debate was over which school (the upper middle class or the older, lower class elementary school), would receive bilingual immigrants, and which would receive the gate students. The bilingual students were left at the lower class neighborhood school, and the GATE students were sent to the upper middle class school. Parents and teachers lobbied heavily for this decision and succeeded in their efforts. In Kay's example, teachers and parents did deliberate, did voice their opinions, and did exercise their rights as members of a democratic process. However, what occurred was discriminatory, in that the students labeled "intelligent" by the term "GATE" or "gifted" were in the upper middle class school, and the immigrant students who were seen as deficit were placed in the lower class school.

Training for teachers

Only one teacher, Kay, received support from her teacher education program for working with students of other language backgrounds, whether literacy, English language development, teaching an immigrant student, cultural sensitivity, or support in learning a second language. That one person, Kay, is an avid advocate of bilingual education for a variety of reasons, including that she did have some kind of support. She was also influenced by friends and significant others in her family and community who supported working with persons of other language backgrounds.

Shauna received no support from the California state college where she completed her teacher training. However, she was placed in a bilingual classroom for her student teaching by Carrington College, so she, at least, had exposure to bilingual education. Kay and Shauna believe that experiencing the students in a real situation is where learning for the teacher really takes place. Shauna would ask for what she needed. She did not hesitate throughout her teaching career to ask for, and almost demand, assistance. She received bilingual support and resources that first year. Her pragmatic approach has been to try what is suggested and then empirically decide whether or not it "works." Over the past two years, Shauna has become disillusioned with what bilingual education is or isn't. She experienced how each of three principals could require teachers to increase Spanish, omit support in the primary language bilingual program, or completely ban the English language instruction program, thus affecting and controlling her classroom practice and curriculum.

Brindley attended a California state university. She did not receive assistance in any way to deal with bicultural or bilingual students. Brindley noted, "But, as far as my college classes, none of it dealt too much with different ethnic groups or how to reach those groups, or what problems you might have trying to teach. Basic, it was just the basic, traditional education." Brindley's concern that Spanish speaking community members are not utilized in more significant and productive ways is an excellent critique of bilingual education as it exists today. Janet also attended a California state college. Again, no training was given to teachers to support them in their work with bilingual immigrant or bicultural students. Teachers had no education themselves to support teaching in a second language. Any language other than English is not encouraged.

Madeline sees bilingual education as a political matter, in that funding needs of schools are driving

districts to have token bilingual programs. She believes that bilingual funds are some of the limited resources available and, therefore, districts will apply for them, whether or not sentiment is behind bilingual education (though she sees it as political).

Shauna is concerned because her principal has allowed cheating on tests and possible changes of test scores. Shauna thinks that this has been done knowingly in order to be in good standing with the district, which measures principal, teacher, and student performance by test scores. The state of California also measures districts by the same scoring measure and intervenes if schools do not maintain a certain percentage on these tests. Realtors refer to these test scores when trying to convince purchasers of good schools and neighborhoods in which to live, and then the media publishes test scores in the newspapers. Shauna's principal has sacrificed integrity and honesty for a reputation of having high test scores at her school. Both Janet and Madeline want English only spoken in America. Both want students to abide by American standards. They do not perceive themselves as biased against immigrants. They just want immigrants to conform to values similar to the "Idealized National Identity": hard work, English speaking only, and attendance at school, regularly and with enthusiasm.

It is not that bilingual education does not work. The greater issue is that real people have turned against other real people over the education of immigrant students. Bilingual education is seen symbolically as a threat to being American. It is seen as giving up value, a work ethic, and the status of teachers as good and nurturing people. By one side, bilingual education is seen as a separate movement that will divide the United States of America. By the other side, it is seen as the venue to restore justice and to punish those who are not fair, just, and moral. The question of who is right and who is wrong does not seem to be the correct question. Rather, I would ask, "How can we all be engaged and alive in the process of educating all children who enter our classrooms?"

We do pass on what we learn through systems, as well as through our cultural and familial heritage. Is democracy dying, and is that the legacy we are passing on at home, in school, and in the work place? Democracy does not mean that the majority wins or that the group in power is not morally obligated to consider the human dignity of all persons. To provide an education that is morally good, with social justice at the core for all students, does not exclude society from providing work conditions that are fair and socially just for teachers and other employees.

Kay states,

> To me, it's not about the language. It's not about that. Language is just, that's a side issue. The thing is, you know, do they want these kids to make it or not? Do we want, a larger issue, do we want our kids to be multilingual? To me, it's if they're here, I want them to succeed. I don't want them, them, I mean, the language minority children, to just be in our schools taking up space and not doing anything. They have a right to learn. They're here, let's, let's have 'em learn, just like the other kids. Let's have 'em be with the other kids. Let's get something together where everybody succeeds. I wish we could at least equip them to succeed, you know. So to me, it wasn't language. It wasn't that we have to speak Spanish to them.
>
> Like some people trivialize it to that; I think that's ridiculous. I mean, it's larger, it's educational; we want them to be educated. I don't think a lot of teachers really understand. Or really think about that, do you know what I mean by that? People just think, "Oh, extra money, to pay for that, and everybody's speaking Spanish, and they aren't learning English." And I don't know if people understand the actual process of learning a language.

In America, an organized set of beliefs does affect how we treat others who are not family or community. It is a collective belief system that has rules and values. These rules and values affect how we vote and how we live our lives – the good lives. These values, "Idealized National Identity," contribute to what we do, how we live, and how we vote. Immigrant children and their families are at the mercy of the American public who embraces the Idealized National Identity. Teachers are part of that American public and belief system.

Both political and cultural values of an Idealized National Identity contribute to the political nature of language. Language and immigrant issues contribute heavily to the politics of bilingual education. James Crawford (1989, 1992) recorded an excellent historical accounting of the political nature of bilingual education. However, because it is a federal, state, and local issue, how the public grapples with the moral issue of teaching students in ways that are comprehensible has not had its forum. Bilingual education is a way to make learning comprehensible for students who do not understand or speak English.

We live in a country that is diverse. Yet, from the transcripts of the sample teachers, it would appear that the society is more homogeneous than it is in reality. It is my contention that teachers and schools are purveyors of culture, as are families, civic and religious organizations, and work and play situations. Institutions and people in positions of power pass on their belief systems. Though I do not believe that students are passive receivers of this culture, I do believe that unless education is democratic, in that it teaches all students to deliberate, we are not maintaining the integrity of the Constitution and the meaning and principles of democracy in the United States of America.

Religion, as such, was affirmed in some manner by all of the teachers. I believe that religion in the United States of America is an invisible force used by families (whether or not they attend church), to support and confirm the values that they attribute correctly or incorrectly to religion. This use of religion to reinforce whatever one believes creates another component of an idealized belief system. How schools incorporate citizenship education and values in school, without including religious doctrine, is a continual issue that is implicit in these findings and supports the present day debate about values, morals, ethics, and religion in education.

Parker Palmer (1983) suggests in *To Know As We Are Known/A Spirituality of Education* that love needs to be put back in education. He states that love is sometimes painful. Grappling with the issues surrounding bilingual education seems to deal more with who we are as people and what we are afraid will happen to our concept of what the good life and the good society should be. Some teachers feel it is their moral duty to convert all students to their concept of the good life. Though I value and respect teachers, the awesome responsibility they have, and good they do, I fear that democracy is being harmed when people cannot choose for themselves their good life and good society. Immigrant students and bilingual students and their families deserve the right to determine who they will be and how they will live.

References

Bennett, William, J. (ed.) (1993) *The Book of Virtues: A Treasury of Great Moral Stories.* New York: Simon and Schuster.

Crawford, J. (1989) *Bilingual Education: History, Politics, Theory, and Practice.* Trenton, New Jersey: Crane Publishing Company, Inc.

Crawford, J. (ed.) (1992) *Language Loyalties.* Chicago: University of Chicago Press.

Palmer, Parker (1983) *To Know As We Are Known/A Spirituality of Education.* San Francisco: Harper San Francisco.

Varenne, H. (1977) *Americans Together: Structured Diversity in a Midwestern Town.* New York: Columbia University, Teachers College Press.

5 Adult Education, Community Development and Cultural Diversity in Northern Ireland

TOM LOVETT

Introduction

What I want to do in this chapter is to explore three interrelated processes – adult education, community development and cultural diversity – within the context of a deeply divided society, Northern Ireland. I then want to compare and contrast a number of initiatives in Northern Ireland concerned with the role of adult education and community development in improving community relations. Then I want to examine in detail the work of one of those initiatives, the Ulster People's College, to illustrate how it attempts, in a radical manner, to link together adult education and community development to tackle the problems of community relations and cultural diversity in Northern Ireland.

Cultural diversity

Cultural diversity in Northern Ireland is often seen to mean two communities and two cultures; one Protestant and British, the other Catholic and Nationalist. The emphasis in much of the discussion and debate on cultural diversity is on encouraging empathy and respect for each side's cultural traditions. Thus, culture is linked to religion, politics, history and reflected in attitudes, beliefs, and behaviour at local community level.

There is a danger, however, of painting a picture of two opposing ethnic groups, each with their own quite distinct and separate culture and way of life. This tends to ignore the fact that the people here live in a number of cultures: Irish culture, British culture, popular culture, mass culture, urban culture, high culture, rural culture and working class culture, among others.

Cultural diversity is, in fact, a reality for the great majority of people, unless they deliberately choose to live in closed cultural, religious or ethnic communities. There is, thus, no simple equation whereby two communities translate into two cultures. The issue is much more complex, much more diverse.

Culture is not only a body of intellectual and imaginative work; not just a means of expression in art and music; it is also, and essentially, about a *whole* way of life. Raymond Williams in his seminal work *Culture and Society* (1971) argued, for instance, that the basic distinction between bourgeois and working class cultures was about the nature of social relationships; about the notion of individualism as against the concept of community and collective approaches to resolving social and economic problems.

European cultural theorists also stress that culture is about creating and shaping community life; about, in fact, community development. For them, this is a process of cultural action assisted by cultural animators or community workers. Some even see it as a political process, a form of cultural politics. However, they believe it will remain 'trivial and unoriginal unless the working class regain control of their own culture' (Simpson 1976: 36). This means culture in the broad sense, i.e. the ability to participate in, and shape, their own lives and communities. R. H. Tawney, a famous radical educator and socialist, made a similar point many years ago when he argued that

> what a community requires, as the word suggests is a common culture because without it, it is not a community at all. But a common culture cannot be created merely by desiring it. It rests on economic foundations. It involves, in short, a large measure of economic equality. (cit. in Donnison 1975)

These views may sound old-fashioned after fifteen years of untrampled individualism. However, I would suggest that they will find support amongst many of those involved in community development work in disadvantaged communities, not just in Northern Ireland, but throughout Europe. I also believe they are becoming increasingly relevant in the political debate on both sides of the Atlantic.

It is now evident that 'community' and community approaches to pressing social, economic and moral issues and problems are becoming an important part of the agenda for political parties in Great Britain and the United States of America as they seek to construct new policies that avoid the extremes of state collectivism on the one hand, and possessive individualism on the other hand. This debate is influenced by the work of Amitai Etzioni in his book *The Spirit of Community* (1993), but it also builds on the work in community development over the last twenty-five years and the lessons arising from it.

Community development

This brings me to my second theme, the role of community development in relation to culture and cultural diversity. Community development is about change; about tackling social economic and cultural disadvantage; about seeking social, economic and cultural equality. Community development is about creating the possibilities for people to develop and strengthen their own culture and sense of community. At the heart of this process is a concern with individual *and* collective growth and advancement.

The emphasis in this process is on participation, empowerment and collective approaches to solving problems. It is about building a new sense of community in which people can effectively participate in the decisions affecting their everyday lives. It is searching for the means whereby the freedom offered to men and women by the breakdown of traditional community structures can be harnessed, in a cooperative fashion, to release the potential for constructive development that is inherent in every individual. Thus, it attempts to link freedom and individualism with responsibility and collective approaches to solving problems.

Here in Northern Ireland over the last twenty-five years we have witnessed a major growth in community development activities. This is one of

the poorest regions of the European Union. The Troubles, plus serious social and economic disadvantage, have been both the backdrop, and the spur, to a situation were many men and women, in Catholic and Protestant communities, have been engaged in collective efforts to find solutions to the common social, economic, cultural and moral issues and problems faced by both communities.

This community development process has had a stabilizing influence on the situation here, preventing a slide into total civil war. It has provided links between the two communities and has often been the foundation, the starting point, for dialogue and discussion about political and religious divisions in Northern Ireland.

Some years ago some colleagues and I decided to explore community life in Northern Ireland, particularly working class communities in both urban and rural areas of the Province (Lovett et al. 1983). With the support and resources of Radio Ulster, we interviewed hundreds of men and women, young and old, seeking their recollections and memories of traditional community life, and their views and comments on the tremendous changes that have occurred over the years.

We found that both Protestants and Catholics had very fond memories of a traditional community life where, despite the poverty and hardship, there was a strong sense of belonging; of roots and shared responsibility; of a secure social and moral order. This was compared to the present situation of poverty and unemployment, compounded by vandalism, crime, a changing social and moral order, and all the problems associated with sectarianism and the Troubles.

Yet, the people concerned were not downcast. They were resilient, good humoured and 'enterprising'. They were often involved in efforts to tackle these problems through their participation in community organizations, tenants' associations, women's groups, environmental groups, community enterprise projects, youth projects, cultural projects, and so on. They were resourceful and committed to change, with a vision of the new community they wanted to create.

They, and their efforts, offered a challenge to existing social and political institutions and structures about the way things are decided and done. They illustrated that, although we need agreed political and social structures in Northern Ireland (and between the latter and the Republic of Ireland), we also need to create more democratic, participatory structures at local community level. The whole interviewing experience, and the subsequent radio programmes, called 'Family and Community in Northern Ireland', suggested that, despite deep divisions about politics and religion, people were living in a 'common' culture. One Protestant community activist summed it up thus: 'We are aware that socially and economically we have more in common with our opposite numbers on the Republican side than we have with the Loyalist big wigs. But how are we to put this over?'

Another Catholic community activist suggested that 'if we could have open discussions about the divisions and find out how to understand each other I think this would all change because if we don't get together there will be no future in Ireland'. This view was supported by a Protestant community activist.

> The division between the two communities can be taken advantage of insofar as the two communities can be worked against each other's interests. Whereas if we had a common ground to approach each other on, namely discussions, if we had open and frank discussions we would not be at a disadvantage.

The whole situation was summed up by a leading Catholic community activist:

> No matter what happens to the National question, in the final analysis the community struggle goes on; the struggle against the hopelessness and helplessness of ordinary people to manage to cope in a complex society. We cannot separate politics from the community question.   (cit. in McNamee and Lovett 1992).

It was evident from the views and comments of all those involved in this community development process (and from my own personal experience of, and involvement in, that process over the last twenty years) that they are not concerned with re-establishing traditional community structures, with all that implies in terms of restrictions on human freedom and choice. They want to find ways and means whereby individuals can be freed from present constraints and afforded the possibility of development and advancement through collective action.

The increase in the amount of freedom in the field of personal morality and behaviour exists alongside very limited opportunities and scope for men and women in working class communities to shape their own destinies; to make an imprint, an impression on their own environment. The emphasis in community development is on individualism rooted in cooperation, fraternity and egalitarianism. It rests on an essentially optimistic view of human nature that stresses the collective and cooperative side of people's nature.

It is, in fact, a call for people to have more freedom to shape things; to use their own, and society's, resources to strengthen and support a dynamic, creative community life. It emphasizes the need for empowerment and participation, not just representation, in the democratic process. It is a call for the creation of democratic social and political structures that offer people the possibility of control, on their own terms, of local resources and institutions, to put to use in caring for, and about each other.

It presupposes that it is possible, in modern circumstances, to find a way, through collective action and community development, whereby men and women can become fully integrated into their social environment and find in the life of their community something deeply expressive of their own personality and aspirations. It implies, as Paulo Freire emphasizes, the right of creating and recreating; of deciding and choosing and ultimately participating in society's historical process.

There is no necessary contradiction in believing in the possibility of creating such strong, self-confident communities with differing, and common, cultural beliefs and interests; communities which are not, in the image used by Raymond Williams of traditional working class communities, a closed fist or a fortress, but open, tolerant and responsible. However, if this is to happen, and if we are to create such communities, then those involved need to engage in a process of critical, reflective education.

Community adult education

Adult *community* education, has a vital role to play in supporting and strengthening this community development process. Historically, adult education and community development have been closely linked. The latter is recognized by many adult community educators as essentially a learning process, a situation where people can learn through action, and involvement in tackling real problems. Community development is, in fact, part of the learning iceberg. It is that part of the learning process – social education – that is hidden from view because it does not take place in traditional, institutional, education settings.

It is testimony to the fact that, for many people – particularly those from disadvantaged groups and communities – most things are learnt out of school; most things learnt in school are soon forgotten; we are more, not less, willing to learn as adults; we learn best when we are doing, when we are actively involved in the learning process.

A Council of Europe project on adult education and community development in the 1980s, which examined a variety of initiatives in fourteen European countries concerned with tackling social and economic disadvantage and exclusion, concluded that 'community development and community education provide working answers to a decaying social fabric and an uncertain future' (Council of Europe 1985: 12).

There is at present, particularly here in Northern Ireland, a great deal of debate and discussion about the role of adult education in the community development process. There are a variety of projects and initiatives concerned with providing education and training. However, there is an emphasis on the latter – on providing the necessary skills to make community groups more effective, more professional in their approach to tackling the variety of issues and problems they face.

The danger is that, as a result, community development will concentrate on the purely practical and instrumental; a form of nuts and bolts education that ignores the social, political and philosophical aspect of the whole process. Training to provide skills for community development must be part of a more general education concerned with knowledge and critical reflection. It should be concerned with simple, but fundamental, questions about community and community development, i.e. what is the nature of community at this particular time?; what were the particular characteristics of traditional community life?; how and why has it changed?; what is the role of community development today?; what sort of community do we want to create?; what are the social, cultural and political implications of community development?; what are the forces hindering and supporting community developments?

There needs to be a stronger emphasis in community education on exploring critically the history and development of local communities (a form of cultural and community study), linked to an examination of contemporary community issues and problems. This should be combined with an examination, not only of the role and function of community development, but of the principles and values underlying it. It is here that questions can be explored regarding the possibility of a common culture across the religious divide and the identification of common projects to tackle social and economic disadvantage.

Such a process of community education should also address the social and political implications of this community development philosophy. The whole process should be seen as an examination of people's communities in all their complexity in order to encourage the embracing of options which improve people's sense of identity, integrity, security and dignity.

Such an educational process, allied to community development, would assist people in both communities in acknowledging and appreciating cultural diversity, in realizing and cherishing their common cultural identity. It is essentially a Freirian approach starting where people are; with their views and opinions; with their vision and aspirations; with their culture.

In organizing such a programme, Freire (1972a) stressed that the starting point

> must be the present existential situation reflecting the aspirations of the people. Utilising certain basic contradictions we must pose the existential present concrete situation as a problem which challenges them and requires a response. In such a situation myth creating irrationality itself becomes a fundamental theme. Its opposing theme, the critical and dynamic view of the world, strives to unveil reality, earmark its mythicisation and achieve a full realisation of the human task; the permanent transformation of reality in favour of the liberation of men.

Community development, education and community relations

There have been a number of projects and initiatives in Northern Ireland over the years of the Troubles, which have sought to use community development and community education as major 'learning processes' for tackling sectarianism, improving community relations and encouraging cultural diversity. These included the Workers' Education Association (WEA), the Northern Ireland Council for Voluntary Action (NICVA), the

University of Ulster's Understanding Conflict Project and the Ulster People's College. As part of a major research project exploring the links between community development, education and community relations the Community Research and Development Centre at the University of Ulster undertook a comparative study of these projects and initiatives (Lovett et al. 1995).

All of them saw a central role for community development in community relations work, with adult/community education playing a major part in linking the two processes. Both the WEA and the NICVA initiatives started off with an emphasis on anti-sectarian work; working with community groups and organizations to combat sectarian attitudes and practices. However, this approach was soon abandoned to be replaced with one emphasizing cross-community workshops and seminars on a range of issues related to anti-sectarianism, such as mutual understanding, cultural heritage, history, human rights, prejudice awareness. In this situation, community development *per se* did not play an important role. However, links with the network of community organizations and groups involved in this process across the province was used by both WEA and NICVA to recruit individuals for the programme of seminars and workshops. The NICVA project became disenchanted with this approach and instead began to stress a single identity, intracommunity model. This model was based on community development principles, stressing a bottom-up, participatory, approach with an emphasis on justice, equality and respect for other people's perceptions of their experiences. In this model, community development is regarded as a process with inherent social and moral values. The role of education is to tease these out but within the context of an educational process grounded in everyday concerns, problems and perspectives.

The University of Ulster's Understanding Conflict Project rejected the anti-sectarian approach, initially adopted by the WEA and NICVA, because it believed it had a tendency to be too moralistic. In some senses this criticism was borne out by the decision of the WEA and NICVA to abandon their initial anti-sectarian approach and to move to a more specifically cross-community dialogue and discussion model. The Understanding Conflict Project, like the others, stressed the importance of the community sector, particularly the role it had played over the years in bringing people together to work on common projects and initiatives. It also,

like NICVA, emphasized the essentially participative nature of community development and its close links with community relations and community education. Thus, there was an emphasis on using the community sector network to recruit groups for the project and to stress community development principles in terms of active participation and choice.

However, this project differed from both the WEA and NICVA initiatives in its emphasis on cross-community dialogue and discussion; on interpersonal, as well as social and historical issues. The stress was on intercommunity work within a strong Christian, moral approach, building new relationships of trust and acceptance using group work techniques. There was an emphasis on the important role emotion and experience played in the whole issue of community division and in building new relationships and structures.

The Ulster People's College (UPC) approach had many similarities with the NICVA model, particularly the emphasis on building from the bottom up, using people's experiences in tackling social and economic problems as the foundation for discussion and dialogue about divisions and differences. It also placed this approach within the context of human rights, justice and equality. However, the UPC work is carried out both on an intra- and intercommunity basis that stresses the search for a common social and political agenda across the religious divide. Thus, stress is laid on the social and moral principles underlying the community development process and how these relate to community relations. But, there is also an emphasis on social and economic conditions and structures. As far as community education is concerned, importance is attached to the use of the radical pedagogy of Freire: an adult education learning process that attempts to link the personal and particular to wider social, economic, political influences and structures. Community education is thus seen as the necessary bridge between community development and community relations. The whole object of this 'bridging' process is to remove sectarian divisions and strengthen the community development movement so that it can play a major part in social, economic and political regeneration.

The four case studies can be placed on a continuum, from the personal to the structural, in terms of their philosophy and approach to the relationship between community development and community relations and the role of community education in those two processes. They all recognize the importance of the community sector and the community development process. However, the actual work ranges from an approach stressing the importance of emotion and the need for personal change and commitment (Understanding Conflict) at one end of the continuum, to an emphasis on understanding the role of social and economic structures in shaping and maintaining sectarian attitudes and community divisions (UPC) at the other. In between are the WEA, and NICVA, the former, adopting a straight-forward educational approach offering a rational analysis and discussion of issues and problems surrounding community divisions and concerned with challenging and changing attitudes and perceptions, but divorced from the community development process *per se*; the latter taking a more community development process approach to its work, with and in communities. This initiative, and that of the UPC, have most in common in their espousal of community development as a force of change in Northern Ireland, with education acting as a critical tool for those involved in, and committed to, that process.

The Ulster People's College

The Ulster People's College, however, was the only initiative that challenged seriously the prevailing two cultures, two traditions and ethos of much community relations work in Northern Ireland and, instead, offered a radical interpretation of cultural diversity. I now want to examine its educational approach to the latter.

The Ulster People's College was established in 1982 by a group of people active in community development, community education and community relations. Its philosophy and approach was strongly influenced by that radical adult education tradition (Paulston 1980) concerned with the working class and the disadvantaged, and committed to the fight for justice and equality. It was also influenced by the cultural action pedagogy of Paulo Freire.

The College's educational approach is issue- and problem-orientated. It is not primarily concerned with access, second chance or certification, although it is involved with the latter. It is openly committed to radical social change and the concept of individual and collective growth and development. As well as providing space for workshops and

conferences on various social, economic and political issues as they arise, the College is developing an alternative curriculum based on the issues and problems facing men and women in working class communities throughout Northern Ireland. It is also seeking to explore ways and means whereby men and women can play a larger part in the reconstruction of local working class communities through the establishment of new forms of social and economic structures designed to meet local needs in a collective fashion. The College has two major educational concerns:

1. **Social and economic problems**: To assist people in both communities who are concerned with, or involved in, the search for solutions to the many common problems facing Catholics and Protestants in the province, for example housing, unemployment, low wages, poverty, vandalism, changes in family and community life, lack of social and recreational facilities.
2. **Cultural and political divisions**: To help the two communities in Northern Ireland to communicate with each other, to appreciate and understand their prospective traditions, to clarify the values and attitudes (social, political religious) inherent in those traditions, to search for their common history, to provide in fact a basis for a study of themselves. In identifying the later labour history is an important instrument but this whole area of exploration utilizes many instruments, language and literature, mythology and folklore, history and theology, economics and politics.

At a practical level its educational aims are:

- To promote a debate on the political situation in Northern Ireland.
- To look at the political and constitutional options facing people in the province.
- To look at the nature of the 'two traditions'.
- To assess the role of the labour movement and its potential for the future.
- To analyse and assess the political role of the major churches – Presbyterian, Roman Catholic and Church of Ireland.
- To investigate the areas of civil and religious liberty, and church and state in general – in particular, the social role of the major churches in relation to the development or otherwise of the secular state and pluralism.
- To look at the question of culture and identity.

- To look at the social and economic differences between the two communities and between North and South.
- To identify areas for further study and debate.

Educational programme and methods: an anti-sectarian approach

The primary educational programme at the College takes the form of short informal courses of up to ten weekly sessions. These are targeted at four groups:

1 young people;
2 women;
3 community activists/trade unionists;
4 peace and reconciliation groups.

The structure of these courses follows a specific educational method. They begin by asking people to look closely at their own community, exploring the economic, social and cultural factors that influence their lives. The purpose of this approach is based on the idea that a strong sense of where people are coming from is of fundamental importance in confronting the things that divide them from others.

The next stage of the courses seeks to identify in what areas, and at what depth, there are common concerns across the 'sectarian divide'. This analysis provides the basis for an exploration of whether there is, or can be, a 'common culture' or a common project which, though 'fragile' and uncertain, can evoke a commitment from members of the two communities. Common themes and problems that generally arise are in the areas of unemployment, health, housing, education and the relationship between the institutions of church and 'the common people'. An exceedingly important area, which the College concentrates on specifically, is the situation of women. Among women's groups in Northern Ireland, an awareness of common struggles is particularly strong.

Only when time has been taken to establish community identity and areas of common cultural and social concern, do the participants on the course turn directly to community divisions in Ireland. This is done by looking at history, religion, identity, politics, once again using materials produced by the College.

An important point as regards this process and method is that members of both communities are together throughout the course. Another approach that the College is using is to work with the groups separately and then bring them together for a residential weekend at the College to complete the discussions. These two different methods give a flexibility to the depth of the discussions. Certain things can be aired more completely when only members of one's own community are present. Ongoing contact can allow stronger relationships between the groups to develop organically.

A final emphasis to be made at this point is that the College's whole educational approach seeks to be solidly anti-sectarian and not simply non-sectarian. In other words it seeks to explore the causes of sectarianism and not simply the feelings evoked. By looking at causes students are in a better position to discuss the 'lines of action', along which these causes can be removed. Thus, the College would not see it as adequate to 'respect the two traditions' but would look for assessments of what elements in the two traditions are progressive and what elements are in need of redefinition.

Longer courses

Arising out of much of the pioneering work done in this field, the College now offers two part-time year-long courses. These courses, which have been certificated by the University of Ulster, are offered jointly by the two bodies. The first course, in Community Relations, is aimed particularly at providing the skills and knowledge necessary for effective cross-community work, particularly for those involved in work in the community with youth, community organizations and women's groups. The second course, in Community Development, seeks to give participants the knowledge and skills required for local community development, with a special emphasis on community economic and social regeneration.

A primary aim in both courses is to try and involve the participants' supporting organization or community in the course work. The courses thus try to integrate with the work in local communities rather than simply giving a certificate to one person for their own career prospects.

Occasional seminars and conferences

Along with the regular educational work of the College, there has also arisen a tradition of holding occasional seminars and other courses addressing areas and issues of current and continuing interest. Following the basic ethos of the College, these events all seek to analyse events and issues that affect ordinary people from the perspective of ordinary people. Thus, a seminar was held on the situation of life sentence and SOSP Prisoners – in Northern Ireland, a person under the age of 18 who commits an offence that should entail a 'life sentence' is instead detained for the Secretary of State for Northern Ireland's Pleasure – focusing on the life sentence review procedure within the prisons. This seminar was attended by prisoners' families and support groups from the loyalist through to the republican side. A seminar was held on the Ulster Defence Association's 'Common Sense' document, as an important contribution to the political debate by an organization formed and led by working class people. A seminar was held on the Irish Language, which sought to explore reasons for the difficulties facing the language revival in Northern Ireland. A very interesting feature of this day was the presence of people from the Protestant community, which led to an important debate on the nature of identity and political options upon which much of the revival hinges.

Another seminar held in the College was on Socialism and Sectarianism. Jointly organized by the College and the Belfast Trades Council, it began an important debate on the responses of the labour movement to the problem of sectarianism in Northern Ireland. A series of seminars were held on the community response to the peace process and on the reaction to the breakdown of the IRA ceasefire. Finally, a number of courses have been held looking at the issue of church involvement in the Northern Ireland problem. The most recent course has specifically taken a radical perspective in trying to analyse the way in which the churches have approached the question of power and powerlessness in Ireland. Many of these events have begun processes that continue in the form of future plans for follow-up meetings, reports and publications and formal groups which continue to reflect on these themes.

A neutral venue

Finally, the College provides a neutral venue, with supporting services and resources, for a wide range of organizations and groups concerned to explore community divisions and/or identify common projects in their own particular field of endeavour. It also acts as host for groups from the Republic of Ireland, UK, Europe and America concerned with the Northern Ireland problem and anxious to know more about it. The College, in this instance, acts as an educational 'guide'.

Effectiveness of the College's work

In trying to assess the work of the College in 'Bridging the Sectarian Divide', it is important to reiterate that the College seeks to be anti-sectarian in its approach. Thus, simply bringing people from both communities together is, in itself, not the main purpose of the work. The College has to identify at least two main strands involved in this kind of work in Northern Ireland.

The first is developing the 'middle ground', trying to identify the elements of a common agenda that is not acknowledged by the prevailing 'stereotypes'. Another way of putting this is to say that there is a 'third way' between the Nationalist and Unionist positions. It would see a plurality of opinions on this among those who work in the People's College, some hoping for a unity among the people, others holding that a resolution of the constitutional question is necessary. All would hope that this plurality is defended.

The second aim, around which there is unanimity within the College membership, is to promote social change. If sectarianism is a result of specific social and class conditions, then working to create an anti-sectarianism society involves trying to change those elements of our present situation that promote sectarianism. In this process, education about social structures, government policy, people's responses and, perhaps most important, clarification of identity gives people the information upon which decisions can be made and options clarified.

Having these aims firmly in mind, how do we assess the College's educational work? First, it recognizes the need to do more work on this, by following up those who are using its resources, and looking more deeply at methods of assessment. Empirical tests looking at attitude change are notoriously difficult to evaluate and are difficult to pitch in the light of comments above about the 'middle ground'. Some of the comments from people who have completed the courses indicate positive results from any perspective.

'I realise now that many of my ideas were silly.'

'The history sessions helped me to understand why we are where we are.'

'I'm much clearer who I am.'

These elements testify to the usefulness of having sessions on contentious areas such as history, identity and politics. They also testify to large and important areas that simply do not receive adequate attention within the educational provision currently available.

Another aspect which is important to restate is that, by targeting certain groups, the College hopes to widen the impact of the courses. Instead of simply giving chances for individual personal development, it emphasizes the importance of collective educational effort. Thus a group from a youth club, a group from a women's group, an activist from a community group or trade union means that there is more chance for further distribution of ideas.

Conclusion: education across the community, about the community

Paulo Freire's concept of 'Cultural Action for Freedom' (Freire 1972b) sums up what the College is trying to do in all its educational work: examine and explore people's communities in all their complexity in order to encourage the embracing of options that improve people's sense of identity, integrity, security and dignity. An emphasis on these manifestations of popular culture and politics from the base of society gives the People's College a specifically important function. One cannot think of many places in Northern Ireland where representatives of organizations from both extremes of the political spectrum can feel able to come for open exchange and discussion. This brings a complex, and hard-to-handle edge, to many of the debates. Another important contribution to cross-community work is for activists and practitioners at the 'coal-face' of community relations to have a neutral and accessible platform to debate the complex issues involved in community work.

It is important to note that the Ulster People's College arose from a specific context. The explosion of community activity during the early part of

the Troubles in the 1970s led to the belief that there was an alternative to community politics that would transcend the sectarian divide. It was partly a growing awareness that this transcendence was an illusion which led the College's founders to set up a cross-community education centre (Lovett et al. 1983). Without an opportunity to explore precisely the issues that divide local communities, it was felt that continuing antagonisms would prevent coherent and effective campaigns on all kinds of pressing issues affecting working class communities. Thus the dual aims of the College's presence arise from long experience.

The Ulster People's College has survived over the last seventeen years because of its rugged individualism and the commitment of its founders and supporters to a specific educational agenda within the context of the search for peace and justice in Northern Ireland. It has had to struggle to maintain its independence. It has been accused in the past of being a 'Marxist' or 'Communist' college. A great deal of energy has gone into seeking financial assistance from trusts and charities to keep the College open. It had, until recently, no full-time director or permanent staff and was run entirely by a group of dedicated volunteers. Their vision and determination has meant that, despite the retreat of progressive adult education forces over the last ten years, at least one initiative has managed to survive as a testimony to the strength of the radical tradition in adult education and has striven to strengthen the 'common culture' across the religious divide in Northern Ireland.

References

Council of Europe (1985) *Adult Education and Community Development.* Strasbourg: Council for Cultural Co-operation.

Donnison, D. (1975) *An Approach to Social Policy.* Dublin: National Economic and Social Council.

Etzioni, A. (1993) *The Spirit of Community.* New York: Crown Publishers.

Freire, P. (1972a) *Pedagogy of the Oppressed.* Harmondsworth: Penguin.

Freire, P. (1972b) *Cultural Action for Freedom.* Harmondsworth: Penguin.

Lovett, T., Clarke, C. and Kilmurray, A. (1983) *Adult Education and Community Action.* London: Croom Helm: chapter 7.

Lovett, T., Gillespie, N. and Gunn, G. (1995) *Community Development, Education and Community Relations.*

University of Ulster: Community Research and Development Centre.

McNamee, P. and Lovett, T. (1992) *Working Class Community in Northern Ireland*. Belfast: Ulster People's College.

Paulston, G. R. (1980) *Other Dreams, Other Schools: Folk Colleges in Social and Ethnic Movements*. University of Pittsburg: Centre for International Studies.

Simpson, J. (1976) *Towards Cultural Democracy*. Strasbourg: Council for Cultural Co-operation, Council of Europe.

Williams, R. (1971) *Culture and Society*. London: Penguin.

6 Women in the Entertainment Industry: A Social and Global Perspective

LINDA SEGER[1]

What is our responsibility?

The camera is a lens that turns its eye on some little corner of the world. It not only records what it sees, but interprets what it sees. It pulls in the light, the images, the stories, leaving some things out, taking others in, changing the view, always selecting one thing, not another.

What the camera sees is determined by the film-maker's view of the world – What is important? What is a good story? Who should it be about? What is my responsibility as a film-maker?

The answers to these questions are determined by the experiences, background, creativity, culture and gender of the film-maker. "If we think of the evolution of films as a kind of mirror which reflects changing society, we must concede that the mirror has always been limited in its reflection, and possibly distorted", says Christine Mahonna. "Our society conditions men and women . . . it could be that they both see male and female roles through the same distorted lens" (1972: 7).

Even when the subject matter might be similar between a woman and a man, the approach is often different, because of the point of view. "As movie makers what we do for a living is that we mirror the culture", says Dawn Steel. "But the culture that we mirror depends on what we're looking at."

The camera not only reflects society, it shapes society. In so doing, it can change us and change our world. What existed before, now exists with a new consciousness. What we didn't know, now we know. Our perceptions change. New attitudes are formed. What we never cared about before, now we see differently. This leads to new judgments, new decisions, new opinions, new actions.

Since film has been dominated by the male point-of-view, a great deal of women's experiences have been left out. Some of these are stories about love, relationships, children, mothering, overcoming oppression, victimization. Others have been little known stories about women's heroism and victories. Some of those experiences have been glaring social wrongs, which no one noticed until somebody turned the camera in that direction.

Certainly, there have been thousands of sensitive films written, directed and produced by men who have cared deeply about our society. Many have dealt with problems that affect all of us – pollution as a result of corporate irresponsibility, war, violence, the destruction of the rain forests, the lack of business ethics.

But many social problems affect women disproportionately in regards to men because they affect the powerless, the disenfranchised, and the victims to a greater extent than the dominant culture.

According to government studies, two-thirds of the world's illiterates are women. There have been several films about illiteracy – all about men. *Stanley and Iris*, written by Harriet Frank Jr and Irving Ravetch, and directed by Martin Ritt, focused on the story of an illiterate man (played by Robert de Niro) and the woman who taught him to read (Jane Fonda). *Bridge to Silence* written by Cynthia Cherbak and directed by Karen Arthur, told the story about a dyslexic man who had problems reading. For women, illiteracy does far more than keep them from getting a job. It's a way of keeping them oppressed, unable to make informed decisions, unable to exert any control over their lives. The woman's story of illiteracy has not yet been told.

In almost all sexual harrassment incidents, women are the victims. The first commercial film that dealt with that subject – *Disclosure* – was about a man. He fought back successfully and triumphed, although for a woman in that same scenario, she might have lost her job, her reputation, and suffered the stigma for years.

More women than men are stalked. Perhaps the best known film about this subject was *Fatal Attraction* – about a man stalked by a woman.

Talk about responsibility

Many women film-makers feel a responsibility to look carefully at the message they're sending, the stories they're telling. "The images that we make go out into the zeitgeist of life" says producer Dawn Steel.

> It can't help but affect you when the images are negative. How can a woman feel good about herself walking out of a movie like *Showgirls*? How can you feel good about yourself when you see abusive images of women, or stupid images of women? But when you get bombarded by positive images, – that effects you as well. My responsibility, as pretentious as this sounds, is to raise the consciousness of women about themselves. And self-image comes from images. Images of yourself.

If all entertainment sends some sort of message, this responsibility can weigh heavily on sensitive film-makers who know the power of their media. Is their responsibility to solve the problems of the world through media? Most would answer no. Is their responsibility to be responsible? Yes.

Few women deny that television and film have a powerful impact on this society. But how far does it go? "I have come to believe that there is an ability for media to change society" says Trina McQueen, president of the Discovery Channel in Toronto, Canada. She continues,

> but that ability is not universal and not total and not predictable. We have a social responsibility for what we put on television, absolutely. I really do believe that what we put on television can, to a certain extent, affect the behaviour of the people who watch it. It has an impact.

Many women have trained themselves to be sensitive to this impact because they've had to. They've had to learn to see children's problems before they say it, to read the mood of the husband when he can't articulate it, to understand instinctively when something is wrong with a friend. Producer Janet Yang believes that this sensitivity is, perhaps, "inherited, or genetic. I think our pores are just more open than men's. It's a curse in one way and a

blessing in another." Having this sensitivity leads to the question: Who or what are film-makers responsible to? How do they exercise that responsibility?

For some, their first responsibility is an artistic one – simply to be true to themselves. "I think my responsibility is to write as authentically as possible and write what the character deserves" says Hilary Henkin, writer and producer of *Romeo is Bleeding*. "Am I true to the voice of the character I am writing? It's a matter of working with integrity." "What is the truth of the character?" asks Australian producer Sandra Levy.

> If I find something that is true and if I believe that I'm doing it as well as I can, then I'm fulfilling that part of responsibility. I would not be comfortable with making sexist, racist material, or exploitative material. I hope that the material that I make that travels the world has more going for it than just the lowest values of human interaction. Perhaps women are looking for this because few of us come into this business because we want to make money. We feel we have things to say. We have observations to make. We have creative relationships to explore. So what we want to do is express a view of characterization and a view of drama which is the truth.

For writer Diane English, creator of *Murphy Brown*, there's a responsibility to present a balanced point of view.

> Murphy Brown is a character with a distinctly liberal point of view. But that does not mean we have not been very responsible. We have several continuing characters . . . who have the opposite point of view. Jerry Gold is a character Murphy might marry – yet he does not support gun control, and he calls Murphy on every aspect of her liberal agenda. We give him equal time, and find their arguments make good debates. The airways are public airways, and there are more than just liberals watching *Murphy Brown*. I don't believe the audience should only see one side of the debate.

Diane English was interested in exploring political and social satire because "it questions the people calling the shots. It gets the audience involved because it's about important public events that are bigger than we are, more dramatic" (English 1991: 17).

"The question of responsibility is a balance that I struggle with all the time in my work" says writer Anna Hamilton Phelan who wrote the scripts for *Mask* and *Gorillas in the Mist*. "I have an enormous sense of responsibility to my gender. And about race. As I get older, I realize it's a part of my being.

It's not going to go away. So, I just go with it and do the best I can."

It's particularly difficult because these topics are not easily sold. Putting the positive into one's work is not always seen as dramatic, high concept, or commercial. "Sometimes it's like battling through molasses to get a good film done," continues Phelan.

> Sometimes I want to just walk away from the whole thing. But the only way to battle media is with media, to keep feeding it with more positive things because it's out there. It is so much a part of everyone's lives now. You cannot deny it.

As a writer, her sense of responsibility includes providing an important balance through the characters that she creates. "Sigourney Weaver once said to me, 'Anna, if you and other writers stop writing about female characters, then our daughters and our granddaughters will have no female images on the screen to identify with at all.' That's an enormous obligation and responsibility."

The producer's sense of responsibility can be even greater. "I feel many levels of responsibility," says Janet Yang,

> first to myself, and what I put my name on. I feel a responsibility to my company and to the company that finances us. I feel a responsibility to women. I feel a responsibility to Asian Americans. I feel a responsibility to the public at large. Somehow within yourself, you recognize where those balances of responsibilities lie. It's something that requires, I think, some real consideration.

There is also moral responsibility. Sallie Aprahamian, a British director and script editor asks,

> Where does our moral responsibility come in? Every subject has an issue and moral to it. In telling a story, we have a whole series of options before us which relate to society's responsibility, individual responsibility, the prejudices that might exist over a character's behaviour. For instance, the majority of love scenes show people falling into bed without any debate about contraception or love or consequences or responsibilities. Writers and producers might not want to deal with it. They might say that raising these issues gets in the way of the scene, but the reality is that every show presents a message.

No matter how much responsibility these women might feel, the stories they want to tell are not well accepted by the male decision-makers. "People who actually talk about issues, who openly say they're going to deal with issues, are not looked on fondly by most producers" says Sallie Aprahamian. "The new shows created by British TV do not perceive themselves as about issues. They're comfortable period pieces, a bit of music, a nice central character that we all like – he's a really good guy – set in a beautiful countryside."

But every film, whether directly about special issues or not, does communicate ideas and issues. It's the nature of the medium. It can't help it. If it's an underdog triumph film (like *Rocky*, or *Places in the Heart*) it says "you can do it". If it's a story about war and combat, the message might be about glory and honor (*Glory*), "we'll get along" (*Hogan's Heroes*), heroics (*The Guns of Navarone*), or even about the stupidity of war (*Gallipoli*). From television we receive messages – which may or may not be true – about the lives of the rich and famous, the working class, the professional women, the beautiful and young. For many decision-makers, it's not the message that's important, it's the question – "does it entertain?"

Social message or entertainment?

Film and television viewers demand to be entertained – and smart programmers recognize this if they want to keep their jobs. Not only is the demand for entertainment part of every movie, dramatic series, and situation comedy, but the demand is part of educational television, documentaries, and interactive media. If we don't enjoy it, we won't watch it.

Is entertainment incompatible with the desire to be responsible? It would seem not. Women film-makers recognize these two elements can and must go together. Most mainstream women film-makers shy away from any desire to do message drama. That is not their intention. In fact, most understand the dangers of dealing with issue-oriented material.

Sallie Aprahamian explains that social issue films must be dealt with carefully:

> It always must be story and character led, not led by the issues. If you don't have a vibrant character, it doesn't matter whether the issue comes into your show or not. It comes back to the quality of the story again and again, then to your moral point of view, and how you tell it.

Diane English know that one can lose audiences when dealing with issues. It depends on the execution of how issues and entertainment are put together. English also believes that

> in a strictly storytelling sense, debates dealing with moral issues create better television. Having a strong point of view is often more entertaining than not having one. It's all in the execution. We work hard to make sure our shows are funny . . . We need to be very, very funny because there is a point of view, challenging material and topics which require people to think. If the show wasn't entertaining on some level, people wouldn't allow us to do what we do.

Sunta Izzicupo, vice president of television movies at CBS, sees a similar distinction that must be made between entertainment and social issues.

> The best movies of the week start by telling a good story, with honest non-exploitive characters, with a compelling script. If it also has socially redeeming qualities, that's all the better. But I think that when you set out to do a socially redeeming, "important" movie, you often fail because it's bloodless. The story has to bring people in first, and then you can hit them with a message or sway their beliefs, or antagonize them into action – whatever you want to do.

But the pay-off of creating a show with issues and entertainment can be bigger, because it reaches people on more levels. Myth consultant Pamela Jaye Smith sees that these fit naturally together: "Entertainment is the easiest form of teaching. It opens doors. Because film hits so many senses at once – the visual, the aural, and implies the sense of touch – film and television have a powerful impact on the brain". She continues, "Unfortunately, not everyone working in media understands this power, so you have many people playing with a loaded gun, not even knowing what a gun is."

Even when a film is purely entertaining, what is being entertained needs to be considered. Zanne Devine, vice president of Production at Universal Studios says,

> A writer once said to me, "Making entertaining movies is not bad. It's all about what you choose to entertain in people." I am not interested in entertaining people's violent feelings toward women, or the violent images that go along with those feelings. I don't like it in my life and I don't want to bring it into the world. I'm interested in contributing all kinds of things. Not this – however you define it – whether it's violence, rape, derrogatory comments, sexual metaphors. I don't want to

advocate making a particular movie because I don't want blood on my hands.

French director Agnes Varda sees that the film artist is almost honor-bound to respond to the problem.

> It might seem ridiculous to just make a film when you see what's happening. The world is such a mess. Two-thirds of the world population doesn't have running water. Millions of women still have clitorectomies and wear veils and have to obey the father. Women are underpaid. Racism is back. It makes you ashamed to be a human being. But since we are on the edge of entertainment, whatever meaning we wish to give it, we can still approach art as a medium to touch and move people, to learn something about life. And we have to be entertaining. We have to give them something which can show good humor, good emotion, that communicates something. We can still reach different people on the level of sensitivity through a universal feeling.

But will it make money?

It's not enough to just be entertaining. There's another balance that is demanded of film-makers. Their films must be commercially successful, they must make money.

"There's a tension between the social message and film and television as a commercial enterprise" says producer-executive Sara Duvall. "We work in a unique field that demands that we be successful on a commercial level. Nobody is in the business to lose money, to make a film that no one wants to see, to exercise their art without recognizing that film is a collective experience – people don't make films just for themselves."

But are responsibility and commercialism incompatible? Although many believe they are, there is plenty of evidence to the contrary.

Executive Geraldine Laybourne, former President of Nickelodeon, sees that they are actually mutually inclusive.

> I have a very strong sense of responsibility and it's first and foremost to our audience and secondly to our shareholders. Basically we believe that what is good for kids is good for business, and it certainly has proven out that way – Nickelodeon has grown at 28% for the last five or six years and continues on that track.

The best films have been all four – true to an artistic vision, socially responsible, entertaining, and commercial. In the process, they have also shaped society. Some of the most profound changes have come about through movies-of-the-week (MOWs). Many of the most influential television movies have either been produced or directed or written by women, or have changed women's lives by tackling controversial subject matter that particularly affects their lives.

Making changes

Since the television movie-of-the-week began in 1964, MOWs have become a form particularly able to deal with social issues. NBC produced *A Case of Rape* in 1974 – one of the first films that dealt honestly with rape and its aftermath. The issue of domestic abuse was opened up through *The Burning Bed* in 1984. *The Rideout Case* (or *Rape and Marriage*) raised the issue that marriage didn't mean that a man could do whatever he wanted with his wife. *Friendly Fire* dealt with a woman who lost her son to friendly fire in the Vietnam War. *Fallen Angel* and *Do You Know the Muffin Man* raised issues about child molestation.

Australian-Asian film-maker Pauline Chan sees that women are often more able to address these problems because they're the outsiders.

> Because men are the people who are running the show they want to think that everything is working perfectly. They're supposed to be doing a good job. So, they don't want to know about a problem. They would prefer to think that they are little problems that don't need addressing. But the women don't feel that sense of responsibility because they're not running the show. They can be the objective bystander. In a sense, the outsider has a better possibility of making change because she can observe in a more objective way. She's not in the thick of it. And she can just sit there and after a while she looks and she says, "You know, I think things could be done better."

Women turn the lens on their domestic world, and see problems that have not been addressed, or even talked about. *Something About Amelia* was one of the most important MOW, turning its eye on the issue of incest. The film aired in 1984. "Sixty million people watched this film on one night" says its director, Randa Haines.

> I remember being amazed by the power of that medium to reach that many people. Very wisely ABC put hot-line numbers into each area for people to call. There were thousands of phone calls and thousands of letters from people saying "I'm in that situation," "I'm a father in the situation," "I'm a child in that situation." Children called after school the next day as well as hundreds of women who were 50 years old who'd never told anybody what had happened to them. It really opened up a floodgate of emotional and social response. Schools and psychologists and social agencies began to talk about it.
>
> People felt less alone. They began to share what happened. They realized they could find help. It was the beginning of an awareness that is very much present today.

Although it alone may not be responsible, studies show that movies actually have more impact than message programming. According to Dr. Richard T. Hezel, information programs on social problems that are designed to impact behavior often have low ratings and the impact is minor. But "made-for-TV movies, on the other hand ... may frequently achieve larger gross behavior impact than information programs, in part because of their larger audiences, their forceful dramatic presentation of the social problems, and perhaps because of audience tolerance for incidental information that is presented indirectly within an entertainment format" (Hezel 1985).

Producer/director/actress Lee Grant has used both the documentary and MOW form to explore issues of oppression, discrimination, and social irresponsibility.

> I began as an actress who was blacklisted during the 1950s. I'm so grateful to that experience because my social consciousness came from this event. I had been traumatized. I have a strong Cassandra sense of the future – as if I can see the handwriting on the wall. I often feel, "if this is not given a voice, we're in real trouble." Documentaries were a great outlet for me.

Her first documentary was called *The Willmar Eight*. "This was about eight women who went on strike against a bank in Willmar, Minnesota. It changed bank legislation, opening up jobs for women." After making a number of documentaries about subjects ranging from battering to sex change to the family court system, Grant began parlaying them into movies of the week for television:

> I made *Down and Out in America*, which said everything that I ever wanted to say about what the Reagan years did to this country. We used a crisis situation from *Down and Out* to make *No Place*

Like Home – about a working class family who thought they were safe. We set it in Pittsburgh where all those iron factories and steel mills closed down. They ended up going right through the safety net on to the street.

Women On Trial was an exposé of the family court system in Houston, Texas. *Nobody's Child* was about a normal child who was put into a mental institution because her family couldn't handle her.

All of these films had an impact on society. "*When Women Kill* was about all kinds of women who kill – many were battered women who killed their husbands. When I did that film, spousal abuse wasn't something you could bring up in court so a lot of these women were doing 15 years to life in prison for a situation that was just totally out of hand. Now the battered woman syndrome is acceptable in courts."

In my interviews with women, I was surprised at the number of women who felt passionately committed to making their films count for more than just entertainment. Some used religious and spiritual words to articulate this passion, calling it a "calling," or a "missionary zeal" or a "passionate commitment." They spoke with energy, intensity, and passion. However, none of these women were focusing on the message as message. This was not about proselytizing or converting. Most were focusing on their desire to tell a truth that had not been told before, but which they considered vitally important. They felt someone, or women in general, or an ethnic group, had been wronged. Or felt that there was some situation that simply had to be addressed and film was the best way to do this.

Some women were adamant about not using the words "responsibility" or "message," and even kept emphasizing "entertainment." Yet, when I looked at their work, or listened to them talk about the films they were most proud of, their sense of responsibility was clear.

The overall message was one of balancing responsibility, artistry, and truth.

Gauging the response

On many of these socially conscious films, response is gauged in a number of ways. Most have an 800 number placed at the end of the film, as *Something About Amelia* and *Dangerous Intentions* did, and hundreds or thousands of people may call for help,

advice, or to share their response. In many cases, social service agencies receive responses for several days, or up to a month, often doubling or tripling the number of calls they normally receive. Producers and networks talk to sociologists and psychologists, who tell them that consciousness has been raised about the issue, or that the movie helped their clients.

With other films, response is more difficult to assess. "A controversial film like *Serving in Silence* (produced by Barbra Streisand's company – Barwood Films, and written by Alison Cross about a lesbian colonel in the army) will receive both positive and negative responses" says Roz Weiman, a vice president of NBC.

> The positive responses ranged from people saying, "It's a pleasure to see such an articulate, well-acted film" to those much more specifically addressing the issue. People were delighted that they were able to see a very positive portrayal of a person who is a lesbian as well as a military person because it comforted them, gave them a sense of strength because they were lesbians themselves or had lesbian family members. We did get some very touching notes from mothers of lesbians, family members who identified and were touched by the portrayal of the family reaction.[2]

These issues are not just being addressed with the movie-of-the-week form, but have been addressed in series as well. Barbara Corday was one of the co-creators of *Cagney and Lacey*, which aired from 1982 to 1987–88 and was one of the first television series created by women, about women. "Traditionally there have been a great many comedy shows that have starred women – from *I Love Lucy* to *Ann Southern* to *Roseanne* to *Murphy Brown* – but few women have had their own one-hour drama shows. When I first worked at ABC in 1979 it was a fairly accepted slogan that women couldn't carry a one-hour show."

Once the show went on the air, it became a critically acclaimed series, winning a number of Emmy Awards. The show was one of the first times that social issues were dealt with in the context of a series. "Within the show, we dealt with problems of rape, alcoholism, racism, sexism. A series has the ability to constantly pick at people, saying, 'remember this, remember this, remember this.'"

What was the response?

> The mail was extraordinary. We got beautifully typed letters as well as letters written on the back of

a shirt cardboard, which showed us that we were reaching a cross section of the population. People particularly responded to the character of Mary Beth Lacey who was a housewife, a working class mom – she had kids, had a husband. They were trying to make ends meet. We had mail from women who felt that for the first time on television people in their situation were being seen and being portrayed not just sympathetically but in an empathetic, realistic way. We were mirroring what was really going on out there. We were talking about daycare problems and childcare problems and husband/wife problems and who makes more money and who still wears the pants and how does that affect sex – all these things that nobody had ever talked about on television before. We dealt with issues about date rape before anybody else. We did alcoholism. We did pornography, breast cancer, sexism in the workplace – every social issue of the day that you could possibly have done.

We didn't just deal with women's issues. We did one episode where Mary Beth was taken hostage. Police departments all over the country used that episode to train policemen about how to act in a hostage situation.

Corday is even more pleased with the impact the show made on modeling relationships. "The things that I loved most about this show were the unspoken images, such as Mary Beth walking in from work and Harvey's making dinner and she gives him a kiss, he gives her a kiss and they start to talk and she doesn't say, 'Oh, honey you made dinner, thank you so much.' Dinner is for everybody. It's not one person's job to make dinner. Those are the kinds of things we were able to do in ways that were very subtle but people got it."

In spite of their success, shows about social issues have not been encouraged. Why? If media is so powerful, if socially conscious films have been artistically and commercially successful, why do women feel there is still such an unwillingness to green light the social problems they consider important?

"I don't think it's a conspiracy" says Janet Yang. "I just think men don't notice. They don't know better. It's a lack of exposure, a lack of education. It's also the economic pressures and not knowing what was possible. Not having the awareness and the voices to bring something new to the screen."

And there's another reason. Films about social problems, that explore social problems, are often not encouraged because a large share of the market – for both television and film – is international. "We're always told that our movies are too 'soft' for

a foreign audience," says Sunta Izzicupo. "They're about our own domestic social issues. And other countries are often not interested in those topics. We're usually told that the foreign market wants male action, and women-in-jeopardy movies."

Whether domestic or foreign, every image touches those who see it. No more is the influence of a film just within its borders. Now the international market is the largest buyer of American films, with up to 60 per cent of the profits from a movie coming from the foreign markets. That brings up new issues about responsibility.

Global interrelationships

We live in the global village. The images that we convey now affect the remotest areas of the world. There are few places on earth that are not affected by television or film.

Producer Gale Anne Hurd recounts going to a very remote island in Micronesia which had only one generator to power up a television or video recorder. There, she discovered that everyone had seen *Terminator 2*:

It was terrifying. I didn't want to invade their culture with something that would impact them the way it did. Here were these peaceful people living in paradise and they had all become fans of Arnold Schwarzenegger and urban, action-oriented entertainment. At that moment, I realized that whatever you may think your responsibility is, it's overwhelming. It changed my perspective on the influence that I have as a producer.

Baywatch is now seen in the Middle East, *True Lies* in China. In Japan the husbands rent American home videos for their stay-at-home wives. What happens to cultures affected by Sylvester Stallone's image of violence? By *Baywatch*'s image of women? By *Showgirls* image of sexuality? What happens when every culture is distorted by images of American life?

The effect of television on other cultures is enormous, and sometimes unexpected. A number of executives spoke about their concern that television is destroying culture. One executive, who asked not to be named, said,

So many cultures are being destroyed because of the influence of *Baywatch*, or *Dallas*, of the constant images of beautiful young women. Suddenly, their black or brown skin isn't beautiful anymore.

Television is telling them you have to be blonde, blue-eyed and white. We're destroying the value systems of these countries by exporting these images of sex and by exporting the violence of a *Pulp Fiction* or *Die Hard* or the latest Jean-Claude Van Damme or Arnold Schwarzenegger or Chuck Norris film.

"There's so much money coming from foreign," says Anna Hamilton Phelan, "that the buyer cares less about script and less and less values writers and producers and even directors and more and more values stars. Since the early 1990s, studios began preselling their films before they were made. They just had to say 'We got Arnold Schwarzenegger' and nobody cared about anything else. They didn't care about how good the movie would be, they just knew that if they had Arnold, they could make a profit."

Tom and Arnold, Bruce and Harrison drive the foreign market leaving little room for the women's point-of-view and for the outsider who wants to raise global consciousness. But that doesn't stop this desire to influence. "As conscious and awake people we can recognize we have a field of influence," says myth consultant Pamela J. Smith.

> The more awake and aware you are, the wider your field of awareness and influence is. So that it's not just "me" the individual, my family, my company, my culture, my stockholders. It gets bigger and bigger and bigger. You hope you have people creating these films who are simply, by definition, more aware. If the film-makers are aware of their influence, and act responsibly, you can take these images and bring them into people's homes and all of a sudden what you've done is you've opened their eyes. That's one of the reasons why film-making is so immediate, so powerful. It's like taking a light and shining it into the dark.

Does it matter what is being watched around the world? Barbara Pyle, vice president of Environmental Policy at Turner Broadcasting Systems is convinced that it does: "It's an absolute fact that people emulate behavior that they see on television." Pyle has been studying ways television is used to address many social and environmental problems.

> The media can affect society positively. I've been documenting this particular phenomenon since 1984. It was pioneered by Miguel Sabido in Mexico. In a soap opera produced in Peru called *Simply Maria*, one of the characters was a maid. In this story, she brought a Singer sewing machine, went to night classes, learned how to sew, and was able to quit her job. She opened her own sewing shop and was very successful. The maids were watching this soap opera, and when she went to school, they went to school. When Maria bought a sewing machine, they did. It was so successful that you could not buy a Singer sewing machine for months, because they were so back-ordered. Once Sabido saw what this program could do by accident; he asked, "what if we did this on purpose? What if we produced soap operas and incorporated into them the value of having a small family, the value of being able to control your own fertility, the value of getting a decent education? What if we use them to show that you can be 'macho' without being violent?
>
> They've done several of these telenovellas in Mexico. They deal with issues such as the empowerment of women, population, education and many more issues that everyone should care about – woven into these shows in a very clever way. Local production companies and television stations have started to do this kind of programming in the Philippines, India, and in many other countries.
>
> I am heartened to see that the soap operas for social change are really taking hold. There was a recent meeting in Los Angeles hosted by Population Communications International in which soap opera producers and directors from the United States attended to learn the details about how these soaps actually work and possibly to adopt some of these methods for North American soap operas. It's things like this that really give me hope.

Cecile Guildate Alvarez is an international film-maker whose work has been featured by Barbara Pyle in *People Count*, a series about the issues debated at United Nations Summits and Conferences. Alvarez has been a television producer in the Philippines since 1962 at the age of 18.

> Unfortunately, too many of the executives have this so-called happy formula that the masses want only sex and violence – it's the general commercial fare. We in the Earthsavers Movement and my colleagues in the Philippine Center of the International Theatre Institute are trying to present an alternative diet for the minds of our people. We've been doing docudramas about the death of students from hazing, trying to wake them out of this stupor of drugs. We do stories on the plight of overseas Filipinos. We deal with crime and corruption and reflect on the burning issues of the day because we have faith that media arts is a catalyst for social change.

Alvarez sees television as vital to resolving basic

identity issues of the Philippines. "The identity crisis of the country is not going to be resolved unless we forge our own identity. The face of the country will never be full unless we've really included all of this rich variety of ethnic strains. And we can't be mesmerized only by Madonna and McDonald culture."

Film-maker Maria del Carmen de Lara from Mexico has made documentaries on prostitution, abortion, AIDS, and garment workers in dangerous situations. "Most of my work in these last two years has been about women's sexuality and gender. It's very important now to talk about gender in Mexico. Many of the problems are affecting women more than men, and women are the victims of male dominance."

Her 1979 film on abortion began a discussion and has changed laws. Her film about AIDS has raised consciousness. "AIDS has become a problem in Mexico. The husbands go the US to work in the fields. They go to the city. They don't use condoms, they have sex with women in the US, or share a plastic doll and return with AIDS. But they never tell their wives that they are infected. In the US, the AIDS programs don't deal with Latin Americans so these workers aren't educated about it." By making documentaries about these subjects, de Lara has been able to begin a discussion, educate the women, and raise consciousness about an issue that has a profound effect on Mexican society. "It's difficult to know the real impact" says Carmen de Lara, "but many of the men are now asking to be tested."[3]

Women are working separately within their own countries, and together through co-productions. They still are limited by numbers. Although 35–50 per cent of executives at studios and companies are women, men still outnumber women writers about 5 to 1, and outnumber women directors about 10 to 1. Although more films have women producers, often the woman is only one producer among five or six men. Film schools do better – about 40–50 per cent of students are women, which could affect the industry within the next five years. Different

cultures do better: In 1995 New Zealand had one of the best records for women writers (35 per cent) and women directors (21 per cent). India has one of the lowest – with only about 5 per cent women in these roles. In many countries such as Germany, Sweden and Australia, about 35–40 per cent producers are women. In England in 1995, nine of the thirty-eight recurring hit drama series were devised solely or partly by women.

To change the influence of women, women need to support each other, speak out about the importance of these issues while still being diplomatic, to connect with women nationally and internationally, and to continually raise our own consciousness. Can we make a difference? The answer is clear. It is a difference that impacts on business on every level and ripples out around the world.

Notes

1 From *When Women Call the Shots: The Developing Power and Influence of Women in Television and Film* Copyright 1996 by Linda Seger. Published by Henry Holt and Co., Inc., New York. Reprinted by permission of Linda Seger.

2 *Serving in Silence* was produced by Barbra Streisand, Glenn Close, Craig Zadan, Neil Meron, Cis Corman, written by Alison Cross and directed by Jeff Bleckner.

3 This same problem was addressed by Lebanese director, Janane Mallal in her film, *Badrieh*, for the Lebanese Broadcasting Corporation International C 33 channel. The woman and her children with AIDS becomes an outcast in her own village. This documentary won a first prize in Health Reporting in CNN, and helped reintegrate the woman into her village.

References

English, D. (1991) Profile. *The Journal*, : 17.

Hezel, R. T. (1995) The impact of commercial television entertainment programs on human service agency requests and reports. Unpublished article for the National Association of Broadcasters.

Mohanna, C. (1972) A one-sided story: women in the movies. *Women in Film Journal*, : 7.

7 Harnessing Folklore and Traditional Creativity to Promote Better Understanding Between Jewish and Arab Children in Israel

SIMON LICHMAN AND KEITH SULLIVAN

'There was nothing at all at the school, nothing, and then the mother turned up with her mother, and I said I was a bit worried, and she said, "We're going to get the clay now", and I said, "Are we? How?", and she said, "Get into your car". So we drove up to a moshav [communal farm], and she said, "This is the field where we always get our clay". They said we needed black mud because red and brown was no good, so I picked up mud that looked exactly the same as the mud they'd collected and they said, "No, that's not black, leave it to us". Then I asked, "How are we going to take it back to school?", and they said, "In the boot of your car", which didn't have lining or anything, so it was stuck in the boot, and then they said, "Now we need straw". So we went to a wheatfield and we gleaned the field just like Ruth in the Bible, at which point a man comes along on a tractor and says, "Can I help you?" There was me looking like me and two traditionally dressed Bedouin women on a Jewish moshav. "Hello, I'm Dr Simon Lichman from the Ministry of Education". I told him we were going to build a tabun [clay pita oven] with seventy Arab and Jewish children in a school yard, and this man looks at me and he says, "Right! Take as much as you want".

So we put the straw in the car and went back to the school where the children were also collecting mud. We started building the oven in the school yard and somehow it wasn't working, and the woman said to me, "Can we go to my yard because it's just not working here, and the truth is I've been begging my mother to build me a tabun and she never has". So, I checked with the teachers and school principal, and since it was very close, we all went to her yard and we built this oven. The grandmother didn't really want the children to help because she was building a tabun and she wanted a good one, but the children did help as much as they could. It was a big event.

At the end of the day what we had was a fine pita oven, made traditionally, with over eighty Jewish and Arab children, parents and grandparents on a spontaneous home visit, with three generations of the host family – the daughter in the programme, her mother and grandmother, as well as her younger sister (who is now in the programme)'.

Introduction

The Traditional Creativity in the Schools Project focuses simultaneously on three problem areas in Israeli society: cultural pluralism; the transmission of home-culture between generations; and coexistence between neighbouring Arab and Jewish communities. Its aim is to provide a positive context within which groups of children, parents, grandparents and educators can work together during activities that focus on aspects of traditional creativity in folklore and home-culture; and to build bridges of understanding between the two main groups in Israel, Arabs and Jews.

Members of extended families are brought into the process in their capacities as expert tradition bearers, and have a crucial role in planning programme content. Children focus on their own heritage, learning about each other's cultures as they experience their own. An atmosphere of pluralism is encouraged through the acceptance of differences between groups, as well as the discovery of similarities.

While living side by side, the Jewish and Arab communities have very little contact with each other outside of the workplace and other formal settings and, as a result, little understanding of or sympathy for each other's cultures and values. Yet, although the divide is large and based on a complex history, there is also much in common between these two Semitic peoples. The Project uses folklore and traditional creativity in education as a means of allowing Jewish and Arab children, and their families, to work together in sharing part of their rich cultural heritages with the hope that it will encourage if not mutual acceptance then at least peaceful co-existence between the two groups. It is also intended to nurture and support the values of respect for and tolerance of cultural and religious difference.[1]

The authors of this chapter are an Israeli folklorist and educationalist, Simon Lichman, Director of the Centre for Creativity in Education and Cultural Heritage in Jerusalem, who conceptualized, developed and implemented the Project and who provides the insider's perspective; and Keith Sullivan, an anthropologist and educationalist from New Zealand who provides the eyes of the outsider. The chapter was developed in an ethnographic fashion.[2] It describes the Project and how it works, the driving forces behind it and the outcomes of the Project. The methodology used to write this chapter is a reflection of the methodology used in the Project, in that it is ethnographic and reflective rather than analytical and evaluative.

Setting the context

Education in Israel

In 1994, there were approximately 1,150,000 children at school in Israel. There are four education sectors: 81 per cent of pupils are in the Hebrew sector (i.e. they are largely Jewish); 14 per cent are in the Arab sector; 3 per cent in the Bedouin sector and 2 per cent in the Druze sector.[3]

When the State of Israel was established, the Arab communities were asked whether they would prefer to be part of the same school system or to have their own. It was decided that two school systems should offer the same basic education, but the language of instruction in the Arab schools would be Arabic with Hebrew as a second language, and the language of instruction in the Jewish schools would be Hebrew. It was felt by the Arab communities that their children would thus best retain their culture. Consequently, there is a variety of Jewish and Arab schools, which differ markedly in themselves and also range from those with no religious instruction to those that are religiously orthodox.

As a response to what was seen as the increasing radicalization amongst youth in both the Jewish

and Arab communities, in 1986 the Israeli government established the Department of Education for Democracy and Coexistence within the Ministry of Education and Culture.

The idea for the Department was predicated on the assumption that formal and informal educational activities have the power to combat existing stereotypes and preconceptions and to develop tolerant behavioural patterns, which centre around accepting differences and acknowledging that all people are equally important. (Department of Education for Democracy and Coexistence Staff 1993: iv)

The Department (ibid.) identified four important areas in relation to the issue of coexistence:

- Education for life in a democratic society – education for tolerance, for accepting differences, for awareness that all people are equally important, and for socio-political involvement.
- Education for life in a multi-cultural society, with emphasis on promoting the relationship between Jews and Israel's Arab citizens.
- Educational involvement in current events, providing the teachers with the tools to better deal with controversial political, cultural and value-orientated issues.
- Education towards peace.

When the Ministry of Education was first approached in the early 1990s with the idea for a creative, long-term project that could realistically meet some of its ideals, it agreed to support the Traditional Creativity in the Schools Project, giving it 'teaching hours', which in effect put Project programmes into the curricula of participating schools. The Project has been granted funds for salaries and running costs.

However, this support has varied in relation to the educational emphases and interests of each government administration. Some funding comes through the local and regional councils' education offices.[4] Larger grants come from independent foundations and institutions.[5]

The Project has received enough of a budget to ensure that it can run, but it has not been able to reach its potential, or to develop programmes in new schools, or new programmes to address the needs of other communities under stress. The Project has been unable, as yet, to fund a fully-staffed Project Centre, and must rely on a group of regular and dedicated volunteers.

The nature of the Project

Setting up the Project has been complex. Its ultimate objective is that the individuals involved (children, parents, grandparents, teachers), having worked together for several years, will become role models of tolerance, mutual respect and coexistence. The expectation is that Arab and Jewish children will learn more first about their own folklore and also about the cultures of the various ethnic and religious groups that their own class comprises; and that second, they will learn more about each other through access, contact and the sharing of traditions for which there is usually no vehicle.

By working simultaneously with paired classes (Jewish and Arab) and by bringing them together to create, observe, play and talk, the Project provides a unique bridge that can be crossed safely and securely. Not only do the children and teachers have access to this contact, but also the parents and grandparents. With various family members helping to create a mosaic of family history and cultural heritage, it is expected that there will be a refreshed relationship between the generations, with parents and grandparents acknowledged by the schools as having wisdom to impart.

The project has been running since 1991 between pairs of Jewish and Arab schools. Classes participate for a 3-year cycle (grades 5–7; 9/10-year-olds to 12/13-year-olds). The programmes begin in the schools every September and run throughout the school year, ongoing from one school year to the next. Depending on funding in any given year, new pairs of fifth grade classes are added as the seventh grade 'graduates'. By 1995, there had been programmes in four schools involving 750 children, 200 active family members, and 35 teachers and principals. By 1999 the Project was running in ten schools.

Although there is a basic programme structure, the specific units of study are chosen in consultation with the school staff and pupils, based on folklore and traditions found in the pupils' homes. Pupils ask their parents and grandparents questions about these subjects and bring information and examples to class. Weekly background lessons are given by Project staff and teachers in each of the paired classes separately. The paired Jewish and Arab schools meet for Joint Activities, built around family members as folk artists, every six to eight weeks in alternate schools (taking into account long holiday periods such as Channuka, Christmas, Ram-adan and Passover – which means three to five times per year). There are regular feedback classes and children create exhibitions and joint end-of-year community events.

Building bridges

In 1995–96, the Project was running in two pairs of Jewish and Arab schools in Ramle and Jerusalem, in communities where the likelihood is that participants will see one another in the course of their daily lives. Ramle, a city in central Israel, has a mixed population of approximately 60,000 residents, of whom 25 per cent are Arab and 75 per cent are Jewish. Here the schools are within walking distance of each other, and there are many common meeting places throughout the town (marketplace, parks, town centre).

In the Jerusalem region, an urban Jewish school is paired with a rural Arab school that services two villages close to the city. These two schools were chosen because they each have a strong sense of themselves as a community and because participants can introduce one another to a world view that differs greatly from their own. Among their common meeting points are a widely used nature reserve next to the Arab villages, and Jerusalem city parks and shopping malls.

By working with twinned schools, a model is set up of cooperation, mutuality and cultural relativism. While coexistence may correctly describe the broadly bilateral nature of Israeli society, it implies that people may know one another without having to accept one another, that they may have to live alongside each other but not see into each other's worlds. The Project embodies structures and strategies for contact, sharing and learning that surpass most other avenues of communication between Jews and Arabs in Israeli life. While beginning as a response to integration, it goes far beyond reaction and embodies a creative and imaginative vehicle for exchange.

Whereas people respond positively to the idea of children researching their home-cultures, they often feel threatened by the idea of meeting members of the 'other' community. The positive attitude to the children learning about their traditional heritage somehow takes these participants past their anxiety and they eventually understand how the Project helps to break stereotypes by creating real possibilities for contact in which participants explain who they are in relation to their own cultures first (for example, as grandparents who make dolls), and then as coming from the other community.

Another essential ingredient of the Project is the simple way in which parents find that they have something concrete and unique to offer in an educational setting. Apart from parent–teacher meetings, parents – and even less so grandparents – mostly have little chance of coming to school. In fact, there are parents who come to Project activities who have never before been to their child's school during school hours, let alone visited another school. School can be intimidating. Immigrant parents in particular ask, 'How can we get into the school, our children are being integrated, we're left behind, we need to understand the school system, we need to keep up with our children's learning'.

In this specific context, everybody has the same level of expertise – parents, children, grandparents – regardless of their cultural background. The Project gives Arabs the possibility of hosting Jews, and Jews the possibility of hosting Arabs. Teachers and pupils have the possibility of visiting each other's schools. In some cases this formalized framework for meeting develops into personal relationships that carry on outside Project activities. While the aim is to create situations that provide the opportunity for knowing one another in a general way and breaking broad negative stereotyping, these personal relationships are an exciting by-product of the Project's presence in the communities.

Feedback from the parents indicates how much they appreciate being involved in their children's education. They enjoy the fact that the children talk to them, and it allows them to show the children things that they have been longing to share. At home, the Project creates an 'enforced' situation of tradition-bearing in that parents or grandparents answer questions 'for school', but once the question/answer/story sequence is in motion the children listen attentively, partly because they then have to transmit the information in class, but more often because once the process begins, they find the material itself interesting. Parents say that the Project opens up new areas for dialogue at home.

The Project

This is the Project Director's description of what he does in each year of the Project.

The first year: traditional play

'In the first year, we use the world of games, games that the parents and grandparents played. The pupils learn about the significance of play in society and the relationship between the games they play and the games their parents and grandparents played. We consider a world before the advent of television and the ensuing "theme" games and shop-bought toys related to television programmes such as *The Care Bears*, *My Little Pony* and *Ninja Turtles*, or Disney productions like *Aladdin* or *Pocahontas*. We ask such questions as, "What games did you play?", "Where did you play them, indoors or outdoors?", "Where did your toys come from?", "Who made them?" and "What were they made out of?".

Based on the answers to these questions we can see which parents and grandparents will be good to work with and we design an activity for both classes together around their skills. The first Joint Activity is usually based on outdoor games. I send the children home with specific questions: "What outdoor games did your parents/grandparents play?", "Can you describe them?", "What are the rules?", "Were there any festival/seasonal games?", "Did you skip; if so, were there any words – can you write them down?".

We work with the Jewish and Arab schools separately each week but at the same time. In the Joint Activities, Jewish and Arab parents and grandparents lead mixed groups of children in, for example, skipping games, 5 stones, 7 stones, marbles, elastic cord jumping games and hopscotch. The children teach one another their own variations of these games and also play them according to the adults' rules.

We usually find that a number of parents and grandparents made different kinds of dolls as children, or do so now for their own children. In the second Joint Activity then, the groups often make dolls and soft toys together.

In class preparation the children are shown examples of all kinds of dolls. We ask them, "What do you need to play with this doll?", "What world does it come from?", "Does it have its own story", "What do you need to make a story with/for it?", "Does it need a name?".

I've got finger puppets of the Four and Twenty Blackbirds nursery rhyme, and a three-faced Little Red Riding Hood. I've got two-headed dolls that offer the possibility of building a story, as each face relates to the other (old/young/green hair/red hair), and dolls whose personality comes from the characteristics given to them by the people who made them.

In the Joint Activity, parents, grandparents and children have made rag dolls, stick dolls, hand puppets, finger puppets, box puppets, soft toys, dolls' clothes and dolls' houses. The children collect materials such as cloth, buttons, socks, wool and cartons, and the Project brings in large quantities of scrap materials.

In learning about natural materials traditionally used in making toys, a third unit of study might be wooden toys, with children examining traditional wooden toys such as spinning tops, egg-in-the-cup, diabolos, yo-yos, and model cars and trains. With wood, we talk about the place of trees in the world, what trees give us, especially here, where they prevent soil erosion; oxygen, shade, all these kinds of things. We show them pictures of trees in England, fields bordered by rows of trees, pictures of individual trees standing out in a landscape. We ask them to bring tree stories from the Bible and the Koran, see if the parents know any local tree stories, think about the raw material, ask for lists of things found at home that are made from wood.

Again, what happens in the Joint Activities depends on what information the children bring. Parents, grandparents and children make a variety of simple wooden toys, which they then take home, such as cars, boats, painted puzzle blocks and mobiles.'

The second year: the food we eat

'I begin this year with an introduction about hunters and gatherers and the whole idea of finding and collecting food, of growing food and of herding. We show as many pictures as we can from various books. We talk about the difference between humans and other animals and the way animals relate to their environment, and the conceptualization of tools and their use. Then I send the children home with all kinds of questions about what foods are made at home, what foods used to be made at home, and whether there are any family specialities.

Sometimes I send them home and ask them to bring a list of all the milk products in their home, then we send them back to find out which of these milk products their grandmother made, and if she made them where did the milk come from, etc.

Questions like, "Do you have any animals at home?", "Do you have any pets?", "Do you have any animals kept for food purposes?", "When your parents were children or when your grandparents were children, were there any?".

The first unit of study is usually pickling, since it is a tradition maintained in most Jewish and Arab households. After children have enquired about traditions of pickling at home and brought recipes, they draw a "cultural" map that includes the history of everyone's traditions. Children collect ingredients, pickling agents and jars for the Joint Activities. The fun element is ensured because there is such a wide variety of different fruits and vegetables that are pickled, and many different processes.

Fathers, mothers, grandfathers and grandmothers come and don't exactly argue about how to make pickles, but they do watch each other. They exchange recipes and discuss the various ways of preserving food. Last year in Ein Rafa, one of the Jewish grandfathers on a visit to the Arab school brought a little jar of his own secret spice for the pickles and at the end of the day he gave it to one of the teachers.

In studying traditional breads, the background classes are about the "starch diet", everyday and ceremonial breads, and national tastes. The children discover what bread used to be made at home in their parents' and grandparents' childhoods, who made the bread, how much was made at one time and how it was distributed. They bring varieties of homemade and shop-bought breads, jams, preserves, spreads, and humus, olive oil and zatar herbs, traditionally eaten in the Middle East with pita bread.'

The third year: learning from ourselves – learning from each other

'In the third year of the Project, the classes learn what can be done with collections of ethnographic material. Using the subject of each unit of study as a starting point, they consolidate the information they have collected in the previous two years of their programme, moving deeper into their traditions. They also collect new material from their own oral traditions – lullabies, work-songs and family stories. They bring family photographs and create bilingual active community archives through which they see home-culture becoming a clear means of learning about each other and about themselves. The examination of the process of collecting folklore, and the way in which it is transmitted from generation to generation, is a prominent feature of the background lessons and class discussion.

By this time the children are 12 and 13 years old. The boys have become more difficult at this stage, often hiding any interest they have in their studies, while the girls seem to become more intellectually inquisitive. But because we've started with them as 10-year-olds (in the Fifth Grade), we have this special relationship and they really enjoy what they do in the Project, so that although they want to be "anti" as they are in their other classes, they sometimes find that a little difficult.

In these Joint Activities, the pupils learn each other's songs and introduce their family stories. They annotate photographs of their past Joint Activities, reinforcing both their sense of having shared experiences and the knowledge they have acquired of each other's lives. They design and mount photographic exhibitions that are open to their communities.'

The project: implementation and design

Apart from the Project Director, in 1995–6 the staff consisted of a programmes coordinator (who ran the classwork in Ramle); an evaluator who worked on documentation, activities design and communications skills through video; a photographer who worked on documentation and ethnography; and the form teachers and school craft teachers. The temporary staff for Joint Activities included student teachers (some of whom received credit towards their degrees), and a range of volunteers with a variety of interests and skills who took on crucial functions. Sometimes a parent or teacher from one of the centres (Jerusalem or Ramle) volunteered in the other centre, which created an intimate atmosphere between Project participants.

In keeping with an anthropological/folkloristic view of education, the Project was envisaged as a fluid system, its malleable nature ensuring a flexibility needed when dealing with a multiplicity of generations, cultures, personalities, roles and even institutions. The constant factor is the attitude to the significance of culture and the positive dynamic between culture-groups and generations. The Project itself, as manifested in the specific programmes will reflect the anthropologist's sensitivity to the specific community or set of communities in which the Project has been established.

The programmes are primarily adaptable, meeting the needs of each specific school-community. They are continually modified according to experience. As with reading the text of a play that is only 'complete' in performance, the 'final version' of the basic programme varies with every 'performance' or implementation situation.

The Project Team must be able to recognize what changes need to be made to the model, allowing the specific programme to suit the specific class. Each group of children, even of the same age, is seen as a new community with it own composition and dynamic. A programme needs to be flexible enough to be inclusive of new communities rather than have them adapt to preconceived programme goals.

Project activities are open. Although family members who have the knowledge and skills that suit the particular subject are invited, anyone who wants to participate is always welcome. There is also a spectrum of children's responses, ranging from those who want their parents to be part of the programme to those who are reluctant to have their parents be in school at all.

The configuration of each Joint Activity depends on the parents and grandparents who participate that day. For example, two Traditional Outdoor Games Days (held in Ein Rafa School in November 1996) were designed around four grandparents, a great uncle and aunt and twelve fathers and mothers who brought games they had played as children in London, Israel and Lebanon such as marbles, skipping, hopscotch, 7 stones and 'ball-against-the-wall' games. The children played according to their own and each other's contemporary rules, and according to the rules of older generations, and they also learned games they had never seen before.

A Jewish grandfather from London and a Jewish mother from Israel found that their games were almost identical, although geography and a period of forty years separated their childhoods. The grandfather brought the game complete, consisting of 2-inch tapered wood chips and a bat (called 'Tippecat'); the mother brought it partly-made (called 'Dudes') and finished carving the wood chips and fashioning the bat during the day so that the children could participate in both their playing and their making.

A second home-made game (called 'Cannon'), brought by a visiting Jewish great uncle from

London, consisted of four sticks placed on an empty tin can, the team that is 'in' having to knock the sticks off the can. An Arab grandfather from the neighbouring village of Ein Naquba found this game to be very similar to '7 Stones' which an Arab mother from Ein Rafa taught. Here, the tower is built from stones, as the name suggests, and knocked down by a ball.

The children clearly loved these games. 'Cannon' was the kind of anarchic school yard game that had everybody half laughing, half playing hard; 'Tippecat' or 'Dudes', more difficult to learn, was practised painstakingly by many of the children and some of them have since shown members of the Project Team equipment that they have made for it themselves in order to continue playing the game and teaching it to their friends.

There was a natural flow between languages and teaching between the children, parents and the grandparents of each community, and between the children and the older generations of their own community. Each class taught the other class games that included words (in either Arabic or Hebrew). When one of the Jewish grandfathers who grew up in Lebanon was asked if he could play in both Arabic and Hebrew, he replied, 'But it's marbles, I only know the terms in Arabic as I played them!' Weeks after the meeting, the children were playing these games and enjoying the word skills acquired.

The schools recognize that teachers working with this Project gain significant in-house training and enrichment while, at the same time, being able to contribute from their own expertise and experience. The curriculum followed by each class is determined by the working relationship between Project Staff and each form teacher. The form teachers are encouraged to take the units of study in any direction that might suit the rest of their curriculum or the own particular interests.

For example, one of the teachers who has worked with the Project for many years comes from a small Arab village himself and is saddened by the way Arab culture is changing. He works in a city school and remarks how city-based children are alienated from much of their tradition. He has been able to use the Project to show his own perception of culture under stress, teaching the children as a primary tradition bearer. For example, when working on ceremonial dance, he turned the classroom into a dancing studio leading everyone through the steps. His input gave the programme additional depth.

While it may be hard to prove the Project works without a thorough process of evaluation, for these researchers there is no doubt that it does provide the children with a different way of seeing their home-culture and those family members who represent and transmit that culture.[6] In the school setting, the Project has found a neutral context for transmission so that children can experience learning about their own tradition in the light of their classmates' interest in the tradition bearers (their parents and grandparents). Thus, experiencing a variety of home-cultures and belief systems, linked specifically to each member of the group, is an experience in presenting oneself, a self that consists partly (not entirely) of each participant's home-culture (see Goffman 1959).[6] Where this is successful, the children can be seen tacitly accepting aspects of their home-culture in their presentation of self that they might formerly have rejected outright as 'old fashioned' and 'primitive'. Even where this interest in home-culture is limited to the Project intervention, it has opened a chink in the armour often placed around the emerging adolescent personality that in Israel is bound up with a disassociation from traditional ways of life.

The reasoning behind the scheme

As a PhD student, the Project Director[7] researched folk drama in England and became interested in the way that ritual can be used by communities to articulate and address issues of contemporary concern without spelling it out.

The second inspiration came from involvement with a Folk Artists in the Schools Programme in Camden, New Jersey. The Programme Director here worked with ordinary traditional items and processes, and brought folk artists into the schools, such as a Puerto Rican eight-string guitar maker, blue grass musicians and a shoe maker. The Programme ended with a Community Arts Fair.

The lesson to be learned here was the way in which the folklorist was able to put a community's folklore 'to use' by involving children in it as an 'event'. Thus, they benefited from experiencing their own traditions while not necessarily having to be, or become, traditional themselves, or to be in a traditional setting for the transmission of this culture to occur (see Hufford 1979).

In the process of creating a unified national culture and integrating immigrants from diverse backgrounds into Israeli society, there is pressure for people to join the mainstream, with the result that home-cultures in both the Jewish and Arab sectors are often rejected by the younger generation. In reaction to the 'melting pot' model adopted in the formative years of Israeli history, there was a period of 'ethnic pride' in the early 1970s. However, this too had its drawbacks in that the various ethnic and national groups created interest camps without necessarily encouraging a deeper understanding of their heritage. Children became increasingly alienated from their parents and grandparents, dismissing their home-cultures as irrelevant to their lives, while the older generation lost their traditional audience for the transmission of their culture.

It was felt that with a national policy of integration and the development of an Israeli sense of identity, the links with the past and a sense of continuity with parents, grandparents and forbears was in danger of being lost. At the same time there was a lack of understanding both within the multi-ethnic mix within Israel's Jewish population and between the Jewish, Muslim and Christian populations. In the Jewish sector of society, the classroom may include family backgrounds from several countries and continents. In the Arab sector of society there are Muslims and Christians, Druze and Bedouin communities, which may also have family ties with, for example, Lebanon, Syria, Jordan and Egypt.

The Project was designed for the cultural, ethnic and religious mix of any Israeli classroom, as well as the twinned classrooms of schools from communities between which there is conflict or negative stereotyping, such as Jews and Arabs, orthodox and secular, new immigrants and veterans.

A major purpose is to create ongoing contact between people who have few opportunities for getting to know each other in a natural setting. It is believed that real change happens over a period of time and where a broad cross-section of society or a community is involved (children, parents, grandparents, teachers, principals and school inspectors). While recognizing the need for the school communities to meet one another more frequently, the time spent in the programme between Joint Activities is seen as preparation for the next meeting and, as such, means that the children constantly have one another in mind. This mindfulness is the beginning of awareness of the other and of their otherness as something to be respected as well as appreciated.

Outcomes and values

The Traditional Creativity in the Schools Project has run against many odds for eight years now, and as teachers, children, parents and grandparents pass through it, its values and outcomes begin to emerge.

Talking with those who have taken part gives an indication of what is happening, of some of the surprises that have emerged from it. Necessarily, these outcomes and values are qualitative, impressionistic, sometimes magical and often moving.

In general terms, the Project has developed an ongoing relationship between each pair of Jewish and Arab schools, as the confidence of the communities has been gained. The children show sustained interest in each other's way of life and in their own heritage. They call for information about various customs and express a stronger desire to learn Arabic and Hebrew respectively. They enjoy seeing their parents and grandparents in Project activities and encourage them to participate. Outside of Project activities, there is ongoing communication between some children, which does not stop at times of tension.

The school principals involved thus far have indicated that the programme contributes to the overall atmosphere of coexistence within their school communities. They work to maintain the relationship between the schools, and furthermore argue that with more scope (more classes, more schools), the Project could have an even greater impact. The principals in both Ramle and Jerusalem have made the Project a priority in their yearly planning.

The people: identity not integration

Inter-generational and inter-cultural relationships
The Project provides participating children with a framework through which they can ask their parents and grandparents questions about their lives, the 'history' they have experienced and the way they lived as children. Most parents and grandparents cooperate and those who come to the schools for a particular Joint Activity are always ready to come again, even if the next activity is not directly in their area of expertise. Building active archives out of the data collected from home encourages the children to consolidate what they have learned about their own

traditions, and then about each other's community. The products in themselves are active records of the cooperative spirit with which the two school communities view one another and of the specific families' involvement with their children's education.

Personal contacts between children

Outside of the Project, some children from each community have played together, either by design or through chance meetings in parks and markets. In the Jerusalem area there is now a group of about ten children who have visited one another's homes during the course of the last two school years, while others keep in touch through telephone conversations and letters. Many of them exchange small presents when they meet at the Joint Activities.

In Ramle, because both schools are in the same city, there are more opportunities for Jewish and Arab children meeting each other outside the Project. For example, in 1995 there were two fifth grade girls whose grandmothers were neighbours. They had watched each other growing up but had never spoken. From the first Joint Activity they began to play together outside school hours, visiting each other's homes and meeting each other's circles of friends.

Parents and grandparents: belonging and participating

Among the participating family members, there are men and women of parent and grandparent generations, including more and less religious and secular Christians, Arabs and Jews. This mix of ethnicity, generations, genders, religious backgrounds and degrees of orthodoxy has added to a natural atmosphere of coexistence.

For both Arab and Jewish parents, to find themselves in each other's schools, being treated as 'parents' and appreciated as having a significant contribution to make to *all* the children's education, is in itself an extremely positive experience. The grandparents work not only with their own grandchildren but also with other children and they talk about the hope this experience has given them. For the most part, the children of each group relate with excitement, warmth and curiosity to what the grandparents offer. The fact that they have this experience in the company of others makes it more memorable, becoming a collective, not only an individual, experience.

Beyond the stereotype

One of the main and simplest objectives of the Project is that once people have done this type of work they can no longer pass each other on the street as if they are faceless. The divides that separate people and are hardened into prejudice and fear are narrowed by the sort of contact that is the life-blood of Project programmes. 'Otherness' is reduced because contact has been made for perhaps three years between children, parents and grandparents who may not ordinarily have been able to meet each other. Even if people are not comfortable in each other's society, they now see faces and lives that they have come to know quite well where before they only saw something unknown.

Resolving the conflict: contact and respect

The children learn about one another's environments in several natural ways. First, when they visit one another's schools, they see some of the surrounding village or city, and then they get to know the inside of the schools themselves. The children look around each other's classrooms, and ask the teachers and children about the pictures and decorations on the walls, and look at schoolbooks. They are curious about each other's school day, playground activities and school subjects.

Although making personal friendships is not an objective in itself, it reflects the atmosphere of the Joint Activities in which developing friendships are possible. All the children relate to one another on some positive level, from simply enjoying working side by side, smiling at one another, passing materials and tools, to playing the same games as part of the same team, and knowing names and gradually learning more about each child as an individual and as part of a group.

There have been moving spontaneous responses to tragic events that reinforce the realization that this kind of project really does offer its participants opportunities to show or share their feelings with those people who could otherwise be generalized into the category or 'you too are the enemy'. When these children discuss the conflict they do so within the context of understanding each other through knowledge, neither 'side' being seen in terms of a stereotype. In many instances there is a clear change of feeling in those hurt or affected by violence between Arabs and Jews, as the 'otherness' and facelessness of Jew and Arab is replaced by the identity of individuals.

The beauty and optimism of the Project is manifest very clearly in the following account from the Director:

'Several years ago, a pair of fifth grade classes were invited to a puppet theatre by one of the Jewish mothers who is a professional puppeteer, to see her new show. About three days before the performance, the tragedy in Hebron took place.[8] Both schools decided to postpone this meeting.

That week I went to both schools. In the Jewish school, one of the teachers had the idea that the children write "blessings", personal messages of warmth and affection. For example, one child wrote, "Although I wasn't in Hebron, this is a shocking thing, and I hope that none of your family has been injured". The children said to me, "We'd like you to take these blessings to the school, but there's one condition. You must explain that because we're Jewish and because the gunman was Jewish doesn't mean that we are guilty. We're sending these blessings because we know these children, they've become our friends and we feel for their pain. We want them to understand that all Jews, and especially these Jews that they know, are not in any way behind this kind of action". The idea came from one of the teachers but the children immediately connected with the idea and turned it into something concrete showed that the children in their own minds were searching for some way to mark this.

The Arab children were so moved by these blessings, and their teachers could not believe that the Jewish children and teachers had reached out to them as a whole community. One of the Arab teachers started to cry. He said, "I can't believe that the children wrote these, I can see that they did, I can see it wasn't parents, I can see it wasn't teachers, I can see what's in their hearts. We go to Jerusalem, we have work contacts, but I have never had this kind of contact, I've never had the opportunity to experience this kind of comment on our situation".

This happened during Ramadan. It's customary at the end of Ramadan for Arab families to give sweet foods to their neighbours even if they aren't Muslims. The Jewish children thought it would be an idea to send a tray of sweets. We chose four representatives, and I took the children to the Arab school. It was an amazing moment. One of the Arab teachers said, "Before we move into the sweets, the children have some questions to ask you", so I had four Jewish 10–11-year-olds facing fifty Arab children. "We want to know where you stand. We got your letters and you've brought us these sweets, but we need to know more, we need to know what you feel about living together". Two of the girls said, "Look, our position is quite simple, we think that we have to work out a way of living peacefully with whoever is living in this area. We don't want to lose Israel, we don't care how much land Israel has as a country. What we really care about is leading as peaceful lives as possible. Any death is one death too many, so we are shocked by what happened. We are also shocked when Jews get killed".

One of the Jewish boys said, "Well, the truth is that I am actually very frightened. This happened in Hebron but I see Jews being killed often as well. How can I tell when I pass an Arab by on the street if he's concealing a knife or a bomb? I feel like a target".

It was a whole conversation. They all said what they needed to say. Some of the Arab children said, "How do you think we feel, that's how we walk round all the time", and he said, "We don't have to count how many Arabs, how many Jews, it's not a question of balance. If we all feel this way, I don't have a solution, but us meeting together makes a difference". The next year when we did the pickles, this boy's grandfather came to the Arab village, quietly made pickles, explained to any child who was interested, went home, and was very happy. I only found out afterwards that the year before he had been stabbed in the Old City on his way to pray at the Wailing Wall.

On the strength of this first letter exchange, some of the children started to send letters through me, I became a postman. They would send each other letters and sometimes presents – a pencil, a rubber, beads – and they would call each other on the telephone.

Several years back when a bus was blown up in Tel Aviv by Arab terrorists, one of the Arab teachers asked her class, "Would those children in Jerusalem want to know how we feel?" The responses were graphic. One letter said, "I saw on the television the pictures of the people who were blown up on the bus and it made me sick. I was horrified by the violence. I am not prepared to live in a world like this". "This is the tree of remembrance" – it is traditional in both Jewish and Arab cultures to plant trees as memorials – so this girl drew a picture of a tree planted on Dizengoff Street in Tel Aviv where the bus was blown up. Another letter says, "If peace were a mountain, I'd climb it every day".

We were due to have a pickles day for another pair of classes a few days after this bus was blown up. The teachers at the Jewish school asked what we should do and I said that they must make that decision, although I thought it would be a shame not to go to the Arab school. They decided to go. We always begin with me or a teacher saying what we are going to do even though it may be really straight-forward. One of the Arab children stood up and said, "We are not part of that, each one of us is shocked, it's not what we believe in, it's not what we think life should be like, and we want you to understand that we feel your pain and we're so happy that you've come and you haven't chosen to halt our relationship. Peace talks are one thing but we're the people who are living in this world. It would be a shame to break our relationship because somebody else did something".'

Conclusion

In its eight years, the Project has brought together people from vastly different and sometimes hostile worlds. Throughout, there is the intractable reality of people prepared to believe the worst about each other, people caught in a negative situation, a situation not of their own making but, in the final analysis, theirs to be complicit in or to change.

The value of a project like this is that not only does it return traditional home-culture to the present generation and honour their parents and grandparents; it can also help bring people to the realization that it makes more sense to offer children a world in which there is the possibility of coexistence, than to encourage them to accept a world consisting of communities of people who cannot get along with each other, who cannot recognize the value of each other's ways. The speed with which these children, parents and grandparents respond to the interest of their counterparts, extend hospitality and friendship and accept it, and find themselves benefiting from the cultural pluralism of their society, has been the fulfilment of the hope that generates this work.

Notes

1 Whereas other projects on divided societies focus on peace processes, differences and, in the case of Northern Ireland, on sectarianism (such as Tom Lovett's project at the Ulster People's College, see Lovett 1990, 1993, 1994), the Traditional Creativity in the Schools Project does not try to deal with conflict and to find solutions. Instead it deals with commonality, through people doing things together and sharing traditional knowledge.

2 The findings of this paper are based on the development

and implementation of the project by Simon Lichman in Israel and on ethnographic research carried out by Keith Sullivan in Jerusalem and Ein Rafa in August and September 1995. Keith and his partner, Ginny Sullivan, interviewed and tape-recorded Simon Lichman, the creator and driving force behind this Project, and his partner, Rivanna Miller. Keith interviewed and tape-recorded Doron Shohat, Director of the Department of Education for Democracy and Coexistence in Jerusalem. He also visited the two elementary schools involved in the Greater Jerusalem project, where he spoke with the principals, teachers, support staff and children and made observations in classrooms and in the playgrounds. Interviews and conversations were conducted in English with interpretation to and from Hebrew and Arabic where appropriate.

3 Sprinzak et al. *Facts and Figures about Education in Israel 1994.* These figures relate to Israel proper and do not include the West Bank and the Gaza Strip.

4 For example, Matei Yehuda Regional Council and 'Manchi' (the Department of Education of the Jerusalem Municipality).

5 For example, The Jerusalem Foundation, the Doron Foundation for Education and Welfare, The Abraham Fund, The Josephine Bay Paul and C Michael Paul Foundation, The Lord Ashdown Charitable Settlement (through the Doron Foundation) and the PEF Israel Endowment Funds for Innovative Education.

6 When Doron Shohat, Director of the Department of Education for Democracy and Coexistence, was interviewed, he said that because of the long-term and delicate nature of the Project, it was felt that an evaluation of it would be inappropriate.

7 Dr Lichman had studied the well-known mumming play performed each Boxing Day by the Marshfield Paper Boys of Gloucestershire. This research started at the Institute of Dialect and Folk Life Studies at the University of Leeds, England, and was completed at the University of Pennsylvania, USA. See Lichman 1981.

8 When a Jewish settler entered a mosque and opened fire, killing a number of worshippers.

References

Department of Education for Democracy and Coexistence Staff (eds) (1993) *The Department for Democracy and Coexistence: Information Booklet.* Jerusalem: Publications Department, Ministry of Education.

Goffman, I. (1959) *The Presentation of Self in Everyday Life.* New York: Doubleday Anchor Books.

Hufford, M. (1979) *A Tree Smells Like Peanut Butter: Folk Artist in a City School.* Trenton, New Jersey: New Jersey Council on the Arts.

Lichman, S. (1981) *The Gardener's Story and What Came Next: A Contextual Analysis of the Marshfield*

Paper Boys' Mumming Play. PhD thesis, University of Pennsylvania: Department of Folklore and Folklife.

Lovett, T. (1990) Community education and community division in Northern Ireland. *Convergence*, 23 (2): 25–33.

Lovett, T. (1993) To fight sectarianism and search for peace: the Ulster People's College in Ireland. *Convergence*, 26 (4): 33–43.

Lovett, T. (1994) Bridging the sectarian divide in Northern Ireland, The Ulster People's College. *Adults Learning*, 5 (6): 155–7.

Sprinzak, D., Bar, E. and Levi-Mazloum, D. (1994) *Facts and Figures about Education in Israel 1994*. Jerusalem: Ministry of Education, Culture and Sport.

8 Heads I Win, Tails You Lose: The Politics of the Disabled World

LEONARD A. PARKYN

Disablement is a tragedy in terms of human suffering and frustration, and in terms of numbers. The number of disabled people in the world today is estimated at 450 million, of which one third are children and four-fifths live in developing countries. Population growth and the increasing proportion of older people can only magnify the problem.

Unless decisive action is taken now the number of disabled people could double by the end of the century.

Leeds Castle Declaration on the Prevention of Disablement (Wilson 1983)

The above declaration was one of nine put forward by a unique international group of scientists, doctors, health administrators and politicians who met to suggest measures to prevent disablement throughout the world.

The politics of the disabled world or the world of disabled politics is a complex one. There is no aspect of the human condition or experience that does not have a disability dimension.

The current trend in disability politics appears to wish to explore issues such as language and linguistics, empowerment, legislation and equal opportunities. This chapter will explore some of these issues, but will also offer alternative considerations for debate. Further to this diverse, some may say unrelated, factors and anomalies will also be presented for discussion as a cause or factor in disablement politics.

The world of disability politics raises many questions: this chapter does not attempt to provide answers but rather to identify areas for consideration. You, the readers, are left to draw your own conclusions to open-ended statements and views. Further, this chapter does not examine the relationship between politics and disability cultures.

The percentage of disabled people in the world has been estimated by the World Health Organisation (WHO 1978) to be in the region of 10 per cent. Lynch (1994) considers that 'based on the 10 per cent figure, the total number of impaired people in the world was approximately 450 million in 1980, 500 million in 1990, and is expected to rise to well over 600 million by the end of this century (approximately 40 per cent of this population may be expected to comprise school age children)'. To add weight to the preceding figures, and to indicate the potential growth in the number of disabled adults, the United Nations Children's Fund (UNICEF 1991) concluded that in developing countries there were approximately 140 million children with significant impairment. UNICEF went on to illustrate how disability was related to geographical factors, in that it is estimated that the number of children with significant impairment is 88 million in Asia, 13 million in Latin America and 18 million in Africa compared to 11 million in Europe and 6 million in North America. Lynch (op. cit.) continues by stating that 'one family in four is estimated to be affected by impairments in one way or another'.

The view of Mittler (1992) sums up much that is pertinent in world and disability politics in that 'the tragedy is that much impairment is either preventable or reversible. Each year 35 million children die and another 35 million become impaired; half these deaths and impairments are preventable by the use of knowledge already in our possession'.

The Leeds Castle declaration (Wilson 1983) was the forerunner of many governments' action in combating some of the causes of disability. The epigraph to this chapter was the first declaration and statement. There were seven significant others; in summary they were:

- Much of the underlying impairment is preventable. Worldwide expansion of a programme of immunization could save 5 million children a year from disabilities caused by measles, whooping cough, tetanus, diphtheria and tuberculosis.
- Impairment due to malnutrition, neglect and infection could be prevented by inexpensive improvement in primary health care (these conditions affect at least 20 million people each year).
- Opportunities for improvement in regard to other disabilities are dependent on sharing knowledge with the public. Many disabilities can be averted or postponed in later life.
- Disability need not give rise to handicap. Failure to apply simple remedies very often increases disability, and the attitudes and institutional arrangements of society increase the chance of disability placing people at a disadvantage. Sustained education of the public and of professionals is needed urgently.
- Avoidable disability is a prime cause of economic waste and human deprivation in all countries. The technology that will prevent or control most disablement is available and improving.
- Research should be encouraged, especially in the biomedical field, to develop revolutionary new tools to strengthen all interventions.
- Mobilization of the political will to act is a necessary basis for any successful programme. 'The need for disabled people to act and raise issues before the global community is supported'.

A programme of action to prevent disablement is seen as logical. 'It would ensure that the next generation did not suffer from the present degree of avoidable disability, and would constitute a most appropriate, effective and long lasting contribution to the health and happiness of mankind' (Wilson 1983).

The Leeds Castle declaration has formed the basis of many movements in the disability world. However, for the majority of people, their knowledge of what goes on locally, nationally and internationally is via television (terrestrial and satellite), radio, magazines and newspapers and, possibly, advertising.

Media is a powerful tool in the shaping of peoples lives, values and ideas. The use and abuse of language and imagery can alter people's percep-

tions of any given situation. 'Ethnic cleansing' is a sanitized version of murder or genocide, those with 'learning disabilities' are more socially acceptable than 'educationally subnormal'. Barnes (1992) quotes Hevey (1992) in the opening of his book on disabling imagery and the media when he states, 'the history of the portrayal of disabled people is the history of oppressive and negative representation. This has meant that disabled people have been presented as socially flawed able people, not as disabled people with their own identities'.

The Disability Discrimination Act (1995) was introduced to give disabled people new rights in relation to employment, goods and services and the buying or renting of land or property. The Act is a legislative first step in changing behaviour and, hopefully, attitudes towards the disabled often amplified and reinforced by the media. Barnes (1992) sees commonly recurring media stereotypes based on cultural images of disablement and socially unacceptable behaviour. These stereotypes portray the disabled person as:

- pitiable and pathetic
- an object of violence
- sinister and evil
- super cripple
- an object of ridicule
- their own worst and only enemy
- a burden
- sexually abnormal
- incapable of participating fully in community life
- normal.

Barnes presents many examples of negative disabled images to support these categories and depictions; however, the point is strongly made that these views of disabled people are not mutually exclusive, frequently one will be linked to another.

> This is particularly the case with fictional characterisations. The disabled person is evil, for example, is often combined with the disabled person as sexually degenerate. The point is that the overall view of disabled people is decidedly negative and a threat to the well-being of the non-disabled community.

Barnes explores this view with an analysis of the disabled person as a burden and how the German Third Reich used the disability image in 1930s propaganda films that justified and exalted their 'euthanasia programme'. In these films, disabled people were dehumanized, described as 'existence without life', and presented as an unnecessary burden that must be got rid of. Purely as an aside, Hitler's final solution and the resultant Holocaust were an abomination and outrage. However, it is worth noting that the extermination gas chambers were modelled on the humanitarian wishes of German parents who wished to have their 'subnormal' children put to sleep to ease suffering. Further, the evil and vicious experiments of Dr Mengele on Jews, gypsies, blacks, non-Aryans and the disabled led later in the twentieth century to some radical improvements in some surgical techniques, in particular the study of neurology. Also, one has to be clear that it was not only in Hitler's Germany where solutions were postulated. Sandow (1994) quotes from the Report of the Departmental Committee on Sterilisation produced by the Eugenics Society (1934). This report takes it for granted that disabled children are seen as a burden to themselves and society. The Eugenics Society states:

> We believe that few parents with any sense of responsibility who had had a defective child would not wish to examine the possibility that they were the victims of a hereditary weakness; and we feel strongly that they are entitled, if they wish it, to the protection of sterilisation. We attach special importance to this recommendation because of its value in relation to the social problem group. There is abundant evidence that this group contributes much more than its numerical proportion to the total volume of defect, and an equal or even larger proportion of children of lower intelligence. This is not surprising, since the economic inefficiency of the defective tends to depress him to the lowest economic level.
>
> Defectives drift to the slums. Like marries like, and not only is the incidence of defect greater in this group, but the proportion of carriers is correspondingly greater.

Sandow balances the Eugenics Societies view well with that of Morris (1991) who discussed Nazi policies on euthanasia and sterilization in relation to current medical thought.

> The arguments about whether disabled people's lives are worth living, and whether the medical profession should enable us to be 'released from misery' are as threatening today as they were in Germany in the 1930s and early 1940s. In such a context, we must insist that our lives have value. We need to question fundamentally the assumption that to be disabled, to be different, means that life is not worth living.

Later in this chapter, I explore Wolfensberger's (1994) views concerning the growing threat to the lives of handicapped people in the context of modernistic values, an analysis of 'death-making' policies in the Western world.

Returning to the world of media and the arts, there are criticisms of how the disabled are portrayed in the theatre, television, poetry and on film. Turner (1996) states that:

> It is 15 years since the National Film Theatre ran a season on disability, so the short season called Freaks is long overdue. Much has changed since that first season, and this new venture showcases the work of a new generation of film and video makers. Disabled film makers have started to take control of the way disability is portrayed in the moving image media. . . . This event celebrates the trend in disability-led film/video projects which tell the real truth about disabled lives and counter all the dubious imagery elsewhere in the media.

Davies (1996), a television critic, exposes misleading or negative images of the disabled and disability when he expresses the view that

> I'm sick of saying it, but drama is the biggest and most powerful key to current social attitudes and behaviour towards disabled people. When drama consistently gets it right, society may begin to learn. Sadly, there are still now one-off TV films that reinforce negative perceptions of disability.

Batten (1996) offers a classic example of the reinforcement of negative perceptions of disability in the story of Martin Guerre, based on true events that took place in Toulouse, France. The story is one of assumed identity, exposure, litigation and he wins – a good yarn; however, what has this to do with disability issues? Batten tells us:

> One character, who is never named (the case with most of the cast) has a limp. He also has every negative image of disability conceivable: mental inferiority (staring on at events with an expression not far removed from Crossroads' Benny); social marginalisation (being pushed out of the action) and ridicule of his disability (having his crutch kicked from under him) – all your old favourites are here. Possibly the most offensive example is the object of his emotional desires – a scarecrow. It just confirms it, doesn't it – us cripples are incapable of forming a 'normal' relationship.

French (1994) quotes Shakespeare's (1993) observation about the disability movement and political power in that:

disabled people, like children, are meant to be seen and not heard, they are meant to be grateful not angry, they are meant to be humble not proud. In challenging all those preconceptions and discriminatory ideologies, the movement is making progress every day, even before attaining the central political objective.

Disability politics is often seen as the empowerment of individuals and groups, the gaining or working towards equal opportunities and rights, and the recognition that disabled people wish to be treated and valued for what they are rather than what may have happened to them or the condition of that experience. Exley (1981) uses a statement that makes the point very well: 'I am not a disability, I'm me. I have dyslexia and I've had polio but I'm not "a dyslexic" or "a cripple", I'm me'.

The disability movement has traditionally been concerned with recognition of their needs and desires. One of the means by which recognition may be achieved is by the challenging of language and its use. Long gone are the days when people with a variety of disabilities were described as idiots, imbeciles, ineducable, retarded or crippled.

Oliver (1995) states that:

> We do not use language just to describe the world and name our own experiences of it. Nor does language merely enable us to deconstruct the world and the practices we engage in. It can enable us to conceptualise a better world and begin the process of reconstructing it. We can only believe that attempting to do so is 'mind control' or 'linguistic terrorism' as far as disabled people or those with special needs are concerned, if we believe that everything is fine and the worlds we inhabit do not need deconstructing and reconstructing.

Oliver believes that language has a major role to play in the improvement of quality of life achieved by changed practice and better policies. Language is seen as a political issue related to power, control, and manipulation (similar to Hevey's view and also that of Barnes). Language can name, classify and identify users and participants. By the appropriate use of language the disabled as a diverse group, whose experiences may be universal, can identify themselves with an idea, philosophy or group. Language can create the environment for change or encourage stagnation and corruption.

Oliver (1995) wished to make two points regarding the use of language in relation to what is considered 'politically correct', the function of language and associated issues of domination and control:

> terminology that is ridiculed is usually not the terminology people use to talk about themselves – the vast majority of democratic organisations of disabled people want to be called exactly that; disabled people, not some name thought up by our critics and in respect of danger, it is not unusual for right wing critics to use terminology like 'mind control' or 'thought police' in respect of those of us who think what we are called is important.

Language is about communication and power. Language can motivate, empower, enable and free people. Disability politics and movements are about voicing issues and concerns, and the betterment of the wider world. Disabled people are seeking a better world or, as Blumer (1995) expressed it, 'social movements can be viewed as collective enterprises to establish a new order of life'.

As I have said, 1995 saw the passing of the Disability Discrimination Act. This Act met with much opposition from disability groups, organizations and individuals on the grounds that the legislation did not go far enough, had little in the way of enforcement, was no more than tokenism and was a placebo for the population as a whole. Advocacy organizations have raised the issues of equality, valuing diversification and recognizing the needs of the disabled as a generic group, giving people power to control and direct their own lives. French quotes Oliver (1993) when he states:

> it is often assumed that empowerment is a process by which those in society who have power can dispense some of their power to those who don't have any.... However, it is more realistic to see empowerment as a collective process on which the powerless embark as part of their struggle to resist the oppression of others and/or to articulate their own views of the world.

History has taught us that groups who are marginalized, oppressed or rejected must fight for their own liberation. An example of this is illustrated by Leach (1996) who suggests that:

> when disabled people began to assert their rights they often used as their model the theories and tactics of other groups (for example, women, black people, the gay community) that were fighting for political influence. In addition, by demanding the right to control both their own lives and their own organisations disabled people were also challenging the power of the disability-related professions.

People can change laws but not always attitudes; however, legislation is at least a starting point (usually with teeth!). So what has happened in legislative terms in the rest of the world?

Australia had the Disability Discrimination Act (DDA) 1992. Its aims were to:

1 Eliminate, as far as possible, discrimination against persons on the grounds of disability in the areas of:

   • work, accommodation, education, access to premises, clubs and sport;
   • the provision of goods, facilities, services and land;
   • existing laws;
   • the administration of Commonwealth laws and programmes.

2 Ensure, as far as possible, that persons with disabilities have the same rights to equality before the law as the rest of the community.

3 Promote recognition and acceptance within the community of the principle that persons with disabilities have the same fundamental rights as the rest of the community.

In 1983 Canada gave some constitutional protection to disabled people. New Zealand has the Human Rights Act 1994 that Davis (1996) sees as 'designed to consolidate and amend earlier race relations and human rights legislation and give better protection for minority rights in New Zealand in line with United Nations declarations extensively includes disabled people among its provisions'.

The nature of medical care, the application of scientific progress and surgical techniques have changed dramatically in the past decade. DNA manipulation, cloning, transplants, microsurgery, abortion, genetic engineering and selection all have implications for the living, unborn and, indeed, those not even conceived. There is a powerful ethical and political debate about approaches to a range of quasi-medical techniques that may improve the lives of the disabled or indeed end them.

Fullbrook and Wilkinson (1996a and b) have examined from a philosophical and legal perspective the ethics of xenotransplantation. Fullbrook and Wilkinson (1996a) consider that there 'now exists, potentially, the scientific and medical knowledge to transplant animal organs into humans, a procedure called xenotransplantation'. The rationale behind the idea is that demand for transplanted human organs exceeds supply. For this reason, alternative methods have been sought. The use of animals is seen as one way to deal with the problem. It is seen as positive that the potential reduction in the lack of human organs, financial savings and the potential improved likelihood of survival and quality of life can be offset by some negative concerns. These concerns include issues related to:

   • animal rights;
   • human rights;
   • religious objections and concerns;
   • the use of animals – methods used to increase the number of organs available;
   • potential psychological damage (feelings of 'alien intrusion' into patients' bodies);
   • inability or unwillingness of care/support staff to work in this arena of specific surgical techniques;
   • possible risk of infections and viruses across species (human and animal);
   • market forces (financial aspect) relating to the supply and patenting of animals;
   • pressure (covert) that might be applied for potential recipients to select cheaper organs;
   • lack of monitoring (policing) of practical health problems and limited accountability and control by authorized agencies.

Wilkinson (1996) illustrates aspects of choice (on the part of care staff) by using the example of abortion, when he states that the

> issues of abortion involves opinions about whether an embryo is or is not a full human life. In the case of transplant surgery, the issues are less definable: ethical questions of the right to 'play God' are compounded by practical issues such as potential health risks and the possibility of organ rejection.

Wilkinson highlights two important issues; one is that of self-image (and religion) the other is the potential result of cross-species infection.

The obvious difficulty in, say, using a pig's heart for transplantation is self-image. 'Some patients may object to the idea of animal parts in their bodies, or may have to cope with objections from friends and family'. Jews and Muslims may have tremendous difficulties receiving part of an animal seen as unclean. While some may permit it in a life-saving situation, long-term problems might result from the way they experience a process that is totally at odds with their culture (see Miles 1995).

The Nuffield Report (1996) explores the ways in

which new viruses could emerge or develop from the liaison of different animal tissues.

> We know comparatively little about the spread of infections across species, but the report recognises a possible risk of passing endogenous retroviruses to offspring, causing mutations in human genetic material and increasing the risk of cancers. It is possible that any recipient of a pig's heart will face a future in strict quarantine to monitor viral action. Here some will decide that life at any price is not necessarily the most desirable option. (Wilkinson 1996)

Fullbrook and Wilkinson (1996b) urge caution when they conclude we are living and exercising some choices in such a way as to have far reaching medical, cultural, ethical and humane effects in stating, 'it is better to reflect now on what we as a society intend to do rather than find ourselves on a slippery slope from which there is no recovery'.

Wolfensberger (1994) considers that there is a growing threat to the lives of handicapped people in the context of modernistic values. He argues that the (Western) world is in the process of radical changes in lifestyles and values: 'the new ones can neither sustain a functional societal policy, nor positive valuing of the lives of all sorts of impaired people'. He talks about deathmaking, which is seen as all actions (or inactions) by humans that directly or indirectly, overtly or subtly, quickly or slowly, abbreviate the lives of humans. Deathmaking categories include:

- medical abortion;
- killing impaired newborns (by injections, starvation, dehydration and withholding treatment);
- withholding water and/or food;
- killing of people seen as suffering or dying by the use of lethal drugs or 'culturally normative forms of violence' (asphyxiation);
- withdrawal of health care (often from the poor);
- the application of psychoactive drugs;
- the abandonment of impoverished 'ghetto' populations;
- 'the dumping of handicapped people out of institutions or other services and into abandonment in the community, where they often end up idle, lonely, in dire poverty, in trouble with the law or with drugs and alcohol, in jail or prison, and as victims of street violence';
- the systematic promotion and support of suicide.

Wolfensberger considers that handicapped individuals, groups or communities are in danger of 'deathmaking' if they have one or more specific conditions, seen as:

- being severely physically impaired (cerebral palsy or quadriplegic);
- being profoundly, severely or moderately mentally retarded;[1]
- having long-term and major behavioural or mental difficulties (long-term residents or 'hardened criminals');[1]
- deinstitutionalized and abandoned.

Twelve other categories or 'at risk' people are also listed, including the elderly, senile or chronically ill, prisoners, the poor, unwanted children (pre or post birth), homeless and the derelict, the terminally ill, severely sick (with multiple sclerosis or degenerative arthritis for example). Those at significant risk are individuals who fall into more than one deathmaking category.

It is interesting to note that bioethics (as postulated by Fullbrook and Wilkinson 1996a and b) is principally pro-life, since the early to mid-1970s, however, there has been a 'wind of change'. In the 1960s 'euthanasia and eugenics were equated with the Nazi experience, and categorically rejected. Abortion was unequivocally interpreted as killing, and as permissible – at most – in extreme cases of risk to the life of the mother'. Now these sensitive matters are seen in balance – contrasting and equally valued views. Wolfensberger reminds us in relation to balance that:

> all sorts of deathmakings get presented as options worthy of consideration – much as at Nazi conferences, there occasionally were discussions of both the pros and cons of killing Jews.
> (Nowadays, people habitually seem to find it incredulous that there could have been arguments against the killing of Jews in Nazi circles. We therefore mention one such pro-and-con discussion, namely, at the January 1942 Wannsee conference near Berlin; where the blueprint for the killing of Jews was hammered out. Hitler himself had at first favoured an expulsion of the Jews rather than their genocide).

Divorkin (1993) poses the questions

> do we, by prolonging a life which we cannot see as

---

[1] Wolfensberger's (1994) own terms.

being in any way of value to the person, undermine the sanctity of human life, or do we obey the golden rule that it is not for us to project our values onto the life of another?

The response to this type of question often depends on individual experiences and beliefs.

Finally Wolfensberger (op. cit.) makes a powerful philosophical, ethical, passionate and political point about people in general that has been often adopted by the disabled:

> every person is as valuable as any other person. The value of human beings does not depend on how much pleasure or utility they afford to others, or on how much they cost, or how much they will suffer in life, or how much suffering they bring to others, or how good or evil they are. . . . A person, and a person's life, is of the same value at every moment of existence.

The world of the beautiful and the engineered is now with us. Davies (1997) in a report titled 'We abhor freak shows, so what are we doing to Samantha?' expresses the desire for the perfect and the non-acceptance of the diverse. Davies examines the experience of John Merrick

> cruelly dubbed the Elephant Man, he lived in the squalid, malodorous backroom of a freak shop on the Whitechapel Road. For one shilling passers-by could enter the shop and gape as the 'freak' turned slowly to reveal the shocking extent of his deformity.

So what accounted for the headlines concerning Samantha, 6 months old? Horror of horrors, plastered across the front page of newspapers because – wait for it – she was born with 12 fingers and 12 toes.

> Samantha, above all else, is a healthy, radiant-faced baby. To reduce her to a mere 'freak', a genetic oddity served up for public curiosity, diminishes all those involved, just as surely as the punters who paid to view John Merrick were diminished by their thoughtlessness, cold-hearted voyeurism. (Davies 1997)

Curphey and Laurance (1997) exposed another genetic-related issue and the British Association of Insurers in so far as 'people applying for life insurance are to be required to disclose if they have taken genetic tests to predict whether they are at risk of inherited disease'.

As a result of this action, medical practitioners expressed concerns that some people could be deterred from asking for tests and that the policy 'would create an uninsurable underclass'. The British Medical Association (BMA) has expressed concern about the increasing use of health information for non-medical purposes. Curphey and Laurance quote the National Consumer Council (NCC) when they state that

> by using genetic test information when assessing risks, insurance companies could create an ever-increasing ghetto of uninsurable people. People with inherited diseases and their descendants could be denied cover and the idea that insurance is about pooling risk would fly out of the window.

Not only could people be discriminated against because 'something may happen', their children and family members also experience selection by famial history. However, screening of this nature could prevent, by early identification, conditions that lead to debilitating illnesses – diabetes, cancer, Alzheimers and heart disease. Insurance has become a disability issue and has been in the political arena since the 1980s when some insurers insisted that applicants declare whether they had ever taken an HIV test, even if the result was negative.

Dolly the sheep has caused more genetic controversy when it was declared that the Finn Dorset lamb is the identical twin of her mother. Laurance and Hornsby (1997) stated that 'the chilling prospect of a woman giving birth to an identical twin of her own father was raised by doctors yesterday after the announcement that scientists have for the first time succeeded in creating a clone of an adult animal'. Clearly ethical questions have been raised by this development in science.

Cloning of animals, humans and plantlife is causing concern across the world in terms of creating perfect life, avoiding 'unacceptable variations', developing organs for spare part surgery and making organisms less prone to disease. Laurance and Hornsby relate the case of a woman who asked how she could clone her father who had died; 'she wants to bring him back to life as a baby, perhaps even carrying him in her own womb'. It has been suggested by Laurance and Hornsby (op. cit.) that cloning techniques could assist

- people with serious illnesses such as leukaemia, who could produce an embryo 'twin' for spare part transplant or transfusion purposes
- dictators who wish to produce carbon copies of themselves

- parents who fear they might lose a child to cot death and would produce an identical replacement as a precaution
- entertainment moguls wanting to re-create dead stars.

Human cloning is not allowed in the UK. However, in countries with less stringent regimes, it is open to abuse.

Human selection and rejection is now with us. Rogers (1997) has revealed that 'doctors believe they have already produced the worlds first human clone, now a four year old boy living in Belgium created by accident during experimental infertility treatment'. The boy and his twin were created from a frozen fertilized egg, rubbed or stimulated by a glass rod. The fears of Laurance and Hornsby (1997) may be justified.

Medical science gives hope and relief for many. It is possible that genetic engineering and associated techniques could have helped sufferers of conditions such as Rapadillino syndrome, where children are born without forearms or kneecaps.

It is thought that there are only seven cases of Rapadillino syndrome in the world. Pope (1997) reported that 'surgeons are to carry out a pioneering operation to create limbs for a baby born with a rare inherited condition which has left him with bones missing in his arms and legs'. Surgeons have developed a technique where a thumb will be created from a finger and will reconstruct a forearm using a fixor rod, tendons moved and pinned. The question raised concerns genetic manipulation set against diversity of the species in relation to pain and suffering of all concerned. A disability issue with political overtones – do we fund this avenue of research at the expense of other techniques? It is all about dilemmas and values.

So how in this modern world can we create so many different and new methods to disable?

> The bucket was filling up. Flies whirred around it as the surgeon performed his third amputation of the morning, removing a limb made useless by the world's most indiscriminate weapon. The patient moaned softly as his leg was dumped in the bucket. The stump was stitched. Cambodia had a new cripple, a boy of 13.   (Malone 1996)

Shortly before her death, television, radio and newspapers focused on the high profile campaigning work of Diana, Princess of Wales in Angola, publicizing the effects of landmines on mainly innocent populations. Valley (1997) states that today 'there are estimated to be 110 million unexploded mines scattered over 64 countries, which maim more than 1,900 civilians a month. Between 5 and 10 million more are produced each year'. Landmines, also known as anti-personnel mines, are designed to kill, disable, create terror and tie up staff (military, medical, transport and social) in a logistical nightmare. Parkyn (1997b) in a radio interview pointed out the evil and vicious nature of landmines and the hypocrisy of governments worldwide who manufacture these weapons that blow off limbs and then, to ease the politicians' or military conscience, provide tied overseas aid to enable foreign powers to purchase artificial limbs – strange circles.

The Hazardous Areas Life-Support Organisation (the HALO Trust) is a non-political, non-religious British registered charity that specializes in the removal of the debris of war mines and UXO (unexploded ordinance). It is interesting to note that much of landmine devastation is centred in the Third or developing world. Where do these mines come from?

- 85 per cent are Russian;
- 10 per cent Chinese;
- 2 per cent Vietnamese;
- 3 per cent a mixture of American, Portuguese, Rumanian, French and Italian.

It is worth noting that HALO 'has only found 3 British mines – all old anti-tank mines manufactured in the 1950s' (HALO 1996). The Chinese make the 72 Alpha which is about the size of a powder compact and costs about $4 to make. It costs about $1,000 to clear.

It is amazing to think that so much 'creative effort' has gone into making a destructive weapon at a time when there is so much need in the world. But man's creativity goes further now. In an attempt to avoid injury and death, technology has created 'a new computer system that could save thousands of lives and prevent crippling injuries by detecting mines and other military equipment stored underground' (Hadland 1996). It is further stated that the development, pioneered by the US Army Research Laboratory based in New Mexico, consists of a device carried on a mobile crane and uses ground penetrating radar technology to detect hidden munitions. Using Mercury's Race computers, mines can be located in 2 to 4 minutes, where previously it took 2 to 4 hours.

Landmines are now classed as 'dumb' or 'smart'.

A dumb mine remains active until it decays, which could be up to seventy years. A smart mine de-activates itself after a pre-determined period of time, typically 2–5 years.

It is interesting to note that a report (Smithers and Bowcott 1977) concluded that the British government is committed to an eventual world-wide ban on mines, in the short term it is prepared to concede the retention of 'smart mines that self destruct after a time'. The apparent change of heart and forward move in thinking must be considered in relation to the view of Palmer (1996) who said:

in September 1991, Asia Watch and Physicians for Human Rights published a report which described the awesome toll from the saturation of Cambodia with mines, for which all parties of the conflict, and their respective sponsors, bear responsibility. The report also provided evidence that Cambodian guerrilla armies received training 'in the use of mines and explosives against civilian as well as military targets' from at least two foreign nations: China and the UK.

Those without sin cast the first stone.

From a publicity perspective, the work of Diana, Princess of Wales raised the landmine issue internationally. However, there are concerns about the effectiveness of the campaign. Jefferson (1997) who is actively involved in making safe mines and UXOs stated:

I am typical of most mine clearers – as opposed to antimine lobbyists, charity PR spokesmen and journalists – in that I do not believe that a ban on landmines will do anything to help solve the problem of landmine devastation. That may sound paradoxical, but it is true. People do not want to hear this, but the call for a mines ban is unworkable, undesirable and worse, counter productive. The campaign diverts attention and funds from the real issue. It enables governments to claim that they are spending money on dealing with the problem of landmines, whereas in fact they are spending money on discussing the problem, on hosting conferences, on carrying out 'assessment missions', on promoting 'mine awareness' campaigns – on almost everything, in fact, other than the messy business of actually getting the mines out of the ground.

What has this got to do with disability politics? Put simply, disability is primarily caused by accidents, prenatal difficulties or trauma, including surgical techniques. Why deliberately add to the population of disabled people as a means of mass control? People with disabilities experience first hand the problems, discrimination and lack of support service. Why add numbers as a matter of governmental policy?

Binyon (1996) stated that:

all countries meeting in Geneva wanted to toughen the present UN regulations. There is agreement to make all anti-personnel mines detectable; the remaining obstacles, coming mainly from Russia, India and China, centre on the difficulty of monitoring a ban and the timescale needed to phase out mines from military stocks, with China arguing for a period of 20 years.

There may be hope for the future. Is there a wind of change? Capella and Linton (1996) suggested that public opinion now supports a ban. Twenty-one countries now favour a total ban. Support ranges from 92 per cent in Denmark to 58 per cent in Japan. Capella and Linton develop the view that

at least 23 governments have indicated they would support an outright ban. Britain, China, India, some non-aligned countries and America believe that anti-personnel mines still have a military value. Britain has declared a moratorium on exports of 'dumb mines'. Campaigners in Britain, including Sir David Puttnam, will hand a petition to John Major today calling on the government to support a global ban on landmines. The UK Working Group on Landmines has gathered 180,000 signatures.

The struggle goes on.

Over the course of history there have been many battles and victims in the name of religion. The Crusades, the Irish situation and Tibet have all been associated with religion, its doctrines, practices and leaders for example. At one time the Protestant church considered the disabled as the sons and daughters of imps and the result of physical and spiritual diabolical liaisons. However, in more modern, and some may say, enlightened times, various aspects of religion can be seen from a disability perspective.

Religion of course, is not all violent or uncaring. In a study that explores aspects of disability in an Eastern religious context, Miles (1995) considered that a significant percentage (70 per cent) of disabled people live 'in countries and contacts upon which Western ethics and philosophy infringe only peripherally'. People with disabilities are seen in a variety of ways in Eastern Religions, for example:

- considered as holy and having second sight;

- employed by the wealthy (as curiosities);
- excluded from religious ceremonies and legal standing;
- feared and thought to be under retributive punishment;
- regarded as lucky protection from evil.

What must be appreciated is that because many Eastern religions are based on rebirth, Karma and working towards enlightenment, disability is seen as 'retributive consequences' – or as you sow so shall you reap. Miles (1995) uses the example that if in a former life you steal a lamp you may be reborn blind. It is worth noting that in a socio-religious context the poorer East has different priorities – education provision or help for the disabled, care versus independence, health services for the young set against support for the aged.

Miles (1983) carried out a survey with 273 adults and children in the North West Frontier (Pakistan) into the attitudes towards the disabled. The results indicated the following attitudes:

- mockery, trick-playing, fear and rejection;
- pity mixed with fear; pity overcoming fear;
- alms-giving as a religious duty; alms-giving with compassion;
- idea of society's duty: must be a place where they can be cared for;
- ascription of caste status and social needs, i.e. they should be put together with others like themselves;
- should be enabled to live their own lives as far as possible;
- should have access to the rights and resources available to anyone else;
- positive action to make rights and services available;
- should have the right to be different – equality, dignity, opportunity;
- do 'they' perhaps have some views of their own?

The above sounds familiar to Western experiences. World religions have much in common, it may be a question of understanding, appreciation and tolerance. Miles (1995) concludes that as

> global efforts are made to improve the situation of disabled people, against massive inertia and competing claims, and perhaps some backlash, it is unwise to maintain Eurocentric neglect of historical beliefs and attitudes inherited from the world's major non-Christian religions, towards disability. Some of the beliefs and the practices associated

with them may now seem bizarre; yet all have their own socio-cultural logic and can be instructive challenges to western practices. Some might well not be derived or disowned by modern adherents of the eastern religions. Some, alternatively, may be presented with pride as evidence of the originality and universal merit of those religious traditions.

Keep the faith!

Connor (1996) comments on the view that 'society is being threatened by a degenerate underclass which is breeding faster than the most intelligent'. The argument is put forward that the growth in a less intelligent under class is threatening the future of mankind and civilized life. The view is also expressed that improvements in health care, screening, advanced surgical techniques combined with 'an increasingly immoral society are leading to less intelligent people having more children at an earlier age'. Connor quotes various professors and doctors who argue that 'people of weak "moral character" are having more children than those with strong morals, self discipline, and a willingness to work and abide by the law'. Men with criminal records 'have 70 per cent more children than those who have not been involved in crime'.

At a time when countries, races and cultures are seeking or gaining freedoms, potentially restrictive practices are being suggested. What could be next; forced birth control, selective mating, mandatory abortions for the less intelligent?

The disabled are becoming a collective force to be reckoned with. Individuals, groups, organizations, agencies and political parties are now being formed or modified to take on disability issues and concerns. The arts movement has done much to raise awareness concerning disability and political issues. Political change is coming. Governments East and West, North and South now recognize disability issues. Governmental and non-governmental organizations are beginning to examine policies and accepted practices to see if they are the cause or maintainer of disability.

The technological age is enabling worldwide mass communication between disability groups and organizations. The use of electronic systems allow for global information exchange. Knowledge is power. With more countries enacting laws that allow for the common person to access previously considered confidential information, the history of disability issues is being discovered, built on and rewritten.

Times are changing. The disabled are rightly taking more control of their own lives. Parkyn (1997a) in discussing the role of education in changing the lives of the disabled stated that

> as the world approaches the end of the twentieth century and the start of a new millennium there are still powerful debates about the quality and opportunities for adults with learning difficulties and disabilities to access educational provision. Empowerment, choice, equal opportunities, civil rights and the transition into adulthood are areas that readily generate discussion, argument, action and reaction.

It is evident that the disability movement is becoming more powerful, more vocal and taking more direct action. However the disabled are still a minority group therefore access to services, the media, to quality housing, benefits and other accepted activities is limited. Whichever way the coin is tossed at present the disabled all over the world are still losers.

However, Massie (1994), in a publication for the Commission on Social Justice, made a number of pertinent points concerning people with disabilities and their lives in relation to power, politics and control. In summary Massie considered that:

- disabled people normally experience more difficult and more expensive lives than non-disabled people (low incomes, restricted employment choices and opportunities and higher living costs);
- there are various ways of defining disability – the medical model is popular but the social model is more relevant and analytical;
- full participation in society is limited due to

  i   personal discrimination (when applying for jobs or requesting service)
  ii institutional discrimination, also known as structural, caused by the way in which public buildings, transport and housing is designed;

- anti-discrimination legislation is required based on civil rights and not charity;
- employment laws, regulations and directives that are monitored, enforced and supported by political will are required;
- a re-examination of priorities is necessary – 'money spent now in segregating disabled people could be saved in the future by designing an environment where accessibility is the priority for disabled and non-disabled people';

- there is a need for issues concerning autonomy and choice in relation to community care to be addressed in that disabled people may wish to be able to select between services and cash so individuals can design their own care packages;
- a 'no-fault' compensation system would reduce the need for disabled people to seek legal redress concerning the acquisition of their disability;
- a 'comprehensive disability income scheme' would promote equality and opportunity;
- disabled people accept that the world cannot be changed overnight.

> However, political commitment to civil rights for disabled people can immediately begin to improve opportunities and influence the long-term process of changing attitudes to disability. The sooner we choose to make a start, the sooner social justice will be a reality for disabled people.   (Massie op. cit.)

Perhaps, with a new century close at hand the world will change constructively and positively for all, and the disabled are an important part of that all. Woolley (1993) concludes with the view that 'from the celebration of our difference and shared experience, great movements and a better world can evolve'.

Education is a way of affecting change. Unfortunately much 'education' is also a method by which stereotypes are maintained and reinforced or concepts, perceptions and attitudes passed on. Education and the agents for transmitting knowledge, skills and attitudes have a major role to play in the raising of awareness concerning disability issues. The disabled world is a complex one with many interrelated dimensions and aspects.

Progress can illuminate the uniqueness of disability for the individual and at the same time explore the universality of the disabled world. Education can illustrate the multi-faceted nature of disability politics and how it influences and permeates all aspects of the human condition. Perhaps, education can lead the way in helping to create a more positive, constructive and balanced world for the disabled population as a whole.

Evolution for the disabled is a hard path and painfully slow. Perhaps revolution in direct political action is called for. A final point by Massie (1994) sums up many issues of concern:

> Disabled people are no longer content to allow others to rule their lives. Disabled people want, and increasingly demand, to be consulted on their

needs, and to be involved in the planning of provision to meet those needs.

This requires representation in the processes deciding what, as well as how, services are to be delivered.

Such involvement is not only a respectful way of working; it can only result in better services.

It follows, therefore, that disabled people should be co-opted onto all relevant Government committees and advisory bodies, and be actively involved in determining public policy which affects them as disabled people.

They do, of course, also have a role to play in contributing to wider social politics.

References

Barnes, C. (1992) *Disabling Imagery and the Media – An Exploration of the Principles for Media Representations of Disabled People.* Halifax: The British Council of Organisations of Disabled People and Ryburn Publishing.

Barron, B. (1996) The Mine Clearers. BBC Radio 4, 6 November.

Barton, L. (1996) *Disability and Society: Emerging Issues and Insights.* London: Longman.

Batten, D. (1996) Theatre. *Disability Now*, September Edition. London: Scope. 23.

Binyon, M. (1996) Red Cross study questions military value of weapons. *The Times*, 29 March: 15.

Blumer, H. (1995) Social movements. In S. Lyman (ed.) *Social Movements: Critiques, Concepts, Care-Studies.* Basingstoke: Macmillan.

Campbell, J. and Oliver, M. (1996) *Disability Politics, Understanding Our Part, Changing Our Future.* London: Routledge.

Capella, P. and Linton, L. (1996) Total ban ruled out as talks seek tighter rules for landmines. *The Times*, 22 April: 11.

Connor, S. (1996) Professor predicts genetic decline and fall of man. *The Sunday Times*, 22 December: 5.

Curphey, M. and Laurance, J. (1997) Life insurers demand gene test results. *The Times*, 19 February: 5.

Davies, J. (1997) We abhor freak shows, so what are we doing to Samantha? *The Mail on Sunday*, 9 March: 37.

Davis, K. (1996) Disability and legislation. Rights and equality. In G. Hales (ed.) *Beyond Disability, Towards an Enabling Society.* London: Sage.

Davies, C. (1996) Television. *Disability Now.* September Edition. London: Scope. 23.

Disability Discrimination Act (1995) London: HMSO.

Divorkin, R. (1993) *Life's Dominion: An Argument about Abortion and Euthanasia.* London: Harper Collins.

Eugenics Society (1934) Report of the Departmental Committee on Sterilisation. London: HMSO.

Exley, H. (1981) *What's It Like to Be Me.* Watford: Exley.

French, S. (1994) 'The disability movement'. In S. French (ed.) *On Equal Terms, Working with Disabled People.* Oxford: Butterworth Heinemann.

Fullbrook, S. D. and Wilkinson, M. B. (1996a) Animals in human transplants, the ethics of xenotransplantation (1). *British Journal of Theatre Nursing*, 6(2): 29–32.

Fullbrook, S. D. and Wilkinson, M. B. (1996b) Animals in human transplants, the ethics of xenotransplantation (2). *British Journal of Theatre Nursing*, 6(3): 13–18.

Fullbrook, S. D. and Wilkinson, M. B. (1996c) Some dilemmas of living wills. *British Journal of Theatre Nursing*, 6(1): 13–17.

Hadland, G. (1996) Race lifts pace of saving lives. *The Times*, 13 March: SP/13.

Hales, G. (ed.) (1996) *Beyond Disability, Towards an Enabling Society.* London: Sage.

HALO Trust (1996) The HALO TRUST, Pamphlet c/o The Halo Trust, PO Box 7712, London, SWlV 3ZA.

Hevey, D. (1992) *The Creatures Time Forgot: Photography and Disability Imagery.* London: Routledge.

Jefferson, P. (1997) In the *Sunday Telegraph*, 2 February.

Laurance, J. and Hornsby, W. (1997) Warning on human clones – fears follow production of sheep from single cell. *The Times*, 24 February: 1.

Leach, B. (1996) Disabled people and the equal opportunities movement. In G. Hales (ed.) *Beyond Disability, Towards an Enabling Society.* London: Sage.

Lynch, J. (1994) *Provision for Children with Special Educational Needs in the Asia Region.* Washington: The World Bank.

Malone, A. (1996) Cambodia in grip of killer with no soul. *The Sunday Times*, 24 March: 1/21.

Massie, B. (1994) *Disabled People and Social Justice* (The Commission on Social Justice). London: Emphasis.

Miles, M. (1983) *Attitudes Towards Persons with Disabilities Following IYDP (1981).* Peshawar: Mental Health Centre.

Miles, M. (1995) Disability in an Eastern religious context: historical perspective *Disability and Society*, 10(1): 49–69.

Mittler, P. (1992) International Visions of Excellence for Children with Disabilities. Speech presented at the International Convention of the Council for Exceptional Children, Baltimore, M.D., USA. In J. Lynch (1994) *Provision for Children with Special Educational Needs in the Asia Region.* Washington: The World Bank.

Morris, J. (1991) *Pride Against Prejudice: A Personal Politics of Disability.* London: The Women's Press.

Nuffield Report (1966) *Animal to Human Transplants: The Ethics of Xenotransplantation.* Leeds: Nuffield Council for Bioethics.

Oliver, M. (1993) Disability, Citizenship and Empowerment. Workbook 2 of the course *The Disabling Society.* Milton Keynes: The Open University.

Oliver, M. (1995) *Insider Perspectives: The Voice of Disabled*

People – Politics and Language: Understanding the Disability Discourse. Sheffield University M.Ed. Course material.

Palmer, A. (1996) Landmines. *The Sunday Times*, 14 April: 3/9.

Parkyn, L. (1997a) How much is that doggie in the window – a critical overview of adult education for those with learning difficulties and/or disabilities – is the tail wagging the dog? In K. Watson, C. Modgil and S. Modgil (eds) *Quality in Education, Educational Dilemmas: Debate and Diversity, Vol. 4.* Cassell: London.

Parkyn, L. A. (1997b) Landmine interview. BBC Southern Counties Radio, 8 February.

Pope, N. (1997) Surgeons give hope to baby without bones. *The Sunday Times*, 2 March: 11.

Rogers, L. (1997) Revealed: doctors accidentally clone twins. *The Sunday Times*, 9 March.

Sandow, S. (1994) *Whose Special Need? Some Perception of Special Educational Needs.* London: Paul Chapman.

Shakespeare, T. (1993) Disabled people's self-organisation: a new social movement? *Disability, Handicap and Society*, **8**(3): 249–64.

Smithers, R. and Bowcott, O. (1997) Diana in political minefield. *The Guardian*, 15 January.

Turner, M. (1996) Film. *Disability Now.* September Edition. London: Scope. 23.

United Nations Children's Fund (1991) *State of the World's Children, 1991.* New York: Oxford University Press.

Valley, P. (1997) 'Queen of hearts meets the heart of darkness'. *The Independent*, 15 January: 8.

Wilkinson, M. B. (1996) At the edge of knowledge. *Nursing Times*, **92**(43): 26–8.

Wilson, Sir John (1983) *Disability Prevention: The Global Challenge.* Oxford: Oxford University Press.

Wolfensberger, W. (1994) The growing threat to the lives of handicapped people in the context of modernistic values. *Disability and Society*, **9**(3): 395–413.

Woolley, M. (1993) Acquired hearing loss: acquired oppression. In J. Swain, V. Finkelstein, S. French and M. Oliver (eds) *Disabling Barriers – Enabling Environments.* London: Sage.

World Health Organisation (1978) *Classification of Disability.* Geneva: WHO.

Part Two

Education for Citizenship

9 Citizenship Education and Cultural Diversity[1]

JANET EDWARDS AND KEN FOGELMAN

What does citizenship mean to teachers?

Not uncommonly we begin a session with trainee, or practising, teachers by asking them to brainstorm in answer to the questions, 'What is citizenship?', 'What words come immediately to mind when you begin to think about the meaning of citizenship?' Among the first words offered are usually some of the following: belonging, community, nationality, rights and responsibilities, attitudes and values, democracy, participation. If we then take these in turn, and perhaps attempt some categorization, the discussion may produce groups of words such as: **belonging** to a place, city, nation, group; contributing to a **community**, shared values, mutuality, culture; **nationality**, immigration control, residence rights, passport; **rights**, legal rights, human rights, equality; **responsibilities**, obligations, duties; **attitudes and values**, beliefs, morality, common good, tolerance; **democracy**, having the vote, subject or citizen; **participation**, taking part, contributing to society, volunteering, community service, active citizenship.

What has education to do with citizenship?

Citizenship has for long been a contested concept. Educating young people in citizenship is not a new phenomenon in English schools. Batho (1990) has identified activity since the last decades of the nineteenth century, and much was written on the subject between the wars, in response to the rise of totalitarianism in Europe (e.g. Association for Education in Citizenship 1935). However, in most schools it was not part of the established curriculum, and approaches were varied and individualistic. In the 1970s and 1980s the term was scarcely heard in curriculum discussions, although a number of organizations, such as the Council for Education in World Citizenship, and individuals were promoting what might now be seen as particular elements of citizenship education, such as community service (e.g. Precey and Marsh 1989), political awareness (e.g. Stradling 1975) and human rights education (e.g. Starkey 1991). Also, during these decades the growth in social studies, environmental studies, law, sociology, psychology, personal and social education, health education and careers education and other subjects beyond the traditional academic school subjects was marked.

In 1985 The Swann Report was published under the title of *Education for All* (DES 1985). The Committee of Enquiry was asked to look into the educational needs of children from all ethnic groups (with particular attention to children of West Indian origin). The Report makes it clear that the ideal society is a pluralist one where diversity is acknowledged and respected within a 'commonly accepted framework of values, practices and procedures'. There were challenges for education posed by the Report, and strategies for change became high on the agenda. The task was to move towards cultural pluralism and policies for multicultural and anti-racist education were given a high profile.

Attainment of cultural pluralism is lodged squarely in the policy, structures, practices and beliefs not only in the educational system but in society at large. It is not an individual problem; it requires both a political commitment and institutional efforts. The school cannot and should not remain neutral in these matters. It should not passively reflect society, it must actively seek to change the attitudes and behaviour of its future citizens.

Cultural pluralism challenges schools' traditional role as the transmitters of the dominant culture. In this process it should engage both those who experience injustice and discrimination and those who are members of the dominant culture in the challenge to racism.   (Verma 1989: 239)

This aspect of education for citizenship became a focus in schools, but mainly in areas of mixed ethnic representation. In all-white schools there was less emphasis and the topics focused on tended to be aspects of personal, health and social development. Gender issues were raised as were aspects of the law, environment and human rights. Political education tended to be neglected and there was little attempt to educate for citizenship but rather for personal autonomy and independent living. Where there was attention to community education it tended to be with a local focus rather than a national or international one. Religious Education almost everywhere became truly comparative in its inclusion of a study of the major religions of the world but little philosophy or moral education was taught.

Citizenship education is an aspect of the curriculum that has been more prominent in England in the 1990s. Two main publications marked this change. The National Curriculum Council (NCC), in 1990, named Citizenship as one of five cross-curricular themes (the others being Health Education, Environmental Education, Economic and Industrial Understanding and Careers Education and Guidance).

> The aims of education for Citizenship are to: establish the importance of positive, participative citizenship and provide the motivation to join in; help pupils to acquire and understand essential information on which to base the development of their skills, values and attitudes towards citizenship. (NCC 1990a: 5)

and 'Education for Citizenship develops the knowledge, skills and attitudes necessary for exploring, making informed decisions about and exercising responsibilities and rights in a democratic society' (NCC 1990b: 2).

Objectives for education for citizenship were categorized as knowledge, cross-curricular skills, attitudes, moral codes and values. Although none of the cross-curricular themes had the statutory status of the national curriculum, eight components of citizenship education were described by the NCC as 'essential':

- Community
- Pluralist Society
- Being a Citizen
- Family
- Democracy
- Citizen and Law
- Work, Employment and Leisure
- Public Services. (NCC 1990b: 5)

The second important document was *Encouraging Citizenship*, the report of the Speaker's Commission on Citizenship (1990). This identified the study of citizenship as involving:

- understanding the rules
- the acquisition of knowledge
- the development and exercise of skills
- learning democratic behaviour through the experience of the school as a community, and from the experience of the school as an institution playing a role in the wider community.

The Commission stressed that the opportunity for learning provided by community experiences would provide an indispensable springboard to encourage students to make a voluntary contribution in later life. The Report identified skills, both intellectual and social, that are necessary to understand and address issues of rights and responsibilities.

Thus, the documentation that could give justification for education for citizenship exists, but the non-statutory status of citizenship education in the UK and the perceived overload of the curriculum since the introduction of the national curriculum have combined with a general lack of teacher confidence and expertise in these areas to result in relatively little development in practice in many schools. Many schools aim to prepare their pupils for citizenship, and when pressed teachers will name a wide range of activities that they see as relevant to achieving this aim. Several recent surveys (Fogelman 1991, Saunders et al. 1995, Kerr 1996) indicate that there is rarely coherence, consistency, institutionalization and progression in these activities. 'Most schools include the intention to teach citizenship in their mission statements but there is no evidence that it is taught systematically' (SCAA 1996). Furthermore, accreditation of citizenship activities is not easy as the appropriate systems are not in place. What is not assessed and accredited may not be valued highly.

McLaughlin (1992: 236) draws a distinction

between minimal and maximal concepts of citizenship in terms of

> the identity that it is seen as conferring upon an individual, the virtues of the citizen that are required, the extent of the political involvement on the part of the individual that is thought to follow, and the social prerequisites seen as necessary for effective citizenship.

His critique of the National Curriculum guidance on citizenship leads him to the conclusion that it is impossible to read the document in an unambiguously maximalist way but suggests it does not offer a clearly worked out concept of citizenship. He agrees with other writers (see Carr 1991) in concluding that 'the guidance will need to be interpreted by individual schools, where fundamental disputes are likely to take place'. He concludes that

> the problems encountered by any attempt to engage in education for citizenship in any maximalist sense in the context of a pluralist democratic society are often underestimated . . . Leaving the controversial matters involved to surface in a rather random way at school level is a recipe either for continuing conflict or for failure to educate for citizenship in a significant sense. (p. 244)

The broader concept of citizenship education is closely related to moral education and values education – indeed, in some contexts these terms appear to be used interchangeably. The Office for Standards in Education (Ofsted) inspection of schools requires reports to be written on Spiritual, Moral, Social and Cultural Education (SMSC). It may be that this requirement is significant in encouraging schools to pay more attention to citizenship (or moral or values) education. The inspection schedule requires inspectors to:

> evaluate and report on the strengths and weaknesses of the school's provision for the spiritual, moral, social and cultural development of all pupils, through the curriculum and life of the school, the example set for pupils by the adults in school; . . . judgements should be based on the extent to which the school . . . encourages pupils to relate positively to others, take responsibility, participate fully in the community, and develop understanding of citizenship. (Ofsted 1995)

This is quoted from the Nursery and Primary Guidance, but similar wording appears in the Guidance for Secondary School Inspection. At the time of writing, a thorough and wide-ranging consultation is taking place, initiated by SCAA, on spiritual and

moral development. There is a general acceptance that there needs to be more coherence in the approach to SMSC development and that research and development work needs to be done on such aspects as: ways of tracking SMSC through the subjects of the curriculum; international comparisons in provision; and the possibility of pupil assessment in these areas of the curriculum. Similarly, there is some indication that attention is being paid to the way Initial Teacher Training might better prepare teachers for their role in school-based activity relevant to the inspection of SMSC.

These developments have taken place in the context of some public debate, fostered by politicians and the media. The issues of value complexity which underlie such a debate should not be underestimated. The contrasting perspectives which have emerged confirm McLaughlin's (op. cit.) assertion that, 'such a debate is likely to reveal deep differences of opinion on a number of issues. It also runs the risk of being conducted at a level of fruitless abstraction'. But, he goes on to argue,

> an effort must be made to achieve general agreement on both: i) the public values which should articulate the practice of a substantial form of 'education for citizenship' and ii) the broad character of defensible practical policies and strategies required for this educative task, including those relating to the handling of controversial issues with pupils. A failure of such an effort in a pluralistic liberal democracy bodes ill for citizenship itself in that context. (p. 245)

While the Dearing Review of the curriculum (Dearing 1993) made no specific reference to a body of knowledge relevant to education for citizenship, there was a clear acknowledgement that the educational challenge has relevance to a very broad range of aspects of life including citizenship.

> Education is not concerned only with equipping students with the knowledge and skills they need to earn a living. It must help our young people to: use leisure time creatively; have respect for other people, other cultures and other beliefs; become good citizens; think things out for themselves; pursue a healthy life-style; and, not least, value themselves and their achievements. It should develop an appreciation of the richness of our cultural heritage and of the spiritual and moral dimensions to life. It must, moreover, be concerned to serve all our children well, whatever their background, sex, creed, ethnicity or talent. (p. 18)

Education for citizenship is not a new concern. It has had a place in the curriculum of some schools in some European countries since the last century. However, it is a matter of particular debate in recent years for a number of reasons. There is widespread concern about a perceived loss of morality and declining respect for national leaders and other authority figures; drug abuse, crime and violence are much reported in the media; materialism and selfishness appear to be on the increase; a rise is perceived in intolerance, racism and ethnic conflict and cities are in crisis; the breakdown of traditional family patterns and the changing technologies and employment patterns may lead to less stable lifestyles; child abuse appears to be on the increase; often low pupil motivation, poor attendance at school and little effort applied to school work are taken to reflect a low value placed by them and their families on education; the decline, particularly among young people, in proportions of the population committed to religious groups or political parties appears to indicate rising levels of disaffection, social exclusion and apathy; there is concern about low levels of participation in local, national and European elections; our pluralist society contains a wide range of cultural backgrounds, family patterns and religious beliefs which may make community understanding hard to achieve. Many such concerns have been summarized by the Hansard Society in its proposals for a commission into Education for Democratic Citizenship: A Commission of Enquiry into the Causes, Consequences and Solutions to Political Disaffection Amongst Young People in the UK Today (Hansard Society 1996). The Society expresses its belief that, while attention is rightly being paid to citizenship in the context of caring for others and knowing one's legal rights, the same level of attention has not been paid to preparing and encouraging people to understand and use their political rights. The Society sees the growing disaffection with traditional political structures amongst young people, their reluctance to register to vote, the rise in extremist and racist organizations' popularity, and the general growth in anti-political activity as real threats to the survival of the state in its present form.

It is easy to agree that schools do have a role in making at least some contribution to addressing such issues. Equally easy is to generate a substantial set of questions which this raises. For example, is it realistic to aspire to a shared set of common values in our culturally diverse society? Should priority be given to local and national issues as against perspectives of European or global citizenship? Where should citizenship education be placed in the curriculum – is a discrete subject preferable to a permeation model? What models do our schools provide in promoting such values as tolerance and understanding? Are systems of discipline and rules based on rights and responsibilities, or can they sometimes appear arbitrary and irrational? What opportunities do schools provide for young people to develop and practise the skills of participative citizenship? Do schools foster links with and understanding of the local community and provide opportunities for students to engage in community service? Is this service built into the learning process with adequate preparation and follow-up?

Schools do have a part to play in influencing young people's attitudes, values and social skills. Clearly other influences are at work – family, friends, peer group, media, politics, religion. Partnerships between school and community can assist collaborative working towards positive participative citizenship. These require teachers to have the confidence and skill to handle controversial issues even-handedly and sensitively and this in turn requires the support and confidence of politicians, parents and community leaders. Many teachers feel that they are not helped by their low status in society and that they are blamed for ills that may have their roots beyond the school and outside the remit of educationalists.

Some views on ways forward

Lynch (1992) argues convincingly that what is required is a vision of responsible global citizenship.

> The imperative of the 1990s is to share internationally the values of democratic pluralism in a process which will reinforce global interdependence and active membership of a world society. For educators the challenge of the 1990s is to deliver not just education for citizenship of a pluralist democracy but education for active global democracy, founded on universal values about the nature of human beings and their social behaviour.   (p. 2)

This approach recognizes local, national and international levels, and social, cultural, environmental and economic domains.

Schooling for citizenship must take account of

every level and domain within a global context of human rights and social responsibilities contributing to the achievement of democratic values and behaviour in pluralist societies and in a culturally diverse world. (p. 3)

Development of the concept of citizenship from the narrower bounds of familial group or tribe, through the age of city-state and single-state nationalism to the age of global rights and responsibilities and the internationalisation of the lives of all inhabitants of this planet . . . we do not have to choose between local and ethnic loyalties, national citizenship and global community . . . Education for global citizenship . . . has to generate the knowledge, skills and insights necessary for creative and active participation, as well as for positive and creative dissent. It has to empower students intellectually and socially, to make conflict creative and seminal of progress. (pp. 16–17)

Lynch believes in the crucial role of primary education in political socialization and potential for democratic citizenship. He lists basic values that should be transmitted for creative citizenship as including: freedom of conscience and religion; freedom of association, peaceful assembly and protest; respect for the freedom of others (p. 30). He suggests (pp. 22–3) that, if schools are to be effective as educators for global citizenship, their activities might include:

- a democratic classroom ethos;
- collaborative and cooperative approaches;
- active participation, including simulation, role-playing;
- emphasis on character, which will include conflict resolution;
- rational, holistic approaches to knowledge and learning;
- help for pupils in evolving and clarifying their own value systems, using situations involving value dilemmas;
- emphasis on open rather than closed tasks and questions;
- multiple approaches, including different media, strategies and locations;
- inclusion of pedagogies involving social responsibility and actioning;
- high intellectual expectations in both cognitive and affective domains;
- explicit commitment to global human rights as the basis for all interaction in the classroom;
- linked, supportive assessment methods, orientated to student success.

Education, he argues

must address social, environmental and economic outcomes and must prepare children for future roles of citizen and neighbour, as much as producer and consumer. Moreover, if there is to be greater peace and harmony for the children of the world, education has a crucial role in educating for tolerance and mutuality and away from ethnic and religious hatred. (p. 24)

Lynch's starting point is clearly global and internationalist. However, similar conclusions are to be found in a recent report written from a UK perspective (Ali Khan 1996). Its first key recommendation is that,

Responsible global citizenship should be recognised as a desired core learning outcome. Enabling responsible citizenship should be recognised as a core business of learning institutions and a legitimate purpose of lifetime learning. This recommendation is of fundamental importance and may be regarded as a prerequisite for whole-hearted Further and Higher Education sector engagement with the challenge posed by sustainable development. (p. 3)

The report provides an appraisal of the progress made in the development of environmental education, against the background of the 1993 report *Environmental Responsibility* and reveals considerable indifference to the report's recommendations on the part of the institutions concerned and recommends required further action.

In the introduction to *Teaching for Citizenship in Europe*, a report based on a project sponsored by the European Commission through the ERASMUS scheme and by bursaries from the Council of Europe, Osler (1995) writes,

The challenge remains of developing approaches to citizenship education which meet the needs of a multi-cultural Europe, in which members of minority communities are often struggling to claim their rights. An appropriate education for the twenty-first century is one which: [quoting from Osler 1994] encourages the development of an inclusive rather than exclusive understanding of national identity and citizenship. This revitalised view of education would promote an understanding of the rights and responsibilities of democratic citizenship not dependent on ethnic affiliation or identification but recognising and supporting diversity both within and between societies. This view of education for active, participative citizenship might therefore acknowledge diversity, interdependence and differences in perception, and might approach areas of study from a variety of cultural perspectives, encouraging students to recognise shared values.   (p. 4)

This report explores inclusive and exclusive understandings of citizenship using examples from countries that have undergone recent political change, as well as issues in the older democracies, to discuss ways forward to meet the challenge posed by the Council of Europe (1983):

> Our education programmes should encourage all young Europeans to see themselves not only as citizens of their own regions and countries, but also as citizens of Europe and the wider world. All young Europeans should be helped to acquire a willingness and ability to preserve and promote democracy, human rights and fundamental freedoms.

Lorentzen (1992: 99), a Norwegian, describes his vision of the future of education for citizenship in his country:

> this development must first and foremost be related to a larger process of change that will characterise the Norwegian Society in the next decennium. We will have to face the rapid growth of pluralism in culture, politics and religion. Our society will to a much larger extent become a multi-cultural society, with its conflicts and challenges. This calls for a much more professional attitude to citizenship education, within research, teacher education, textbook production and methodological support to teachers.

He goes on to describe the advantages and disadvantages of either creating citizenship as a discrete subject or as an integrated part of all school activities and concludes his chapter by emphasizing the importance of pupils' participating in community activities. 'Through their participation and experience we hope to help the pupils to reach the level of knowledge, skills and attitudes that will be necessary to function as reflective and critical members of a democratic, multi-cultural, Norwegian society' (p. 100).

A German contribution from the same volume as Lorentzen (Fritzsche and Knepper 1992) stresses the importance of prevention rather than correction, and multi-perspective education.

> Thus what is called for is an education designed to impart an ability to empathise and to cope with conflict as well as to tolerate stress; an education which will erect barriers in good time against the susceptibility to authoritarianism. This demands a

pluralist education programme giving access to a multitude of viewpoints.   (p. 114)

From a more local perspective, Brighouse (Foreword to Steiner, 1996) writes:

> The urgency of the issue of global education is obvious if you work and live as I do in Birmingham, a city of a thousand trades and a hundred ethnic communities where the diversity of the many strongly held faiths, on the one hand, and faithlessness on the other, add to the potential wealth and the present challenge of those who would educate tomorrow's citizens. We struggle to see bilingualism not as a problem but as a rich opportunity to create a city in the United Kingdom that is truly multilingual. Whether one lives in Birmingham or not, the reality for those who teach in Britain today is that they must think globally while teaching locally.

He then offers five principles that he suggests should govern such an approach.

Schooling and education should be based on:

- the goal of everyone achieving success rather than allowing for success for some and failure for others;
- the assumption that intelligence is multi-faceted not general, environmentally affected as well as inherited, and limitless not fixed;
- the assumption that learning is a lifelong not a 'once and for all' activity;
- the assumption that competition is best when ipsatively rather than normatively based (by 'ipsative' I mean based on competition against 'oneself' rather than others);
- the assumption of inclusive not exclusive packages.

We might console ourselves that if progress is possible locally in matters within our grasp, then the next generation will find some of the solutions.

We have quoted at some length, but in order to demonstrate that there is an impressive consensus to be found in a variety of sources, writing from a range of perspectives – global, European, national and local. Each of these authors expresses clearly a vision of education for responsible global citizenship, democratic participation and human rights.

The above examples are all from relatively recent publications. Other, less recent formulations of similar visions could have been used. If there is such a consensus, and it has existed for some time, then we have to ask why such approaches are not routinely represented in the curriculum and why related activities are not commonplace in our schools? How can it be that there is still difficulty in achieving such aims?

Problems and constraints

Undoubtedly the first problem area is in achieving shared value agreements across cultural, social, religious and ethnic groups. Vine (1992) argues that the central objectives of education, to enable young people to function effectively in their social worlds and to develop their potential to achieve a fulfilled life, require a contribution from moral education. But to agree on what is to be taught and how to teach it is not easy. Western liberal democracies are internally fragmented into subcultures that make it extremely difficult to reach unanimity of values or pluralist ideals of equitable and harmonious relations between their major subcultural groupings of citizens. This gives rise to educational dilemmas that result in disputes about the goals and strategies of moral education.

> If we are unable to reach agreement about just what moral pedagogy is meant to do for a society's future citizens, then our education systems will be obliged to cope with profoundly uncomfortable challenges. Countries like Britain are already facing distressing moral dilemmas about values education itself . . . Should we respect the sincere beliefs and earnest desires of an increasingly 'fundamentalist' Islamic subculture, mostly representing one politically disadvantaged ethnic minority? Or should we insist upon pedagogic approaches which appear to have the best long-term potential for minimising the 'racial' element in unavoidable conflicts between dominant and minority groups? (Vine op. cit.: 170)

While he concludes that providing all children with the same basic moral and social preparation will not necessarily ensure that present and future sources of conflict will be overcome, he believes in the need to continue to debate, refine and put into practice the multi-cultural moral curriculum. Leicester (1992: 37) argues for education providing

> a forum for debate about resolving conflicts of value – both general debate (can we construct an agreed procedure?) and debate about particular disputes . . . Specifically moral education in pluralistic societies could be based on developing those qualities and values in pupils which will contribute

to a just and harmonious pluralism. Thus an essential requirement is for an anti-racist dimension to moral education. The pupils, as developing moral agents, should develop a commitment to eliminate racism and to acquire knowledge and skills relevant to this . . . Moreover, if the pluralist society must, paradoxically, also impose liberal values, let its education at least seek to ensure that pupils do learn to respect the various cultural traditions and the equal rights of all citizens. It is my belief that a multicultural education for all children in common schools will encourage further convergence of values. Those values required for the effective functioning of a just and harmonious pluralist society should be exhibited in the micro society of the school itself. This 'should' is both a moral ought, deriving from liberal values, and a pragmatic must for effective moral education. Thus my final picture is of a just community school, serving the whole community and teaching antiracist pluralist values through its very functioning. Such an institution would recognise the right of all cultural groups to have a voice in negotiating what, in practice, just and pluralist provision will be like.

Approaches such as Leicester's do offer a route through the dilemma of what values, decided by whom. However, there is still the question of what kind of society we believe education should promote, particularly, though not exclusively, in the multi-cultural context. There is evidence all around us that there is not a unanimous view on this within our own society.

Therefore, how does this influence the commitment and responsibility of the teaching profession in attempting to educate the citizens of tomorrow?

Societies have to choose between social assimilation where one predominant culture is advocated (minority cultures are absorbed into the culture of the majority or a more balanced blending of two or more interacting cultures takes place) or cultural mosaic where the distinctiveness of cultural subgroups is encouraged (Amir 1992). Is it a stark choice made consciously or is a compromise possible? And, of course, there is unlikely to be a single, stable answer.

> As the ethnic texture of nations such as USA, Canada and UK continues to deepen, educational programmes related to ethnic and cultural diversity will continue to emerge and take various shapes and forms. New challenges will continue to evolve in pluralist democratic societies. The extent to which these challenges will be transformed into opportunities will be largely

dependent on a nation's vision, knowledge and commitment.   (Banks 1992: 93)

This suggests that a nationally expressed vision is a requirement for educational opportunities to answer challenges posed by cultural diversity, and current debates in the UK can be interpreted as an attempt to clarify such a vision. This may lead to teachers being instructed to create appropriate opportunities to answer the challenges, but there is a danger of this being based on an over simple assumption of a values consensus.

Gutmann (1996) attempts an answer to the question – how can a multi-cultural society educate its members for democracy? She puts forward a pragmatic compromise between the apparently competing aims of securing common values and respecting cultural differences. Schools

> can teach students how to engage together in respectful discussions in which they strive to understand, appreciate, and, if possible, resolve political disagreements that are partly rooted in cultural differences. Mutual respect that rests only on recognition of cultural diversity is an incomplete democratic virtue. Recognition needs to be accompanied by a willingness and ability to deliberate about politically relevant disagreements. A culturally diverse citizenry dedicated to deliberation strives for reciprocity in political relationships. It seeks agreement on public policies that are justifiable (as far as possible) to all citizens who are bound by them. Reciprocity is not a goal likely to be fully realised. Rather, it is an on-going aspiration, constitutive of democracy understood as a political ideal. By teaching skills and virtues of deliberation, schools can contribute to bringing a democracy closer to its own ideal.   (pp. 160–1)

This seems to suggest that teachers need to be trusted to engage their students in an ongoing process of debating controversial issues, and that the processes of negotiation, empathy, putting oneself in the shoes of another, and of compromise are at the heart of good education for citizenship. How can these processes be developed and invested with importance and status in competition with more traditional knowledge-based subject disciplines? On the other hand are they really in competition? The processes described may have validity as ways of studying academic subjects. Styles of learning that promote democracy and reciprocity could have a wider application across the curriculum.

However, such ideas can imply asking teachers to adopt methods and organize classrooms in ways with which they are not familiar or comfortable. For example, Fullinwider (1996: 16) concludes that the operations of democratic institutions 'require a citizenry with particular habits of mind and particular commitments. These habits of mind and commitments constitute the political culture that students must be educated to value and sustain'. Such habits of mind may not be immediately compatible with the patterns of power and control in the traditional classroom.

The relevance of the 'commitment' element in Fullinwider's statement is illustrated by Bell's (1995) report on a nine-country study on teaching about Europe in primary schools, which took place in the 1980s. He describes the rationale for the project as deriving from the view that developing a European dimension was not simply about the content of teaching about Europe but also about the process of becoming a European citizen. The conceptual model that derived from this project offers a provisional theory of the linkage between a European dimension of the curriculum and the practice of teaching and training for European citizenship. Education for international understanding is seen as occupying a central place in the model while related fields, which interlock with this central one, are education for intercultural understanding, education for the global environment, education for European citizenship, education for economic and industrial understanding, education for national identity, education for personal identity. In describing the development of educational attempts to respond to cultural diversity, Lynch (1989 – quoted in Bell 1995) provides a rationale for a European education programme which would focus both on tolerance, as a necessary condition in order to safeguard ethnic concerns for autonomy, identity and unity, and on human rights. Lynch concludes that:

> the first principle of the curriculum must be to strike a judicious balance between celebrating legitimate difference . . . and insights about the things that all human societies should hold common; active, skills based learning experiences based on well formed knowledge components should develop a capacity for reflective decision making; implementation strategies must be rigorously audited through continual assessment and evaluation.   (from Bell 1995: 16)

In the context of cultural diversity, much of the debate leads to questions of equality and society's interpretation of it. Malik (1996) argues that under the guise of promoting 'multi-culturalism', 'pluralism' and 'diversity', anti-racists have become equivocal about the ideal of equality. 'Far from objecting to the pigeon-holing of people according to their race, many anti-racists now prefer to celebrate the differences between peoples.' Malik believes that this abandoning of the quest for equality in favour of the claim to a diverse society is no solution. In an article in the *Independent on Sunday* on 23 June 1996, Malik writes,

> The world is already a diverse place, not because we have consciously made it that way, but because we have failed to overcome the inequalities that currently exist. Like racists, the anti-racists have come to believe inequality is in the nature of things and cannot be changed. Like racists, anti-racists too have come to view the world through racial eyes. The only consequence can be the continued marginalisation, even ghettoisation, of black communities, but this time in the name not of discrimination but of diversity. Anti-racists' stress on pluralism and diversity is disastrous. We cannot fight racism so long as we continue to view the world through racial eyes. The challenge facing us today is not to embrace 'difference' but to transcend the whole language of race and to put the case clearly for equality.

Responding to such ideas, clarifying their own views, and translating them into classroom practice is a daunting challenge for the teacher.

The earlier quote from Lynch and reference to the Ofsted framework emphasized the importance of audit, assessment and evaluation. Teachers in this country are increasingly familiar with such processes, and they are important if we are to know what is happening in our schools and identify and develop what is most effective. However, if, as we and others have argued, citizenship education should entail new, sometimes riskier, approaches and more readiness to tackle controversial issues, then this may not be helped by the increasing emphasis on accountability. There is clearly a danger that, faced with more rigorous inspection, teachers may play safe and be reluctant to take such risks with unfamiliar methodologies. Classroom control and examination success are challenges enough without choosing the added challenge of more informal, potentially difficult (although potentially more effective) strategies.

Even if we are able to agree that citizenship education is important, that it should have a place

within and beyond the formal school curriculum, that we can reach consensus on at least some fundamental values and develop effective strategies for exploring others, then we must also recognize the constraint that will be at the forefront for most practising teachers – where does it fit in, when can I do it? Many other countries have the tradition of a protected slot for some version of citizenship education, but this is not the case in Britain. Most teachers are still struggling with coverage of the statutory requirements of the national curriculum and will hardly welcome suggestions for additional areas to be covered. Although the Dearing Review (op. cit.) aimed to free 20 per cent of the curriculum for use at schools' discretion, most teachers view this with some cynicism. In the present climate there is nothing to be gained by arguing for a new statutory subject.

It has already been argued that there are links with the other subjects of the curriculum. Following the cross-curricular approach advocated by the NCC (1990a and b), several publications have explored these links in more detail and suggested methods of cross-curricular planning (e.g. Edwards and Fogelman 1993, Morrison 1994). However, this can only be the beginning. If there are to be significant developments in citizenship education then this will have to be in the context of overall school policies which give it priority and establish structures for coordination, development and support.

Conclusions

While the above arguments have largely been developed from considerations of what is problematic, they do point to some constructive ways ahead, in terms of issues that need to be resolved both at a national level and within the classroom. They are also the basis for beginning to suggest classroom strategies that are likely to prove effective for citizenship education. These will entail what are generally characterized as more active methodologies such as role play, simulations and service-learning (see CSV 1997), as well as calling upon resources from beyond the classroom and the teacher, such as the media and input from relevant members of the community. Such approaches can underpin McLaughlin's 'maximalist' conception of 'education for citizenship' which requires a full educational programme 'in which the development of a broad critical understanding and a much more extensive range of dispositions and virtues in the light of a general liberal and political education are seen as crucial'.

Those who have been campaigning on behalf of citizenship education for the last decade or more may well be justified in believing that the door against which they have been pushing is at last beginning to open. The attention it is currently receiving from bodies such as SCAA and Ofsted support such optimism. In the next few months further developments can be expected in the form of published guidance from SCAA. The surveys already cited demonstrate that teachers are positive about such developments and in agreement about their importance. Equally though, they are uncertain and unconfident, not only about content and about curriculum time, but also about what resources are available and what will be recognized as good practice. Thus, even clarity of purpose, guidance and information will not be enough. If citizenship and values education are to be an established and effective part of the school curriculum in the future, there will also need to be substantial investment in in-service education and ongoing support for development.

Note

1 This chapter was written in 1996. Since then there have been significant developments in Education for Citizenship.

In 1998 Professor Bernard Crick chaired the *Advisory Group on Education of Citizenship and the Teaching of Democracy in Schools*. The final report of the group was published in September 1998. The report states the Advisory Group's view that Education for Citizenship should be a statutory entitlement for all pupils (in Key Stages 1 to 4) and suggests learning outcomes for all key stages.

The Qualifications and Curriculum Authority (QCA, successor to SCAA since the time of writing the chapter) has proposals currently (July 1999) out for consultation (*The Review of the National Curriculum in England – The Secretary of State's Proposals*). These suggest a statutory status for Citizenship in Key Stages 3 and 4 (to become statutory after 2001). In Key Stages 1 and 2 an advisory framework for PSHE includes Citizenship as an identifiable strand. In the Autumn 1999 definite arrangements for the year 2000 and beyond should be available.

The *Report of the Advisory Group on Education for Citizenship and Democracy in Schools* (ref. QCA/98/245) and the consultation papers *The Review of the National Curriculum in England – The Secretary of State's Proposals* (refs QCA/99/405, 406 and 407) are available free from QCA Publications (tel: 01787 884444 fax: 01787 312950). The web site address is: http://www.qca.org.uk/news/index.htm

References

Ali Khan, S. (1996) *Environmental Responsibility: A Review of the 1993 Toyne Report*. HMSO for the Welsh Office, Department of the Environment and Department for Education and Employment.

Amir, Y. (1992) Social assimilation or cultural mosaic. In J. Lynch, C. Modgil and S. Modgil (eds) *Cultural Diversity and the Schools: Volume One – Education for Cultural Diversity: Convergence and Divergence*. Brighton: Falmer Press.

Association for Education in Citizenship (1935) *Education for Citizenship in Secondary Schools*. Oxford: Oxford University Press.

Banks, J. (1992) Multicultural education: approaches, developments and dimensions. In J. Lynch, C. Modgil and S. Modgil (eds) *Cultural Diversity and the Schools: Volume One – Education for Cultural Diversity: Convergence and Divergence*. Brighton: Falmer Press.

Batho, G. (1990) The history of the teaching of civics and citizenship in English schools. *The Curriculum Journal*, **1**(1): 91–107.

Bell, G. (1995) *Educating European Citizens: Citizenship Values and the European Dimension*. London: David Fulton Publishers.

Carr, W. (1991) Education for citizenship. *British Journal of Educational Studies*, **XXXIX** (4).

Council of Europe (1983) *Recommendation No. (83) 4 of the Committee of Ministers to Member States Concerning the Promotion of Awareness of Europe in Secondary Schools*. Strasbourg: Council of Europe.

CSV (1997) *A Guide to Community Service Learning*. London: Community Service Volunteers.

Dearing, R. (1993) *The National Curriculum and its Assessment: Final Report*. London: SCAA.

DES (1985) *The Swann Report: Education for All*. London: Department of Education and Science.

Edwards, J. and Fogelman, K. (1993) *Developing Citizenship in the Curriculum*. London: David Fulton Publishers.

Edwards, L., Munn, P. and Fogelman, K. (eds) (1992) *Education for Democratic Citizenship in Europe – New Challenges for Secondary Education*. Lisse: Swets and Zeitlinger.

Fogelman, K. (1991) Citizenship in secondary schools: the national picture. In K. Fogelman (ed.) *Citizenship in Schools*. London: David Fulton Publishers.

Fritzsche, K. and Knepper, H. (1992) Authoritarian challenges for political education or the re-emergence of the authoritarian and the renaissance of a theory. In L.

Edwards, P. Munn and K. Fogelman (eds) *Education for Democratic Citizenship in Europe – New Challenges for Secondary Education*. Lisse: Swets and Zeitlinger.

Fullinwider, R. (eds) (1996) *Public Education in a Multicultural Society: Policy, Theory, Critique*. Cambridge: Cambridge University Press.

Gutmann, A. (1996) Challenges of multiculturalism in democratic education. In R. Fullinwider (ed.) *Public Education in a Multicultural Society: Policy, Theory, Critique*. Cambridge: Cambridge University Press.

Hansard Society (1996) *Education for Democratic Citizenship*. Unpublished paper.

Kerr, D. (1996) *Citizenship Education in Primary Schools*. London: Institute for Citizenship Studies.

Leicester, M. (1992) Values, culture conflict and education. In M. Leicester and M. Taylor (eds) *Ethics, Ethnicity and Education*. London: Kogan Page.

Lorentzen, S. (1992) Democracy through participation: a Norwegian model for citizenship education. In L. Edwards, P. Munn and K. Fogelman (eds) *Education for Democratic Citizenship in Europe – New Challenges for Secondary Education*. Lisse: Swets and Zeitlinger.

Lynch, J. (1989) *Multi-cultural Education in a Global Society*. Brighton: Falmer Press.

Lynch, J. (1992) *Education for Citizenship in a Multicultural Society*. London: Cassell.

Lynch, J., Modgil, C. and Modgil, S. (eds) (1992) *Cultural Diversity and the Schools: Volume One – Education for Cultural Diversity: Convergence and Divergence*. Brighton: Falmer Press.

Malik, K. (1996) *The Meaning of Race*. London: Macmillan.

McLaughlin, T. (1992) Citizenship, diversity and education: a philosophical perspective. *The Journal of Moral Education, Special Issue: Citizenship and Diversity*, **21** (3).

Morrison, K. (1994) *Implementing Cross-Curricular Themes*. London: David Fulton Publishers.

NCC (1990a) *Curriculum Guidance 3: The Whole Curriculum*. York: National Curriculum Council.

NCC (1990b) *Curriculum Guidance 8: Education for Citizenship*. York: National Curriculum Council.

Ofsted (1995) *The Ofsted Handbook: Guidance on the Inspection of Nursery and Primary Schools*. London: HMSO.

Osler, A. (1994) Education for development: redefining citizenship in a pluralist society. In A. Osler (ed.) *Development Education: Global Perspectives in the Curriculum*. London: Cassell.

Osler, A., Rathenow, H. and Starkey, H. (eds) (1995) *Teaching for Citizenship in Europe*. Stoke-on-Trent: Trentham Books.

Precey, R. and Marsh, J. (1989) *Community Links with GCSE*. London: Community Service Volunteers.

Saunders, L., MacDonald, A., Hewitt, D. and Schagen, S. (1995) *Education for Life: The Cross-Curricular Themes in Primary and Secondary Schools*. Slough: NFER.

SCAA (1996) *Education for Adult Life: the Spiritual and Moral Development of Young People, Discussion Papers: No. 6*. London: School Curriculum and Assessment Authority.

Speaker's Commission on Citizenship (1990) *Encouraging Citizenship: Report on the Commission on Citizenship*. London: HMSO.

Starkey, H. (ed.) (1996) *Socialisation of School Children and their Education for Democratic Values and Human Rights*. Lisse: Swets and Zeitlinger.

Steiner, M. (ed.) (1996) *Developing the Global Teacher*. Stoke-on-Trent: Trentham Books.

Stradling, R. (1975) *The Political Awareness of the School Leaver*. London: Hansard Society/Politics Association.

Verma, K. (ed.) (1989) *Education for All*. Brighton: Falmer Press.

Vine, I. (1992) Moral diversity or universal values? The problem of moral education within socially segmented societies. In J. Lynch, C. Modgil and S. Modgil (eds) *Cultural Diversity and the Schools: Volume One – Education for Cultural Diversity: Convergence and Divergence*. Brighton: Falmer Press.

10 Citizenship Education for Adolescent Offenders

DONALD BIGGS, ROBERT COLESANTE, JOSHUA SMITH AND GARY HOOK

Introduction

The children and youth who live in the central cities of the United States are often described in the most derogatory terms and the communities in which they grow up are described as violent, impoverished and dangerous places. It's no wonder that so many citizens in the United States seem to be asking, "What's wrong with those kids that live in the hood?" Many of the approaches to working with these inner city youth seem to be based on an assumption that something is broken and needs to be fixed. In some cases, the something is broken and needs to be fixed. In some cases, the something is the youth. In other cases, it is the parents, the schools or the community. The trouble with these descriptions of inner city youth and their communities is that they, for the most part, reflect the perspectives of outsiders and they emphasize remediating deficits rather than developing resources.

In this chapter, we will describe a citizenship education program that was developed in Albany, New York. It was held in summer 1995 over a 4-week period in an inner city middle school. Participants included graduate and undergraduate students from the University at Albany, as well as high school and middle school students from inner city communities in the Capital District Region. The participants from all levels of education were primarily people of color. The goals of the Institute reflect the voices of citizens who live in these inner city communities. Many of whom told us that they wanted more community-based programs for their youth that would develop their strengths and engage them in the life of their community.

The Institute was designed to promote increased youth involvement in a central city community through a democratically based citizenship educa-tion program. A primary function of the Institute was development of social responsibility in the form of citizenship skills that would empower youth to make improvements in their community. However, it was also important to us that increased social responsibility is not only a valued outcome in itself, but it can be instrumental in acquiring new know-ledge and the development of critical thinking skills. Our view of citizenship was not based on blind conformity to the present but a responsible approach to change.

Incarcerated youth

A major social problem in the United States is the growing number of incarcerated youth who are housed in rehabilitation/correctional facilities. The popular media and the professional literature both describe these youth in very derogatory terms. They are represented as "criminal types" and/or as suffering from psychological, social or moral def-icits. As a consequence, many of the rehabilitative programs in these facilities seem to emphasize the need to fix whatever is wrong with these youth. We believe that many of the problems besetting those who are trying to build effective rehabilitative pro-grams follow from the fact that they represent these youth as having something broken that needs to be fixed. The usual question being asked is, What's wrong with these youth? (Cuban 1989). Youth agencies have developed a wide variety of counsel-ing and psychological education programs that are supposed to fix or cure these youth. In contrast, we have assumed that these young people have strengths and resources to be developed as well as problems to be remediated. We also assume that these youth could benefit from increased community involvement in their own rehabilitation. We argue that they share many characteristics with other youth in our society and that their rehabilitation would be fostered in an environment that develops a "sense of community" in their residential units and provides a democratic structure in which they can play responsible roles in these communities. Put simply, our position is that these youth will only become socially responsible citizens if they have opportunities to engage in responsible activities while in the rehabilitative facilities.

Involvement in community activities is perhaps one of the most effective ways of promoting the development of leadership, achievement, and social responsibility among urban youth (Nettles 1991, Wentzel 1991). Since the incarcerated youth share many similarities with urban youth, who are also often represented as "at risk," we thought there were good reasons for believing that increasing youth involvement in their rehabilitation communities would yield a number of positive benefits for the youth and the community at large. We believed that they are most likely to value justice and democracy if they have first hand experiences in community problem-solving about issues of justice and democracy in their daily lives.

Given the research on adolescent development and community involvement (Nettles 1991, Heath and McLaughlin 1993) we wondered if we could develop a program of community involvement for youth who are incarcerated in these facilities. First, we had to set up a process by which the youth and staff could develop a sense of community in the residential units. Then we needed to structure a democratic model of community involvement that was credible to both residents and staff. The administration agreed to set up an experimental group structure in the residential units that would allow residents to provide consultation on problems of group living. The goal was to build a democratically run governance group for promoting youth involvement in these residential communities. We helped residents and staff assess problems and plan a citizenship program which included fairness meetings and town meetings that would address issues of justice and democracy. The incarcerated youth were to be involved in a democratically based citizenship education program that allowed them to have a voice in decisions that might impact their lives in the youth facility.

Adolescents and young adults in the United States are more likely than any other age cohort to commit violations of the law. Between 1965 and 1988, the arrest rates for aggravated assault, murder and non-negligent manslaughter increased substantially in this population (FBI 1987). Since 1955, the courts have been referring more and more adolescents who have committed either status or index offenses to juvenile rehabilitation programs. Status offenses and minor delinquent acts are as common among middle income as lower income adolescents. Self reports of delinquent activities among Anglo and African American adolescents are very similar, but a number of studies indicate that African American adolescents are seven times more likely to be arrested for the same type of crime as are their Anglo counterparts (Henggeler 1989).

Clearly, there is no consensus among researchers about either the causes of delinquency and misconduct among adolescents or the nature of appropriate treatments. However, this adolescent population, no matter what the nature of their specific delinquent acts, all have citizenship problems in that their actions have conflicted with the concept of the "common good" in society. Their views of their rights and obligations are in conflict with those of others in their communities.

We propose that programs for incarcerated youth should foster the development of social responsibility by creating a citizenship program that expects these youth to act in socially responsible ways. They must also learn that they are part of a community of residents in the facility and that their individual interests can be enhanced by participating in responsible group actions. Problems of living in a residential community are represented as both group and individual problems which can impact the welfare of individual residents and the group as a whole.

In some ways, the just community approach has similar goals to those of character education. Simply stated, we are trying to encourage peer communities to support positive, pro-social behaviors and inhibit those behaviors that negatively impact the welfare of their community. We would like to second Walberg and Wynne (1989) who argue that citizens, educators, and parents who want to improve character among youth need to influence the quality of their peer groups. They recommend that groups need to be formed that allow youth to be assigned responsibilities for improving the common life of their communities.

Background

The setting

This state youth agency in the Northeastern United States provides a continuum of residential and community care facilities. Those admitted to non-secure facilities may be adjudicated juvenile delinquents, persons in need of supervision (PINS), or persons on probation by the family court. Limited secure programs involve youth who are 7 to 15 years of age who have committed acts that would constitute crimes if committed by adults. The secure programs are designed for juvenile offenders or youthful offenders 13 years or older who are convicted in adult criminal courts of murder, 2nd degree, or youth over 14 years of age who have committed crimes such as homicide, kidnapping, arson, assault, rape, sodomy, aggravated sexual abuse, burglary, or robbery. The community-based programs are the least secure facilities. They house adjudicated juvenile delinquents, persons in need of supervision, or persons placed on probation by the Family Court or the Adult Court. As youth demonstrate improvement in their behaviors, they may be transferred to the less secure community-oriented facilities.

At most facilities, residents receive academic and vocational instruction, as well as counseling services. They live in separate units in the facilities that are supervised by child care workers. Residential units have group meetings several times a week. Sessions usually begin by having each resident describe his or her experiences during the day while staff members and other residents provide feedback. Very often residents discuss disputes with other residents, teachers, and/or counseling staff. These groups also provide staff with opportunities to discuss issues involving residents who are failing to meet their program responsibilities.

The consultation process

In spring 1990, the Director of a non-secure youth facility located in a country setting in the Northeastern area of the United States decided to do an evaluation of the group program in his facility. A consultant (the senior author) was asked to work with the staff and residents to identify ways of improving the groups. The consultation model involved reciprocal collaboration with staff and residents. The goal was to identify issues that the staff and residents thought that the groups should address. It was also necessary to differentiate between the staff needs and the residents' needs that were to be addressed in their group settings. The consultant tried to identify relevant concepts and methods that would provide a framework for thinking about the goals and structure of the groups. The consultant did not provide prescriptions for improving the groups. Instead, he focused on identifying goals for the groups that both residents and staff agreed upon. One of the major obstacles to improving the groups was the perception among residents and staff that the responsibility for the groups was entirely in the hands of the staff. Thus an immediate short-term goal was to increase responsibility and/or ownership among residents for the groups. We wanted to change the sense of ownership so that residents perceived the meetings as *their* groups, and we wanted the groups to become a mechanism for building a sense of community in the residence units.

The consultant met with the staff and residents, who identified a set of problems concerning interpersonal conflicts among residents that they wanted to deal with in their daily group sessions. These disputes, often referred to as "set-up" games or "playing", were usually verbal in nature but could evolve into more serious physical conflicts among residents. The staff wanted the residents in their groups to take more responsibility for dealing with some of these verbal games which they considered to be very petty. The residents felt that the staff often over-reacted to these games.

Residents played games with their peers that usually included making verbal insults that were designed to get one or another to act in such a way that they would be disciplined by the staff. These games could have negative consequences for either or both residents but they usually were not considered serious disciplinary infractions. When these set-up games preceded fights, it was difficult to identify which culprit was responsible for starting the dispute.

The fairness program

The facility staff and residents proposed that each unit develop a "fairness program" to deal with verbal set-up games and other kinds of verbal hassling among residents. These verbal conflicts were considered real life moral problems. The residents were asked to play a role in preventing the problems from escalating into fights that could have negative consequences for them. The groups were to take responsibility for figuring out the circumstances that contributed to a dispute, listen to both disputants and recommend actions that needed to be taken in order to prevent the dispute from occurring again. The meetings would be run democratically, and follow a flexible procedural order. The fairness issues would be discussed openly by voicing reasons and not by attacking other residents. The group would vote on what they considered to be the causes of a dispute and the merits of various alternative strategies for resolving it. Their recommendations were considered as being advisory to the staff.

The fairness program included unit fairness committees which were to act as review and fact-finding groups when residents or staff registered complaints against residents whose interpersonal disputes were adversely influencing the welfare of the group. Members of the committee could recommend that the complaint be handled by staff or it could be discussed at a unit fairness meeting.

The fairness meeting had three goals:

1 To achieve a collective understanding of the problem situation that gave rise to the conflict;
2 To identify individual and community goals in resolving the dispute and recommend appropriate actions that would prevent it from occurring again;
3 To establish an agreement about how each of the disputants would act in the future and recommend sanctions if they failed to meet the terms of the agreement.

A major goal of the fairness program was to talk about issues of fairness and justice in their daily lives and to provide responsible experiences in community problem-solving about these issues. Residents were expected to establish and follow collective norms regarding order, civility and democratic processes. Staff were to ensure that the residents adhered to orderly procedures in their meetings, and were to ask questions that clarified issues and/or challenged residents to think aloud and discuss their reasons for their judgments.

The just community

In summer 1991, the staff reviewed the fairness program and proposed that a "just community program" be developed that would include town meetings as well as fairness meetings. This program assigned residents collective responsibilities for helping to maintain and improve the quality of life in their units. The idea was to provide democratic and orderly group experiences in which the residents could learn about citizenship and collective responsibility in their residential units (see McLaughlin 1992).

The just community program employed two types of meetings for teaching citizenship skills in the residence units. The town meetings promoted social cooperation among residents so as to enhance group morale in the units. They provided opportunities for the residents to take collective responsibility for defining their common good and the collective norms regarding individual actions that affected the *welfare* of other residents and staff. The fairness meetings were to also provide a justice structure for mediating interpersonal conflicts among residents. In these sessions, residents were to assume collective responsibility for preventing verbal conflicts from escalating and becoming disciplinary issues.

The town meetings were to teach respect for the "common good" by considering the impact of individual actions on the rights of others and the rights of the community. They were to involve residents in making recommendations about preventing problems in group living and promoting positive social programs in their residential units. These meetings also tried to develop collective norms that were directed toward building the concept of a residential group as a community. The essential quality of these norms is that they expect members to be concerned about the rights and welfare of others and the welfare of their group. An infraction such as stealing would be discussed as both a violation of another person's individual rights and a violation of a community norm involving trust among its members. The idea was to develop a sense of community so that residents perceived themselves as members of a group with norms that protected the common life of them all. These meetings also provided opportunities for residents to consult with staff regarding how to develop and maintain a positive sense of community in their units.

The just community program included fairness

meetings that dealt with any arguments or disputes among residents that were adversely influencing the quality of life in a residential unit. The goal was to increase understanding of how a justice system works within a community. Fairness meetings were to model conventional moral reasoning (Reimer et al. 1983). The conventional view of morality takes the perspective of the individual in relationships with other individuals: youth are to look at their actions in terms of consequences for other persons and the group as a whole. The idea is to realize and take into consideration the fact that a community has the legitimate right to expect individual citizens to act in accordance with its moral norms. The fairness meeting approaches individual problems among residents from the viewpoint that they are all members of a community that has accepted standards for determining the rights and obligations of its members.

The group was to help the two residents in a dispute figure out the nature of their argument and then advise them about how to prevent disputes from arising again in the future. Group leaders were taught basic mediation skills that they were to utilize in the fairness meetings. Their meetings began with the two residents who were involved in a dispute moving their chairs to the middle of the circle and a mediator sitting between them. Then they would model a group mediation approach to the dispute which included the group members in the mediation process. Their group task was to achieve a common understanding of the issues in the dispute, how the dispute should be resolved and how it might be prevented from occurring again in the future. The group could recommend "homework" sanctions that would involve the assignment of reading or writing tasks related to the issues underlying the interpersonal dispute.

In the first part of a fairness meeting, the mediator asks the disputants to spell out their experiences, behaviors and feelings during the dispute:

1 What *experiences* or things happened to them? e.g. "He kept calling me names".
2 What *behaviors* or actions were taken by the disputants? e.g. "He hit me".
3 How did each of them *feel* during the dispute? e.g. "I was angry".

Each person and the mediator summarizes how they believe the dispute started and the group members are asked for their opinions about the situation.

The chair then asks the disputants and group members to identify the problematic behaviors of the residents that seem to be self-defeating and/or they have the potential to lead to undesirable consequences for the resident and/or the unit and the facility. These are the behaviors that must be reduced or eliminated.

In the second part of the meeting, the chair asks the two residents to describe how they would like to see the dispute resolved. What were their goals during the dispute and what are they now? How would the group like to see the dispute resolved? What does the group want the disputants to do? The two residents are asked whether either of them tried to resolve the dispute. The mediator concludes by summarizing the discussion and asking for recommendations for resolving the dispute.

If the fairness meeting involved arbitration, the chair would ask residents to propose and then vote on possible "homework" sanctions for one or both residents; these would be recommendations to the staff. The sanctions might involve the assignment of educational tasks that would improve knowledge and skills needed for dealing with the issues involved in the dispute. Disputants may be asked to prepare a group discussion or to make a report on a special topic such as anger control, moral reasoning, or victim awareness. The sanctions were not to involve punishing residents or embarrassing them in front of their peers.

Youth facility programs 1993–1994

In spring 1993, the authors initiated discussions about the just community program with staff and residents in two residential centers and two group homes. One of the residential centers houses about sixty boys ranging from 13 to 20 years of age, most of whom are juvenile offenders or juvenile/youthful offenders who have been tried in adult courts. These residents have usually committed the most serious crimes of all those youth who are under the responsibility of the Youth Agency. The other residential center is a non-secure facility housing approximately twenty-five residents. Each of the two group homes houses about ten residents. They are considered to be transitional programs that provide youth with opportunities to test their new personal, educational and vocational skills in community settings. They are the least restrictive of the residential programs.

In summer 1993, staff and residents at each of the three kinds of youth facilities reviewed the background of the original program and developed their own plans for implementing just community activities. All of these proposals emphasized the goal of citizenship education. The idea was to use community problem-solving activities having to do with discipline and welfare issues to teach a concern for the common good. They developed models of fairness meetings and town meetings that involved residents providing consultation with staff regarding how to prevent group problems and how to capitalize on opportunities for improving the quality of life in their residence units. Their approach involved small group activities that provided practical experiences in democratic decision-making and collective responsibility (Power et al. 1989).

The planning groups were responsible for three tasks:

1 To develop guidelines for residents to use in formulating unit by-laws or constitutions. These included identifying criteria for selecting group leaders and for removing them when they fail to meet their obligations.
2 To develop guidelines for training residents in group leadership and mediation skills.
3 To develop group norms and expectations regarding orderly and appropriate behavior of residents in town meetings and fairness meetings.

The proposal for one residential center included an advisory group that focused on peer teaching about various personal and social issues of residents. The idea was to identify real problems in the units that deal with aggression, anger, and/or moral reasoning and then ask residents to read material on the topics and lead group discussions on them.

Conclusion

The just community program described in this chapter was concerned with promoting responsible involvement in the residential communities of incarcerated youth facilities. Democratic consultation processes are at the heart of the approach. For staff and residents to overcome their traditional reliance on authoritarian control patterns of group management, they have to take democratic values seriously, as well as control values in their daily interactions. Delinquent youth have a wide assort-

ment of problems but the central problems that have landed them in these facilities are their citizenship problems. They must learn to live cooperatively with other citizens, respect the laws of the society and learn the citizenship skills that will allow them to represent their interests and obtain fair treatment when they feel that they have been treated unjustly. The State Youth Agency places youthful offenders into relatively stable and orderly residential groups under adult direction and monitoring in which they can learn to be responsible citizens. However, these groups should provide residents with practical experiences in group problem-solving where they learn to respect the common good and the collective norms of community life. They must learn that all members of a community are "at risk" when individual members don't observe the code of discipline that guarantees their security.

The most powerful agent for change in youth rehabilitation facilities is these peer groups. Thus it is necessary for staff to positively influence the norms of these groups. It is also important that residents learn through their group experiences how to influence their peers and how to engage in cooperative problem-solving.

The just community approach provided a means of consulting with residents about issues of discipline and general welfare. Residents were to decide through democratic procedures the nature of their collective advice to staff. Most of these youths perceived issues of discipline, maintenance of order and conflict resolution as the sole responsibility of staff. They often didn't perceive themselves as members of a community who have any responsibilities for the quality of life in their units. As a consequence, they made little effort to mediate problems between themselves or take any pro-social actions to prevent small interpersonal problems from escalating into major disciplinary issues. Because the residents sense no responsibility for their collective lives, the staff were expected to solve these problems by becoming increasingly more controlling over the lives of residents. Although most residents have been involved in assertive or violent acts in society, much of their collective and individual problem-solving behaviors in the facilities could be characterized as passive, institutionalized and dependent. Consequently, many of them were initially not willing to assume responsibility for the fairness and town meetings. But, as staff began to adapt authoritative rather than authoritarian roles, residents became much more willing to participate in their residential communities.

We learned the wisdom behind Ralph Mosher's observation about democratic high schools always having their feet in the water (Mosher 1979). From Fall 1993 to Summer 1994, we observed our just community proposals nearly drown over and over in a sea of institutionalized resistance. We found out that many residents and staff never really thought that the program would be implemented and thus would not try out this new approach. An exception to the trend was found in the original residential center where a creative counselor, Augustine Amissah, initiated both fairness meetings and community meetings in his unit. With his aid, we had established a beach-head and were then able to develop the credibility of the just community approach for dealing with practical problems in living in the residence units.

We wish we could end our story on a positive note; a kind of; "Then everyone lived happily ever after!" Although the just community program still has many advocates, the staff and some residents continue to tell us that it is an alien and impractical idea for working with incarcerated youth. Obviously we just don't know how bad these youth are!

References

Cuban, L. (1989) The "at-risk" label and the problems of urban school reform. *Phi Delta Kappan*, **70**: 780–91.

Federal Bureau of Investigation (1987) *Uniform Crime Reports*. Washington, D.C.: U.S. Department of Justice.

Heath, S. B. and McLaughlin, N. W. (1993) *Identity and Inner-City Youth: Beyond Ethnicity and Gender*. Columbia University, NY: Teachers College Press.

Henggeler, S. W. (1989) *Delinquency in Adolescence*. Newbury Park, CA: Sage Publications.

McLaughlin, T. H. (1992) Citizenship diversity and education: a philosophical perspective. *Journal of Moral Education*, **21** (3): 235–50.

Mosher, R. L. (1979) A democratic high school: damn it, your feet are always in the water. In R. Mosher (ed.) *Adolescents Development and Education*. Berkeley, CA: McCutchan Publishing Company.

Mosher, R., Kenny, R. A. and Garrod, A. (1994) *Preparing for Citizenship: Teaching Youth to Live Democratically*. Westport, CT: Praeger Publishers.

Nettles, S. M. (1991) Community involvement and disadvantaged students: a review. *Review of Educational Research*, **61** (3): 379–406.

Power, F. C., Higgins, A. and Kohlberg, L. (1989) *Lawrence Kohlberg's Approach to Moral Education*. New York: Columbia University Press.

Reimer, J., Paolitto, D. P. and Hersh, R. H. (1983) *Promoting Moral Growth – From Piaget to Kohlberg* (2nd edn). Prospect Heights, IL: Waveland Press.

Walberg, H. J. and Wynne, E. A. (1989) Character education: toward a preliminary consensus. In L. P. Nucci (ed.) *Moral Development and Character Education*. Berkeley, CA: McCutchan Publishing Corporation.

Wentzel, K. R. (1991) Social competence at school: relation between social responsibility and academic achievement. *Review of Educational Research*, **61** (1): 1–24.

11 Citizenship Education, Cultural Diversity and the Development of Thinking Skills

PATRICK J. M. COSTELLO

Introduction

The purpose of this chapter is to examine the theory and practice of citizenship education with particular reference to cultural diversity. I begin by offering an account of the development of education for citizenship in the UK. This is followed by an examination of the implications of such education for promoting cultural diversity. In particular, I shall focus on international education programmes such as world studies and global education, which aim to contribute to the development both of citizens and of such diversity. Having argued that teaching the skills of critical thinking, reasoning and argument is central to any adequate notion of 'international education' and of 'education for citizenship', I suggest that the absence in these programmes of explicit guidance on the teaching of such skills is a significant omission. Finally, I conclude the chapter by discussing how citizenship education, which promotes cultural diversity and the development of pupils' thinking skills, might take place in primary and secondary school classrooms through the teaching of personal, social and moral education.

Education for citizenship

One should begin by noting that a concern that schools should provide children with the knowledge, skills, attitudes and dispositions which they will require in order to play a full part as citizens in the society to which they belong and, indeed, in the wider world, is not recent in origin. Over sixty years ago, the Association for Education in Citizenship (AEC) published a volume entitled *Education for Citizenship in Secondary Schools* (1936). In the Preface to the book (p. vii), the President of the Association, W. H. Hadow, referred to citizenship education as being of 'common and urgent interest' and argued as follows (ibid.):

> Citizenship is the heritage of all of us, and we share the responsibility of bringing it to the highest stage of efficiency which the nature of the subject admits. Some topics, e.g. history, geography, economics, and politics, are immediately germane and relevant; in other cases, such as biology, mathematics, art, and literature, the connexion may be more indirect but the line of approach is equally continuous, and the whole makes up a corpus of Education no branch of which can be safely neglected. The work of the classroom can be strengthened and corroborated by external activities, directed to the one end of inculcating the best kind of life, with as little as possible of bias and partisanship and with the utmost of concentration and dispassionate judgement.

More recently, the authors of *The National Curriculum 5–16: A Consultation Document* (DES/Welsh Office 1987: para. 4) suggested that

> Since Sir James Callaghan's speech as Prime Minister at Ruskin College in 1976, successive Secretaries of State have aimed to achieve agreement with their partners in the education service on policies for the school curriculum which will develop the potential of all pupils and equip them for the responsibilities of citizenship . . . in tomorrow's world.

In the late 1980s, an increasing emphasis was placed on the importance of citizenship, allied to calls for a return to 'traditional values'. Indeed, such was the importance given to this theme that several ministers in the Conservative government added their voices in its support (see Costello 1990). For example, as Home Secretary, Douglas

Hurd called for 'lessons in how to be a good citizen ... to be made a GCSE exam subject' (Greig 1988). Angela Rumbold, while Minister of State for Education, asked 'the national curriculum subject working groups to pay attention to cross-curriculum themes that [are] "important in ensuring that citizenship and awareness of other people's needs are part and parcel of the lessons which are given to children"' (Hugill and Surkes 1988). At the 1988 Conservative Party conference, Hurd suggested that 'The challenge of the 1990s is to rekindle our strong tradition of citizenship' (Sharrock and Linton 1988); and Kenneth Baker, as Secretary of State for Education, urged the need for 'a moral code in schools to bring back traditional values' (Murphy and Irvine 1988).

As is evident from the AEC quotation given above, the approach advocated by the Association was one that sought to promote citizenship education through subject disciplines. As we approach the millennium, the idea that schools should prepare children to live as future citizens is once again becoming increasingly prominent and, although the core and foundation subjects of the National Curriculum are important vehicles to encourage this development, the emphasis in recent times has been on much broader conceptions both of the aims and purposes of such education and of how it might be introduced to pupils.

Since the advent of the National Curriculum Council's discussion document *Education for Citizenship* (1990), the relationship between schooling and the formation of citizens has become the subject of keen debate. Although teachers would argue that it has always been part of their responsibility to develop in children an awareness both of the latter's rights within society and their accompanying responsibilities to it, the emergence of 'citizenship' as a cross-curricular theme gave a firm foundation to such work. While a number of books have addressed the nature of 'citizenship' (Barbalet 1988, Jordan 1989, Heater 1990) several have also been published by educationists aiming both to elucidate the notion of 'citizenship education' and to suggest ways in which it might take place in schools (Fogelman 1991, Baglin Jones and Jones 1992, Lynch 1992, Edwards and Fogelman 1993, Morrison 1994, White 1996. See also Costello 1995).

The NCC's booklet outlines a number of objectives under the headings 'Knowledge', 'Cross-curricular skills', 'Attitudes' and 'Moral codes and values'. With reference to the first of these, it was suggested that pupils should develop knowledge and understanding of:

1   The nature of community

- the variety of communities to which people simultaneously belong: family, school, local, national, European and worldwide;
- how communities combine stability with change;
- how communities are organized and the importance of rules and laws;
- how communities reconcile the needs of individuals with those of society.

2   Roles and relationships in a democratic society

- the nature of cooperation and competition between individuals, groups and communities;
- similarities and differences between individuals, groups and communities – diversity and interdependence;
- the experience and opportunities of people in different roles and communities.

3   The nature and basis of duties, responsibilities and rights

- the role of custom and law in prescribing duties, responsibilities and rights;
- fairness, justice and moral responsibility. (p. 3)

I should like to make two comments about this list. First, it is clear that the notion of 'cultural diversity' is central to each of the three categories outlined above and therefore to the knowledge-based aspect of education for citizenship itself. Second, although 'knowledge and understanding' is a pivotal component, something more is required if this cross-curricular area of study is to be instrumental in developing pupils' critical thinking skills. Accordingly, the NCC suggested a set of cross-curricular skills, attitudes and moral codes and values, by reference to which knowledge and understanding might be contextualized. I shall return to these later in the chapter.

As I have argued elsewhere (Costello 1997), two events have contributed to the call for a renewed emphasis on the importance of citizenship education. The first of these was the Archbishop of Canterbury's 'crusade to stop the moral and spiritual decline of the nation' (Thomson and O'Leary

1996: 1). Opening a House of Lords debate, the Archbishop argued as follows:

> It would be a failure if our schools were to produce people with the right skills and aptitudes to take on our economic competitors, but who cannot string two sentences together about the meaning and purpose of life or who have no idea what it means to be a good citizen and a moral person.   (ibid.)

The second concerned the call from Frances Lawrence, widow of the murdered headteacher Philip Lawrence, for 'a national effort to reinforce citizenship and family values, raise the status of authority figures and outlaw violence' (Young 1996: 6). In her 'Manifesto for the Nation', Lawrence suggested the need for 'new primary school courses in good citizenship' and 'an emphasis in teaching on effort, earnestness and excellence' (MacAskill and Carvel 1996: 1). She argued as follows:

> I would wish to see the emergence of a nationwide movement, dedicated to healing our fractured society, banishing violence, ensuring that the next generation are equipped to be good citizens and urgently debating how the moral climate can be changed for the better . . . I should like to see lessons in good citizenship begin early in a child's school career. Schools should inculcate an appreciation of the civic bond, the respect we owe to others and the duties we owe to society . . . I worry that too few people are encouraged to think seriously about the nature and progression of the country . . . I would hope to encourage an engagement with the important issues, a generation that thinks rigorously about the moral questions behind politics instead of taking refuge in sneering at them.   (Lawrence 1996: 14)

In what has been referred to as a 'victory' for Mrs Lawrence, the new Labour government has indicated its intention to introduce proposals under which children would be taught 'how to be model citizens' (Prescott 1997: 1). In addition to citizenship education taking place through subjects such as history and geography, it is possible that free-standing classes, to be called either 'citizenship' or 'civics' would be introduced by schools.

Citizenship education and cultural diversity

The NCC's *Education for Citizenship* suggests that this cross-curricular theme consists of eight com-

ponents, one of which is 'roles and relationships in a pluralist society'. In a section of the document devoted explicitly to this aspect, the NCC (1990: 6) argues as follows:

> A democratic society is based on shared values and a variety of cultures and lifestyles can be maintained within the framework of its laws. This component helps pupils to appreciate that all citizens can and must be equal. It increases awareness of and works towards resolving some of the tensions and conflicts that occur between groups which perceive each other to be socially, racially, ethnically or culturally different. In this context, it explores diversity, fairness and justice, co-operation and competition, prejudice and discrimination.

The following areas of study are suggested as possibilities (ibid):

- the interdependence of individuals, groups and communities;
- similarities and differences between individuals, groups and communities and their effects;
- the existence of differences in perception and the ways in which these may be reconciled;
- Britain as a multi-cultural, multi-ethnic, multi-faith and multi-lingual society;
- the diversity of cultures in other societies;
- a study of history and culture from different perspectives;
- international and global issues;
- the origins and effects of racial prejudice within British and other societies.

Such areas are useful because they enable children to focus on a number of problems that they may face at school, in the home and in wider society. A graphic account of many of these difficulties is set out in *Children and Racism*, a research study of telephone calls made to ChildLine during the year ending on 31 March, 1995. As the authors argue (ChildLine 1996: 7):

> It is not easy to research the impact of racism. Race and culture are slippery concepts – they do not have agreed clear definitions. For example, which nation, race or culture do children of mixed national, cultural or colour inheritance identify with or claim as theirs? This altogether depends on their relationship to different aspects of their inheritance, and on how they perceive that these are valued both in general and by those close to them. It is this very uncertainty in definition, the fluidity of boundaries between so-called categories, which renders absurd rigidly applied public

policies differentiating people in racial or cultural terms.

In discussing the relationship between citizenship education and cultural diversity, there are a number of important factors to consider in this study. The first concerns the fact that 'openly racist harassment and bullying plays a large part in the daily experience of many black and ethnic minority children' (p. 2). Given this, the notion of 'citizenship' as an entitlement that accords rights as well as entails responsibilities, is to some extent a theoretical construct which makes little impact on the lives of many of those on whom it is, supposedly, conferred. Second, the authors suggest that

> there is a generation gap in attitudes, that whether adults want it or not, many young people are making and will make relationships across cultural, religious and race frontiers ... In resisting this movement, adults create misery and unhappiness for themselves and their young people, and, in the end, cannot succeed in halting an unstoppable tide towards new and diverse relationships and identities.   (p. 3)

The role of citizenship education in focusing on themes such as 'similarities and differences between individuals, groups and communities and their effects' and 'the existence of differences in perception and the ways in which these may be reconciled' is therefore of the utmost importance, especially when one considers the views of children themselves expressed as follows (pp. 19, 21, 36, 42–3):

> I'm bullied at school. They call me 'Paki' and shout, 'You don't belong in this country'. Reeta, aged 10, had written it all in her diary but not yet told anyone.

> My brother and I are the only Jewish boys at the school. The others call us 'nigger' and 'chocolate biscuit' ... I've told my parents and the teachers and they say ignore it ... it's really getting me down ... I thought of killing myself last week but then I decided not to ... You're the only people I can talk to ... said David, aged 9.

> I have race problems at school and so does my brother. We're picked on all the time. I get punched and kicked and had my head put down the toilet.

> I'm going out with a black boy. My parents are Asian. They would go mad if they knew.

> I have a black boyfriend. My dad is racist ... he's said that if I don't pack him in I can just leave home.

> Joanna, 15, was fed up because her parents were Jehovah's Witnesses. 'They don't celebrate Christmas ... all my friends have a good time and lovely presents ... if they send me cards, my parents tear them up.' She had tried telling them she didn't want to be like them and had run away in the past but she was brought back.

> I'm finding difficulties with cultural differences ... things like going out to discos and even coffee shops are out for me. My parents insist I should be home and studying all the time. I see good things in both cultures. I just don't want to feel under pressure all the time like I do now.

Such views are important not least because children's voices illustrate all too clearly both the complex relationship between 'citizenship' and 'cultural diversity' (Tomlinson 1992, Verma and Pumfrey 1994) and also the fundamental importance of research which seeks to explore topics such as prejudice and prejudice reduction (Aboud 1988, Lynch 1987); 'race' and culture in education (Chivers 1987); 'race' and ethnicity (Gillborn 1990); 'race' and racism (Gill, Mayor and Blair 1992, Troyna 1993, Gaine 1995, Hewitt 1996); anti-racism, politics and schools (Epstein 1993); children's friendships in culturally diverse classrooms (Deegan 1996); and the role of teacher education in plural societies (Craft 1996).

Citizenship, cultural diversity and international education

Themes such as 'education for citizenship' and 'cultural diversity' feature prominently in approaches to teaching and learning which, for the purposes of this chapter, I shall refer to collectively as 'international education'. These include world studies (Fisher and Hicks 1985, Hicks and Townley 1982, Hicks and Steiner 1989), global education (Pike and Selby 1988, Greig, Pike and Selby 1987, Fountain 1990, Steiner 1996), humane education (Selby 1995), futures education (Hicks 1994, Hicks and Holden 1995), peace education (Hicks 1988) and green education (Randle 1989). Although each of these programmes has a distinctive outlook (Rowley and Toye 1996), they have much in common, sharing similar aims, objectives and approaches to pedagogy.

Fisher and Hicks (1985: 8) define world studies as 'studies which promote the knowledge, attitudes and skills that are relevant to living responsibly in a multicultural and interdependent world'. Arguing that world studies can be taught to children of all ages and abilities, the authors give substance to the above definition by suggesting that the subject encompasses

(a) studying cultures and countries other than one's own, and the ways in which they are different from, and similar to, one's own;

(b) studying major issues which face different countries and cultures, for example those to do with peace and conflict, development, human rights and the environment;

(c) studying the ways in which everyday life and experience affect, and are affected by, the wider world. (ibid.)

One important reason offered by Fisher and Hicks for teaching world studies is 'learning about others', a theme concerning which they argue as follows:

The study of 'other people', that is, in countries and cultures other than our own, or at times in history other than our own – helps pupils avoid making false generalisations. These frequently arise from an 'ethnocentric' world view in which people judge others exclusively by their own cultural norms. Learning about others can also help pupils learn about human nature – that is, about themselves. (ibid)

Pike and Selby (1988: 63–9) offer a detailed list of objectives for global education under the headings 'knowledge', 'skills', and 'attitudes'. The importance accorded to cultural diversity is evidenced by objectives such as (ibid.):

How others see us: students should learn about their own culture, lifestyle and identities through studying how other people view them.

Prejudice and discrimination: students should understand the nature and workings of prejudice, in themselves and others, and how such prejudices can lead to personal and social discrimination by means of age, class, creed, ethnicity, gender, ideology, language, nationality or race. They should also know about measures to combat discrimination at personal, societal and global levels.

Oppression: students should know about the oppression of groups, in their own and other societies, for reasons of their age, class, creed, ethnicity, gender, ideology, language, nationality or race. They should have an understanding of personal attitudes and social structures which nurture oppression, the part they as individuals play in this process and the contribution each can make towards its diminution.

Diversity: students should be willing to find the beliefs and practices of other cultural and social groups of value and interest, and be prepared to learn from them.

Commonality: students should appreciate the essential worth of others and the commonality of needs, rights, aspirations, behaviour and talents which binds humankind.

Susan Fountain's book, *Learning Together: Global Education 4–7* (1990) provides an excellent introduction to the subject for young children. Having asked 'What is global education?', she outlines four 'critical factors': knowledge of interdependence; perspective consciousness; 'state of planet' awareness; and 'awareness of human choices' (pp. 1–3). Responding to the question: 'What do these concepts have to do with young children?' Fountain rejects the view that the latter are incapable of understanding notions such as 'justice', 'rights', 'resource distribution' and 'interdependence'. While it is certainly true that secondary school children are able to grasp such ideas at a more sophisticated level, Fountain argues that: 'in the course of the school day, in their relationships with peers and adults, young children do in fact have simple, concrete experiences which contain elements in common with larger world issues' (p. 3). It is suggested that nursery and infant children frequently:

- Call each other names, sometimes gender- or race-related (prejudice);
- Exclude others from play for arbitrary reasons (discrimination);
- Argue over materials (resource distribution);
- Protest that rules are 'not fair' (human rights);
- Fight (peace and conflict);
- Use consumable materials, sometimes unwisely (environmental awareness);
- Find that by sharing and working together, more can be accomplished (interdependence);
- Negotiate to find a solution to a problem that both parties will find acceptable (perspective consciousness);

- Discover that some adults have power in the school to make decisions, or that older children may be allowed to do things that younger ones are not ('state of planet' – or in this case, 'state of school' – awareness);
- Decide what activities they will take part in: write letters, pick up litter, or plant flowers in the school grounds (awareness of human choice and action). (pp. 3–4)

The practical activities that are suggested in each of the three texts referred to above demonstrate, in a very thorough fashion, the extent to which global education can (and should) permeate the curricula of nursery, infant, junior and secondary classrooms. They are stimulating as well as informative and, most importantly, they encourage children (and teachers) to think for themselves (Costello 1992). However, one would expect that as international education is orientated towards the discussion and promotion of values, these activities would draw more heavily and systematically upon the explicit teaching of thinking and valuing. When Fisher and Hicks (1985: 15) suggest that 'The important goals of world studies teaching . . . focus on learning to learn, solving problems, clarifying values and making decisions', one wonders why 'thinking how to think' has been left out.

Elsewhere, I have argued that the teaching of logical and ethical reasoning is essential to any viable conception of 'international education' (Costello 1990) and of 'education for citizenship' (Costello 1993, 1995). In short, I suggested, young children should be introduced to philosophy (Costello 1996). This stance has been supported by Rowley and Toye (1996) and much excellent work has been undertaken in Britain (see, for example, Citizenship Foundation 1992, Rowe and Newton 1994, Murris 1992). In addition to the development of philosophical thinking, I would suggest that children also need to acquire proficiency in the skills of argument. Before outlining, in the next section, how this might take place, it is necessary to answer the question: why is the explicit teaching of thinking, reasoning and argument required within programmes of international education? In order to do this, I shall focus on *World Studies 8–13: A Teacher's Handbook* (Fisher and Hicks 1985).

In a section entitled 'Questions and Values', the authors (p. 18) suggest that:

If pupils are to grow more aware of their own values and priorities they . . . should be provided with opportunities [to] choose, prize and act, that is: (a) choose freely; (b) choose from alternatives; (c) choose after thoughtful consideration of the consequences of each alternative; (d) cherish and be happy with their choice; (e) be willing to affirm their choice in front of others; (f) do something as a result of their choice; (g) do this repeatedly, as part of their everyday life.

In evaluating a particular action, children are enjoined to ask themselves three questions: 'Who gains and who loses? Is it wise or unwise? Is it just or unjust?' (ibid.). While Fisher and Hicks are to be commended for encouraging pupils to engage in discussions which require them to clarify and develop their values, nevertheless it is the case that before children can be expected to make informed value judgements they must be able to recognize what, in fact, is to count as a *moral* argument. However, materials promoting a consideration of the nature of morality are conspicuous by their absence in *World Studies 8–13: A Teacher's Handbook* and in other classroom texts that fall under the banner of 'international education' (Costello 1990). Although it is true that some mention is made of the importance of activities involving 'critical thinking' (Fisher and Hicks 1985: 25, Huckle 1989: 13, Hicks 1994: 12) and 'argument' (Huckle ibid., Pike and Selby 1988: 55), no programme is offered to develop them. In what follows, I offer a rationale for such a programme and some examples of teaching materials which have been developed to support it.

Teaching critical thinking and argument

The important contribution to be made by the teaching of critical thinking and argument to the promotion of cultural diversity is outlined succinctly by Pike and Selby (1988: 55); 'It is through [the] interplay between cognitive and affective learning, the analytical and the experiential, learning through reasoned argument and emotional insight, that diversity can be valued yet equality promoted'. In *Education for Citizenship* (1990: 3), the NCC identifies 'arguing a case clearly and concisely' as an important communication skill to be developed through this cross-curricular theme. In addition (p. 4), it is suggested that pupils should 'be helped to develop a personal moral code . . . to explore values and beliefs' and that they should have 'respect for rational argument'. Schools should provide opportunities for children to:

- compare values and beliefs held by themselves and others and identify common ground;
- examine evidence and opinions and form conclusions;
- discuss differences and resolve conflict;
- discuss and consider solutions to moral dilemmas, personal and social;
- appreciate that distinguishing between right and wrong is not always straightforward;
- appreciate that the individual's values, beliefs and moral codes change over time and are influenced by personal experience (e.g. of the family, friends, the media, school, religion and the cultural background in which an individual is raised). (p. 4)

The Commission on Citizenship (1990) suggested the following skills and experiences as being essential for effective citizenship (see Rogers 1992: 108):

- the capacity to debate, argue and present a coherent point of view;
- participating in elections;
- taking responsibility by representing others, for example on a school council;
- working collaboratively;
- playing as a member of a team;
- protesting, for example by writing to a newspaper, councillor or local store.

More recently, the School Curriculum and Assessment Authority (SCAA) has also been instrumental in placing the teaching of critical thinking skills, the notion of 'education for citizenship' and the teaching of moral values at the forefront of educational debate (Costello 1996). How might such work take place in the classroom? Recently, together with a colleague, Maggie Bowen, I developed a programme for promoting values education. Entitled *Issues in Personal, Social and Moral Education*, the series consists of four volumes: *Deadly Habits?*, *The Rights of the Child*, *Family Values*, and *What are Animals' Rights?* (Bowen and Costello 1996a, 1996b, 1997a, 1997b), together with a teachers' handbook (Bowen and Costello 1996c).

Issues is intended primarily for use with pupils at Key Stage 2 but is also a useful resource for teenagers with special educational needs. The aims of the series are to:

- provide teachers with a resource to meet specific National Curriculum requirements;
- increase pupils' knowledge and understanding of a range of topical issues in personal, social and moral education;
- enable teachers to develop pupils' value systems;
- develop pupils' skills in speaking, listening, reading and writing;
- promote pupils' reasoning and argument skills;
- encourage pupils to work cooperatively and to respect one another's viewpoints;
- encourage independent thinking and decision-making.

Each book aims to develop argumentative skills beyond the requirements of the National Curriculum. Pupils are introduced to a range of information related to a particular theme and incorporating a selection of moral and values issues that will help them to develop self-awareness, decision-making skills and the ability to think and behave in a reasonable and responsible manner. Topics in the series are divided into three sections. In the first, pupils are given a collection of relevant data outlining key issues for discussion. These have been taken from a variety of sources and provide a broad perspective against which the topic in question may be viewed. The second section contains a selection of pictorial representations each with a number of discussion points. Finally, in section three, a story featuring several important themes provides a basis for discussion and argument. This approach has been adopted to enable a variety of teaching methodologies to be used in the classroom and to cater for pupils' individual learning needs (Bowen and Costello 1996c).

Using a model that focuses on the processes of argument (see Appendix 1), developed as part of a two-year funded research project (Andrews, Costello and Clarke 1993; Andrews 1995; Costello and Mitchell 1995), the six volumes attempt both to introduce children to current issues in personal, social and moral education and to offer a structure by reference to which critical thinking skills may be taught, learned and assessed. Examples of materials for use in the classroom are offered in Appendices 2 and 3 (Bowen and Costello 1997a, 1997b).

In conclusion, I suggest that proficiency in thinking, reasoning and argument is central to the educational enterprise. While recent calls for the introduction of a Critical Thinking A Level are to be welcomed, it is important to begin such work with pupils of a much younger age. Since, as Fountain (1990: 1) suggests, 'Even in the early years of schooling, children . . . show that they are forming rudimentary conceptions, and misconceptions, about issues of peace and conflict, human rights, racism, sexism, global development and the environment', the need for curricula which are respectful of and which seek to enhance pupils' thinking skills in primary and secondary schools is a necessity.

Appendix 1: assessing progress in argument

Processes of argument

The pupil is able to:

1 express a point clearly
2 take a point of view, express an opinion
3 make a personal value statement
4 express a preference
5 give an example
6 give several examples
7 give appropriate examples
8 make a comparison
9 draw a contrast
10 use an analogy
11 use supposition
12 use persuasive language
13 give a reason
14 give a variety of reasons
15 give appropriate reasons
16 quote evidence
17 weigh up evidence
18 refer to own experience to support arguments
19 appeal to authority (of various kinds)
20 stick to the point, be relevant
21 show a degree of logic in the development of the argument
22 repeat an argument in another form
23 take into account others' points of view

Specific to oral argument

24 listen and respond to others' points of view
25 sum up the progress of a discussion or argument
26 speak at length, linking several points together
27 avoid diversion
28 speak with authority, and without hectoring or aggression

Specific to written argument

29 vary the structure of written argument
30 write in various forms (e.g. letter, dialogue, essay)
31 use appropriate connectives (e.g. although, nevertheless, on the other hand)
32 introduce and conclude well (if necessary)
33 write in a lively, readable way
34 be sensitive to the purpose of the argument, and to the audience.

Appendix 2: family valued

The bell rang in the playground at Ashlands Primary School. Afternoon break had come to an end. Class 5J lined up together and waited for their teacher, Mrs Jenkins. Back in the classroom, the children took out their English workbooks. The previous day, Mrs Jenkins had asked them all to write about someone in their family and today they were going to discuss the written work.

Kurshid was the first pupil to speak. He told everyone about his cousin, Imtiaz. Imtiaz was four years older than him, but had always been a good friend. He took Kurshid to play cricket in the summer and to watch football matches at his secondary school in the winter. Often the two boys would go for a Coke afterwards – Imtiaz called it his 'treat'.

Jenny was next. She spoke of her Aunty Emily, her mother's younger sister. Aunty Emily lived alone in a flat in London and Jenny and her mum would often visit for a few days in the school holidays. 'We always have great fun shopping and feeding the pigeons in Trafalgar Square', Jenny told the class with enthusiasm.

Reuben was keen to tell everyone about his grandmother. He explained that she had come to live with him last year when her husband died. 'Grandma always has such fascinating tales to tell', Reuben said. 'She tells me all about the things she used to do as a little girl. Boy, did she have some fun!'.

Thomas gave a brief speech about his Uncle John. He told the class that Uncle John was not a relative, but his father's best friend. Uncle John worked as a fireman and would often let Thomas see all the equipment housed at the fire station.

Unfortunately, the lesson had to end before any more children could speak. Mrs Jenkins praised the class for all their hard work. The children lined up and walked quietly to the cloakroom to get ready to go home. Collette stayed behind. 'What is it, Collette?', asked Mrs Jenkins. Collette told her teacher that the lesson had made her feel sad because it had reminded her that her favourite cousin, Amy, was soon going to emigrate to Australia. 'I don't know what I'll do without her', she said. Mrs Jenkins and Collette sat and talked. After their little chat, Collette left the classroom smiling.

Questions to discuss

1   Is there someone in your family that you particularly like? Why?
2   Why do you think Kurshid said that his cousin was also his best friend?
3   Do you think that Aunty Emily gets lonely living by herself?
4   What kinds of stories might grandparents tell their grandchildren?
5   Is it O.K. for Thomas to call his dad's friend 'Uncle John'?
6   Why do some families emigrate?
7   What do you think that Mrs Jenkins said to Collette to make her feel better?

Appendix 3: all the fun of the circus

Leo, the lion cub, was bored. He had been on holiday from lion school for two weeks and did not have anything to do. 'I'm tired of doing nothing,' he told his mother, 'can't we go out for the afternoon?'. 'Not today, I'm afraid,' his mother the lioness replied, giving him her usual irritable look. 'I'm busy. I've got to do the hunting and then prepare the evening meal. I haven't seen your father all day – he's probably out somewhere sunning himself'. Leo stretched out on the ground. It was a very hot day and the sun beat down on him remorselessly. 'And don't get under my feet,' his mother growled, moving towards him with a purpose. 'If you want to do something useful, practice your roar. If you're going to be king of the jungle one day, you've got to learn to roar. Then, when you're walking about, all the other animals will know you're coming and they will stay out of your way. Also you need to practise walking. Never walk

quickly. This might give others the impression you're nervous. Practise a slow walk with your head held high in the air. They should teach you these things at lion school – I don't know why we send you there.'

Leo got to his feet and walked away – slowly. He tried to roar but his throat was a little dry and he coughed instead. 'Hello, Leo, why are you coughing? Are you unwell?'. Leo turned round. A huge lion filled the clearing. 'Hello, dad! I'm fine – where have you been?' 'Walking down by the river. I heard a new circus was in the area and I went to have a look. 'Can we go please, dad? Can we? I'm bored!' said Leo. 'Tell you what,' replied his father, 'let's ask your mother and we can all go together. It's much too nice a day to be hunting'. Leo's mother agreed to accompany them reluctantly. 'I wish *I* was on holiday', she said quietly to herself. But Leo knew that, secretly, his mother was looking forward to the trip.

After a pleasant stroll, the lion family arrived at the circus. There was a large crowd waiting to be admitted. Lots of Leo's friends were there with their parents. Leo wanted to go off to join them but his mother whispered: 'No, Leo, let them come over to us. Remember what I said this morning'. One by one, the other young animals walked over, their parents a few steps behind. 'Hello, Leo', said Paul and Percy the piglet twins. Leo nodded with his head as high in the air as he could manage. Roberto, the young rhinoceros, bounded over. 'Hi, Leo. This circus should be fun. Shall we go to the front of the queue?'. Leo's father had already begun to walk towards the entrance. On seeing this, the other animals jumped back and allowed him to pass through the crowd. Leo watched how slowly he walked. 'It must be good to be the king', he thought to himself.

Once inside the large tent, Leo and his family found a comfortable spot right next to the ring. The rhinoceros family tried to follow but Leo's dad frowned at them. 'Better sit well back,' Roberto's father said, 'we'll see more from here'. The circus animals were already in the ring but Leo was confused because he didn't recognize any of them. 'What sort of animals are these, dad?' he asked. 'Humans, of course.'

Looking out from the nearest cage, two male adults were throwing plastic balls to each other and catching them in their mouths. A sign attached to the bars said 'No feeding the humans'. 'That one's got a beard like you, dad!', shouted Leo. His father laughed. 'Yes, and they've been trained to roar like us as well. They're very clever really.' In the next cage, two young girls were performing gymnastic exercises on a wooden beam. One became distracted by the noise the audience was making and fell to the ground. 'Ha, ha, ha, ha', laughed Harriet the hyena, 'Did you see that? I'm really enjoying this!' 'Hee haw' bellowed Desmond the young donkey, 'when's the show going to start?'

Suddenly, the lights were dimmed and two elephants trumpeted the entrance of the performing humans. A family of six people came into the ring on all fours. They were dressed in their best clothes and were being ridden by monkeys. 'Let's see who can go fastest!' screamed the ring master, a huge bear. The humans raced across the ring trying to be the first to reach some food at the other end. One of the adults won and grabbed the prize – a huge grapefruit – and began to eat it noisily. Leo watched carefully. After a while, he said to his father: 'I know that one day I'm going to take your place as king of the jungle but, if you don't mind me asking, isn't this cruel?'. 'Of course not, Leo,' his father replied. 'As you can see, these humans are well looked after. They get enough to eat, we give them a place to live and all for doing a few tricks. In fact, we're actually doing them a favour because, if they lived in the wild, they wouldn't last for very long at all. I thought you would have learned this at lion school. Really, I don't know why we send you there!'

Questions to discuss

1 What sort of things should Leo be taught in lion school?
2 Why did Leo's mother not allow Leo to join his friends?
3 Why did Leo not reply to Paul and Percy? Should he have done so?
4 Why did Roberto suggest that Leo and he go to the front of the queue? Should they have done so?
5 What do you think about the idea of a circus that only contains humans?
6 Why does the sign say: 'No feeding the humans'?
7 Should Harriet the hyena have laughed when one of the girls fell from the wooden beam? Could Harriet help laughing?
8 Why were the six humans dressed in their best clothes?

9 Why does Leo think the circus is cruel?
10 Are the humans being well looked after as Leo's father suggests?
11 Is performing in a circus preferable to living in the wild?

Acknowledgement

I am grateful to Craig Donnellan of Independence Educational Publishers, Cambridge, for permission to quote material from *What are Animals' Rights?* and *Family Values*. Information on these and other IEP titles may be obtained from: Independence Educational Publishers, P.O. Box 295, Cambridge CB1 3XP, UK.

References

Aboud, F. (1988) *Children and Prejudice*. Oxford: Basil Blackwell.

Andrews, R. (1995) *Teaching and Learning Argument*. London: Cassell.

Andrews, R., Costello, P. J. M. and Clarke, S. (1993) *Improving the Quality of Argument, 5–16: Final Report*. Esmée Fairbairn Charitable Trust/University of Hull.

Association for Education in Citizenship (1936) *Education for Citizenship in Secondary Schools*. London: Oxford University Press/Humphrey Milford.

Baglin Jones, E. and Jones, N. (eds) (1992) *Education for Citizenship: Ideas and Perspectives for Cross-Curricular Study*. London: Kogan Page.

Barbalet, J. M. (1988) *Citizenship*. Milton Keynes: Open University Press.

Bowen, M. and Costello, P. J. M. (1996a) *Deadly Habits?* Vol. 1 of *Issues in Personal, Social and Moral Education*. Cambridge: Independence Educational Publishers.

Bowen, M. and Costello, P. J. M. (1996b) *The Rights of the Child*. Vol. 2 of *Issues in Personal, Social and Moral Education*. Cambridge: Independence Educational Publishers.

Bowen, M. and Costello, P. J. M. (1996c) *Issues in Personal, Social and Moral Education: Teachers' Handbook*. Cambridge: Independence Educational Publishers.

Bowen, M. and Costello, P. J. M. (1997a) *Family Values*. Vol. 3 of *Issues in Personal, Social and Moral Education*. Cambridge: Independence Educational Publishers.

Bowen, M. and Costello, P. J. M. (1997b) *What are Animals' Rights?* Vol. 4 of *Issues in Personal, Social and Moral Education*. Cambridge: Independence Educational Publishers.

ChildLine (1996) *Children and Racism*. London: ChildLine.

Chivers, T. S. (ed.) (1987) *Race and Culture in Education*. Windsor: NFER-Nelson.

Citizenship Foundation (1992) *Primary Citizenship Project.* London: The Citizenship Foundation.

Costello, P. J. M. (1990) Education for citizenship and the teaching of world studies. *World Studies Journal,* 7 (3).

Costello, P. J. M. (1992) Review of Fountain, S. (1990) *Learning Together: Global Education 4–7. Curriculum,* **13** (3).

Costello, P. J. M. (1993) Educating reflective citizens. *Citizenship: The Journal of the Citizenship Foundation,* **3** (1).

Costello, P. J. M. (1995) Education, citizenship and critical thinking. In J. I. Fields (ed.) *Young Children as Emergent Philosophers,* special edition of *Early Child Development and Care,* **107**.

Costello, P. J. M. (1996) Values and the teaching of philosophical thinking. *Curriculum,* **17** (3).

Costello, P. J. M. (1997) Reasoning and argument in values education. *NAVET Papers* (National Association for Values in Education and Training), **15**.

Costello, P. J. M. and Mitchell, S. (eds) (1995) *Competing and Consensual Voices: The Theory and Practice of Argument.* Clevedon: Multilingual Matters.

Craft, M. (ed.) (1996) *Teacher Education in Plural Societies: An International Review.* London: Falmer Press.

Deegan, J. G. (1996) *Children's Friendships in Culturally Diverse Classrooms.* London: The Falmer Press.

Department of Education and Science/Welsh Office (1987) *The National Curriculum 5–16: A Consultation Document.* London: DES/Welsh Office.

Edwards, J. and Fogelman, K. (eds) (1993) *Developing Citizenship in the Curriculum.* London: David Fulton.

Epstein, D. (1993) *Changing Classroom Cultures: Anti-Racism, Politics and Schools.* Oakhill: Trentham Books.

Fisher, S. and Hicks, D. (1985) *World Studies 8–13: A Teacher's Handbook.* Edinburgh: Oliver and Boyd.

Fogelman, K. (ed.) (1991) *Citizenship in Schools.* London: David Fulton.

Fountain, S. (1990) *Learning Together: Global Education 4–7.* Cheltenham: Stanley Thornes.

Gaine, C. (1995) *Still No Problem Here.* Oakhill: Trentham Books.

Gill, D., Mayor, B. and Blair, M. (eds) (1992) *Racism and Education: Structures and Strategies.* London: Sage Publications.

Gillborn, D. (1990) *'Race', Ethnicity and Education: Teaching and Learning in Multi-Ethnic Schools.* London: Unwin Hyman.

Greig, G. (1988) Hurd's citizen GCSE set for schools. *Daily Mail,* 10 October.

Greig, S., Pike, G. and Selby, D. (1987) *Earthrights: Education as if the Planet Really Mattered.* London: The World Wildlife Fund/Kogan Page.

Heater, D. (1990) *Citizenship: The Civic Ideal in World History, Politics and Education.* London: Longman.

Hewitt, R. (1996) *Routes of Racism: The Social Basis of Racist Action.* Oakhill: Trentham Books.

Hicks, D. (ed.) (1988) *Education for Peace: Issues, Principles and Practice in the Classroom.* London: Routledge.

Hicks, D. (1994) *Educating for the Future: A Practical Classroom Guide.* Godalming: World Wide Fund for Nature.

Hicks, D. and Holden, C. (1995) *Visions of the Future: Why we Need to Teach for Tomorrow.* Oakhill: Trentham Books.

Hicks, D. and Steiner, M. (eds) (1989) *Making Global Connections: A World Studies Workbook.* Edinburgh: Oliver and Boyd.

Hicks, D. and Townley, C. (eds) (1982) *Teaching World Studies: An Introduction to Global Perspectives in the Curriculum.* London: Longman.

Huckle, J. (1989) 'Lessons from political education'. In D. Hicks and M. Steiner (eds) *Making Global Connections: A World Studies Workbook.* Edinburgh: Oliver and Boyd.

Hugill, B. and Surkes, S. (1988) Rumbold on responsibility. *The Times Educational Supplement,* 14 October.

Jordan, B. (1989) *The Common Good: Citizenship, Morality and Self-Interest.* Oxford: Basil Blackwell.

Lawrence, F. (1996) My manifesto for the nation. *The Times, Features,* 21 October.

Lynch, J. (1987) *Prejudice Reduction and the Schools.* London: Cassell.

Lynch, J. (1992) *Education for Citizenship in a Multi-cultural Society.* London: Cassell.

MacAskill, E. and Carvel, J. (1996) Moral crusade gathers pace. *Guardian,* 22 October.

Morrison, K. (1994) *Implementing Cross-Curricular Themes.* London: David Fulton.

Murphy, P. and Irvine, C. (1988) Baker argues for a school values code. *Yorkshire Post,* 14 October.

Murris, K. (1992) *Teaching Philosophy with Picture Books.* London: Infonet Publications.

National Curriculum Council (1990) *Education for Citizenship.* Curriculum Guidance 8. York: NCC.

Pike, G. and Selby, D. (1988) *Global Teacher, Global Learner.* London: Hodder and Stoughton.

Prescott, M. (1997) Schools to teach good citizenship. *The Sunday Times,* 25 May.

Randle, D. (1989) *Teaching Green: A Parent's Guide to Education for Life on Earth.* London: Green Print.

Rogers, P. (1992) Education for the international responsibilities of citizenship. In E. Baglin Jones and N. Jones (eds) *Education for Citizenship: Ideas and Perspectives for Cross-Curricular Study.* London: Kogan Page.

Rowe, D. and Newton, J. (eds) (1994) *You, Me, Us! Social and Moral Responsibility for Schools.* London: Citizenship Foundation/The Home Office.

Rowley, C. and Toye, N. (1996) Learning to listen, beginning to understand: the skills of philosophical inquiry. In M. Steiner (ed.) *Developing the Global Teacher.* Oakhill: Trentham Books.

Selby, D. (1995) *Earthkind: A Teachers' Handbook on Humane Education*. Oakhill: Trentham Books.

Sharrock, D. and Linton, M. (1988) Electronic tags hailed as part of assault on 'dependency culture'. *Guardian*, 13 October.

Speaker's Commission on Citizenship (1990) *Encouraging Citizenship*. London: HMSO.

Steiner, M. (ed.) (1996) *Developing the Global Teacher*. Oakhill: Trentham Books.

Thomson, A. and O'Leary, J. (1996) Carey's moral crusade upsets schools. *The Times*, 6 July.

Tomlinson, S. (1992) Citizenship and minorities. In E. Baglin Jones and N. Jones (eds) *Education for Citizenship: Ideas and Perspectives for Cross-Curricular Study*. London: Kogan Page.

Troyna, B. (1993) *Racism and Education*. Buckingham: Open University Press.

Verma, G. K. and Pumfrey, P. D. (eds) (1994) *Cultural Diversity and the Curriculum, Vol. 4, Cross-Curricular Contexts, Themes and Dimensions in Primary Schools*. London: Falmer Press.

White, P. (1996) *Civic Virtues and Public Schooling: Educating Citizens for a Democratic Society*. New York: Teachers College Press.

Young, S. (1996) Party leaders leap on Lawrence bandwagon. *The Times Educational Supplement*, 25 October.

12 Values Education and the Humanization of the Curriculum

DAVID ASPIN AND JUDITH CHAPMAN

I

Education has been defined by Warnock (1978) as being largely concerned with the undertaking of preparing our younger generation to face the challenges of the future. This preparation involves at least three elements: preparation for the world of work; preparation for the life of imagination; and preparation for the life of virtue. We want to argue that each of these will have its typical excellence and that each of them can be addressed within the framework of programmes for quality and effectiveness in schooling.

This chapter will concentrate on the idea of educating for excellence in the life of virtue. This we might delineate as including the realm of moral, political and personal values, particularly those obtaining in relations between ourselves and others. These values are perhaps best exemplified in the social principles and institutional practices embodied in modern forms of democracy and the part played by citizens in them.

We follow Aristotle in maintaining that the principal human excellence is that of rationality. However, following Wittgenstein, we see this rationality as embodied and deployed in the various forms of human discourse, language and communication – in all the many styles and modes in which they have been developed and articulated. We argue that our understanding of values and of the language of 'ought' is as objective and cognitive an enterprise as any other area of human rationality and communication; that both can therefore be learnt; and that such learning can be subjected to rational and objective appraisal, criticism and amendment.

As against holders of subjectivist doctrines of various kinds on these matters, we maintain that it does make sense to talk of excellence in the matter of values, without in the least countenancing or proposing a view of value infallibility or absolutism, and that values education demands and indeed underlines the appropriateness of encouraging individual responsiveness, spontaneity, sensitivity – as well as imagination and creativity – in matters of culture and value. We support the view that talk of values, inasmuch as it *is* objective and cognitive, is as intelligible as any other realm of human discourse. Furthermore we contend that the centrality of and preoccupation with value matters and concerns are now so important for our community's life, that schools have a positive responsibility to undertake the education of the community's young in preparation for engagement in those valued activities that will play a pivotal part in their lives as private individuals and as citizens.

We therefore advocate values education as a proper subject for inclusion in any set of proposals, such as those being currently considered by the OECD, to redefine and to humanize the curriculum. We believe that the objectivity and rationality of value discourse in general, and moral and aesthetic awareness and understanding in particular, require schools as educating institutions to work out ways in which they can provide an effective education in this most important realm of all human activities.

Schools and the educators within them will best do this by showing how value concerns, and the social and moral relations in which those concerns are embodied and exercised, are expressions of larger-scale conceptions of life and value. The character of the individual judgements and activities in which we engage in our discussions on matters of value and in our moral relationships is, as Best (1992) argues, determined at the level of the culture of a community – that network of language patterns, social practices and moral conventions that give human beings their most fundamental conceptions of the meaning and value of life.

It is therefore among the community's most important concerns to engage in the moral enterprise of preparing the coming generation for a future that, it is hoped, will be better than that which we received from our forebears, and one that will allow greater access to sources of individual and social well-being, flourishing and advancement than those we have already enjoyed. Attention to and promotion of this aspiration will be seen as best developed in a cooperative relationship subsisting and operating between the community, the family and the individual student; the forum in which that relationship gets greatest point of purchase and finds greatest opportunity for expression will be in the informal educational surroundings of the family and the formal educational enterprise of the school. For it is in the interplay between both the family and the school that the greatest number and most wide-ranging opportunities for personal and social growth, development and enrichment will be offered and savoured.

This ethical impulse, we believe, finds especial expression, with respect to the idea of education for citizenship, in the concept of democracy. We take the fundamental presuppositions and values of this particular model of government to be almost entirely moral in character: democracy is that form of life to which adults as autonomous moral agents are necessarily committed in the arrangement of their social relations, the institutionalization of their political principles, and the construction of satisfying and enriching patterns of personal life choices, above and beyond any other.

That impulse is further animated by the concern of modern participative democracies to address and cater for the different needs and interests of the various communities of which they are constituted. Among the prime principles of democracy are those of tolerance, freedom and equality; attention to the moral and political obligations generated by regard for those principles becomes particularly important in the case of those democracies containing a plurality of different cultures and communities. For the place, value and potential contributions made to the polity by those cultures and communities to be acknowledged, allowed space for development, and understood puts a premium upon the acceptance of their plurality as constituting an important part of the overall fabric of that society. Education for citizenship in such an environment will pay special regard to the need for tolerance and intercultural understanding.

An emphasis upon such principles and the work of schools and other educational institutions in promoting them, can contribute significantly to the quality of life for all members of our community. It is for this reason that attention to values issues and concerns in the programmes of those planning for effectiveness in schooling is vital and indispensable. The dominant imperatives here are functions of the consequences that flow from our communities' acceptance of the need for an education that will prepare generations of their future citizens for meeting all the exigencies of, and capitalizing upon, the opportunities offered by their future life as citizens. The obligations and opportunities of that life are particularly manifested in the various institutions of the various forms of political arrangement in which wide ranges of cooperative (and competing) individual and plural forms of life, with all their characteristic value concerns, can be made available, balanced and allowed expression in a modern participative and multi-cultural democracy.

II

Stress on and promotion of the ideas and goals lying behind education for citizenship require the values of the democratic form of life to be explored, elucidated and incorporated as a proper subject for inclusion in any set of proposals to redefine and humanize the curriculum. For it is especially these values that our community deems that schools should teach and at the acquisition of which our students should aim: communities want students to develop, as one of the outcomes of their schooling, the ability to talk, judge and act with a considerable measure of knowledge, understanding and insight on vital matters relating to community accord and personal fulfilment.

An acceptance of the possibility of objectivity in matters of value and culture will allow students to develop the requisite degree of maturity for these purposes and schools to increase their standing as quality institutions by working out curriculum guidelines, ways of teaching, and modes of organization, in which they can provide an effective education in this most important realm of all human affairs. In these matters schools can offer educational assistance and leadership, and thus contribute to the improvement of quality in the lives of a community's inhabitants.

This discussion on values education is therefore concerned *inter alia* with an education for citizenship in a democracy, and the ways in which this can provide a rationale and programme for the humanization of the curriculum and for the increase of quality schooling. We see this as a vitally necessary undertaking in a time when the major thrust of curriculum activity in many countries is driven by economic imperatives, the demands of technocratic rationality, and mechanistic versions of school effectiveness. We believe that the current preoccupation with these concerns, to the exclusion of many others, threatens the equally, if not more, important values of moral awareness, interpersonal sensitivity and cross-cultural understanding in the home, the workplace and the wider community.

We want to argue that the best forum for the promotion of such valued concerns is via the democratic form of life, to which we believe we are all necessarily bound, in virtue of our epistemic commitments and intellectual engagement in the pursuit of knowledge, discourse and truth – the chief stock in trade of educating institutions in the modern liberal state. We hold that this commitment necessarily issues in the induction of our young people into those modes of speech, realms of knowledge, and networks of interpersonal relations that constitute our lives as human beings. These find especial expression in the various ways and means in which a community decides to institutionalize, organize and administer its educational systems, institutions and schools. It is within the democratic school that young people will receive the best possible preparation to take their place as mature and well-informed citizens of a participative democracy (cf Chapman, Froumin and Aspin 1995).

III

At this point we might find it useful to consider what constitutes a value, or set of values. We suspect we are all aware that the question of the existence and nature of a logical domain of 'value', and its relationship to a (supposedly separate) world of 'fact', has been the subject of considerable philosophical controversy over the last fifty years and still provokes discussion.

This discussion has been, perhaps, nowhere more in evidence than in the field of educational research

and theory, where, until relatively recently, the answer to the question raised above has been given decisively by empiricists, positivists and verificationists of various kinds, most of whom have elevated the psychometric and quantificatory modes of investigation as the paradigm for all educational enquiry. For most of those working within this paradigm, the realm of 'values', if indeed such things were deemed to exist at all, was very little talked about. 'Values' were regarded merely as subjective reactions or idiosyncratic expressions of individual feelings; 'value judgements' were regarded as logically equivalent to an expression or evincement of personal taste. By such people values were held to be separate from the realm of 'facts' and generally, as such, beyond rational enquiry. By some, values were allowed a limited credence as causal factors among those motivating conduct; by these people it was thought that, though values themselves were beyond investigation, the effect of people's values on their actions could be neutrally perceived and factually described as phenomena observable in individual behaviour or inter-personal interactions in the social world. And to give such descriptions the methods of the natural or social sciences were and indeed by some continue to be judged as entirely appropriate.

However, recent work in the epistemology and methodology of the natural and social sciences has moved decisively away from the emphasis upon measurement and the so-called 'value-neutral' description of so-called totally objective 'facts'. This emphasis was typical of an earlier era in research, when workers believed completely in the academic tenability of the empiricist paradigm and tended only to design, develop and apply research projects and instruments exclusively based upon it. Indeed that view had already been shown long ago by Dewey (1907: 309) to rest upon a fallacy, which he described thus:

> The fallacy of orthodox logical empiricism is . . . [that] it supposes that there can be 'givens', sensations, percepts, etc., prior to and independent of thought or ideas, and that thought or ideas may be had by some kind of compounding or separating of the givens. But it is the very nature of sensation of perception . . . already to be, in and of itself, something which is so internally fractionalised or perplexed as to suggest and to require an idea, a meaning.

What Dewey called a fallacy was attacked as one

of the two philosophical dogmas exposed to telling refutation by W. V. Quine (1971), and ably redirected towards the rebuttal of some key theories of educational policy and administration by Evers and Lakomski (1991). One of the basic tenets of that dogma, according to Quine, is the positing of an absolute divide between what are held to be the 'neutral', factual and 'value-free' statements – regarded as distinctive of mathematics and the natural sciences, which are thus paradigms of 'objectivity' – and those of other such realms of discourse as ethics, politics and aesthetics, which are held to be non-factual, value-laden and irredeemably subjective.

We take it that this tendency has now been decisively refuted by the powerful epistemological arguments advanced against such notions by Popper (1969), Lakatos (1976) and Lukes (1982), and has been replaced by a view of science that goes beyond both factualism and relativism (cf. also Bernstein 1983). This view of science rests upon the remark of the French physicist Pierre Duhem (1914) that any set of empirical phenomena is always under-determined, in the sense that it will admit any of a number of interpretations and explanations, not all of them necessarily compatible with each other. This makes science less an activity of inductive probability and much more one of theory comparison and competition; crucially, it means that there are now many more models of valid research than that restricted to positivist and verificationist paradigms.

Most important, the post-empiricist approach in particular has made it possible for theorists and researchers working in the field of policy and administration to speak intelligently and validly about the realm of values and, in doing so, to move decisively beyond the narrow empiricism of the positivists who dominated the field up until the 1980s, and the relativism of much work during the course of the 1980s that was so heavily influenced by subjectivists working in the interpretative paradigm.

The post-empiricist approach to research might be designated pragmatist and anti-essentialist: it deems the provision of millenarian answers to difficult questions to be not merely practically but logically impossible, and the production of uncontentious theories and definitions of concepts to be a pipe-dream. Having rejected absolutism and eschewed relativism, post-empiricist researchers are therefore seeking to arrive at some set

of provisional theory-constructs, that will *pro tempore* resist falsification, and to work out and operate with a set of *ad hoc* agreements that will constitute a pragmatic consensus which can then be applied to the solution of problems that are in principle amenable to treatment (cf. Aspin and Chapman 1994).

Such approaches to analysis, research and policy-construction enable us to transcend the narrow empiricism, neo-Marxist cynicism and post-modernist relativism that has been applied to, required of, or discernible in much previous academic work in the field of policy, curriculum and administrative studies. Instead, the post-empiricist approach enables us to address the question of values in a systematic and rigorous way. It provides us with a method for identifying values and for teasing out their presuppositions and implications, as they exist in the concrete life and daily reality of the school and the community. This method allows us to ask whether our intermediate theories are defensible, to test them against other bodies of knowledge and theory, and, in so doing, to generate new understandings and areas of agreement from which recommendations and prescriptions for useful and relevant educational policies and administrative practices may be drawn.

IV

The foregoing considerations enable us to reject a number of theses about facts and values. These include the supposed separation of discourse relating to matters of fact and value; of subjective and objective appraisals and judgements; of descriptive and normative uses of language; and of the separation of human rationality from the world of feeling. They also enable us to dispose of the long-held empiricist contention that the logics of mathematics and the natural sciences offer us paradigm examples of objectivity and verifiability, to the standards of and requirements generated by which all educational undertakings and curriculum provision should conform as regards intellectual respectability and educational acceptance.

On the contrary, we argue that the main burden of the counter-arguments to the now largely discredited thesis of empiricism has served to show that there is no such distinction as that supposed to subsist between fact and value, or between policy examination and policy formation (or, come to that, between science and philosophy). For Quine, Popper, and many others, all thought, language and enquiry are inescapably and *ab initio* theory-laden, far from value-free, and a mixture of both descriptive and normative elements. Indeed, argued Kovesi (1967), in all discourse and enquiry, there is an unbroken continuum, at one end of which lies 'fact' and the other end of which lies 'value'. 'Description', for such thinkers, is a way of 'evaluating' reality; 'evaluation' is a way of 'describing' states of affairs.

Two useful distinctions help us to see how inextricably inter-connected such activities as 'description' and 'evaluation' really are. One of these is that made by Anscombe (1958) between what she calls 'brute facts' and 'institutional facts', according to which mere objects in haphazard relation are transformed into patterns of meaning and significance by their enclosure in institutional surroundings of various sorts. Without the institution and values of banking and monetary exchange, for example, a coin is just a lump of metal; without the institution and values of marriage, all we have is two people holding hands standing in front of a person dressed in white; and it is because of the objective meanings and values instantiated in such institutions that I may hand over considerable amounts of my own money to a complete stranger, or offer my abdomen to an unknown person holding a sharp piece of metal. This distinction was employed by Searle (1969) to show how, in matters relating to the making of promises and the incurring of obligations, descriptive and normative uses of language collapse into each other.

Searle's reference to the institutions of 'promising' and 'owing' remind us of the crucial distinction made by Austin (1962) between what he called 'constative' and 'performative' uses of language. The former we employ simply to inform people about states of affairs ('Today is Wednesday'; 'The Pope is blessing the crowds'; 'I believe Australia will win'); the latter we deploy as forms of action, in order to get people to do things or to bring about particular outcomes ('I congratulate you'; 'I award you the degree'; 'I bequeath to you all my property'). It is, of course, the latter that plays greatest part in our daily lives, to the point at which Austin eventually came to the conclusion that all our uses of language are 'performative', in that they are shot through with the kinds of intention, aspiration and

volition that lie behind the whole of human action. To that extent they serve as injunctions, prescriptions and evaluations of various kinds. All that is necessary, then, is to engage in some kind of linguistic anthropology to distinguish between the ends aimed at and the values being commended in and by the different categories of speech-act that we perform.

Such arguments permit us (Evers and Lakomski 1991, Aspin and Chapman 1994) to develop a new approach to the identification of values and the elucidation of problems in educational policy and administration. For on the above view, all our talk on these matters is conceived of as being in itself a 'theory', embodying a complex 'web of belief', shot through differentially with descriptive and evaluative elements, according to the contexts and purposes for which our theories of education, policy and administrative action are brought to bear and applied in our world. In this enterprise, we do not attempt to reduce everything to some absolute foundations of 'fact' and 'value', 'theory' and 'practice', or 'policy' and 'implementation', in the (vain) attempt to educe some 'analyses' of concepts and theories, that can be completely 'correct' or 'true'; or to produce some fundamental matters of indisputable research 'findings', about the objectivity and existence of which there can be no dispute.

What is important in these matters of working out the value or effectiveness of policies, and endeavouring to achieve excellence in them, is not to establish which analyses are 'true', which facts are 'correct', or which 'values' are universally or even widely shared, but rather, in our endeavours to identify and promote effectiveness and quality in schooling and education generally, to query which theories, which beliefs and which values we should be least willing to give up, not simply on which (unexaminable) tenets we should rest our educational policies and theories. The identification and examination of *values* is clearly therefore an ineliminable part of this process.

Conceived of in this way, an enquiry into the effectiveness of any policy or programme of education is like any scientific enquiry – an unending quest to develop and articulate theories dealing with problems, determining and predicting advance in a particular field, such as education for citizenship, and then, by critical theory appraisal and comparison, to show which of them is better and for what purpose.

V

For the purposes of this discussion, we shall take the term 'values' to refer to those ideas, conventions, principles, rules, objects, products, activities or procedures that people accept, agree to, treasure, cherish, prefer, incline towards and place importance upon. Such things they make objects of admiration, high levels of aspiration or goals of endeavour in their lives and commend them so to others. This last comment enables us to argue, as against subjectivists and relativists of various persuasions, that value judgements are different logically from, and much more than, mere matters of taste and individual preference. We see values, and the judgements deriving from them, functioning as the rules, conventions or principles implicit in certain modes of communicating and manners of proceeding, that furnish and act as a *standard of discrimination* (a criterion) against which other communications and procedures can be measured and assessed, and ranking high in a scale of comparison among objects etc. of the same class. Their interpersonal significance we regard as commendatory, action-guiding and generally prescriptive.

An examination of value discourse seems to suggest that there is a number of different kinds of value: moral, religious, aesthetic, social, political, educational, technical, economic, and so on, though some of these (for example social, political, economic, educational) are claimed (by Aristotle, among others) to be sub-classes of one prime value – the moral. It is right that we should raise the question of whether all these various species of value are indeed distinct and logically different (as ethical value is, for instance, clearly different from the aesthetic – or so it seems to us, at any rate) or whether all forms of value and value discourse do not all in the final analysis come down to being species of the one genus – the moral. There is also the further important question of how such judgements are to be justified – if indeed they can be and, if so, by what kinds of argument.

This last question we can leave for the time being. We might for the moment simply advance the view that, so far as the values of citizenship are concerned, they seem to us to include a number of different elements – the social, political, economic and technical *inter alia* – but, above and beyond all these, to be primarily *moral* in character.

To typify the main features of moral discourse concerning the nature of values for citizenship, and following Anscombe and Austin, we should like to argue that the commitment of human beings to the various nexus of obligation and patterns of individual and interpersonal significance is best exemplified in our use of language and our development of individual and community relations in the institutional forms of various kinds in which our values and systems of value are instantiated. That commitment starts with our birth and increases as we come to maturity. Being the creatures we are, and living as we have to under the limitations of the natural laws and the social conditions and constraints surrounding us, we could not possibly survive, much less flourish, without being enmeshed in and having to conform to the protocols, conventions and norms of the various institutions human beings have conceived, established and improved, in order to stabilize their identity, understand and control their environment, and endeavour to give some point and purpose to their lives.

The chief of these institutions is found in the various forms of communicative interchange that human beings have articulated, cultivated and refined as ways and means of rendering their common experience of the world they share intelligible and variously significant. It is in and through this institution above all that they have found it possible to form and give expression to their progressively deepening and increasingly sophisticated conceptions of their lives and all their main concerns. In this institution all the elements of meaning, value and intention combine, interact and coalesce in an inextricable enmeshment. These enmeshments are then played out at the level of the community and in the various forms of relationship, institutions and agencies, in and by means of which the life of that community is carried on.

This encourages us to claim, as against some moral theorists such as John Wilson (1970, 1990), that we do not simply choose to 'accept' or to 'play the game' of morality and that this 'choosing' depends in turn upon our 'acceptance' of the institutions in which morality is characteristically exercised. We argue instead that, in virtue of the kind of creatures we are and the characteristic form of life we share, and given the ways in which, as fellow constituents in it, we explicate it and elaborate upon it between ourselves. The presence, function and coercive imperatives of sets of values and regulative principles are part and parcel of the language and institutions into which we, in our community, are gradually initiated. To change the metaphor, they are part of their whole warp and weft, of the inherited integuments and valued traditions of which we in turn become bearers and beneficiaries.

Values and values education, therefore, (and *a fortiori*, given that political and educational judgements are a function of our commitments to certain moral preconceptions, the democratic institutions in which these find expression) are all concerned with helping us to understand that human life is beset with obligations of one sort and another. As rational beings, sharing with others in that particular form of social arrangement and set of cultures and relationships that we call a community, human beings are bound up in these kinds of obligations and responsibilities, and their observance of these requirements is exhibited in their enmeshments in, and observance of, the various rules and conventions governing all the occasions of social intercourse in which they are called upon, as *actors*, to participate. Nowhere is this more called for than in their responding to the calls of the duties and responsibilities that their role as citizens requires of them.

Attending to and conducting themselves in accordance with such principles becomes especially important and demanding when those communities embody a diversity of cultures, with norms and conventions, that sometimes overlap and intersect with those of other cultures, that also sometimes do not overlap but are consonant with them, and that sometimes also are dissonant from them. In such a case, citizenship places additional burdens of tolerance and mutual acceptance and regard upon those possessed of it, which are nonetheless of vital importance socially, politically and morally, for being different and sometimes difficult to understand, much less accept.

One of the aims of values education, therefore, will be to give us a knowledge of the rules and principles that function in this form of social relationship and set of institutions, and to seek to produce in us, as citizens in it, a grasp of its underlying principles, together with the ability to apply these rules intelligently, and to develop the settled disposition to do so (cf. Aspin 1975). For without such an education in values for citizenship, we should all be significantly impoverished in our attempt to come to terms with the exigencies of our life as citizens and as individuals, and to exercise our informed choice in order to make that process manageable, tolerable, and enjoyable. Certainly, such an educa-

tion will help to make us see that our life in the variegated and many-cultured communities that we share with our fellow-citizens is capable of being improved upon, and that just possibly the conjoint exercise of our intellectual resources, imagination and creativity can help to add quality to them and make them better and worthy of support and engagement.

VI

It is this last realization that has a special bearing upon the question of how we are to characterize values in the relationships people have, and the institutions in which they develop them, when it comes down to ways in which, as members of the community, we institutionalize our civil arrangements in that form of chosen self-governance called 'democracy'. This is a difficult but vitally important task in a plural society when such a democracy encompasses a plethora of cultures and values, not all of which sit easily side by side and between which there is often considerable tension, not to say confrontation (cf. Zec 1980, Walkling 1980, Phillips-Bell 1981 and Brent 1982).

This is especially true, with respect to political values, in the case of the current contention between radically different theories and policies of economic development and direction purporting to offer unique access to and a guaranteed means of securing national self-sufficiency, power and advancement. It is also particularly important to the attempted resolution of such matters of cardinal importance as the constitutional arrangements of any nation state, its relationships with other countries, particularly those of different political orientation or religious or cultural make-up, in its geographic region or economic ambit. And this becomes all the more pressing when such a state is still developing a sense of national identity, when it is composed of a number of different cultures and communities.

We believe that it is possible to apply objective criteria of intelligibility to various public institutions and practices, of a kind to which a value can be attached, that transcends the private preoccupations, sectional interests or hegemonic ambitions of those who are already on the inside of them and employ them instrumentally for their own purposes. Among, and indeed presupposed by such institutions, are those symbolic codes of intersubjective agreement, communication and significance in and by which the community can begin to form, develop and appraise its various modes of communicative interchange, cultural practices, and social relations. From among these, a degree of consensus may be arrived at concerning those forms of life to which the community ascribes particular importance, and with the provision and promotion of which the work of its educating agencies might most reasonably be thought to be concerned. In cooperation with the community, schools then make a selection of those preferred activities they all wish to select for inclusion in the content of its schools' curricula.

Perhaps chief among these are those modes of discourse and cognitive style that we discern as central to their identity, and that we observe as embodied in their use of the languages of science, technology, culture, the arts, politics, morality or religion, and their typical beliefs, standards and conventions – all those matters of life and death in and by which their community's character has been established and may now be comprehended, and its preferred patterns of culture and value articulated, confirmed and extended or amended. The community's concerns for the perpetuation, protection and promotion of its citizens's political powers and responsibilities, cultural and religious freedoms, and rights to individual and social justice will be disclosed, expressed, and given force in the various forms of communication, action and relationship for which its institutions have been established and developed, and to the work and success of which its citizens are presumed to be committed.

One of these institutions – indeed perhaps the most important – is that of education. For it is only in, by and through the institution of education that individuals and future citizens can learn to communicate with their fellows in discourse relevant to the understanding, appraisal and tentative resolution of problems they share, and the exploration, elaboration and exploitation of the possibilities of community improvement and individual enrichment they can envisage and for which they can plan. The requirements this institution generates necessarily entail an education in all the various modes and styles of public discourse, in which these problems and possibilities can be communicated about, addressed, analysed and decided upon (cf. Hirst 1965a). Associated with this will be the attempt to impart an understanding of and a willingness to accept and work with all the various

public institutions, to the continuance, standards and specifications of which they will also have to conform.

Such a wide spread of knowledge and understanding will be crucial to the life of us citizens, inasmuch as all must be prepared to handle the paradox that it is public institutions, according to the requirements of which we have both to respond and be accountable, that both constrain us yet also civilize and liberate us. Our submission to and yet enjoyment of them serves to open innumerable avenues of opportunity to us and to the whole community of which we are a part. Learning to communicate, conform and take advantage of our society's institutions will enable us not only to manage our lives effectively, but also give us the powers to take advantage of the opportunities offered by them and in that way to add untold increments of value and enrichment to them.

That all these forms of discourse – culture, the arts, politics, religion, morality, and justice – and the beliefs and values expressed in them, have equal objectivity and significance with other forms of communication and cognition, such as science, is a contention on which their claims to be included on the curricula of educating institutions may, at least in part, be based. For our part, we wish to maintain that making and defending a value judgement – appraising an object artistically, for instance, or deciding whether to give to charity, or so approving of a particular political programme as to vote for its adoption – is quite as objective an undertaking as framing an hypothesis to explain an apparent anomaly in science, or developing a novel interpretation of some event in history, or deciding upon which form of statistics to employ in describing our current economic situation. All use different, though overlapping forms of description and evaluation; all call up some of our deepest and most cherished beliefs; all involve recourse to deeper values. And, above all, all have abiding and overriding importance at various points in our lives, for the different purposes and commitments for which we variously employ them.

VII

In 1994 we published a study on the question of quality and excellence in schooling (Aspin and Chapman 1994). What emerged from our study of *the use of these terms* in the educational community appears to indicate a wide measure of agreement that in both there are certain 'core' values. These core values are widely observed to subsist in, and then to be looked for, as typical features of the 'quality', 'good', or 'effective' school, and, when found or agreed upon, are seen as ends to be aimed at or values worth promoting in the activities and undertakings of schools. These values may then help to structure and define the direction and aiming points of educational policy and practice.

Among the core values of quality schooling we might point to the following:

- Schools should give their students access to, and the opportunity to acquire, practise and apply those bodies and kinds of knowledge, competences, and attitudes, that will prepare them for life in today's complex society.
- Schools should have a concern for, and promote the value of, excellence and high standards of individual and institutional aspiration, achievement and conduct in all aspects of its activities.
- Schools should be democratic, equitable and just.
- Schools should humanize our students and give them an introduction into and offer them opportunities for acquiring the values that will be crucial in their personal and social development.
- Schools should develop in students a sense of independence and of their own worth as human beings, having some confidence in their ability to contribute to the society of which they are a part, in appropriate social, political and moral ways.
- Schools should prepare our future citizens to conduct their interpersonal relationships with each other, in ways that shall not be inimical to the health and stability of society or the individuals that comprise it.
- Schools should prepare students to have a concern for the cultural vitality, as well as the economic enrichment, of the community in which they will ultimately play a part, promoting the enjoyment of artistic and expressive experience in addition to the acquisition of knowledge and its employment.
- Schools should conjoin education for personal autonomy and education for community enmeshment and social contribution, enabling each student to enrich the society of which he/she is to become a part as a giver, an enlarger

and an enhancer, as well as being an inheritor and beneficiary.

These are cited only as illustrations of some of the values of quality schooling; no doubt there are others. But our research suggests that, whatever other functions a quality school might be said to perform, with the promotion of these values at least it is vitally concerned.

As an aside, we might point out that this list constitutes a somewhat different set of criteria for quality or effective schooling from that which emerges from studies using a strictly quantitative approach, stemming from the Mr Gradgrinds of the educational community (Chapman 1993). Such an approach, that has dominated American and some European models of school effectiveness, runs the risk – and indeed, in the present political climate, it faces the danger – of creating a situation in which the outcomes of education are officially articulated in such a way that the curriculum concentrates on and becomes narrowly related to and prescriptive of exclusively instrumental and economic goals. Indeed, by definition such an approach can concentrate on only those goals that are readily measurable in numerical terms, and these are much more likely to be amenable to instrumental concerns and the values of utility only.

As against the values stressed in that utilitarian approach, however, the point that emerges strongly from our enquiry is that central to the concept of quality schooling is an emphasis upon values much more widely conceived and much less extrinsic in character. What schools are looking for these days is an approach to curriculum that will concentrate, not merely upon vocational competence, economic capacity and management skills, but also, and much more, upon the *humane* values. These comprise such matters as an understanding and appreciation of our society's history, cultural heritage and civic traditions; sympathy for and a willingness to work and live with other people of many different backgrounds, interests and lifestyles; spontaneity, consideration and sensitivity in our interpersonal relations; communication and courtesy; the arts and the special opportunities they offer for imagination and creativity; the importance of ethics in business, sport and personal relations; the search for meaning offered by religion, humanism and other valued life-stances.

Anyone looking into schools' regard for and work in these areas of interest will quickly discover that schools are as aware as anyone of the dangers posed to the values of humanity and individual worth by the depersonalizing effects of large-scale and overbearing concern for the values of economic efficiency and effectiveness. What schools, educators and very many parents want – as well or even instead of a preoccupation with sheerly economic concerns – are educational policies that put economic necessities, and the vocational competences they require, into their proper place within a panoply of other concerns, the chief of which centre upon the values of human dignity, community harmony and social justice.

VIII

The drive for such humane values goes further than merely ensuring that they are offered at various points in curriculum programmes and that our students are simply made aware of and given some limited exposure to them. We believe that the principal reason and motivating force behind our community's increasing concern to see such things taught in our schools incorporates a dual value emphasis. This is an emphasis that is especially pertinent to our enquiry into the forms and goals of our drive for education in citizenship.

One part of that stress in value is, as R. F. Dearden so clearly perceived (Dearden 1975), upon the development of autonomous individuals, with their own powers of independent judgement and the capacity to be self-motivated and self-starting in action, and this implies practice and engagement in appropriate sets of activities; the other is the realization that such autonomous agents must at the same time – and necessarily – be taken up into patterns and networks of mutual inter-relation with other individuals and with the whole community, in all its economic, political and social aspects.

Such inter-relationships form and structure the set of agreements and conventions about an inner core of values (some might say, a value-system) that then, in their totality and interdependence, function to provide us with the various kinds of insight, capacities and strengths needed to deal with the difficulties, problems, tensions and controversies that so beset the field.

This helps us appreciate that the problems relating to the investigation of the concept of values in quality schooling – one that will be effective in giving a good education for citizenship – are not only of a metaphilosophical kind: they also require discussion and agreement at the substantive level. Discussion about autonomy and mutuality translated into the social setting immediately involves reference to questions concerning the ways in which we wish individuals to be, and which form of society we consider will best facilitate their development.

For example, discussions between proponents of social justice, viewed as equality of treatment or of opportunity, and advocates of individual excellence, resting on and incorporating a requirement of complete personal freedom, embody a difference of value judgements of a markedly substantive kind. These differences are most obviously articulated and then transposed into a highly-contentious but binding political reality, that gets its most powerful point of purchase when we come to translate them into the institutions, relationships and practices that make up and give meaning to our lives. One such arena of democratic engagement, for instance, would involve us in the attempt to understand and adjudicate upon the claims of political parties whose programmes are calculated best to express those differences and translate them into social operation; another would be to try to understand and have some sympathy for the different forms of religious, cultural or artistic practice carried on by members of the various communities constituting the social whole, with the aim, not merely of tolerating them, but of seeing whether there was anything of value in them by which our own lives, social relationships and cultural practices could possibly be enriched.

The key questions in values education and quality schooling for citizenship, therefore, are ones not merely of meta-ethics but also concern the form and content of our normative systems of values, codes of ethics and standards of conduct, that shall be translated into particular educational policies and become normative for individuals and society. In our debates about the future of education these questions should be of central concern and should precede any discussions about the actual procedures and practices of organizing and administering a quality education, such as, for instance, whether our administrative structures and financial arrangements shall be decentralized, delegated and devolved to management at the local school site. Our contention is, rather, that agreement on the substance of the values and agenda, which shall underpin our educational norms, conventions and arrangements, must logically come before any discussion of the ways and means of their institutional realization. It is only, we maintain, when we have secured some form of agreement about values and their substance, that we can then tackle the further problems of implementation and operation.

Both parts of this task include reference to the address on and resolution of a number of difficulties and tensions – all of them quite crucial to the undertaking of educating our future generations for citizenship:

- the tension between providing access for all students to a high quality integrated curriculum for individual empowerment and civic responsibility by participating fully in all aspects of the life of the school *and* encouraging a high standard of specialized knowledge and training for those most capable of it;
- the danger that an emphasis on accountability might distort teaching and the curriculum towards an emphasis on the readily identifiable and testable, *at the expense of* longer term and more abstract goals of education, such as an increase in students' awareness of the need for social involvement, moral responsibility and cultural sensitivity;
- the tension between respect for the needs and concerns of the individual person or their culture, *and* the perceived need for some kind of agreed forum in which there can be movement towards increasing social harmony and a sense of national unity on matters of vital political, economic or moral importance;
- the tension between developing a more self-conscious regard for and promotion of the rights and freedoms of different groups, cultures and creeds in a plural community, *and* the realization and willingness to acknowledge and bear all the different costs involved in redressing racial, religious and ethnic discrimination and exploitation, in ways that will provide a ground for reconciliation in the community overall.

It is for this reason that educators planning for an induction into citizenship in modern culturally-plural societies will have to take into account the clear differences in political and ethical orientation operating between parties debating the best way to ensure quality in schooling. These have to do with the commitments that people have to a set of beliefs regarding the nature of human beings, the most

desirable form of society, and the ways in which they can best arrange and institutionalize their relationships for the various purposes they have in mind. Such differences of vision and perspective are fundamental to our conceptions of an education for quality: the relationship between individual and community; the idea of education as a 'transforming power' or a 'privileged possession' and the notion of education as a 'Commodity' or a 'Public Service'; the provision, resourcing and management of educational institutions, goods and services; and our response to questions associated with the restructuring of education and the devolution of decision-making to schools.

As a modest contribution to at least one part of that debate, we should wish, in contrast to the notion of education as a commodity, to contrapose the notion of *education as a public good*, access to which is a prerequisite for informed and effective participation by all citizens in a democratic society. This immediately becomes a question for equity and social justice: acceptance of the requirement implies that we make access to such an education available to citizens of whatever ethnic origin, cultural background or religious commitment; and where such people have difficulty in securing such access, that we then take steps to ensure that they receive it, by different forms of affirmative action or special educational programmes. The same may be said of such services as health, welfare, and housing, all of which, with education, constitute the infrastructure upon which individuals may hope to construct, realize and work at achieving their own versions of a life of quality. It is upon this notion of education as a public good that education for all children was made available in many countries. And in the modern world, in circumstances of so many and such complex demands and difficulties – economic, social and cultural – with which our future generations will have to cope, it is this principle which, we argue, we should be least willing to give up.

Certainly no-one would suggest for a moment that education, health and welfare services are 'free' and require no resources; they have to be funded and supported financially and in a myriad other ways. But these are services that are vital and indispensable to the nature, quality and operation of the society in which we all live and as citizens have a share. Our point is that individuals can only develop as autonomous agents fit to participate in our modern pluralist societies if they are sufficiently informed, prepared and predisposed; if they are secure, healthy and well-fed; and if they have the minimal physical and domestic conditions for perpetuating existence. In our view, the whole of our society has a direct interest in securing, providing and safe-guarding those prerequisite conditions and services on the basis of the contributions that all of us who are to benefit from them shall see it is in our interest to make to the common wealth in a common exchequer.

IX

In addressing such questions as those posed above, what must be noted, of course, is that the social world is much more than a complex conjunction of aggregations of individual human beings. The coalescence and increasing interactions of such beings evolve into an entity of an organic and dynamic character, the totality of which is much greater and much more transformative than merely being the sum of its parts. There is, we are saying, such a thing as society, and it is a heterogeneously evolved organism, the continuing life of which is necessary for the life of its constituent elements. We do not live, in fact we could not start our existence or survive, if we lived on desert islands.

Indeed, the meanings and values of personal freedom and individual choice, so prized and exalted by exponents of the market philosophy, only become possible as an outgrowth of the knowledge and powers that other members of society have opened up to us. It is these that give us an intimation of the complex range and balance of the choices that are available to us, and what choosing, and the calculation of its consequences, might mean. For all of us this comes about through interaction with other members of our community; for most of us this means that the full range of information and structured leading towards the concept of autonomous decision-making has first been made available through our schooling experience.

It is a paradox of our existence that our autonomy requires the work of other persons. It is given to us and increased by our education; and that requires the learning of language and the transmission of knowledge. Both of these are social activities and public enterprises in which at least two people must engage in an interaction predicated upon the assumption of the values of mutual acceptance, tolerance and respect, embodied in the institutions of

society. Without the one, there cannot be the other; and without that key institution called education, there can be neither. Autonomy is the flower that grows out of seeds planted and tended by heteronomous hands.

It is part of our argument, therefore, that, just as there can be no such creature as a completely independent person, so, in a public system of education, there can be no such thing as a completely autonomous or independent self-governing school. To be sure, a certain amount of autonomy may be readily countenanced in certain areas of decision-making. But that autonomy can only be rendered intelligible and made to work within the confines of a relationship with the system, the community, and its educating agencies generally, based on a mutuality of regard and benefit.

Schools conceived thus enjoy a mutual relationship with the system and the community of which they are a part. The system values and ensures the basic protection of rights for all teachers, students and schools; at the same time, schools enjoy a mutual relationship with the community, in which parents and other significant groups are able to have their voices heard in regard to matters of fundamental value and goals. There is also a mutual relationship within the school among school-based personnel, as decision-making is shared, owned and supported.

In return, the school enjoys a greater degree of autonomy in selection of community-related goals and the fitting of resources to meet those goals. It also enjoys a greater sense of its own value and standing in providing community leadership, in promoting the importance of education among all its stakeholders, and in this way promoting the idea of the learning community and the values of life-long learning.

In sum, the model of the relationships between school, system and community should mirror those of the strong, robust autonomous individual in mutual relationship with the society of which she or he is part, and in partnership with all its elements and agencies that make it possible for both of them to realize the values in those interests that define and structure their identities and enable them to find a forum for the discussion of possibilities and to give expression to their choices.

All this, at rock bottom, is what the negotiation of public policy and the payment of taxes in a participative democracy are for. Those of us with differential levels of resources contribute to the exchequer differentially as a result and in proportion; it is that contribution which grants us licence to access those good things that society wishes to be available for enjoyment by all its members. The notion of that contribution brings out the very mutuality and interdependence of our economic arrangements for funding and running our society, and providing appropriate levels and kinds of service for the benefit of all its constituents. This includes those, who because of history, handicap, weakness or sheer misfortune may not able to contribute much to it at the moment but still need its support if they are ever to realize their chances of ever doing so.

This makes of society and its various institutions, especially the school, the very site and forum for two value enterprises. One part of these relates to the ways in which individuals are enabled further to develop their pattern of preferred life-options, and so increase their autonomy. The other relates to the ways in which the younger generation learns to become citizens in mutual association with other members of their school community and representatives of the community more broadly conceived, in a form of interaction in which all sections of the community cooperate mutually for the benefit of the societal whole. Both are indispensable parts of an education for citizenship.

There are thus two parts to making this interaction positive, fruitful and productive. The first raises questions concerning the *quanta* of knowledge and skill that are indispensable preconditions for and parts of the attempt to establish, run and correct the institutions necessary for the stability, security, continuation and welfare of the whole community. The other is the awareness and imagination that are vital to the envisioning, provision and extension of opportunities for individual development and enrichment within it. It is these considerations that make it possible to characterize, flesh out and give opportunity for the institutional expression and individual realization of the values of autonomy and mutuality.

The first part of this formula stresses the importance of the values of partnership and mutuality in the preparation and involvement of students in programmes of education for citizenship. It thereby underlines the need for their introduction to, and immersion in, the whole range of cognitive requirements for full and effective participation in it. The second stresses the immense variety, scope and complexity of activities and engagements having the potential to open up avenues of personal development and enrichment, that will enable individuals to enlarge their horizons and uplift the quality of their life. It draws attention to the range and proliferation of the cognitive repertoires necessary for an informed selection of those activities upon which individuals will think it worthwhile spending their time, energy and resources, both formally in school and afterwards.

In both of these fields of value, there will have to be, in the learning activities engaged in, a sufficient degree of depth to ensure that the judgements made and the commitments entered into are outcomes of and based upon appropriate footings of understanding and insight (cf. Brent 1978). Between the two, there will have to be at least some minimal balance. For our stress on the correlative importance of autonomy and mutuality requires education for and involvement in a balanced mix of activities leading to effective partnerships between citizenship in the community *and* individual autonomy in the selection and working out of a pattern of satisfying life-choices.

We should also see it as an educational *desideratum* that there should be some balance in the latter set of activities and outcomes as well. We should not, we think, be inclined to regard those who choose to spend *all* their time playing the trumpet, practising politics, or even doing philosophy, as showing the benefits of having been educated to have some grasp and appreciation of the nature, scope and potential value of all the opportunities offered by access to a wide-ranging and 'balanced' curriculum. Thus 'balance' becomes as much a value as 'depth' in characterizing the relationship between autonomy and mutuality.

X

This last point presents an issue of major concern in the development of any theory of education for autonomy, citizenship and a life of civility and culture. It raises the question of what a 'balanced' curriculum might look like and how children's learning can be judged to be appropriately 'balanced'. And what this in its turn quickly uncovers is some fundamental underlying questions: What are our schools educating for? What are our children at school to become? What is the right relationship between school and school system, student and state? What types of cognition and conduct shall the state's future citizens need to draw upon, in order to exercise their roles, rights and responsibilities as citizens of a participative democracy? How can the curriculum give them the skills, knowledge and values that they need to face the challenges and exigencies of the future? How can we try to ensure that, in planning for the future, the schools and educating institutions of any democracy will be able to encourage the development in its citizens of the awareness and sensitivity necessary for all the various communities that are found in it, the confidence and freedom to express their own particular interests, their characteristic values and cultural concerns? And how can all these different interests be accepted and allowed their own pride of place, while at the same time contributing to the development of a sense of common identity and shared nationhood, without losing the best of each? The question of values and their place and expression in the curriculum becomes vital and critical at this juncture.

For all the foregoing relates to the obvious but crucial point that values exist, are found in and embodied across the whole curriculum. Values are not definable as though they were an autonomous element in the curriculum, as being in some way a separate subject, with its own body of theory, cognitive content, typical activities, disciplinary procedures or criteria for success. Values permeate everything that we do in the curriculum – including the naming, defining and inter-relating of all its parts. And that is because of the point made above that description and evaluation are inextricably entwined activities.

MacIntyre (1971) put all this well when he remarked that, to describe someone as a 'ship's captain' is in fact to engage in a complicated activity of appraisal: the ship's captain's qualification to be described as such depends centrally upon their constantly exhibiting, coming up to and maintaining certain standards of professional performance, that are held to constitute the minimal criteria of admissibility to the class of those licensed to practise in that profession. In similar manner, Peters (1966) noted that to become a scientist is *ipso facto* to be committed to the values implicit in the procedural principles defining the nature of the subject and prescribing appropriate activities and ends in it.

Thus, it is plain that questions of value in knowledge and the curriculum are not entirely separated from subjects such as mathematics and science, nor solely restricted to the humanities, the arts and

religion, in which matters of value are supposed to be defining features of those particular styles of cognitive activity. Questions of value also underpin, and indeed permeate, the entire syllabuses of all other curriculum subjects, including mathematics and science. Science, engineering and information technology, for example, are in no way value-free, not merely in their application but in their very nature and modes of procedure: they are shot through with value elements that help define, characterize and determine the direction of their activities and the appropriate forms of engagement in them, and give them their typical points of purchase in the extension of knowledge and their place in human life and the concerns of the community. There is indeed a strong sense in which such subjects are humane concerns too.

This consideration licenses us to call into question some of the claims that, because values discourse is replete with utterances that are held by positivists and others of their ilk to be epistemically degenerate, and since educating institutions are centrally concerned with the transmission of knowledge and the initiation of pupils into the paradigm forms constituting public knowledge – mathematics and the sciences – the claims of the arts, culture and religion for inclusion on the curricula of schools are gravely suspect and cannot, without intellectual compromise to the standards of objectivity, impartiality and neutrality, be sustained in an educating institution.

Such an approach, based on such a set of contentions, would, as we hope to have made clear, only carry conviction if (a) verification critiques against matters of culture and value on epistemological grounds were indeed sound; (b) schools as educating institutions were indeed *centrally* concerned with the imparting of knowledge; and (c) the concept of knowledge were indeed restricted to the paradigms of mathematics and the natural sciences, as empiricists have so constantly urged. But the first claim cannot be considered as other than highly contentious if not fatally flawed; the second needs much further consideration; while the third has long since fallen to the powerful rebuttals deployed against such claims by Wittgenstein, Popper and Quine.

It would, of course, be perverse to deny that parents send their children to schools in order for them to acquire knowledge or that schools do not see themselves as being under some sort of obligation so to transmit it (Harris 1979). But it is at least open to question whether the transmission of knowledge should be the central concern of schools as educating institutions; there can be other aims of education and to concentrate emphasis upon this one only is to risk falling into the fallacy of mistaking the part for the whole. As Laura (1978) comments, it might be thought at least as important an aim for educational undertakings to

> suggest that the fabric of society could well be improved by doing far less to ensure initiation into the so-called domains of knowledge and far more by way of instructing children in the art of living with themselves and with each other.

This interplay of epistemological and axiological elements and considerations, in association with reflections drawn from the psychology of learning, the sociology and anthropology of school as a social institution, and the values – both individual and social – attached to and embodied in the institution of schooling by the society in which a school is located, will obviously occupy a central place in discussions about quality education and the development of effective education for citizenship in the 1990s, and into the next century.

XI

In this our undertaking of education for citizenship, we begin to see that no part of the curriculum is in some way or other theoretically privileged or set epistemically apart from the values education enterprise. The Roman poets, of course, with their deep appreciation of civic responsibility, realized this long ago and, in their service to the Muse, took the whole range of human activities, interests and problems as providing them with their charter: '*humani nil a me alienum puto*' ('No part of human affairs do I conceive as lying outside the range of my concern') remarked Terence (*Hauton-timoroumenos* 77), while Juvenal could apostrophize (*Satires* I, 86):

> Quidquid agunt homines, votum, timor, ira, voluptas,
> Gaudia, discursus, nostri est farrago libelli

> (The whole of human conduct – prayers and fright,
> Wrath, pleasure and their moments of delight,
> Their worlds of talk –
> these are the medley of the book I write)

We need not be so expansive or ambitious: suf-ficient unto us is the need to concentrate upon redefining the curriculum in a way that would transcend the narrow economic preoccupations of the present, while avoiding the axiological imperialism of those who would insist upon the teaching of a particular set of 'traditional' or 'family' values, as though these were a universal panacea for all the ills of humankind. We need instead to adopt an approach to the construction of curricula, theoretically and practically integrated, and orientated towards the solution of problems, both of contemporary puzzlement and also of more abiding perplexity (see Brennan 1994). Using problems and a range of human concerns as starting points, we can then concentrate upon building a larger approach to the curriculum that will not only help us meet the challenges posed by current national or individual economic and vocational needs, but will also help us prepare a programme for a larger-scale and longer-lasting imbuing of the curriculum with humane values and orientating it towards humane concerns.

There is nothing grand, elevated or absolutist about this: in our drive towards the humanization of the curriculum, we could quickly put together a list of problems, topics and issues of which Dewey himself might well have approved (Dewey 1938, 1956). Such a list would comprise an intellectual attack on a range of pressing concerns and perplexities and could well issue in tentative solutions that would promote the community's interest and contribute to human welfare. In constructing and following such a curriculum programme we should be embarking upon and engaging in the theoretically highly respectable activity of forging a pragmatic and progressive curriculum research programme, meet to address a range of pressing problems, promote education for community engagement and individual autonomy, resting upon and incorporating a whole range of humane values: civility, courtesy, sensitivity, consideration, tolerance, patience, service, sympathy, courage and cooperation.

As examples of some of those problems from which a rich curriculum diet might be constructed (cf. Aspin and Chapman 1993) we might point, for instance, to such matters as the following:

1 the common concern of many countries to enhance the literacy of their citizens;
2 the need of many countries to acquire the requisite skills and competences to enable its citizens to operate in a world where the amount of

available productive work is decreasing, where advances in knowledge and the information technology revolution will mean that workers will have to be prepared to change jobs four or five times in a working lifetime, where working life is likely to become shorter and shorter, and where – notwithstanding the increasing scarcity of salaried employment – many will also enjoy increasing longevity;

3   the problem of social and workplace relations in such circumstances: how can all people, in times of employment shortage, work together cooperatively and harmoniously so as to enhance productivity and build and enjoy a sense of social and workplace satisfaction and reward, avoiding the social divisions caused by making scapegoats of minority groups in a plural society?

4   the question of interpersonal relations, in a time when the incidence of phenomena such as domestic violence and child-abuse shows no sign of decreasing, when the divorce rate is already high and climbing, when suicide among young people is a phenomenon of disturbing frequency – with all the attendant dysfunctions and social dislocations that these bring about;

5   the problem of constructing healthy lifestyles and a regimen of risk-avoiding behaviours, when the economic and social conditions promote among some sections of the population a sense of hopelessness and anomie;

6   above all, perhaps, is the problem of how to assist human beings to acquire and retain their values of *humanity*, of sensitivity, sympathy, intercultural understanding and compassion, at a time when the emphasis upon what Habermas (1972, 1976) called technocratic rationality, upon technicization and the dominance of particular kinds of economic interest, threaten us with the loss of a sense of individual worth and commitment to a set of values that will help define and enrich the quality of relationships between ourselves and others in a plural society – what we might call the problem of the need for the *humanization* of the present-day curriculum.

There is, then, no shortage of theoretical and human problems, that generate a whole list of varied, demanding and highly relevant subjects for curriculum address, and that can function as a start-

ing point from which the enterprise of redefining the curriculum might well begin (Chapman and Aspin 1993). What is clear is that an informed and insightful attack upon even a few of these problems requires immersion and engagement in areas of enquiry and styles of intellectual activity, of enormous and wide-ranging scope and complexity. So much is necessary so that our coming generation can not only begin to understand the difficulty, complexity and multifariousness of such theoretic and practical problems, but also start to help the present generation try to make tentative moves towards their solution and, in that way, make a vital contribution towards securing the community's future.

It is as a function of our attack on such problems, and our ability to offer imaginative and creative solutions to them, that schools are required to provide access to and instruction in those forms of cognitive operation by means of which the question of understanding, dealing with, and solving those problems, and a myriad others like them, can be most appropriately tackled.

XII

It is this kind of consideration that helps us appreciate that the role and function of good schools, and the mark of quality schooling, does not solely reside in their success in the transmission of valued knowledge. There is much more to quality schooling than that. For what Laura's (1978) injunction helps us remember is that a community's main concern is to see, not merely its cognitive capital and modes of operation extended to and taken up by its next generation, but that its very identity, culture and principal values, enshrined in its institutions, customs and traditions, be bequeathed as an inheritance and passed on intact to its successors.

The point of this is so that they may, with the greater awareness and insight offered to them by their education in them, be able further to refine, embellish and improve upon the most fundamental conceptions of meaning and significance that characterize and define the form of life, in which that community has had its being and from which it has drawn its life-force and inspiration. That is why the debate about values in education and the best form in which citizens can be educated for life in a democracy is of such critical moment now, for it is about nothing less than the ways in which future generations of citizens may come to understand the past, conceive of the present and envision the future of their country and their own place in it. The current debate about the possible move towards a Republic in Australia is evidence of the part being played by Australians in the development and putting into place of a vision and a form for the future that will meet all their needs, aspirations and sense of self – and of the value they lay upon that.

Perhaps this is where this preliminary discussion of the problems of values education should come to an end – with the realization that there will always be debate, discussion and maybe even dissension in a lively and vigorous democracy about what its citizens believe matters most. For that is an indication of how vitally important such conceptions and values are to it and to our ideas of individual significance and community character. Such values and practices are crucial in creating the necessary climate for a sound community, in which the demands and opportunities offered by our search for autonomy and mutuality can be given best and greatest expression. It is at such a point, and in such a climate of openness and contention, that the search for answers to questions as to which are the most important values in our society and in its educating institutions must go on.

It is therefore especially significant that these considerations should be taking place at this time, when in some countries threats to a socially inclusive and harmonious society and to inter-ethnic and inter-cultural respect and understanding have been coming under greater threat than has been evident at any time during the last fifty years. Perhaps we may employ the opportunity offered by events occurring in this time of turbulence, uncertainty and the raising of fundamental questions concerning national identity, cultural awareness, and ethnic and racial reconciliation in today's increasingly plural societies, to identify, clarify and articulate the particular topics, issues and problems that must figure in the educational agenda of those concerned to advance the understanding of our coming generations of young people who are to be citizens in our multi-cultural and plural societies. For in this way educators may be encouraged to try to help make their charges better, more committed and more effective citizens in a more just, socially inclusive and democratic national and international community in the twenty-first century.

References

Anscombe, G. E. M. (1958) On brute facts. *Analysis*, 18.

Anscombe, G. E. M. (1969) Modern moral philosophy. In W. D. Hudson (ed.) *The Is/Ought Question*. London: Macmillan.

Aspin, D. N. (1975) Ethical aspects of sport and games, and physical education. *Proceedings of the Philosophy of Education Society of Great Britain*, **IX**(2) July: 49–71.

Aspin, D. N. and Chapman, J. D. (1993) *Preparing a Rich Curriculum Diet* (Hot Topics – **II**(3): 1–6). Melbourne: Australian Council of Educational Administration.

Aspin, D. N. and Chapman, J. D. (1994) *Quality Schooling: A Pragmatic Approach to Some Current Problems, Topics and Issues*. London: Cassell.

Austin, J. L. (1962) *How to Do Things with Words*. Oxford: Clarendon Press.

Beardsmore, R. W. (1969) *Moral Reasoning*. London: Routledge and Kegan Paul.

Bernstein, R. J. (1983) *Beyond Objectivism and Relativism*. London: Routledge and Kegan Paul.

Best, D. (1992) *Rationality and Feeling*. London: Falmer.

Brennan, A. (1994) Environmental literacy and educational ideal. *Environmental Values*, **3**: 3–16.

Brent, A. (1978) *Philosophical Foundations for the Curriculum* esp. pp. 153–6. London: Allen and Unwin.

Brent, A. (1982) Multicultural education and relativism: a reply to Phillips-Bell. *Journal of Philosophy of Education*, **16**: 125–130.

Chapman, J. D. (1993) Leadership, management and 'the effectiveness of schooling': a response to Mr Gradgrind. *Journal of Educational Administration*, **31**(4): 4–19.

Chapman, J. D. and Aspin, D. N. (1993) *The Implications of the OECD Activity on the Effectiveness of Schooling and of Educational Resource Management: The Curriculum Re-Defined* (Commissioned Paper). Paris: OECD.

Chapman, J. D., Froumin, I. and Aspin, D. N. (1995) *Creating and Managing a Democratic School*. London: Falmer Press.

Dearden, R. F. (1968) *The Philosophy of Primary Education*. London: Routledge and Kegan Paul.

Dearden, R. F. (1975) Autonomy and education. Part III, Chapter 4 in R. F. Dearden, P. H. Hirst and R. S. Peters (eds) *Education and the Development of Reason*. London: Routledge and Kegan Paul.

Dewey, J. (1907) The control of ideas by facts III. *Journal of Philosophy*, **4**(12).

Dewey, J. (1938) *Experience and Education*. New York: Macmillan.

Dewey, J. (1956) *The Child and the Curriculum* and *The School and Society* (combined edition). Chicago: University of Chicago Press.

Duhem, P. (1914) *The Aim and Structure of Physical Theory* (trans P. P. Weiner 1954). Princeton, NJ: Princeton University Press.

Evers, C. W. and Lakomski, G. (1991) *Knowing Educational Administration.* Oxford: Pergamon.

Gellner, E. (1983) The overcoming of relativism. Unpublished lecture at the Royal Institute of Philosophy, 25 February, 1983.

Habermas, J. (1972) *Knowledge and Human Interests.* London: Heinemann.

Habermas, J. (1976) *Legitimation Crisis.* London: Heinemann.

Hare, R. M. (1965) *Freedom and Reason.* Oxford: Clarendon Press.

Hare, R. M. (1973) Language and moral education. In Langford, Glenn and O'Connor (eds) *New Essays in Philosophy of Education.* London: Routledge and Kegan Paul.

Harris, C. K. (1979) *Education and Knowledge.* London: Routledge and Kegan Paul.

Hirst, P. H. (1965a) Liberal education and the nature of knowledge. In R. D. Archambault (ed.) *Philosophical Analysis and Education.* London: Routledge and Kegan Paul.

Hirst, P. H. (1965b) Morals, religion and the maintained school. *British Journal of Educational Studies,* **XIV**:15 ff. See also Flew, A. G. N. Indoctrination and doctrines. Chapter 6 in I. A. Snook (ed.) *Concepts of Indoctrination.* London: Routledge and Kegan Paul.

Hudson, W. D. (ed.) (1969) *The Is/Ought Question.* London: Macmillan.

Kovesi, J. (1967) *Moral Notions.* London: Routledge and Kegan Paul.

Lakatos, I. (1974) Popper on demarcation and induction. In P. A. Schilpp (ed.) *The Philosophy of Karl Popper.* La Salle: Open Court. Reproduced in Lakatos, I. *Collected Works, Vol. 1.* J. Worrall and G. Curtis (eds) Cambridge: Cambridge University Press.

Lakatos, I. (1976) Falsification and the methodology of scientific research programmes. In I. Lakatos and A. W. Musgrave (eds) *Criticism and the Growth of Knowledge.* Cambridge: Cambridge University Press.

Laura, R. S. (1978) Philosophical foundations of religious education. *Educational Theory,* **28**: 310–17.

Laura, R. S. (1979) Rejoinder to Losito: on returning the patches for his own use. *Educational Theory,* **29**: 341.

Lukes, S. (1970) Some problems about rationality. In Bryan R. Wilson (ed.) *Rationality.* Oxford: Blackwell.

Lukes, S. (1982) Relativism in its place. In M. Hollis and S. Lukes (eds) *Rationality and Relativism.* Oxford: Blackwell.

MacIntyre, A. (1971) *Against the Self-Images of the Age: Essays on Ideology and Philosophy.* London: Duckworth.

Partington, G. (1982) Cultural relativism and education. *ACES Review,* **9**: 9–11.

Peters, R. S. (1966) *Ethics and Education.* London: George Allen and Unwin.

Phillips, D. Z. and Mounce, H. O. (1969) *Moral Practices.* London: Routledge and Kegan Paul.

Phillips-Bell, M. (1981) Multicultural education: a critique of Walkling and Zec. *Journal of Philosophy of Education,* **15**(2): 97–105.

Popper, K. R. (1969) *Conjectures and Refutations* (3rd edn). London: Routledge and Kegan Paul.

Quine, W. V. (1960) *Word and Object.* Cambridge, Mass.: MIT Press.

Quine, W. V. (1971) Two dogmas of empiricism. Reproduced in his *From a Logical Point of View* (repr. edn). Cambridge, Mass.: Harvard UP.

Quine, W. V. and Ullian, J. S. (1970) *The Web of Belief.* New York: Random House (Vintage Books).

Searle, J. R. (1969) How to Derive 'Ought' from 'Is'. In W. D. Hudson (ed.) *The Is/Ought Question.* London: Macmillan.

Walkling, P. H. (1980) The idea of a multicultural curriculum. *Journal of Philosophy of Education,* **14**(1): 87–95.

Warnock, M. (1977) *Schools of Thought.* London: Faber and Faber.

Wilson, J. (1970) *Moral Thinking: A Guide for Students.* London: Heinemann Education (for the Farmington Trust).

Wilson, J. (1990) *A New Introduction to Moral Education.* London: Cassell.

Winch, P. G. (1958) *The Idea of a Social Science.* London: Routledge and Kegan Paul.

Zec, P. (1980) Multicultural education: what kind of relativism is possible? *Journal of Philosophy of Education,* **14**(1): 77–86.

For an elaboration of some of the themes discussed in this chapter and for a more detailed discussion of post-empiricist approaches to educational research see Aspin, D. N. and Chapman, J. D. with Wilkinson, V. (1994) *Quality Schooling.* London: Cassell, for whose kind permission to include some material here from that publication we are indebted.

13 A Proposal for Moral and Citizenship Teaching

MARÍA JULIA BERTOMEU AND MARÍA VICTORIA COSTA

Introduction

In this paper we comment and criticize from an ethical and philosophical point of view the ethical and citizenship education contents developed for national curriculum in Argentina. We point out the document's aspects we consider correct and also those we disagree with, as they do not fit with an ideal of democratic education. Our working hypothesis is to show that there is an incompatibility between some of the contents: those aiming to impose a particular conception of the good life and human flourishing, and those advocating a democratic education for tolerance, reasonable dissent and respect for differences. Finally, we outline an alternative proposal for teaching ethics and citizenship based on universal normative principles. Among other goals, we propose the development of moral judgement, the improvement of the perception of particular situations, the critical discussion of particular cases and the promotion of argumentative capabilities to participate in democratic processes.

Ethical and citizen education

With the appointment of Raul Alfonsín as President of Argentina after the elections in December 1983, Argentina regained the democratic system of government. This had been tragically interrupted by a military coup d'état on 24 March 1976, when the army took over the constitutional authorities and started one of the bloodiest periods in the history of the country, producing nearly 30,000 missing and dead people. The difficult process of re-establishment of democracy – similar to others that took place in other Latin American countries – was accompanied by an increased interest in debating the political, psychological, moral, educational and social causes that might have led to the constitutional order's violent halt. A portion of the discussions focused on the problem of what people should be taught in order to strengthen and improve democratic institutions.

These processes of debate and reflection were common in Latin America, where academics and researchers coming from private centers, state universities, governmental institutions and also organizations connected with the United Nations set forth the issue of democracy and education as an aim for the 1980s. Between 1983 and 1985 a series of meetings were held in Brazil and Argentina with representatives from Venezuela, Uruguay, Mexico and Chile. Those meetings had two main objectives: first, to define the role of society, community and the state in the democratization of access to education and knowledge; and second, to formulate educational policies that would facilitate the transition to democracy or to the democratization of politics (Braslavsky and Filmus 1994). Two of the points that received unanimous agreement were the need to strengthen a democratic exercise through the practice of citizen rights and the improvement of individuals' freedoms, and the need to promote changes in those factors that may deepen intolerance, instability or fundamentalism. These goals require the formal and informal communication of a set of democratic values, such as respect for other people's values, beliefs and rights, tolerance to political differences, solution of conflicts through dialogue and mutual cooperation, and political participation and pluralism, among others. Such values would shape the teaching and learning practices taking place in the frame of the formal educational system, and they would also be explicitly acknowledged in the national curriculum.

The recent "Federal Law of Education" passed in Argentina in April 1993, which implies significant changes in the structure of the educational system that cannot be analyzed here, includes ethical and civic education as one of the compulsory subjects for general basic education. Common contents for basic education, grouped in eight different areas – language, mathematics, natural sciences, social sciences, technology, artistic education, physical education, ethical and citizen education – expect to state a set of relevant knowledge to be taught at a national level (Ministerio de Cultura y Educacíon de la Nación 1995). Its selection and organization resulted from a series of surveys carried out along the country, in which influential people – outstanding academics from different disciplines, non-governmental organizations that develop educational programs, business and unions representatives, educational institutions' authorities – and the general public took part. In addition preliminary proposals were discussed in seminars, workshops and meetings of educators.

In this chapter we will analyze critically the final version of the contents of ethical and citizen education, as developed in the law.[1] We will refer to those aspects of the document that we believe to be correct, and also those we disagree with, as not fitting in with an ideal of democratic education. Our thesis is that there is an incompatibility between the compulsory contents for the teaching of ethics and citizenship: while some statements try to impose a certain conception of the good life – such as those referring to a hierarchy of objective values or to a definition of persons in terms of their capacity for transcendence and relationship with God – others advocate tolerance, reasonable dissent and respect for differences. To conclude, we will outline a proposal for moral and citizenship teaching that attempts to overcome the difficulties mentioned. It also avoids the exclusively theoretical approaches that are prevalent in moral and political education in our country. We suggest that dealing with problems of applied ethics, together with practical activities and the fulfillment of projects is a necessary complement for the effective learning of normative issues.

In pluralist and multi-cultural societies, there is a widespread consensus that not even a democratically elected government has legitimate authority to shape educational institutions so that they inculcate any particular substantive conception of the good life, as for example, a religious *Weltanschauung*. This idea represents a version of the state neutrality principle for the scope of education, which is accepted in most countries with a liberal tradition. We think that lack of an adequate theoretical distinction between the right and the good, or between public norms and non-public values, leads necessarily to the identification of moral education with the transmission of substantive conceptions of the good (see McLaughlin 1995a and b). In turn, this leads to either a rejection of all moral education – considered mere indoctrination, or to the unexamined acceptance of a particular dogmatic approach and, consequently, the abandonment of the neutrality thesis concerning education.

Although the problem of the neutrality of the state has given rise to complex discussions that we will not mention here, the recognition of the non-homogeneous and pluralist character of many contemporary societies points out the need to determine precisely what are the limits of legitimate state action. We are interested in underlining the state's responsibility in a democratic society to secure the necessary conditions so that all members of society can pursue their personal or collective self-chosen life-plan. This task is connected with the duty to respect persons as autonomous individuals. Although there are disagreements on whether the promotion of autonomy should be stated as one of the central aims of education, there is agreement that values, cultures, ways of life or conceptions of the good that the students adopted or possessed ought to be respected. In our opinion, in spite of the difficulties concerning its conceptual delimitation and application to the field of education, it is possible to specify and defend an operative notion of autonomy – that could be an attainable goal for most students with the assistance of schooling (Rich 1986) – a program of moral education oriented to the development of autonomy should include instruction in moral reasoning and critical reflection in order that students become able to determine by themselves not only what is right to do but also which personal and political ideals are valuable for them to pursue.

In the processes of selection of the ethics and citizenship contents there was a certain basic agreement regarding the need for an education based on teaching and practising autonomy and democracy. The cognitive basis of democracy was emphasized, that is, citizens' capabilities for argumentative participation in public discourses (Habermas 1983). This view supposes the acquisition of those skills necessary to accept the implicit rules of rational discourses. The search for more reflection and the development of comunicative capabilities were stated as foundations of ethical and civic education, together with acknowledgment of human rights and democratic values. In other words, critical and reflective thinking were considered key tools to incorporate citizens into public processes of decision-making.

However, as we will claim in this chapter, the acceptance of the importance of critical thinking is in open contradiction with the introduction of certain dogmatic ideas in the final version of the document. Among those dogmatic ideas we find, for example, the postulate of the existence of a sole hierarchical order of values, in whose highest point religious values are located, or the teaching of an essentialist rigid conception of masculinity and femininity. Note that such dogmatic ideas, were not the product of an agreement reached by means of argumentative discussion in which different sectors were allowed to participate. Rather, it was the result of hidden negotiations between some people in power and the most conservative sectors of the Catholic church that have had an hegemonic role in the recent history of education in Argentina.

From a theoretical point of view, the actors taking part in the selection and organization of the contents for ethics and citizenship education could be divided into two large groups. In the first one we find defenders of a universalistic conception centered in the primacy of justice over different conceptions of the good, a view inspired by the Kantian and Rawlsian tradition. In the second we find representatives of the Catholic church who – although not opposed to political liberalism – hold omni-comprehensive notions of the good close to the Aristotelian Thomist tradition, and mixed with elements of the material values ethics developed by Max Scheler and Nicolai Hartmann. As the final document gathers views from both approaches, without making an explicit distinction between them, there are some tensions, even though most subjects are treated in terms of vague general statements. We believe that the introduction of certain few but deep changes in the final version of the basic contents for ethics and citizenship education risks transforming it into a document for indoc-

trination that is not consistent with the plurality of beliefs mentioned by the very text of the law.

To the initial characterization of the person appealing to a set of affective, intellectual and volitive capabilities, is added a close relationship between its dignity and the capacity to transcend and consequently to connect with God. This implies binding the person's dignity to a capacity that neither all inhabitants of Argentina wish to develop nor least should develop, except for their free decision to join a religious community. Beyond the promotion of respect for autonomous individual elections, declaring that persons are naturally oriented to transcendence involves inculcating a determined way to understand the good life that transforms moral education into a religious one.

A closer examination of the notion of person as described in the text shows that it presupposes an anthropological conception, according to which mankind is defined essentially in terms of spirituality. Therefore, it seems that human beings can only give full expression to their nature – and also reach individual and social perfection – when their actions and lives as a whole are guided by religious values. Similarly, the family is founded in a natural order and constitutes the primary nucleus or "cell" of society. However, in societies where there is no consensus regarding issues such as divorce or abortion, for example, imposing values linked to the most stable and conservative sectors means disavowing autonomy claims for those willing to secure their own life-plan. In a modern and pluralist society, we cannot accept a religious interpretation of an ethical monopoly that does not represent the variety of goods and values accepted by different individuals and communities.

One thing to notice about the material values ethics on which the proposal we are discussing is partially based is that it makes use of an intuitionist methodology, that is, it appeals to an emotional intuitive apprehension of a values hierarchy. This constitutes an ingenuous resource, insufficient to justify the intersubjective validity and objectivity of the theory. Besides, the notion of person it defends supposes a premise about God's existence, or at least of mankind as naturally inclined to transcendence, neither of which are accepted as true by all rational persons. Without pretending to settle the question concerning whether it is possible to argue in a valid fashion from premises about human nature, we can see that in this document those premises support a static, rigid and closed view of human beings and their development, a view unacceptable to a modern open society. Moreover, this general conception is not hospitable to the exercise of critical reflection and rational debate about moral and political issues, but rather tends to heteronomous and dogmatic inculcation of "indisputable truths".

In accordance with the former, the notion of "gender" was systematically replaced in the document by the term "sex". But if we consider gender as an equivalent for sex, it becomes mainly a biological category, that conveys that gender relationships appeared as founded in a natural order. We think that the distinction between the biological notion of sex, which refers to the possession of certain anatomic and physiological characteristics, and the cultural notion of gender should be maintained. The meaning of gender results from a complex construction, including a set of properties and functions that, in the framework of a particular society, culture and history, are assigned to individuals by virtue of their sex (see Santa Cruz et al. 1994). In this sense, masculinity and feminity are not merely descriptive terms but evaluative, arising from social institutionalization of sex differences.

Since the initial notion of gender is discussed in biological terms in the document, it seems an essential, universal and ahistorical determinant of people's identity. Obviously, it is very difficult in this context to discuss gender relationships, which assign roles and legitimate behaviors as appropriate for men and women. This view cannot offer tools to explain changes in gender relationships that take place in contemporary societies, for example, the redefinition of roles in the family and the labour market, but wrongly suggest that such changes are signs of the moral crisis of the present society. It is true that, as the text holds, from the point of view of the individual identity construction, sex (gender) is a central element. However, it is only a part of a complex organization that includes other elements, such as race, social class, occupation, sexuality, religion, age, and so on. For these reasons, we should be very careful not to inculcate essentialisms and stereotypes about man and woman, adopting instead a point of view sensitive to the richness of diversity of concrete male and female characteristics, as a first step to prevent discrimination.

The text also refers to affective, intellectual and volitive processes of persons, sociability, personal identity construction and education for health.[2] The general characterizations of these subjects make explicit room for the introduction of problems such as the free election of a personal life-plan, self-knowledge, self-respect, the sense of belonging to a community, and personal rights and duties. We also consider positive, in the context of the construction of personal identity, the discussion of the wrongfulness of discrimination and exclusion, which is aimed at inculcating respect and value for oneself and for others, for different cultures, religions and races. What is at stake here is the sense of dignity as an interpersonal feeling that presupposes relationships of recognition between all members of a community. It is the same feeling that has a central role in the citizen's identity construction, and is at the base of solidarity, mutual respect, public life promotion and the successful functioning of democratic institutions.

Regarding the specific contents corresponding to citizenship education, these are included under the heading of "norms". In general terms, there is a prevailing minimalist interpretation of citizenship[3] which stresses its legal sense, i.e., the legal privileges and responsibilities of members of a nation-state which are defined in terms of positive norms and regulations. However, since the document points out that social norms may be an answer to human basic needs but also to diverse conflicting social interests, it leaves open the possibility of analyzing norms and laws from a moral point of view, in order to state if they can be argumentatively justified. Citizenship education includes the study of the national constitution and of human rights and children's rights declarations, that have been reaffirmed by the constitutional text. The main values expressed in this section are those of democratic life, respect for human dignity and appreciation of human rights. The former include the study and criticism of racism, discrimination and stereotyping. Although the document holds that "there is a story of human rights that should be known" (Ministerio de Cultura y Educacion de la Nación 1995: 343; our translation) there is no mention either in this section or in the social sciences section of the human rights violations that occurred in Argentina during the last military dictatorship.

These theoretical conceptions are followed by a description of general procedures, attitudes and competences that the students should develop. This part of the document has a pluralist tone, asserting that critical analysis of values and virtues should lead students to understand the existence of diverse ways of life, and of different conceptions of persons and their happiness, so that later on they can choose freely their own life-plan and have respect for people's plans. Together with critical thinking and the exercise of argumentation, the discernment of values in concrete situations and the capacity to universalize rules, are also mentioned in the text as proper moral competences. There is an innovative treatment of the need to develop moral creativity, understood as personal elaboration of moral issues, that is designed to transcend apparent limits and explore new alternatives. Without using this term, what is at work here is an ideal of authenticity associated with autonomy, understood as self-expression from a personal and collective view. Thus, the development of moral creativity is explicitly connected with the possibility of designing communal or social projects inspired by principles of solidarity and fairness.

In the examination of the official contents for ethical and citizenship education we have advanced some ideas about what should be, in our opinion the core of a more adequate program. We think that the teaching of ethics should be focused in discussing and promoting a public morality, founded in a formal universalistic ethical theory. One of its main goals should be that of enabling persons to take part in public processes of decision-making and developing their capabilities for intersubjective communication within society. This view implies that the state should not impose as true – by means of the educational system – some particular conception of the good life, based on a comprehensive metaphysical, anthropological or religious point of view. Instead, moral education should deal with the universal principles of justice inspired by a notion of moral persons as free and equal, and designed to guarantee to all members of society the enjoyment of those opportunities necessary for elaborating and pursuing their own life-plan. The recognition of equal dignity of all the citizens in a modern, pluralist and multi-cultural society is not compatible with educational policies attempting to uniform or assimilate some people's ways of life to the ethos of a supposed majority group with hegemonic aspirations. The state should ensure, then, diverse moral doctrines and the growth of ideals, appealing to rationally justified principles. On the other hand, the state's promotion of the critical capabilities of future citizens is valuable for evaluating the socio-political reality and performing activities to transform it, according to an ideal of participative citizenship with a commitment to improve the community.

Once we have established a distinction between the right and the good, or between universal and particular values, it is possible to sketch a moral and civic education program that avoids both dogmatism – understood in terms of acritically teaching a substantive conception of the good life or human perfection – and relativism concerning values. On many occasions, the latter assumes a wrong interpretation of neutrality that leads to a decline in the search for criteria for the evaluation of a moral judgement's validity. Conversely, it seems to us that one of the tasks of ethical education is the argumentative defense of the validity of some moral norms or public values, as binding for all persons independently of their metaphysical or religious *Weltanschauung*. These norms are generally enforced by the legal system, although the differences between legal and moral reasoning should be clearly kept. Aided with these universal or public values, it is possible to carry out a certain sort of critical inquiry of particular conceptions of the good, for example, showing the unfairness of those supposing some race or ethnic group supremacy. Another kind of particular values exploration can also be done, attending to the internal coherence of these conceptions, or to the personal commitment of those who proclaim them to act accordingly. By means of classroom discussion some inconsistences could be pointed out, for example, between holding the unqualified value of life in some contexts and accepting the death penalty in others.

There is a well-known approach to moral education called values clarification in which students are asked to clarify their own values through discussion of their opinions concerning different controversial issues and to express their commitment to them in their everyday behavior (see Simon et al. 1972). Among other criticisms, it is generally pointed out that the values clarification approach does not offer students criteria to evaluate and choose between conflicting values, or between moral and non-moral values. However, it contains some important insights that should be taken into account. In the first place, the didactic resources provided by peer conversation can be profitably used by the teacher to introduce moral distinctions in order to separate non-controversial from controversial issues, together with the ideas of pluralism and respect for other people's beliefs. Second, the exercise of clarifying personal values and assessing their relative importance as regards dispositions to action, rightly assumes that morality has to be rooted in personality if its prosecution is to generate an actual commitment.

In addition to the need for introducing evaluation criteria, a program for moral education should not overlook the psychological processes that determine the maturity of the students to conceptualize moral issues in order to teach them in an effective way (Haste 1996). The most systematic attempts to apply moral psychology theories to the educational field arose from Lawrence Kohlberg's investigations. Although there are some limitations in the educational methodologies designed in the light of the cognitive moral development theory, we have to admit that it has opened a fruitful research field where contributions from psychology, ethics and education converge. Kohlberg and his collaborators have shown that moral reasoning capacities develop following a sequence of stages, which can be described as general structures to understand, evaluate and justify moral judgements. The students' level of moral maturity should be a central concern at the time of designing curricular guidelines and teaching strategies.

The first educational application of Kohlberg's ideas, named "Socratic moral discussion", implies the didactic use of hypothetical moral dilemmas initially designed as research tools. The teacher challenges the conceptual framework employed by the students to justify answers to those moral dilemmas, so as to generate critical reflection and, as a general result, to promote a stage change. Thus, students' reasons and their implications become the center of discussion, indicating contradictions, undesirable consequences or alternative solutions. The main objections raised against this approach focus on its exclusive attention to cognitive aspects of morality. While it points to the development of rationality, objectivity, impartiality and universality in moral reasoning, it assumes too simple a relationship between judgement and action, failing to take into account the role of motivations, dispositions and affective processes in moral behavior. A second application designed by Kohlberg and his collaborators – the "just community" approach to moral education – consists of a more ambitious program, which aims at avoiding some of the 'Socratic dilemma discussion' limitations, introducing participatory democracy in the school. This model tries to create a democratic space of reflection and peer interaction, replacing individual reasoning about hypothetical situations by common discussion of school problems. Even

though its implementation is quite complex, this approach has the advantage that the decisions taken become real experiences, whose consequences lead to the improvement of a sense of collective responsibility. Students not only discuss moral problems, but also see how democratic values and norms are institutionalized at school, which is understood as a moral community. In this case, moral education is not exclusively focused on the exercise of judgement skills, but also looks after the promotion of moral behavior (see Kohlberg 1981, 1985).

Regarding the problem of how to teach moral dispositions to action, psychological theory and research may offer a valuable contribution clarifying those complex variables and processes involved in its production, including the perception of the situation, the commitment to principles, norms, values, the capacities to evaluate possible courses of action, the efficacy to reach proposed goals, and so on (see Rest 1985). Empirical studies have shown that some students have difficulties interpreting relatively simple situations, and that there are considerable differences in their sensibility to perceive others' needs and feelings and in their capacities to correctly infer what should be done in a given situation. Moral education programs should outline strategies pointing both to the improvement of judgement capacities and to the exercise of particularistic moral sensitivities. Those theoretical principles, values and norms could be internalized by means of practices of democratic dialogues or the elaboration and implementation of common projects.

These moral principles could also play a larger role in civic education, if the normative foundations of democracy are stressed. In other words, education for citizenship could provide an explicit understanding of democracy as the only political system that guarantees citizens a treatment according to their dignity and rights to participation. Instead of inculcating a mere acritical loyalty to the political community, we believe that its central aim consists of developing comprehension and commitment to democratic values, principles and procedures. Here we disagree with William Galston (1989: 91), who considers that an appropriate citizenship education is the one designed on behalf of a particular political order and it may appeal to a "pedagogy that is far more rhetorical than rational". Critical inquiry about the political system or about alternative ways of life, in his opinion, carries the danger of falling into sceptical reflection and thus impeding the flourishing of life-plans and diversity. Although he does not deny the possibility of an argumentative defense of democratic principles and procedures, he holds that their embracement through rational inquiry can only be effective for a small élite.

Defending a more democratic approach to civic education, Amy Gutmann (1995) holds that the best antidote to skepticism is reflection concerning the reasonableness of democratic principles. With regard to the protection of diversity, it is by means of tolerance, mutual respect and pluralism that this liberal purpose can be secured, and not through discouraging the development of future citizens' autonomy. We agree with her defense of the need to cultivate those character and intellectual traits that enable persons to reflect critically and choose among political conceptions and private ways of life.

Our conception of civic education is founded in a strong maximalist concept of citizenship, similar to the one used by John Rawls in his *Theory of Justice* (1971). This concept is the political equivalent of the notion of 'moral person', retaining the value of autonomy and capacities for defending demands in an argumentative way in the framework of a pluralist and democratic society (see Guariglia et al. 1993, Guariglia 1996). A defense of the democratic life is more effective if it is founded on normative principles instead of a pragmatic consensus or *modus vivendi*, especially in those countries where there is no long democratic tradition, but a history of successive ruptures of the constitutional order. For these reasons, citizenship education cannot consist in a moralizing idealized history as a "pantheon of heroes" in Galston's style, but rather a revision of historical cases from a moral point of view, showing the mistakes that a mature democratic society cannot allow itself to commit again.

Conclusion

After making some critical comments about the selection of contents for ethical and citizenship education in the Argentinian national curriculum, we have delineated an alternative proposal based in a normative universalistic theory. The core of the program we defend is both the development of moral judgement capabilities, inspired in the findings of Kohlberg and his followers, and the improvement of perception discernment and interpretation of conflictive political and moral situations. We consider that certain ideas from Lawrence Blum and Martha Nussbaum are quite helpful in this respect. As moral education programs in our country tend to remain on an abstract level, we suggest the inclusion of case interpretation and discussion, aided with the tools of normative ethics.

We also think that the exercise of values clarification could be useful to encourage self-knowledge in people concerning their own values and pluralist discussion. However, this exercise should not obscure a clear division between considerations of political justice and conceptions of the good life. Besides, the individualistic bias of this approach may be overcome by introducing the discussion of collective values. The stories and narratives that confirm individual and community history could be appraised, but in the context of a normative framework provided by universal principles.

Finally, as regards issues of citizenship education, we believe that it is necessary to start studying and discussing universal democratic principles, such as freedom and equality, human rights declarations and also different conceptions of democratic government. At the same time, those normative concepts could be applied to critically analyze our own country's institutional history and present sociopolitical circumstances, in order to strengthen democratic procedures for the solution of conflicts.

Notes

1 These contents correspond to compulsory basic education from 1st to 9th course.
2 In order to avoid controversies, sexual education was not included in education for health.
3 On the distinction between minimalist and maximalist conceptions of citizenship see McLaughlin 1992, Kymlicka and Norman 1994.

References

Blum, L. (1991) Moral perception and particularity. *Ethics*, **101**: 701–25.

Braslavsky, C. and Filmus, D. (eds) (1994) *Respuestas a la Crisis Educativa*. Buenos Aires: Cántaro.

Galston, W. (1989) Civic education in the liberal state. In N. L. Rosenblum (ed.) *Liberalism and the Moral Life*. Cambridge, MA: Harvard University Press.

Galston, W. A. (1995) Two concepts of liberalism. *Ethics*, **105**: 516–34.

Gilligan, C. (1982) *In a Different Voice: Psychological Theory and Women's Development*. Cambridge, MA: Harvard University Press.

Gilligan, C., Ward, J. V. and McLean Taylor, J. (eds) (1988) *Mapping the Moral Domain*. Cambridge, MA: Harvard University Press.

Guariglia, O. (1996) *Moralidad. Etica Universalista y Sujeto Moral*. Buenos Aires: Fondo de Cultura Económica.

Guariglia, O., Bertomeu, M. J. and Vidiella, G. (1993) *Democracia y Estado de Bienestar*. Buenos Aires: Centro Editor de América Latina.

Gutmann, A. (1989) Undemocratic education. In N. L. Rosenblum (ed.) *Liberalism and the Moral Life*. Cambridge, MA: Harvard University Press.

Gutmann, A. (1995) Civic education and social diversity. *Ethics*, **105**: 557–79.

Habermas, J. (1983) *Moralbewusstsein und kommunikatives Handeln*. Francfort: Suhrkamp.

Haste, H. (1993) Moral creativity and education for citizenship. *Creativity Research Journal*, **6** (1 and 2): 153–64.

Haste, H. (1996) Communitarianism and the social construction of morality. *Journal of Moral Education*, **25** (1): 47–55.

Kohlberg, L. (1981) *Essays on Moral Development*. Vol. 1: *The Philosophy of Moral Development*. San Francisco: Harper & Row.

Kohlberg, L. (1985) The just community approach to moral education in theory and practice. In M. W. Berkowitz and F. Oser (eds) *Moral Education: Theory and Application*. Hillsdale, London: Lawrence Erlbaum Associates.

Kymlicka, W. and Norman, W. (1994) Return to the citizen: a survey of recent work on citizenship theory. *Ethics*, **104**: 352–81.

McLaughlin, T. H. (1992) Citizenship, diversity and education: a philosophical perspective. *Journal of Moral Education*, **21**(3): 235–50.

McLaughlin, T. H. (1995a) Liberalism, education and the common school. *Journal of Philosophy of Education*, **29**(2):239–255.

McLaughlin, T. H. (1995b) Public values, private values and educational responsibility. In E. Pybus and T. H. McLaughlin (eds) *Values, Education and Responsibility*. St. Andrews: Centre for Philosophy and Public Affairs.

Ministerio de Cultura y Educación de la Nación (1995) *Contenidos básicos comunes para la educación general básica*. Buenos Aires: Ministerio de Cultura y Educación de la Nación.

Noam, G. G. and Wren, T. E. (eds) (1993) *The Moral Self*. Cambridge, MA: MIT Press.

Nussbaum, M. (1990) *Love's Knowledge. Essays on Philosophy and Literature*. New York: Oxford University Press.

Rawls, J. (1971) *A Theory of Justice*. Oxford: Oxford University Press.

Rawls, J. (1980) Kantian constructivism in moral theory. *Journal of Philosophy*, 77: 515–72.

Rest, J. R. (1985) An interdisciplinary approach to moral education. In M. W. Berkowitz and F. Oser (eds) *Moral Education: Theory and Application*. Hillsdale, London: Lawrence Erlbaum Associates.

Rich, J. M. (1986) Autonomy and the purposes of schooling. *Educational Philosophy and Theory*, **18**: 34–40.

Santa Cruz, M. I., Bach, A. M., Femenías, M. L., Gianella, A. and Roulet, M. (1994) *Mujeres y Filosofia. Teoría Filosófica de Género*, Vols 5 1 and 2. Buenos Aires, Centro Editor de América Latina.

Simon, S. B., Howe, L. W. and Kirschenbaum, H. (1972) *Values Clarification: A Handbook of Practical Strategies for Teachers and Students*. New York: Hart Publications.

Taylor, C. (1992) *Multiculturalism and 'The Politics of Recognition'*. Princeton: Princeton University Press.

White, J. (1991) *Education and the Good Life. Autonomy, Altruism and the National Curriculum*. New York and London: Teachers College Press.

Wilson, R. W. and Schochet, G. J. (eds) (1980) *Moral Development and Politics*. New York: Praeger.

14 Education and Democratic Citizenship: In Defence of Cosmopolitanism[1]

PENNY ENSLIN

The acquisition of a sense of national identity is commonly regarded as a necessary feature of education for citizenship, likely to promote the development of an appropriate set of citizen values, including an attachment and commitment to one's fellow nationals. Yet the accelerating pace of globalization – 'the rapid growth of complex interconnections and interrelations between states and societies' (Held 1995b: ix) raises the possibility that citizenship understood as membership of a particular nation-state offers too restricted a notion of citizen identity and, hence, of the values appropriate to democratic citizenship. If this is so, it has implications for citizenship education.

In this chapter I explore some of the implications of globalization for education, arguing that trends towards political and cultural globalization give new impetus to the cosmopolitan ideal. In doing so, I argue one critical perspective on the idea that developing a sense of national identity promotes values appropriate to democratic citizenship.[2] My argument will defend two central claims, the first of which is that citizen education based on identity defined by membership of a 'nation' rests on the mistaken assumption that democracy is effectively pursued within the nation-state, whose influence and authority has been reduced by globalization. Hence, second, citizen values should be derived not from the identity that comes from membership of a nation, but from identification with a range of chosen identities and with democratic principles. In arguing this, I endorse the assumption that the development of identity is a necessary component of values education. It is also assumed that the values under discussion are those that are relevant to democracy; there are other fundamental values, such as those pertinent to relationships between individuals, which are not central to this discussion.

In making this argument, I begin in the first section by exploring five features of citizenship, paying particular attention to that of identity and its relation to citizen values. The second section discusses the implications of globalization for the future of democratic citizenship in relation to the nation-state. In the third and final section it is argued that education for democratic citizenship should respond to disjunctures between globalization and citizen identity as membership of a nation-state by encouraging cosmopolitan identities and democratic values. In this discussion I take as my context post-apartheid South Africa as an example of a society in transition to democracy, in which the development of national identity has been suggested as a means of developing citizenship among a population that has recently emerged from an undemocratic and divided past.

Citizenship, identity and values

For the purposes of this discussion I shall take citizenship in a democracy to comprise five related features. First, citizenship bestows on an individual the status of **membership** of a territorially defined political unit in which reciprocal rights and responsibilities are exercised on equal terms with fellow citizens. Second, and relatedly, citizenship confers **identity** on an individual, an awareness of the self as a member of a collective with a shared political destiny, and desirably a shared political culture, which defines the citizen rights and responsibilities exercised with fellow members of that political collective. This identity includes, third, a set of **values**, usually interpreted as comprising a commitment to the common good of the political collective. My question is: what sort of collective should this be; if we are promoting citizenship in the late twentieth century, must we necessarily presuppose and privilege a single, national collective? Citizenship in a democracy involves, fourth, a degree of **participation** in the life of the polity, reflecting the citizen's assumption that she is a political agent, rather than an object of policy. At a minimum – although democracy implies choice in the extent of one's involvement – this involves voting in elections, but it also implies involvement that goes beyond voting, such as active membership of voluntary organizations like churches, unions, and political parties. Furthermore, the citizen's democratic relationship with the state is one not only of obligation to obey the law, but is also a matter of making one's needs known and of defending one's rights and those of others, of contributing to defining the issues that face the polity. For such activities a citizen needs, fifth, **knowledge and understanding** of political and legal principles, an awareness of current events, the ability to weigh up alternatives and to assess the success of state policy, to make known her needs and wishes as a citizen, and to assess whether the state is responding adequately to them and to those of other citizens.

Much of this conception of citizenship is presupposed in post-apartheid South African public philosophy, in which there is a popular commitment to democracy. Crucial to the post-apartheid vision of democracy is the principle that there will now be citizenship for all as equal members of a democratic state. While white inhabitants of South Africa previously enjoyed full citizen status, albeit in a polity whose democratic features were limited, for blacks an ethnically ascribed citizenship in separate states offered few rights and minimal participation. Hence the significance of the common citizenship provided for in Article 3 of the new Constitution of 1996. The views of all are now to be heard, and participation in decision-making will be promoted, for example through public participation projects at the levels of central and provincial government (Republic of South Africa 1996, Articles 59, 72, 118). A commitment to extensive consultation has been exemplified in the process of seeking public comment on drafts of the new Constitution. During the struggle against apartheid unions, civic associations and other popular organizations self-consciously established models of democracy through debate, consultation, mandates carefully negotiated by leadership with its members, report-

back and criticism. All this assumes a public of active citizens, and their need for sufficient knowledge to enable them to participate is presupposed in a commitment to open and transparent government and to freedom of information. These assumptions and expectations further imply, in the words of the *Reconstruction and Development Programme* (RDP) which is the policy framework of the African National Congress (ANC), 'thoroughgoing democracy' (ANC 1994: 7), the establishment of a *culture* of democracy that will pervade the life of the society. If seriously pursued, these democratic goals have radical implications for citizenship in South Africa.

The five features of citizenship in a democracy have important implications for education for citizenship, some of which have been suggested above in relation to the promotion of democracy in South Africa. Most obviously, education for democratic citizenship requires the development of knowledge and understanding about one's society (and about others), its history and constitution, the laws of the land, one's rights and responsibilities as a citizen, and about who has power over one, how and why. Given the active participation envisaged for the citizen members of the new democracy, considerable knowledge and understanding will be required if such a degree of active citizenship is to be sustained so that membership can be more than merely formal, although the significance of formal membership is not to be underestimated. What of the other two features of citizenship? How to promote citizenship identity and values as part of the project of consolidating democracy appears more complex and less clear. One view is that citizen identity and values are best developed by promoting a sense of national identity.

But how should education for democratic citizenship approach the teaching of citizenship identity and values? To answer this question, it is necessary to distinguish between three related senses of identity, which together contribute to the constitution of our selves as citizens, and whose content will differ considerably in a democracy from more traditional societies. First, in order to perceive herself as a member and participating agent the future citizen acquires self-identity as she grows up, a sense of self as enduring through time, as a person who is distinct from others and has needs and wants which she can articulate. A second sense of identity, and a prerequisite for the development of the first, is that of the self as a member of a wider collective, usually but not necessarily understood as a combination of family, neighbourhood, ethnic or language group, class or nation. Third, and closely related to the second, is identity as the values with which one identifies, as part of one's sense of self. Membership of the groups to which one belongs has tended to bring with it given values, duties and loyalties – a commitment to a way of life, with which one is expected if not required to identify. So, for those who articulate citizenship as membership of a nation-state, identification is primarily with the nation and its particular set of values. But modernity has brought with it another way of identifying with a set of values, with those which are chosen, either because one changes one's membership, for example by emigration or by changing one's lifestyle, or by choosing to adopt a set of universal values, like those presented by democratic principles of freedom and equality.

Membership of particular communities has traditionally had a strong if not determining influence on the other two senses of identity. In pre-modern, and to a lesser extent in modern societies too, these three senses of identity were closely integrated. Traditional conceptions of self and values were inevitably derived from collective identities; ascribed identities determined a clearly-defined sense of self-identity, depending one one's rank, and a clear sense of values with which identification was required. This tight integration of the three senses of identity was loosened with the advance of modernity and now of postmodernity, in part because of the spread of democracy itself.

Yet it remains the case that if one belongs to a community that has traditions of hierarchical stratification and authority, with roles and rights strictly set by caste, class, religious or other ideologies, or gender, the extent to which one is allowed to develop a sense of self-identity in which one sees oneself as an agent with wants, rights and plans as well as duties, will be more limited than, say, if one is a member of a democratic society that defines itself in terms of principles of universal human rights, equality and liberty. Membership of such differing political communities will create or prevent the conditions in which traditional values are accepted or questioned. The individual citizen's potential for self-identity as an agent and for participation can be severely curtailed by the self-identity and values made possible by her communal identities, that is by the form of membership available to him or her. Each of the three senses of identity contributes to the constitution of our selves as citizens, and there are complex interrelations between them. While they can and do tend to complement one another, in the achievement and consolidation of democracy they can be in serious tension. In making these claims I do not discount the significance of collective identities in liberation struggles; the idea of the nation played its part in creating solidarity against the apartheid order.

Two important implications of the loosening connections between the three senses of identity should be recognized. First, it is no longer the case that persons simply acquire all three in an integrated, inevitable sort of way. Second, the pursuit of democratic goals can require that traditional identities be questioned, moderated and adapted to allow for the development of a sense of self as an agent in a democratic society. If a culture of democracy is to be created, it is likely to require critical reconsideration and amendment of at least some aspects of the traditional culture or cultures of the population that comprises the polity. Both have implications, in turn, for the role of education in the process of identity acquisition in democratic societies, which is different from that traditionally played by schools as reproducers of the identities favoured by dominant ideologies.

The identities ascribed to students by schools and other institutions have tended to fix their social roles and correspondingly their expectations in life, including their expectations of themselves as agents in the polity and of schooling itself; for girls, blacks and working-class children, this has commonly meant lowered expectations, ambitions and goals.

As feminist writers have emphasized (Friedman 1989, Mendus 1993), the identities we acquire may be chosen and created, as well as given and discovered. While schools teach identities as if they are unproblematically and unavoidably given, the acquisition and practise of identities is far more complex and variable. At different times in our lives it is possible to discover aspects of our identities that we had previously neither noticed nor valued. We may adopt ascribed identities with little awareness of doing so, and with varying degrees of understanding of their origins and significance. If these observations are true, then a feature of the knowledge and understanding needed for active citizenship is the capacity to develop an awareness of given identities and to choose or create new ones, including identities that emerge from doing certain kinds of work, membership of a profession, of a group with common leisure interests, different lifestyles, participation in ecological and other campaigns, and other chosen goals and projects. This implies abandoning the idea that schools are legitimately places where students are told who they are, supposedly, for example, that they are members of a particular nation, rather than providing them with as much opportunity as possible for self-definition, including exit from some collective identities and the adoption of new values. This requires that the curriculum enables them to study their location at a particular time and place and to develop a sense of the self as a participant in a democratic way of life. These claims endorse Jeremy Waldron's observation that the social world is not neatly divided into separate cultures, to one of which we each need to belong (Waldron 1995: 105). The process of globalization has radical implications for the education of identity as a feature of preparation for democratic citizenship.

Globalization, the nation-state and democracy

Far-reaching challenges posed for democracy and citizenship by the process of globalization have been explored by sociologists and political scientists. Tony McGrew (1992: 65) describes globalization as:

> the multiplicity of linkages and interconnections that transcend the nation-states (and by implication the societies) which make up the modern world system. It defines a process through which events, decisions, and activities in one part of the world can come to have significant consequences for individuals and communities in quite distant parts of the globe. Nowadays, goods, capital, people, knowledge, images, communications, crime, culture, pollutants, drugs, fashions and beliefs all readily flow across territorial boundaries.

The internationalization of production, trade and distribution, exchange and finance represents a system which operates beyond the control of nation-states, whose power has also been reduced by the emergence of a range of organizations, corporations and social movements whose influence transcends international boundaries. The processes that constitute globalization, in which rapid change takes place across a now compressed space and time, are the subject of controversy about their fea-

tures, their causes, their significance and their likely outcomes. And the extent to which globalization has occurred to date is debatable. While some posit the emergence of a global or world culture (for discussion see Hall 1992), it seems more plausible that as identities change and some new identities emerge, 'local' and national identifications will remain (Hall 1992, Held 1995a). Hall argues that 'it seems unlikely that globalization will simply destroy national identities. It is more likely to produce, simultaneously, *new* "global" and *new* "local" identifications' (1992: 304).

Yet while national identifications are likely to remain, what of the nation-state? For McGrew globalization challenges the dominant role of the nation-state as 'the primary container of modernity' (1992: 64), while Mary Kaldor argues that 'the nation-state was and is a temporary phenomenon, even though there remains an extremely powerful attachment to the idea' (1995: 69).

This challenge to the nation-state has several features. First, globalization presents to governments of nation-states problems so vast and international in nature, such as Aids, environmental degradation and the international drugs trade, that they are not amenable to solution by individual governments acting alone. Second, the growth of international law and government, through for example human rights agreements and the United Nations Organization, represents a *de facto* surrender of some sovereignty by governments of nation-states. Third, globalization has reduced the power and authority of actual governments, who have lost some of their earlier powers to transnational organizations and corporations and the emergence of social movements whose influence transcends international boundaries.

For Held, this poses problems for our assumptions about the nation-state as the site within which democracy is exercised: 'The problem is that national communities by no means make and determine decisions and policies exclusively for themselves, and governments by no means determine what is right or appropriate exclusively for their own citizens' (1995a: 99). Under conditions of global interconnectedness, Held (1995a: 100–2) questions the viability of traditionally-held ideas of democracy understood as countries governing themselves, of political communities within bounded territories giving their consent in elections, and of governments as accountable to territorially demarcated electorates.

To observe these developments is not necessarily to predict the end of the nation-state as a political unit, or the establishment of world government. Indeed, as Carol Gould warns, 'The concentration of power and authority on such a scale, even if limited by democratic controls, would pose a grave risk of unmatched global tyranny. There would be no effective alternative power to counter such a totalistic authority' (1988: 327). But it is necessary to acknowledge with Held that a changed, cosmopolitan model is needed if democracy is to meet the changes effected by globalization.

> Democracy can only be fully sustained in and through the agencies and organisations which form an element of and yet cut across the territorial boundaries of the nation-state. The possibility of democracy today must . . . be linked to an expanding framework of democratic states and agencies. (Held 1995a: 106)

Held cites as examples of the agencies and forces providing impetus to such an extension of democracy transnational grass-roots movements pursuing environmental and health objectives and international institutions with transnational objectives, including the United Nations. Cosmopolitan democracy could be promoted by the establishment of regional parliaments, such as in Africa and Latin America, similar to the European Parliament, whose role could be extended. The general referenda envisaged by Held's model are endorsed in Mary Kaldor's emphasis on the development of a 'transnational political culture' (1995: 94), through which public opinion could develop across national boundaries by means of a transnational debating forum, which already exists to an extent in international human rights and environmental groups.

For Kaldor, the growth of new horizontal transnational networks and social movements like Amnesty International and Greenpeace creates the conditions for the emergence, alongside territorially-bound national units which are smaller than in the past, of 'a horizontal political culture based on a commitment to solve certain shared global problems . . . combined with a multiplicity and diversity of local popular cultures based on relatively small local and national territorial units' (Kaldor 1995: 88). For Kaldor, this in turn poses, together with the reassertion of national identity, a change in citizens' membership of political units, from territorially-based to issue-based membership.

Thus, in the case of South Africa, democratic goals can be pursued both by citizens participating as members of the new democracy located within South Africa's borders and by seeking with fellow democrats elsewhere the solution of environmental problems, the combatting of the consequences of colonialism, or the countering of gender inequality. This could involve building alliances with green groups against industrial corporations responsible for pollution in other countries, with democrats who share an interest in promoting post-colonial causes in other parts of Africa and Asia, or with feminist groups across the globe opposing patriarchy in all societies. Doing so would reflect two features of democracy in the age of globalization. One is that, depending on the issue in question, democrats may have greater common cause with fellow democrats whose formal citizenship locates them within other nation-states than with those who are formally fellow members of a nation-state. Yet, commonsense assumptions about the nation-state continue to encourage the belief that relations between citizens of different states ought to be conducted by and between governments representing the interests of their citizens in competition with those of other states. Second and conversely, while ideologies of national identity create the impression of a unity of purpose among the members of each nation-state, there are usually fellow citizens intent on pursuing goals that are not always in the interests of all. For example, when traditional leaders in South Africa attempt to retain their influence, women's rights organizations campaign against such interests as being in conflict with the democratic principles of equality and of offices being open to all citizens in free competition.

To recognize these features of the contemporary political context is to acknowledge that democracy itself is already a cosmopolitan project. Democracy is pursued in many societies and we applaud its progress in other parts of the globe. The fall of the Berlin Wall and the end of apartheid were welcomed by democrats elsewhere. Democrats are troubled by abuses of human rights and democratic principles, wherever they take place. This does raise the ongoing and unresolved debate about the extent to which democracy ought to respect and maintain traditions that try to preserve religious laws and hierarchical gender relations. We have to take seriously the assertion of the right to maintain and practise traditions on democratic grounds. However in South Africa, the priority given to the transformation of all institutions and the establishment of a culture of democracy suggests that democracy will require the transformation of traditions of this kind. The process involved should itself be a democratic one of public debate in which aspects of different traditions are reconsidered by those who practice or are subject to them.

If traditionally-held notions of the nation-state as the arena for democracy ought to be replaced by a cosmopolitan conception of democracy, we need to shift our conception of citizenship and of education for democratic citizenship accordingly.

Education: the cosmopolitan ideal

Two of the disjunctures identified by Held between the formal authority claimed by the nation-state and the actuality of globalization point to the implications of globalization for citizenship education. The first is that between national identity and the globalization of culture – 'the pull of national identities and the diverse orientations of contemporary cultural and communication systems' (1995b: 126). While the development of communication through printing has been regarded as a key factor in the formation of political identities – of the nation as 'imagined community' – 'the development of new communication systems creates a world in which the particularities of place and individuality are consistently mediated by regional and global communication networks' (1995b: 123). New experiences, meanings and transnational commonalities have been created by these new communication systems, creating possibilities for a plurality of identities. Film, video and television, as aspects of global communications, have created new forms of awareness and participation in global events and the possibility of new patterns of identification, of the experience of a 'global civil society'.

While Held does emphasize that the outcome of these trends is not clear, and that new forms of communication also have the potential to revive old forms of identity, we can draw some implications for education from these developments. To suggest to students that their identity is describable in terms of a particular nationhood, as distinct from others, is no longer accurate, if it ever was. Societies like South Africa, where there is no common culture, language, or sense of a shared history, are already cosmopolitan societies. Furthermore, students' perspectives and chosen identifications, drawn from

modern media, embrace global youth cultures. There is often a chosen identification with heroes from sport, film and video which represents rebellion against ascribed identities. Youth culture is already cosmopolitan, and to pretend otherwise threatens to undermine the potential schools have to persuade students to reflect on their actual lives in order to be able to be informed, critical citizens. Similarly, the curriculum of schools and especially universities reflects the impact of globalization. Access to various academic disciplines is initiation into practices that are transcultural and international, to a community of scholars whose membership transcends boundaries of nation-states.

Second, there is the disjuncture that posits on the one hand a formal understanding of democratic politics as exercised within the site of the territorially-bounded nation-state. On the other hand is the actuality already noted of recent developments in international law which recognizes powers and rights that transcend the authority of nation-states, the internationalization of political decision-making and of security structures, the transnational reach of contemporary systems of production, distribution and exchange, and the impact of new technologies on production and the location and movement of money.

In educating students for participation in democratic politics in this new context, it is necessary to recognize with Held the declining extent to which democracy can meaningfully be pursued if confined to the context of the modern nation-state. Accordingly, encouraging students to see themselves participating as democratic citizens by virtue of their membership of a particular nation-state is problematic. If, as Held argues, the sovereignty and authority of the individual state has been eroded by globalization, and if the reality is a 'global internationalisation of political decisions and outcomes among states' (1995b: 267), education for democratic citizenship must be located within the context of a cosmopolitan identity and a transnational democratic order. This precludes the teaching of citizenship as one national sense of identity, and demands instead that we develop a reflective awareness of a plurality of identities.

In educating for a plurality of identities, as well as for democracy that transcends national boundaries, the aim is a cosmopolitan self who, as Waldron puts it, is not defined by location, ancestry, citizenship or language, but is constituted by various cultures: 'He [sic] is a creature of modernity, conscious of living in a mixed-up world and having a mixed-up self' (1995: 95). The cosmopolitan individual, exemplified for Waldron by Salman Rushdie, affirms a vision of the self as mongrel and revels in melange, in hotchpotch. Rushdie himself might not be a realistic model for all, and is not intended by Waldron to represent the necessary disposition of all cosmopolitans. Waldron acknowledges (1996: 106) that most people will not have the opportunity or the wish to celebrate the cosmopolitan as Rushdie does. And most people will not become frequent flyers or have access to transcultural occupations and membership of international scientific and academic communities. The cosmopolitan identity that many will embrace is rather one whose attitude towards diversity will be one of openness to difference and of cultural competence, the ability to relate and act successfully across cultures.

The education of the cosmopolitan self rests on an altered conception of the five features of citizenship. Participation as a citizen is not restricted to involvement within the boundaries of the nation-state. Membership, correspondingly, is neither fixed nor unitary. While active membership of the nation-state remains, it is accompanied by a range of other local as well as cosmopolitan memberships, of collectivities of choice, which may change as identification with other issues and groups shifts over time and across different spaces. Under these conditions, the knowledge and understanding required of the democratic citizen is extensive. While the kind of knowledge and understanding focused on national identity is needed to serve the purpose of re-enacting and reproducing traditions, including those newly manufactured, for the cosmopolitan citizen knowledge and understanding is updated regularly as conditions at home and abroad change. It requires familiarity with local and national developments and a comparative perspective on the progress of democracy internationally. More constant than the knowledge and understanding required for understanding local, national and international developments would be the fundamental democratic principles of human rights, equality and freedom. Hence, turning to the place of identity and values in cosmopolitan citizenship, a more enduring feature of the citizen's identity in all three senses would be identification with democratic values. The upshot of this is that in the development of cosmopolitan citizenship there would have to be a detachment of values from identity as commonly understood, from values as derived from one communal membership, to values arrived at by identification with universal democratic principles, which are those of cosmopolitanism.

In the context of consolidating an emerging democracy like South Africa, it is tempting to turn to the promotion of national identity as the means of inculcating citizenship, especially where such factors as the ongoing legacies of apartheid, the high rate of violent crime and continuing non-payment for services following the boycott tactics of struggle threaten stability and development. While promoting national identity might appear to be the best means of repairing the social fabric, its limitations in the face of globalization have been made clear. The teaching of citizenship as an aspect of values education, in a society which is itself already cosmopolitan, should promote democratic principles.

Notes

1 An earlier version of this chapter was presented at the Fifth Biennial Conference of the International Network of Philosophers of Education, Johannesburg, August 1996. Thanks to Nazir Carrim, Mary Tjiattas and Steve Segal for their comments.
2 Such a project, I have argued elsewhere, is also subject to other criticisms (Enslin, 1993/4, 1994).

References

African National Congress (1994) *The Reconstruction and Development Programme*. Johannesburg: Umanyano Publications.

Archibugi, D. and Held, D. (eds) (1995) *Cosmopolitan Democracy: An Agenda for a New World Order*. Cambridge: Polity Press.

Enslin, P. (1993/4) Education for nation-building: a feminist critique. *Perspectives in Education*, **15**(1): 13–26.

Enslin, P. (1994) Should nation-building be an aim of education? *Journal of Education* (Natal), **19**(1): 23–36.

Friedman, M. (1989) Feminism and modern friendship: dislocating the community. *Ethics*, **19**(1): 275–90.

Gould, C. (1988) *Rethinking Democracy: Freedom and Social Cooperation in Politics, Economy, and Society*. Cambridge: Cambridge University Press.

Hall, S. (1992) The question of cultural identity. In S. Hall, D. Held and T. McGrew (eds) *Modernity and Its Futures*. Cambridge: Polity Press.

Hall, S., Held, D. and McGrew, T. (eds) (1992) *Modernity and Its Futures*. Cambridge: Polity Press.

Held, D. (1995a) Democracy and the international order. In D. Archibugi and D. Held (eds) *Cosmopolitan Dem-*

ocracy: An Agenda for a New World Order. Cambridge: Polity Press: 96–120.

Held, D. (1995b) *Democracy and the Global Order: From the Modern State to Cosmopolitan Governance*. Cambridge: Polity Press.

Kaldor, M. (1995) European institutions, nation-states and nationalism. In D. Archibugi and D. Held (eds) *Cosmopolitan Democracy: An Agenda for a New World Order*. Cambridge: Polity Press: 68–95.

McGrew, T. (1992) A global society. In S. Hall, D. Held and T. McGrew (eds) *Modernity and Its Futures*. Cambridge: Polity Press.

Mendus, S. (1993) Different voices, still lives: problems in the ethics of care. *Journal of Applied Philosophy*, **10**(1): 17–27.

Republic of South Africa (1996) *Constitution*. Pretoria: Government Printer.

Waldron, J. (1995) Minority cultures and the cosmopolitan alternative. In W. Kymlicka (ed.) *The Rights of Minority Cultures*. Oxford: Oxford University Press: 93–119.

Waldron, J. (1996) Multiculturalism and melange. In R. Fullinwider (ed.) *Public Education in a Multicultural Society: Policy, Theory, Critique*. Cambridge: Cambridge University Press: 90–118.

15 Beyond the Work-related Curriculum: Citizenship and Learning after Sixteen

KAREN EVANS

Introduction

The concept of citizenship potentially provides a way of understanding the life and work transitions of early adulthood. Becoming a citizen can be seen as more than a simple matter of acquiring civil status with accompanying rights and obligations. Citizenship is being rethought as a process through which young adults exercise responsibility and social contribution while having entitlements to support and provisions that enable them to manage their own transitions to adulthood and pursue their own projects. This requires and embraces competence. This approach to citizenship requires us to consider institutional structures that constrain or enable the acquisition of the various forms of knowledge and competence which are necessary to independent existence and social contribution. In spanning the public and private domains of existence, it enables us to address questions of inequality and of status inconsistency at various stages of the life course.

Independence is central to notions of citizenship. This creates ambiguities for a range of social groups, including women dependent on partners as well as for young adults. In early adulthood, independence occurs incrementally and unevenly on a number of fronts. Step by step, young people achieve independence from parents, not only financially but also by establishing values and beliefs of their own, making their own choices (albeit structurally constrained) and eventually by the physical separation of leaving home, either permanently or for extended periods. This growing independence goes hand-in-hand with the process of establishing separate identities and with development of beliefs about their own competence as functioning and active members of society. These changes are, increasingly, provisional and reversible. Self-efficacy or belief in one's ability to act is central to effective participation in social and economic structures of society. Citizenship thus potentially embraces notions of individual competence, as well as collective responsibility and contribution.

The discussion of citizenship in post-16 education that follows is in three parts. The first section outlines 'minimal' and 'maximal' versions of citizenship and citizenship education – Are they appropriate to the changing social context and situation of young adults? The second section explores further the social dynamics and social conditions of the time and argues that the workplace as the dominant source of values, standards and the curriculum cannot continue to drive developments in the post-compulsory curriculum. The goals of learning must derive from broader frameworks, providing learners with the means and capacities for interpreting and acting in the world as a social whole. The approach that places work at the centre with citizenship as an adjunct is turned on its head. The final section considers how we can educate people as citizens, with the capacities necessary for work and independent economic contribution to society as a significant component of that process. This reverses the argument we have seen since 1976, in which the broader goals of social contribution and equality of opportunity have progressively been replaced by a narrower instrumentalism in education, with subordination of education to the perceived needs of the economy and labour market. Finally, salient features of approaches to post-compulsory education and training which would foster maximal versions of citizenship are outlined.

Education for citizenship

I have discussed in previous work (Evans 1995, 1998) some relationships between the contested concepts of citizenship and competence, and have argued that both have 'minimal' and 'maximal' versions. Education for citizenship in minimal interpretations requires only induction into basic knowledge of institutionalized rules concerning rights and obligations. Maximal interpretations require education which develops critical and reflective abilities, independence of thought on social issues and capacities for active participation in social and political processes. As educators we need to be clear about which version we wish to adopt and that the version chosen is consistent with our wider educational values and vision of what is required for the ethical advancement of society and the state.

The policies of the last two decades in the fields of upper-secondary and higher education have increased steadily the emphasis on the work-related curriculum, with values and standards derived from the government's interpretation of the needs and practices of employers. In further education, too, the Work-Related Non-Advanced Further Education initiatives of the 1980s were carried through into the 1990s in the vocational education and training 'tracks' which the 1996 Dearing Report has sought to strengthen.

Education for citizenship was receiving little serious attention in Britain at the time the Commission on Citizenship was established, with the Rt Hon. Bernard Weatherill MP, Speaker of the House of Commons as patron in 1988. The Commission identified a threat to democracy in an increasingly commercial society, where insecurity and sense of isolation and powerlessness become the everyday experience of growing numbers of individuals, and asked whether we are, as a society, creating conditions of the 'mass society of mutually antagonistic individuals, easy prey to despotism'.

The Commission produced what Morrell (1991) termed a traditional British analysis of citizenship. This followed the classic approach of Marshall (1950) based on civil, political and social elements, and emphasizing individual freedom, rights to participate in the exercise of political power and the right to share 'to the full' in the social heritage. Rights and responsibilities were seen as standing 'in their own right' as Morrell puts it, and not necessarily as a *quid pro quo* arrangement, a deal between the individual and society.

The Commission's work had some influence on the re-emergence of education for citizenship as a cross-curriculum theme in the framing of the National Curriculum. Citizenship was one of five non-mandatory cross-curricular themes identified by the National Curriculum Council, the others being careers education and guidance, economic awareness, health education and environmental education. Schools were guided to teach these themes largely through the mandatory core and other foundation subjects. The National Curriculum Council Report (1990), which elaborated this theme, emphasized 'increasing diversity, Europeanisation, multiculturalism' and put forward a wide range of approaches through which, it states, the foundation can be laid for 'positive, participative citizenship'. As McLaughlin (1992) shows, there are some aspects of the Report that can be read in maximal ways, as well as many that lend themselves to minimalist readings. For example, maximalist interpretations are suggested by the references to awareness of political structures and processes and 'independence of thought on social and moral issues', based on consideration of questions of diversity, justice and inequality in society.

While no explicit statement is made of underlying values, a clear value position is discernible in the emphasis on duties and responsibilities, and on the pluralist conception of society. The latter is reflected in the emphasis on diversity as a source of tensions and the implicit assumption that these tensions can be resolved by consensus around a set of shared values. There is little acknowledgement, for example, of the position that power is contested and that society is made up of competing interest groups with differentials of power and influential operating at all levels. The emphasis is on normative concepts of the 'good citizen' rather than on critical participation in social and political processes. This represents a packaging of social and political values as though they were part of an agreed syllabus for an uncontested subject, despite its apparent breadth and scope.

The Report of the independent National Commission on Education, *Learning to Succeed* (1993), adopted a pluralistic model of society combined with treatments of citizenship that are more open to maximal readings, but also failed to acknowledge the contested conceptual frameworks within which notions of citizenship are discussed and operationalized. Morrell, a member of the Speakers Commission on Citizenship, highlighted the contrast between the way academics philosophize about meanings of citizenship with the apparent unity of views of young people surveyed in an associated study, carried out by Richardson (1990: 35).

> It is unusual to find wide consensus on any issue. Yet in this study, there was one issue which united virtually everyone across the social spectrum. From those who had left school with few qualifications to those in University or beyond, there was a strong call for more teaching of the issues surrounding citizenship in schools.

The Speaker's Commission emphasized that the skills of citizenship need to be learned and that considerations of citizenship should be incorporated in education at all levels, from the earliest years, through further and adult education, and also in professional education and training.

In practice, citizenship education is little in evidence at any level. While nominally present in the form of a cross-curricular theme associated with the National Curriculum, evidence (Whitty et al. 1996) has shown that, in practice, these themes are 'submerged' within the strongly framed National Curriculum subjects, with very limited opportunities for pupils to relate the themes to their everyday lives:

> very few pupils had heard of the term 'economic and industrial understanding' or thought they were being taught any. The findings were similar for education for citizenship except in one school which had a specific citizenship module as part of a PSE (Personal and Social Education) module. (ibid.: 62)

Even where identifiable forms of citizenship education exist, schooling may, in the assumptions implicit in its structures, be promulgating 'passive knower' models in 'civics education' on the rights and duties of citizenship in a democracy; it may in political and debating societies simply be giving openings for the 'movers and shakers' of academic or social élites to practise their skills in a safe institutional environment; or it may through Community Service or voluntary activity, be promulgating versions of citizenship that emphasize citizen duties or voluntarism and private contribution, without the concomitant understanding of wider citizen rights, obligations and roles. Education for citizenship may become ineffectively minimalist, or seriously controversial when maximal in approach. The institutional educator committed to

maximal versions of citizenship is thus potentially caught in contradictions of a fundamental kind.

In post-16 education and training, citizenship education *per se* rarely appears in curriculum offerings, since the virtual demise of 'liberal studies', as a self-contained and much criticized curriculum component. The subsequent encouragement of 'balancing studies' of various kinds for those following primarily academic routes may be seen as an attempt to develop the learner's ability to inquire within and through a broader set of frameworks and perspectives than previously narrowly specialized programmes allowed or encouraged. Such approaches have been beset with problems of not being taken seriously, often being seen as timetable-fillers by students and some teachers. Through what Dale (1985) terms 'ideological characteristics' of vocationalism, values and priorities of egalitarianism in education in the 1960s and early 1970s have gradually been replaced by the needs of industry, the economy and workforce, encouraging not only increased skills training but attitude changes and status adjustment. These ideological characteristics have been contested, and a tendency for gender, race and class-based inequalities to be reinforced by the work-related curriculum has been countered to some degree by other ideological forces and interests which have 'continually reasserted the values of education' (Dale 1985: 7). Pring (1991) has suggested a return to the industrial spirit of the Victorian era was envisaged in the 'new vocationalism' initiated in the late 1970s, with increased emphasis on qualities such as 'a sense of individual responsibility' permeating the curriculum. In 1996, proposals for reform of post-16 education have incorporated versions of moral education and citizenship, but only as adjuncts to the main business of educating for work (Dearing 1996).

Unlike the new 'vocationalism' of the 1980s these relatively marginalized approaches to citizenship and citizenship education continue to be based implicitly on normative models which are themselves grounded in the social dynamics of the 1950s and 1960s. There is some enlargement, to make them more 'inclusive' of diversity of background and experience, but are they adequate for the fragmented and polarized, sometimes marginalized, life situations emerging for many young people as they encounter 'blocked opportunities, reduced access to resources and social exclusion in their endeavours to negotiate their way to adulthood'

(Williamson 1996). In a wider European context, where social exclusion and citizenship have become intertwined as primary policy concerns, it is increasingly recognized that the social processes that are shaping lives reflect the complex interactions of social structures with transition behaviours of the young people themselves – the interplay of structure and agency in unprecedented circumstances of risk and uncertainty. The operation of differentials of power and cultural capital in the transitional years bring stability or instability to the life course. How far do social rights play a part in shaping the life course, how far do individual capabilities contribute to success in negotiating uncharted waters?

For some of those who subscribe to maximal versions of citizenship, education for citizenship is better tackled outside the formal structures of schooling, in non-formal youth or community organizations in which aims, values and structures are more congruent with the processes being learned? But does that marginalize citizenship education, open its proponents to accusations of 'indoctrination', and limit exposure to these forms of education to the voluntary users of the organizations in question?

The contribution of youth and community work

Youth and community work in any society will reflect the development of that society, historically, politically and economically. In developing countries, for example, youth and community work has aims and priorities which often centre on self-reliance, 'citizenship', self-employment and 'development' skills (Evans and Haffenden 1991).

In the former Soviet Union and Eastern Europe of the recent past, youth organizations were closely controlled. They played a central role in pursuit of state objectives, in a context in which there was a broader conception of the scope of education with overt social objectives permeating the curriculum in every sector. Non-formal provision in the USA and Western Europe has been provided through a wide variety of forms of service and institution, but with a common general aim of developing individual maturity and community involvement. While youth and community work in the West suffered from narrow concepts of education, in the Eastern part of Europe, non-formal education had a high priority. However, state control meant that the exercise

of freedom and responsibility were not assured (Marsland 1991).

The Youth Service curriculum in Britain shifted from a focus on physical fitness and the promotion of family values, to an emphasis on personal resources of 'body, mind and spirit' and good citizenship in the post-war years. This need to develop citizenship was highlighted in the Albemarle Report (Ministry of Education 1960) and the concept of social education was brought to the fore. With the Milson-Fairbairn Report (YSDC 1969), a new emphasis was given to more active roles for young people in society and for political education to form an explicit part of social education. In 1982, the Thompson Report (Department of Education and Science) saw the role of youth work as affirming and involving individual young people. This Report had a central concern with alienation (which it saw as often leading to juvenile crime and drug abuse); unemployment; homelessness; the hardship of life in the inner cities and in rural areas. The need to counter racism, sexism, and work with those with disabilities was highlighted. Much emphasis was also placed on greater participation by young people in all levels of the service, and the report reasserted the central place of political and social education in youth work in unequivocal terms. The Youth and Community Service in England and Wales has thus long held values associated with citizenship at its heart.

The Service, in the early 1990s, was called on to justify its continued existence by making explicit its unique contribution to the education and personal development of the young population. It was challenged to say what it can do that other agencies cannot. In parallel with this, it has been increasingly constrained by ever-reducing resources and central governmental interventions, requiring it to identify a core curriculum with measurable outcomes. Despite this, in 1990, the Youth Service and its agencies at national level restated its maximal position on citizenship through local and political education in the following 'mission statement' for the Youth Service:

> The intent of the Youth Service is to assist young people to make sense of the personal, social and political issues which affect their lives; to promote young people's self-awareness, self-confidence and competence in relationships; to encourage the making of decisions and choices (for example, education and training); to support the development of independent judgement by young people and their

ability to express their opinions and values; and to advocate with and for young people the defence and extension of opportunities and choices available to them.   (National Youth Bureau 1990: 35)

Citizenship education in this approach must enable young people both to understand the social processes which produce diversity and reproduce inequalities, and to see how they can act from the social positions they hold. But many young people cease their participation in youth organizations by 16 and do not experience the service in the way envisaged (Evans 1994). For the majority of young people, their understanding of social processes comes through their day-to-day experiences inside, outside, and beyond schooling.

Social dynamics and status passages

Turning to accounts of the changing nature of work and the effects of social change on status passages, what are conditions under which learning for adult life takes place? Which versions of citizenship and competence are required? How can they best be achieved?

In all European countries, young adults are experiencing uncertain status and are dependent upon state and parental support for longer periods than would have been the case a generation ago (Chisholm and Bergeret 1991). Faced with changing opportunity structures, people have to find their own ways of reconciling personal aspirations with available opportunities and their own values in the domains of education, consumption, politics, work and family life. Achievement and recognition of adult status comes at different times to different spheres of life, and status inconsistency may result (Hurrelmann 1988). They may, for example, be supporting a family while on a grant, or still in training. Or they may hold responsible positions in work while remaining in their family of origin, still the child in the household but supporting other members financially. In this way individual roles and status become differentiated across the different domains of life and experience, and defining an individual as an adult and citizen may hinge on multiple roles performed. Young adults may be caught in disjunctions and contradictions of policies that do not recognize the interplay of the private and public domains and are based on invalid assumptions about common characteristics and needs of age ranges. As Jones and Wallace (1992)

have pointed out, age-graded welfare entitlements in particular can lead to gross inequalities, with the recognition of varying domestic circumstances a 'missing ingredient' in the social security criteria of need. To understand transitions to adult, worker and citizen status, we also have to understand the 'private world of family life' (p. 69).

Social changes in the interrelated domains of work, education, family and community all affect transition behaviours, which themselves reflect personal identities and aspirations as well as the opportunity structures with which young adults are faced. The social dynamics against which policies and programmes should now be assessed are those of growing individualization of the life course. According to Baethge (1989), processes of individualization are taking place that are creating inconsistencies and ambiguities in the status of young adults. Inconsistencies need to be identified and addressed if policies are to maximize means of achieving economic independence through competence and active, responsible and fulfilling participation in society, through full citizenship.

Work and status passages

Individualization is also linked with emerging post-Fordist scenarios in the organization of work, where the scene is set for social control via increased surveillance (Ball 1990), or creation of new possibilities for social transformation, with education as the engine for change (Brown and Lauder 1992).

In the work arena, transitions to worker status are defined by institutionalized rules concerning recognized qualifications and credentials. These credentials testify to the knowledge, competence and experience of the holder and their acquisition and application depend on the way in which the various credentials and selection systems are negotiated (Ainley 1994, Raffe 1991). This in turn is heavily influenced by cultural capital, particularly in respect of access to information, advice, social support and personal networks. Young adults bring different transition behaviours to these situations, and success in negotiating these structures and networks can bring stability or instability to the life course. For those who are unsuccessful in gaining entry to jobs, long term unemployment cuts young adults off from the opportunities of the market, from access to work-based credentialling systems and from the exercise of citizenship in any significant sense (Evans and Heinz 1994). Even successful entry to the labour market can bring another set of limitations and instabilities. Early work entry can create premature foreclosure of options and stereotyped work identities. In the 1950s workplaces were described in the Crowther Report (Ministry of Education 1959) as deadening to the minds of young school leavers. Post-Fordist discourses now talk of learning organizations, providing either new opportunities for democratic access to knowledge or bringing new forms of social control, for example, through increased surveillance. Post-Fordist discourses about the social and economic future attempt to normalize a view of the social organization of work and present as inevitable what is in fact contingent and subject to political process (Edwards 1993). The post-Fordist scenario presented by writers such as Brown and Lauder (1982) is one of work transformed by new technology, of multi-skilled highly-trained workforces with high levels of training underpinned by extended initial education which itself acts as the driving force for wider social transformations and democratization. The alternative version of this scenario presented by Edwards (1993) is one in which the disappearance of intermediate level jobs will leave a stratum of jobs demanding high levels of intellectual skill, competence and flexibility and a large mobile sector of casualized labour at all skill levels, operating by selling their services by contract. For those in the increasing ranks of casual labour, narrow competences are unlikely to be of any use over time and membership of a casualized pool of labour kept in ongoing insecurity and instability is also unlikely to be able to engage in full participation in society in the sense implied in the maximal definitions of citizenship discussed earlier.

How have the changing employment situation of the 1980s and 1990s affected young people's attitudes to work? For some time, there was a version of the 'moral panic' over the effects of unemployment of young people's motivations to work. The traditional incentives of 'get good qualifications and get a good job' for the majority of school leavers could not be invoked by teachers, and fears that a generation would be raised lacking the 'work ethic' were pronounced in the early 1980s. In fact, the decline of employment opportunities for young people 'tightened the bonds' between education and employment in a host of ways. The 16–19 Initiative research studies carried out between 1987 and 1991 studied work and training attitudes, and

showed that the value young people attached to training reflected whether or not it led to a proper job. Motivation to train is driven by the hope and expectations of work and it is evaluated accordingly. As Raffe (1991) has put it, education for its own sake is fair enough but training for its own sake is a 'contradiction in terms'. Economic locus of control measures showed that high internal locus of control, or belief in one's influence and control over events, was associated with success both in education and in direct entry to work. These were also associated with political and social beliefs. Work commitment was strong, with only a quarter of respondents disagreeing with the statement that 'having almost any job is better than being unemployed'; but a majority also agreed that 'you do not have to have a job to be a full member of society and that a job is not essential to life satisfaction'. Those closest to the labour market, and in jobs, had the strongest work commitment.

To what extent did our findings in the early 1990s indicate a shift towards post-materialist values in work? When young adults were asked to select the three work characteristics they felt to be most important, a friendly atmosphere at work was chosen by two-thirds of all respondents, supporting the position that work is more than a means to an end for many young adults, who increasingly seek to develop personal identities and relationships through their work as well as life outside work. While non-materialistic considerations were rated highly by all groups, the most disadvantaged young people on the unemployed/under-employed trajectory saw career security and wages as very important. These, of course, were the very aspects of work denied them, and through lack of these, other aspects of social life were affected. Young people following the academic track tended, by contrast, to balance the social and quality aspects of work alongside the material. Attitudes to work are thus strongly affected by social location and experience of the labour market, with materialistic values strongest amongst those most adversely affected by depressed labour market conditions.

All of these findings are significant in the emergence of a casualized workforce. Strong internal locus of control will enable people to play the labour market opportunities available better than those with fatalistic attitudes. The prospect of a 'revolving door' is intended to ensure that work commitment and instrumental work values will remain strong even amongst those most disadvantaged and most marginalized in work opportunities. But training will not be valued and skills and motivation will not be sustained over time unless there are successful outcomes. Casualization and the growth of the proportion of workers in relatively insecure jobs in small and medium companies which do not, by themselves, have a capacity for quality training, means that there is a high danger of skills loss and lack of continuity in social identity construction. One of the major challenges is to provide for continuous development of knowledge-based skill for individuals and with an emphasis on work identities gained through ownership and recognition of skill and membership of defined 'communities of practice' (Lave and Wenger 1995). A second challenge is to provide a modernized framework of social support to ensure access to social citizenship for all, to counter diminishing entitlement and the move towards dependence of citizen rights and obligations on increasingly insecure worker status.

Education and status passages

The expansion of education has produced a new set of structures and experiences between the end of the compulsory phase of schooling at 16 and first entry to the labour market, at ages up to the mid-twenties.

Anglo-German studies showed how far the developments in Britain in post-compulsory education have moved towards the 'workplace as curriculum authority' in introducing experiences related to the work place into educational settings. At the ages of 17 and 19 young people in British cities studied, namely Swindon and Liverpool, identified with work-related experiences much more than their German counterparts in the 'matched' cities of Paderborn and Bremen. The results (Bynner and Roberts 1991, Evans and Heinz 1994) showed that many more have agreed that they have been given responsibility, have been able to make decisions and use initiative and have developed other work-related competences than young Germans at the same age. 'New skills and abilities' and 'thought more abilities were being used', were the comparable results. Some care has to be taken in interpreting these findings as young people in Britain are also so much closer to the labour market chronologically than their German counterparts, entering work at least two years ahead in all trajectories, therefore,

the anticipation of work was much nearer to their interests and concerns. The results also indicate that British provision, in making the curriculum richer in work experiences, was perhaps making up for the relative lack of progression of opportunities subsequently. In Germany, young people valued the experiences they were getting because of the general labour market utility of the credentials they were gaining. This is a marked example of *earning* the right to take responsibility rather than *learning* it through the educational process. In England, the approach was much more to surround young people with a range of work-related opportunities for learning, with the opportunities for progressing from learning into work much more haphazard and risky. There is also a prolonged dependency associated with extended post-compulsory education, which runs counter to the deeply-embedded cultural values and expectations of a significant proportion of the working class population, particularly among males. While access to education is a right of social citizenship, in the post-compulsory phase this has become associated with decreased social citizenship rights in other areas, associated with increased dependency and expectations of family support.

Families

Families can impede or support the transitions of early adulthood. For many young adults the experience of physical separation from the family for extended periods may result in improved understanding and appreciation and is part of the process of negotiating independence, as Banks et al. (1992) have shown. For others, escape from the parental home is seen as the only way to achieve a sense of self and to exercise their own choices, however restricted these may be in reality. For some young adults thrown back into involuntary dependence on family through welfare policies, prospects for achievement of independence and citizenship may be impaired. It can be argued further that it should be a basic social right not to 'have to rely' on their family because alternatives do not exist (Finch 1995).

In the context of social changes and individualized transitions, the parental role becomes even more one of support rather than guidance. Few parents have experience of the options facing their children because of the pace of change in all aspects of work and education. This is an arena in which status inconsistencies for young people are most pronounced. Jones and Wallace (1992) identified the 'basic ambiguity':

> emancipation and citizenship status derive from economic independence, but some recognition of emancipation and access to some citizenship rights are required for the achievement of economic independence. This creates a 'double-bind' to which many young people are subject as they become older.   (p. 92)

The 'double-bind' occurs because young adults are expected to become emancipated and independent – 'to stand on their own feet' – and one of the roles of the family is to assist in this process. The economic dimension is important here. When young people have a degree of financial independence through an independent source of income, their progress towards emancipation is enhanced. They become less subject to parental control and more able to exercise rights both inside and outside the home. Policies have progressively increased the financial dependence of young people on their parents in the 16–18 age range, as access to unemployment benefit have been removed and training rates have assumed parental support. While the case for this can be argued for young people under the age of legal majority, that is the age of legal and political citizenship, after the age of 18 and up to the mid-twenties an assumption is made of financial dependency in the withholding of full adult rates of social security. What are the effects and implications of this?

The interconnections between the three main transitions (or 'careers') of the youth phase become significant here, as Coles (1996) has argued:

1 education, training and labour market careers (from schooling into post-school education and training and jobs;
2 domestic careers (from families of origin to families of destination);
3 housing careers (from living dependent on families to living independently of them).

Often the transition involving education, training and the labour market drives the other two transitions. For example, young people who follow the academic trajectory and live away from home while studying have moved to a form of 'half-way house'. These intermediate households form an important and recognized part of the transition process. For others 'intermediate households' are more risky. These involve staying in hostels or with friends. These carry a risk of moving onto homelessness, particularly where a welcome is outstayed or a 'fixed term' of stay expires, with lack of economic means through unemployment being the major contributory factor.

Many young people go through a period of moving backwards and forwards between their parental home and intermediate housing before moving finally to the independent home. The 16–19 Initiative showed that, by the age of 19, most young people expressed a preference to live away from their families. This constitutes normal development. More than 35 per cent of females aged 19–20 had left home, compared with 27 per cent of males. Ten per cent of 15–16 year old males and 11 per cent of females had left home (Banks et al. 1982). Leaving home earlier was not a problem in itself. It is leaving home *prematurely* that is problematic, when the young person does not have the means for independent living but 'push' or 'pull' factors operate. 'Push' factors are often associated with poor family circumstances and relationships while 'pull' factors are hopes of jobs in some distant and more promising labour market. Lack of access to affordable housing and unemployment are the major underlying causes of the drift into homelessness, where this occurs, and early leavers, who are at most risk of unemployment, are the most vulnerable.

More respondents in the academic trajectories and unemployment/under-employment trajectories had moved away from home. Those on skilled and semi-skilled transitional work trajectories tended to remain at home for longer. In the academic trajectory, the higher level of leaving home reflected 'going away to University'. In the unemployed/under-employed trajectory the higher moving out rate was associated with family pressures and bad housing conditions (push factors) and the pull factors of relatively buoyant labour markets.

Policies are encouraging lengthening dependency both by increasing retention in education and training and by assuming parental support. Those for whom the push factors are irresistible, through family breakdown, for example, will be at greater risk of social exclusion and homelessness than previously, since policies are geared to retention. The policies will reduce those going into intermediate housing. For those who do go into intermediate housing (other than student housing) there is little incentive to continue in education and training unless adequate financial support is available. In Britain, removal of income support, the limited provision of affordable intermediate housing, combined with low training allowances without a housing element or sufficiency to 'pay their keep' has increased dependency and vulnerability.

The thrust of social policy to push young people back on families can increase pressures on the family both financial and personal, and is reflected in rising homelessness figures as young people leave or are pushed out without the 'social scaffolding' to support them.

In many of our European counterparts, different cultural norms apply concerning dependency and age of accession to adult status. Young people are not expected to be earning until their twenties, there is not the same pull of the labour market and strong institutional structures allow for a degree of experimentation, false starts, and provide 'safety net' financial support for those for whom family support is not available. The wage packet as a symbol of growing up in Britain does not hold to the same degree in other advanced economies. In the less institutionalized, less supportive British context, young people need help to break out of the vicious circles operating, but the circles themselves need to be tackled.

Social identities, status passages and community participation

Young adults participate in their communities in a number of ways. As well as being producers at work, they are also consumers and they have a right to participate in the life of their local communities as citizens and voters. Fragmentation and diversification of the opportunity structure are combined with the effects of globalization in which people increasingly become disassociated from their traditional contexts. This means that the search for identity or sense of wholeness and continuity as a person, gains a new intensity (Baethge 1989). Intergenerational transmission of 'virtues' is reduced, and the channels to participation in political and social structures may become obscured. Engagement in citizenship in its maximal sense is thus made more difficult, and the pursuit of 'ego-driven' projects may become paramount, as young adults act to maximize personal opportunity and reduce risk.

Many of these 'choices' are rooted in partly-formed social identities, the senses young people have of who they are and what their capabilities are. Self-definition involves internalizing the definitions and attributes ascribed by others. These subjective identities are associated with social class, gender, race. They also reflect educational credentials and other mediating factors associated with experiences in the labour market and wider social context, with narrowing career options playing a part in shaping identities over time. While the latter are increasing in relative significance as traditional transition patterns become 'fractured' and extended, disadvantage continues to be concentrated in groups defined by class, gender and race in particular localities, as the 16–19 Initiative demonstrated. Social identities are reflected in social attitudes. These have been shown to be organized around institutionalized authority, gender and race, employment commitment and fatalism (Banks et al. 1992), with the more 'political' dimensions of identity less sharply focused and less consistently expressed over time.

Changes in political involvements between 16 and 20 were incremental, with 'only a tiny minority [developing] any serious involvement in politics of the conventional kind' (ibid.: 176). Their attitudes were not organized around political positions but around the politics of the personal. Changes in early adult life involved gradual increases in interest in political issues.

The structures for democratic experience exist in many community groups, yet youth participation in these, in so far as it is quantified, appears small (Evans 1994, Evans and Heinz 1994). Local organizations provide a means by which people engage with public life. They featured in the proposals for the Active Society (YSDC 1969) that aimed to encourage young people's active and critical participation through the vehicles of Youth and Community work. Freire (1974) argued that

> People could learn social and political responsibility only by experiencing that responsibility, through intervention in the destiny of their children's schools, in the destinies of their trade unions and places of employment ... through associations, clubs and councils, and in the life of their neighbourhoods, churches and rural communities by actively participating in associations, clubs and charitable societies.

The approaches of the 'Learning by Participation'

projects of the 1980s (Dalin 1983) aimed to harness both work and wider community experience in these ways, to assist young people in their status passages. However, as Mac-an-Ghaill (1996: 172) argues, such approaches must address fundamentally working class students' experiences of transitions into adult life:

> we need to incorporate a more dynamic perspective that sees schools as well as *reproducing* wider class divisions, also locally *producing* a range of class-based identities, involving social and psychic investments, that students and teachers come to occupy and live out.

Yet the signs are that the media and advertising are creating alternative ways of establishing collective identities, and a sense of belonging around these are often 'global' and centred on consumer goods, Nike trainers being the obvious example. This is significant, given that consumerism is an arena in which citizenship rights are being redefined. Williamson (1996) asks 'whether citizenship is anything more than a rhetorical device when it has been reduced to consumerism and when the social scaffolding which supported it has been dismantled?' (p. 11). The communitarian movement, as articulated by Etzioni (1995), puts forward self-help, family support and community support as means to reconnect people at local level. As employment status and consumer power increasingly determine citizen status and rights, there is a fundamental problem of motivation to be addressed in the communitarian movement, among those disadvantaged in and by the operation of labour and consumer markets. As Williamson (1996: 11) asks: 'There remains questions concerning the relationships between 'status' issues and issues of volition and competence. Where is young people's motivation to develop the latter, if the former are being systematically eroded?'

Many factors can combine to marginalize and exclude young people. As citizenship has become increasingly equated with consumer power under the 'New Right', what is the position of young people unable to gain a foothold in work? Unemployment cuts young people off not only from work, but also from exercising consumer power in their leisure time. Adults' monopolies on local politics and democratic structures may also make it difficult for young people to participate, and the 16–19 Initiative and the Anglo-German Studies found widespread apathy among British

youth, with them being the most politically alienated but also potentially the most politically impotent. But these studies have also shown keen interest in issues such as equality of opportunity and the environment and particular receptivity to changes in lifestyles and values.

Maximal versions of citizenship and competence required

Minimal versions of citizenship and competence are inadequate to deal with the social dynamics of the time, and young people's responses to them, since they neither equip with the critical skills necessary to engage with an uncertain world nor cultivate the sense of shared autonomy and social being, in the broader context within which individual projects and tasks are pursued. Maximal approaches to the development of citizenship and competence have these processes at their centre. Interventions through education and social support must begin with respect for individual autonomy. Young people's subjective emotional experiences of support and satisfaction, their future perspectives of optimism or pessimism and their feelings of control in relation to norms and external expectations are all significant variables. In maximal approaches the educator many exercise *influence* through providing information, discussion of courses of action and their possible consequences, and creating conditions for exposure to different points of view through 'undominated verbal discourse'. All of these create conditions for attitude change, personality development and unfolding of competences (Habermas 1976). The potential for personal competences to 'unfold' is affected by particular societal conditions. The interactions that are necessary in order to develop capacities for social action are thus enhanced or impeded by social structures, and the removal or reduction of structural barriers are as important as the facilitation of personal growth.

Thus, person-centred approaches must be combined with altering the material and social environment so that demands do not become so great that young people cannot cope unaided. When demands exceed the capacity to cope, social citizenship is eroded and social exclusion results for many. While much emphasis is placed on the obligations and responsibilities of the young, the social rights that provide the material and cultural conditions for social inclusion and participation must not be lost sight of. These enable the 'social self' to develop.

Each individual needs to be able to balance and manage 'internal and external' realities, that is their needs felt in relation to the environment in which they operate. Where there is a mismatch between needs felt and the opportunities the environment can provide, dissatisfaction results. Expectations may be 'unrealistic' because they stem from self-concept and identity formation which is at odds with the environment or they may be unrealistic because the environment is overly constrained or hostile and the expectations could be better met through changes to the environment. Individuals may accommodate or resist aspects of the social world, the structural influences around them. They may do so individually or collectively. Individuals need to be able to regulate their behaviour and expectations in relation to the environment, while maintaining and developing a values base, which gives meaning to goals and actions. They need to become 'productive processors of reality' in Hurrelmann's (1989) terms, goal-directed in their behaviour, with the capacities to regulate and adjust their actions, achieve and redefine goals and boundaries and to participate in change (see Table 15.1).

In this sense, they are engaged in the transformation of experience into knowledge and action, the foundations of experiential learning which emphasizes the process of adaptation and learning rather than content or outcomes. These processes lie at the heart of maximal approaches to learning for competence and citizenship, when set in a modernized framework of material and social support.

Embedding maximal approaches in a wider framework of provision

In Britain, transition structures are weakly institutionalized, and post-compulsory education and training arrangements reflect historically embedded narrowness and divisions, with the 'élite' Advanced level and the narrowly based National Vocational Qualifications exemplifying the academic/vocational divide. The curriculum has been progressively shaped by instrumental values and the presumed needs of employers. In particular, the NVQ system is predicated on minimalist notions of competence-based performance, which are of questionable relevance to future skill needs and are outdated quickly. Not only do they fail to develop the broad-based underlying capabilities appropriate to the social dynamics of the time (Skilbeck et al. 1986), but they are also highly individualistic, reinforce structural inequalities and run counter to the development of interdependence (Blackman and Evans 1994). Criticisms of narrowness are offset by post hoc attempts to broaden the curriculum by 'entitlements' and 'transferable skills' which occupy an ambiguous and weak place in the curriculum, and are not comparable in breadth or depth to the 'general education' provided at this stage of education in many European countries.

In England, the preferred response to all difficult financial and family situations is to terminate education and seek a job. Young adults are much closer to the labour market than many of their European counterparts, and enter it at least two years earlier, so in many respects the range of work attributes they have acquired in their early careers is wider

Table 15.1 Variables in youth transitions

Structural attributes	Intervening variables (socialization conditions)	Psycho-social processes	Person-environment behaviours/actions	Outcomes
• Gender • Social class	• Family • Peers • Media	• Identity formation	• Active	• Political participation
• Ethnicity	• Social networks • Locality	• Self-concept and esteem	• Passive	
• Labour market	• Educational institutions			• Economic participation
↓	• Educational qualifications		• Accommodating	
• Structural and ascribed attributes	• Credentials			
	↓			
	• Acquired attributes		• Resistant	• Personal goals

than in other northern European countries. While the narrowness of curriculum content for many users of Further Education (FE) colleges is a weakness, the *processes* and *climate* of learning in the colleges contribute to the status passage to adulthood, helped by the extended age range involved, 16–25 and beyond. Young people report very positively that they are 'treated as adults'. In allowing and encouraging young people to exercise a reasonable degree of responsibility and self-determination, evidence (Evans and Heinz 1994) has indicated that the FE colleges are significantly contributing to the *process* of becoming adult citizens, even if failing to provide broad perspectives via the content of the curriculum.

Beyond dualisms

A set of 'dualisms' limit our approaches to questions of learning and its social and vocational effects (Marginson 1994). Dualism is represented, for example, in the distinctions between the 'vocational and relevant' and the 'academic and liberal' traditions in education. It is also represented in the opposing approaches to 'structure and agency' which argue that individuals determine their own fates and those which argue that agents are subject to, and determined by, external forces. Questions of 'choice or determination' are strongly represented in discussions of career pathways. Much early literature on occupational choice saw individuals as context free agents; Roberts (1968, 1995) took the opposite view, arguing that there was little choice involved. Careers were determined by social structures and individuals were launched on trajectories, with the flight path and end point more or less fixed. The polarized perspectives of 'people make society' versus 'society makes people' have given way to more recent approaches which show that the field of human actions is structured and that these structures can themselves be negotiated, and changed by those who operate within them. Thus we are no longer locked into waiting for the social policies and the broad social structures within which we operate to change fundamentally before educational practice based on alternative values becomes possible.

The arguments that move beyond dualism are about the dynamics of transformation, the 'dialogical relationships' of Giddens. Institutions are continuously created and recreated by the individuals who live and work within them. When we apply these ideas to the relationships between education and work, a new perspective is developed on ways in which 'work-related' education is conceptualized. The challenge in establishing new relationships between education and work is to reduce the gap that separates them without impinging on the unique features of each. Work can be made more educative and education more relevant to work without dissolving one into the other. Further changes need to be made to the world of work and the structures of work and the labour market, as well as to education, if the new relationships between education and work are to be well-founded (Brown and Evans 1991). Moreover, education has a plurality of purposes. As Marginson suggests, it is no more tenable to argue, for example, that a university should be subordinated to the economy, that is government and industry, than it is to claim total self-regarding autonomy for the community of scholars.

Some argue that by broadening vocational education, redefining it to incorporate some aspect of 'liberal' education, it becomes preparation for life. This is one way in which instrumental orientations of the work-related curriculum are brought into the wider domains of education for adult life and citizenship. But can the multiple purposes of education be resolved in a simple 'broadening' of work-related studies in this way? The same analysis could be applied to further education in the 1990s, where generic skills and key skills are emphasized and seen as central to this process of 'broadening' work-related education. They are represented as being in the general interest of society yet they are derived from and defined in terms of the needs of employers. In some contexts, generic skills are construed as being superior to knowledge since the skills are as being somehow timeless and independent, while knowledge is seen as provisional and context bound.

Whether context-free transferability is possible in the way suggested by the proponents of 'key skills' is debatable since the 'freeing' of skills from their contexts can lead to superficiality and detaches 'flexibility' from deeper capability (Barnett 1994). As propounded, key skills also reflect a restricted set of social values, derived from the needs of employers. Education, as distinct from training, must maintain a degree of independence from any particular dominant set of social values, although the prevailing economic conditions will influence those qualities and skills which are emphasized. For this degree of independence, critical skills, and research-mindedness have to be preserved alongside the development of capabilities and competence.

In the approaches based on experiential learning education is distinct from the experience on which it draws. Multiple purposes are embodied within it without collapsing it into the values of the work or community service experience which it seeks to use as a learning resource. If education is to be tranformative, not reproductive, the role of education at all levels is to develop *educated attributes*. These incorporate core skills, key skills and transferable skills in their various manifestations, but go far beyond these. Core/key skills may enable us to survive, to stay afloat in the rapids; they do not encourage us to think about the influences we have on our context, individually and collectively. Are we in danger of a new generation engaged in ego-driven projects with no sense of mutual responsibility? Thatcher's children, perhaps, to whom there is no such thing as society. The Speaker's Commission on Citizenship in 1990 concluded that the skills of citizenship need to be learned, and the greatest challenge of the late twentieth century is to create a society in which all can actively participate, understand, influence, whistle blow, and work together in pursuit of the common good. What are the real educated attributes in this context? They are the intellectual and critical skills that go hand-in-hand with the knowledge society, the information society. They need to be cultivated at all levels, with higher education there to secure and promote the highest forms of learning with understanding, critical skills, creativity and, above all, lifelong learning and inquiry centre stage. 'Knowing how' is not the same as 'knowing why' and the social dynamics of the time demand that we know 'why' as well as 'how'.

Enlargement, inclusion and a redistributive approach

To develop maximal versions of citizenship and competence in ways that are complementary *does* require at the very least an enlargement of the curriculum, irrespective of the post-16 'track' – academic, applied/vocational or work-based – followed. Silver and Brennan (1988) have argued that the enlarged post-16 curriculum should feature:

- studies selected from several disciplines;
- problem-solving related to real world problems;

- breadth of courses and of outcomes;
- concern with long term employment needs;
- concern to produce questioning and critical adults;
- an openness to external influences.

Developing competence and citizenship in maximal terms goes beyond this. It means bringing together some of the successful teaching and learning processes developed in English Further Education, coupled with the breadth of curriculum that is the norm in the wider European context. The effective worker with a *beruf* in German terms has also to be an educated citizen. This means that humanities education plays a continuing role in what the trainee needs to know.

But achievement of maximal versions of citizenship and competence requires still more than this. It requires approaches to teaching and learning that promote a sense of social being and shared autonomy in decision-making and arriving at judgements. There is also a need to move beyond enlargement of the curriculum to strategies for inclusion of groups at risk of social exclusion. Support services are required that encourage pro-active rather than passive transition behaviours and are made available in ways that are less dependent on the cultural capital of users. A 'redistributive' approach to social and financial support provides targeted support where it is needed, to optimize individual or group life chances to negotiate transition structures successfully.

Interventions should draw on support both inside and beyond the walls of educational institutions, involving a range of providers in concerted strategies that can extend individual capacities while adapting the more hostile features of the environment that can defeat and ultimately exclude. Thus, measures must aim to:

1 *encourage active transition behaviours by* developing problem-solving behaviours, 'action competences' and encourage self-managed learning;
2 *make the social/material environment less hostile to those most at risk of exclusion through*:

- social support;
- targeted help and guidance;
- financial support and entitlements for study;
- access to affordable housing.

In the move from **enlargement** to **inclusion**, and from **key skills** to **educated attributes, the workplace** cannot be the 'ultimate curriculum authority' and neither can the 'academy' (see Figure 15.1).

The curriculum must relate, at any age or stage, to a framework for interpreting the world as a 'social whole', to use Sedunary's (1996) expression, while understanding the sources of diversity and differentiation within it. In conjunction with this, inclusive policies, strategies and forms of educational support are needed that value and recognize the capabilities of all, policies that recognize diversity and move away from assumptions about the condition of the age group as a whole. The idea that a curriculum based on bundles of core and technical skills combined with action planning will equip young people for the future is wholly inadequate. Policies need to be based on more holistic analyses of social dynamics and an understanding of ways in which experiences in early adulthood can give stability or instability to the life course (Evans and Haffenden 1991, Evans 1998). Effective education for the future depends on the extent of free and equal access and the 'redistributive' mechanisms for resources and social support employed; the ways in which provision is linked structurally and methodologically, and relates to the life course; the ways in which education links and draws upon different domains of experience in work, community and family.[1] Moreover, future orientated, maximal versions of education for citizenship derive their values from what is required for the ethical advancement of society and the state, and it is these, beyond and above the values of the workplace and the immediate requirement for material economic progress, that shape effective learning for citizenship at all levels.

As Georg Kerschensteiner (1911) founder of the

modern German vocational education and training system argued, the overriding aim of education is to produce a society consisting as far as possible of persons who have independence of mind and who are morally free. Giving as extended an education to as many as possible of its members is to the advantage of the democratic state, which is dependent on its members for its preservation and long term well-being. The challenge is to promote empowered and participatory communities able both to support the successful pursuit of individual projects and to play their part in the social and political processes which will shape the socio-economic scenarios of the future.

Notes

1 A development of the analysis is given in Evans 1998. ESRC Award L-134251011 (Evans K) is contributing to extension of this analysis.

References

Ainley, P. (1994) *Class and Skill.* London and New York: Cassell.

Baethge, M. (1989) Individualisation as hope or disaster. In K. Hurrelmann and U. Engel (eds) *The Social World of Adolescents.* Berlin: de Gruyter.

Ball, S. (1990) *Politics and Policy Making in Education.* London: Routledge.

Banks, M., Bates, I., Breakwell, G., Bynner, J., Emler, N., Jamieson, L. and Roberts, K. (1992) *Careers and Identities.* Buckingham: Open University Press.

Barnett, R. (1994) *The Limits of Competence.* Buckingham: Open University Press/Society for Research in Higher Education.

Blackman, S. J. and Evans, K. (1994) Comparative skill acquisition in Germany and England. *Youth and Policy,* 43: 1–23.

Brown, A. and Evans, K. (1994) Changing the training culture: lessons from Anglo-German comparisons. *British Journal of Education and Work,* 7(2): 5–15.

Brown, P. and Lauder, H. (1992) *Education for Economic Survival: from Fordism to Post-Fordism.* London: Routledge.

Bynner, J. and Roberts, K. (1991) *Youth and Work: Transitions to Employment in England and Germany.* London and Bonn: Anglo-German Foundation.

Chisholm, L. and Bergeret, J.-M. (1991) *Young People in the European Community: Towards an Agenda for Research and Policy.* Brussels: EC Commission on Citizenship, Task Force Human Resources, Youth, Training and Education.

Coles, R. (1996) Vulnerable groups and social exclusion. Paper presented at Conference on British Youth

Figure 15.1   Education for citizenship

Research: A New Agenda, University of Glasgow, 26–28 January.

Dale, R. (1985) The background and inception of the technical and vocational education initiatives. In R. Dale (ed.) *Education, Training and Employment.* Oxford: Pergamon Press.

Dalin, P. (1983) In H. Chisnall (ed.) *Learning from Work and Community Experience.* Windsor: NFER-NELSON.

Dearing, R. (1996) *Review of Qualifications for 16–19 Year Olds.* London: HMSO.

Department of Education and Science (1982) *Experience and Participation* (Thompson Report). London: HMSO.

Edwards, R. (1993) The inevitable future? Post-Fordism in work and learning. In R. Edwards, S. Sieminski and D. Zeldin (eds) *Adult Learners, Education and Training.* London: Routledge.

Etzioni, A. (1995) *The Spirit of Community – Rights, Responsibilities and the Communitarian Agenda.* London: Fontana.

Evans, K. (1994) Patterns of leisure activity and the role of the youth service. *International Journal of Adolescence and Youth,* 4: 179–95.

Evans, K. (1995) Competence and citizenship: towards a complementary model for times of critical social change. *British Journal of Education and Work.*

Evans, K. (1998) *Shaping Futures: Learning for Competence and Citizenship.* Aldershot: Ashgate.

Evans, K. and Haffenden, I. (1991) *Education for Young Adults: International Perspectives.* London: Routledge.

Evans, K. and Heinz, W. (1994) *Becoming Adults in England and Germany.* London and Bonn: Anglo-German Foundation.

Finch, J. (1995) Family responsibilities and rights. In M. Bulmer (ed.) *Citizenship Today: The Contemporary Relevance of T. H. Marshall.* London: UCL Press.

Finegold, D. and Soskice, D. (1990) The failure of training in Britain: analysis and prescription. In G. Esland (ed.) *Education, Training and Employment Vol. 1: Educated Labour.* Wokingham: Addison-Wesley/Open University.

Freire, P. (1972a) *Pedagogy of the Oppressed.* Harmondsworth: Penguin.

Freire, P. (1972b) *Cultural Action for Freedom.* Harmondsworth: Penguin.

Freire, P. (1974) *Education: The Practice of Freedom.* London: Writers and Readers.

Giddens, A. (1996) T. H. Marshall, the state and democracy. In M. Bulmer and A. M. Rees (eds) *Citizenship Today.* London: UCL Press.

Green, A. (1995) The European challenge to British vocational education and training. In P. Hodkinson and M. Issitt (eds) *The Challenge of Competence.* London and New York: Cassell.

Habermas, J. (1976) *Legitimation Crisis.* London: Heinemann.

Habermas, J. (1991) *The Theory of Communicative Action.* Cambridge: Polity Press.

Hurrelmann, K. (1988) *Social Structure and Personality Development.* Cambridge: Cambridge University Press.

Jones, G. and Wallace, C. (1992) *Youth, Family and Citizenship.* Buckingham: Open University.

Kerschensteiner, G. (1911) *German Youth and Education for Citizenship,* 5th edition. Erfurt: Villaret.

Lave, J. and Wenger, E. (1991) *Situated Learning: Legitimate Peripheral Participation.* New York: Cambridge University Press.

Mac-an-Ghaill, M. (1996) State schooling and social class: beyond critiques of the 'New Right' hegemony. *British Journal of Sociology of Education,* **17** (2): 163–76.

McLaughlin, I. H. (1992) Citizenship, diversity and education – a philosophical perspective. *Journal of Moral Education,* **21** (3): 235–50.

Marginson, S. (1994) *The Transferability of Educated Attributes.* Melbourne: Centre for the Study of Higher Education, University of Melbourne.

Marshall, T. (1950) *Citizenship and Social Class.* Cambridge: Cambridge University Press.

Marsland, D. (1991) Trends in youth education and development, East and West. In K. Evans and I. Haffenden (eds) *Education for Young Adults: International Perspectives.* London: Routledge.

Ministry of Education (1959) *15–18* (Crowther Report). London: HMSO.

Ministry of Education (1960) *The Youth Service in England and Wales,* Cmnd 929. London: HMSO.

Morrell, F. (1991) The work of the Speaker's Commission and its definition of citizenship. In K. Fogelman (ed.) *Citizenship in Schools.* London: David Fulton.

National Commission on Education (1993) *Learning to Succeed.* London: Paul Hamlyn.

National Curriculum Council (1990) *Curriculum Guidance 9: Education for Citizenship.* York: NCC.

National Youth Bureau (1990) *Danger or Opportunity?* Leicester: NYB.

Pring, R. (1991) The curriculum and the new vocationalism. In G. Esland (ed.) *Education, Training and Employment Vol. 2: The Educational Response.* Wokingham: Addison-Wesley/Open University.

Pye, D. and Mac-an-Ghaill, M. (1996) Inherent Contradiction and the Search for an Answer: Young People in the New Vocational Context. International Sociology of Education Conference, University of Sheffield, 2–5 January.

Raffe, D. (1991) Beyond the mixed model. In C. Crouch and A. Heath (eds) *Social Research and Social Reform.* Oxford: Oxford University Press: 287–314.

Richardson, A. (1990) *Talking about Commitment.* London: The Prince's Trust.

Roberts, K. (1968) The entry into employment: an approach to a generational theory. *Sociological Review* **18**: 165–84.

Roberts, K. (1995) *Youth and Employment in Modern Britain.* Oxford: Oxford University Press.

Sedunary, E. (1996) Neither new nor alien to progressive

thinking: interpreting the convergence of radical education and the new vocationalism in Australia. *Journal of Curriculum Studies*, **28** (4): 369–96.

Silver, H. and Brennan, J. (1988) *A Liberal Vocationalism*. London: Methuen.

Simons, D. (1966) *Georg Kerschensteiner*. London: Methuen and Co Ltd.

Skilbeck, M., Tait, K. and Lowe, M. (1986) *A Question of Quality*. London: Institute of Education, University of London.

Speaker's Commission (1990) *Encouraging Citizenship*. London: HMSO.

Whitty, G., Aggleton, P. and Row, G. (1996) Competing conceptions of quality in social education: learning from the experience of cross-curricular themes. In M. Hughes (ed.) *Teaching and Learning in Changing Times*. London: Blackwell.

Williamson, H. (1996) *Youth Work and Citizenship*. Paper presented at the British Youth Research Conference: A New Agenda, University of Glasgow.

Youth Service Development Council (1969) *Youth and Community Work in the 70s*. London: HMSO.

16 Comparing Discourses: Democratic Values, the Coalition of Essential Schools and the Eight Year Study

TOM C. WILSON

Introduction

Michael Foucault (Ball 1990) writes of *discourses* which are about what can be said and thought, but also who can speak, when, and with what authority. Words and concepts change their meaning and their effect as they are deployed within different discourses. Meanings are derived, then, not so much from languages but from contexts with their histories, institutional practices and power relationships. Additionally, discourses constrain the possibilities of thought and beyond what can be said, they are about what cannot be or is not said. Thus, they are constituted by exclusion as well as inclusion.

This exploration takes a look at two discourses: a discourse of democratic value as characterized by key words and a discourse of school reform. The former equates key words as value indicators wherein the meaning of democracy is revealed through the degree of their occurrence. The latter probes the meaning of two school reform movements within the United States (the historic Eight Year Study 1932–40 and the contemporary Coalition of Essential Schools), and then compares these meanings, these sub-discourses with a discourse on the meaning of democracy, at least, as each meaning is revealed at the level of written language. Because this exploration does not examine the institutional settings, practices and contexts in which the reforms play out or are said to play out, they may only approach discourses as Foucault might define them. Yet since, in a strong sense, words are all we have, it seems to be reasonable to look at them as they are found in texts as indicators of possible meaning. We can allow them to speak to us in order that we can come to know, or at least have a modicum of confidence about, an author's world view. The exclusion or inclusion of particular words cer-tainly provides a vocabulary that fosters insight into the position of a text with respect to a particular discourse.

This importance of words within a vocabulary is captured by Raymond Williams (1983) who calls our attention to the importance of key words "we share with others, often imperfectly when we wish to discuss many of the central processes of our common life" (p. 14). Key words are those which are necessary for an understanding of our society and reflect the values within that society. While it may be comfortable to think of key words as per-manent, Williams is quite clear about the danger of ascribing fixed or "proper meaning" (p. 17) to any particular word. This is so because of:

> a history and complexity of meanings; conscious changes, or consciously different uses; innovation, obsolescence, specialization, extension, overlap, transfer; or changes which are masked by nominal continuity so that words which seem to have been there for centuries, with continuous general mean-ings, have come in fact to express radically different or radically variable, yet sometimes hardly noticed, meanings and implications.   (ibid.)

However, the situation is far from random. At any given time, certain words in cluster can be said to constitute a particular discourse as "elements of an active vocabulary – a way of recording, investigat-ing and presenting problems of meaning in the area in which the meanings . . . have formed" (p. 15). Yet there is more to it than time and place. Williams continues:

> the problem of meaning can never be wholly dis-solved into context. It is true that no word ever finally stands on its own, since it is always an elem-ent in the social process of language, and its uses depend upon the complex and (though variably)

systematic properties of language itself. Yet it can still be useful to pick out certain words, of an especially problematic kind and to consider, for the moment, their own internal development and structures ... for it is only in reductive kinds of analysis that the processes of connection and interaction can be studied as if they were relations between simple units.   (pp. 22–3)

The Eight Year Study and the Coalition of Essential Schools

The following procedure "picks out" four problematic key words (freedom, equality, community, democracy) as expressions of key values that characterize a democratic discourse. Two texts that explain the Eight Year Study (EYS) and the Coalition of Essential Schools (CES) are then scrutinized to determine the usage of the four key values. Yet, before proceeding to analyse the texts, some sense of both EYS and CES needs to be provided.

Launched in 1932, the Eight Year Study was designed to question the belief that it was necessary for high school students to take a required course of academic study in order to be successful in post-secondary education. In collaboration with colleges and universities, some thirty high schools were released from the precise subject and unit requirements for college and university admission and the post-secondary institutions agreed to admit students based on two criteria:

1 Recommendation from the principal of the high school that the student could creditably carry on college/university work.
2 A recorded history of the student's high school, including activities, interests, results of examinations, aptitude and achievement scores, and other evidence of the quality and quantity of the candidate's work.

This understanding then allowed the thirty schools to alter their curriculum in terms of what they thought to be in the best interests of the students. The results of the study documented that the graduates of the thirty schools, when matched with students from traditional high schools, had done as well as or better than the control group of students. Wilford Aiken (1942), Chairman and Director of the study, was able to conclude in the early 1940s that:

1 The assumptions that preparation for the Liberal Arts College depends upon the study of certain prescribed subjects in the secondary school is no longer tenable.
2 Secondary schools can be trusted with a greater measure of freedom than college requirements now permit (p. 118).

In sum, Aiken wrote:

The purposes of the school cannot be determined apart from the purposes of the society which maintains the school. The purposes of any society are determined by the life values which the people prize. As a nation we have been striving always for those values which constitute the American way of life. Our people prize individual human personality above anything else. We are convinced that the form of social organization called democracy promotes better than any other the development of worth and dignity in men and women. It follows, therefore, that *the chief purpose of education in the States should be to preserve, promote, and refine the way of life in which we as a people believe.* (pp. 132–3)

The text chosen for analysis of the EYS is Aiken's (1942) *The Story of the Eight Year Study*.

The Coalition of Essential Schools (1984)[1] is an extension of A Study of High Schools, an inquiry into American secondary education conducted from 1981 to 1984 under the sponsorship of the National Association of Secondary School Principals and the National Association of Independent Schools. As part of its findings, the Study identified five "imperatives" for better schools:

1 Give room to teachers and students to work and learn in their own, appropriate ways.
2 Insist that students clearly exibit mastery of their school work.
3 Get the incentives right, for students and teachers.
4 Focus the students' work on the use of their minds.
5 Keep the structure simple and flexible.

The rationale for these imperatives is detailed in the first of the Study's three publications, *Horace's Compromise: The Dilemma of the American High School* (Sizer 1984). Established in 1984 as a high school–university partnership, the Coalition of Essential Schools (1984) is devoted to strengthening the learning of students by reforming each school's priorities and simplifying its structure. Brown University joined in this partnership with schools that are diverse in character, geographically dispersed, and representative of both the public and private sectors. Each school evolves a plan appropriate to its own setting. Within these schools, the focus of the programme should be on helping students to use their minds well and on producing a high school graduate with the ability to show his or her knowledge and skill – to exhibit mastery – in a variety of areas deemed important by local and external authorities. This suggests that the high school diploma should signify genuine competence, specifically in the areas of reading, writing and fundamental mathematics. These Essential Schools should also be places where decency prevails; where social and professional relationships are typified by tolerance, generosity, and fairness. The philosophical bedrock of the Coalition is spelled out in Nine Common Principles:

1 The school should focus on helping adolescents learn to use their minds well.
2 The school's goal should be simple: that each student master a limited number of essential skills and areas of knowledge.
3 The school's goals should apply to all students.
4 Teaching and learning should be personalized.
5 The governing practical metaphor of the school should be the student as worker.
6 The diploma should be awarded upon a successful final demonstration of mastery for graduation.
7 The tone of the school should stress values of unanxious expectations, of trust and of decency.
8 The principal and teachers should perceive themselves as generalists first and specialists second.
9 Total student load per teacher of 80 or fewer pupils; substantial time for collective planning by teachers; competitive salaries for staff and an ultimate per pupil cost not to exceed that at traditional schools by more than ten percent.

The text chosen for this analysis was *Horace's Compromise* (Sizer 1984), which captures the essential rationale for CES.

With some understanding of each of the two reform movements now in mind, the examination of democratic discourse through key value analysis can be re-visited.

Analysis and procedures

For this task, the political value conceptualization and methodology of Milton Rokeach (1973) is central. He defines a value as "an enduring belief that a specific mode of conduct or end-state of existence is personally or socially preferable to an opposite or converse mode of conduct or end-state of existence" (p. 5). Thus, Rokeach classifies values as terminal (end-states of existence) or instrumental (modes of behavior). He assumes that individuals differ not so much on the possession of values *per se*, which are relatively small in number, but rather on the importance that one gives to particular values in relationship to other values. The rank order or hierarchy of terminal or instrumental values on a "continuum of perceived importance" then constitutes a value system.

Examples of terminal values follow (the words in parenthesis which follow each value word are "value categories" that expand the meaning of the particular value):

• A comfortable life (a prosperous life)
• Freedom (independence, free choice)
• Equality (brotherhood, equal opportunity for all)
• True friendship (close companionship).

Instrumental values include such values as being:

• Capable (competent, effective)
• Broad-minded (open-minded)
• Loving (affectionate, tender)
• Imaginative (daring, creative).

The question then becomes one of ascertaining how Rokeach's efforts could inform our examination of democratic discourse in school reform movements. Rokeach argues that political ideology,[2] in terms of a liberal–conservative dichotomy, is not a phenomenon that can be ordered along a single continuum (p. 165), but rather is best understood as a "language of values" (p. 168) incorporating the two values *freedom and equality* from the list of terminal values. He writes (p.169):

> It may be hypothesized that all major varieties of political orientation will have to take an explicitly favorable, a silent, or an explicitly unfavorable position with respect to two values in particular – *freedom and equality* – . . . [and] . . . the major variation in political ideology are hypothesized to be fundamentally reducible, when stripped to the barest essence, to opposing value orientations

concerning the political desirability of *freedom and equality* in all their ramifications.

As previously noted, the meaning of key words needs to be understood in their relationship within a given context (Foucault) and at the same time honored for their internal development and structure (Williams). What then are the meanings of freedom and equality in Rokeach's analysis? The definitions he offers for equality (brotherhood, equal opportunity for all) and freedom (independence, free choice) further indicate his sense of the two key words. Yet he sees them in terms of each other wherein "the meaning of freedom and equality is to be sought in their relation to one another within a particular set of values" (Rokeach 1973: 183). And it is the contextual inclusion and strong emphasis of *both* equality and freedom that characterizes a democratic vocabulary and discourse. However, such relationship does not answer fully the question of meaning, for it seems clear that each can be defined differently. Karl Mannheim (cited by Rokeach op. cit.: 183) delineates at some length the different conceptions:

> Revolutionary liberalism understood by liberty in the economic sphere is the release of the individual from his medieval connections with state and guild. In the political sphere they understood by it the right of the individual to do as he wishes and thinks fit, and especially his right to the fullest exercise of the unalienable Rights of Man. Only when it encroaches on the liberty of fellow citizens does freedom know any bounds according to this concept. Equality, then, is the logical corollary of this kind of liberty – without the assumption of political equality for all men it is meaningless. Actually, however, revolutionary liberalism never thought of equality as anything more than a postulate. It certainly never took it as a matter of empirical fact, and indeed never demanded equality in practice for all men, except in the course in economic and political struggles. Yet conservative thought twisted this postulate into a statement of fact, and made it appear as if the liberals were claiming that all men were in fact and in all respects equal . . . [therefore] political necessity compelled the conservatives to develop their own concept of liberty to oppose that of the liberals, and they worked out what we may call the qualitative idea of liberty to distinguish it from the revolutionary egalitarian concept. The counter-revolutionary opposition had a sound enough instinct not to attack the idea of freedom as such; instead, they concentrated on the idea of equality which stands behind it. Men, they claimed, are essentially unequal, unequal in their gifts and abilities, and unequal to the very core of their beings. Freedom therefore can only consist in the ability of each man to develop without let or hindrance according to the laws and principles of his own personality.

Thus, two ideological groups would both give high allegiance to the value of freedom yet the meaning they ascribe to it might vary considerably. Rokeach (op. cit.: 183–4) states the case as follows:

> It is one thing to value *freedom* highly and ignore or be silent about *equality*, and it is quite another thing to insist that *freedom* is not truly possible unless it goes hand in hand with *equality*. To American conservatives, freedom probably means lack of restraint on individual initiative and the freedom to achieve superior status, wealth and power: to socialists, freedom probably means sufficient restraint on individual initiative to ensure greater equality for all. To American conservatives, social equality is perhaps seen as a threat to individual freedom; to socialists, there can be no freedom without social equality.

John Dewey also discussed the forms of freedom and the symbiotic relationship between freedom and equality. Westbrook (1991: 165) writes that Dewey characterized a moral democracy as including both a negative and positive sense of freedom. The latter proclaims freedom from restraint while the former is cast in terms of "effective freedom" in which the opportunity exists for individuals to actualize their capacities to become the best they can. Yet Dewey recognized that effective freedom required the means to achieve it and merely removing restraint is hardly sufficient: ". . . the freedom of an agent who is merely released from direct external obstructions is formal and empty" and therefore, effective freedom necessitates equality, not in the sense of equal results or equal distribution of goods, but in the sense of "providing all members of a society with the means of self-realization" (p. 165).

Based upon the above analysis, the position taken herein consists of two propositions:

1 For a discourse to be considered democratic, it must place high value on both freedom and equality while less or non-democratic discourses place a low value on either or both of the values.
2 For a discourse to be considered democratic, freedom is understood in its relationship to equality and one cannot exist without the other.

To test his *equality/freedom* value hypothesis, Rokeach counted the absolute and relative frequency of the words (as values), *freedom* and *equality* from 25,000 word samples from writings that he believed represented four major political ideologies: Fascism, Communism, Socialism, and Capitalism. And beyond mere word count, Rokeach used the aforementioned "value categories" (p. 172) as it was necessary for the judges who counted to make decisions in terms of which were more or less synonymous with *freedom* and *equality*. Writings selected for content analysis for each ideology included:

1 A. Hitler, *Mein Kampf* (Fascism)
2 N. Lenin, *Collected Works* (Communism)
3 Various works from N. Thomas, E. Fromm, T. Bottomore, P. Medow, and M. Titmuss in E. Fromm's, *Social Humanism: An International Symposium* and *Let Man Prevail: A Socialist Manifesto and Program* (Socialism)
4 B. Goldwater, *The Conscience of a Conservative* (Capitalism)

The results support a four-component model of political ideology as illustrated by Figure 16.1 (Rokeach, p. 170).

EQUALITY HIGH

Communism   Socialism

FREEDOM LOW   FREEDOM HIGH

Fascism   Capitalism

EQUALITY LOW

Figure 16.1. A four component model of political ideology.

Figure 16.1 indicates that the values of freedom and equality do discriminate among the four ideologies. Hitler ranks both equality and freedom low. Lenin ranks equality high, freedom low. The capitalists, or perhaps better, American Conservatives, are high on freedom yet low on equality. The difference in the rankings within the American and Russian samples supports the conclusion of Jaeger (1943) some thirty years prior to Rokeach:

> the social conflict between Liberty and Equality can be a clear issue . . . and . . . the United States and the Soviet Union . . . are, by their pasts, at opposite poles in this conflict, the United States combining the maximum of Liberty with the minimum of Equality, and the Soviet Union the

maximum of Equality with the minimum of Liberty. (p. 123)

It is only the Socialists who place both freedom *and* equality high. From these findings Rokeach (op. cit.: 190) concludes that the value ranking derived from political documents offer strong evidence of general ideology.

> if we know nothing more about a person than where he stands with respect to the two distinctly political values we should be able to predict his position with respect to all major ideologues and toward the major reference persons and groups associated with the major ideologies.

Further, he claims that beyond political documents, "there seems to be no reason why the present method cannot be extended to extract the values in other kinds of documents – historical, literary, biographical, and so on" (p. 186).

Rokeach's conclusions thus provided a grounding to determine the democratic discourses within two educational, as opposed to political, texts.[3] Once again, the argument here is that a high rank for both freedom and equality is essential for an authentic democratic discourse rather than a low rank on either one. Freedom is consistently ranked quite high by most Americans; it is equality that tends to discriminate, and it is hard to argue that a low rank of equality is more democratic than a higher rank. As Rokeach concludes, "application intended to decrease the importance of such political values as *equality* and *freedom* are ethically indefensible" (p. 337). Yet, more is required. While accepting Rokeach's argument for the critical necessity of equality and freedom to capture meaning within political discourse, it seemed prudent to include several other words as further indicators of democratic discourse in order to escape a potential charge of a reductionism stemming from the use of only two values. The two additional words selected are *community* and *democracy*.

Community is a popular word. Perlstein (cited in Kahne, King and Westheimer 1996: 843) reports 96,439 citations from a subject search using the Educational Resources Information Center (ERIC) data base. While popular, it is subject to a multiplicity of meanings both historically (Williams 1983: 75–6) and currently (Kahne, King and Westheimer 1996: 843–57). The latter authors assert distinctions among communitarian, liberal and democratic communities. While not making the distinction completely clear, they seem to place strongest emphasis upon the democratic by including Dewey's (and unnamed "others") requirements of "a sense of unity, common bonds, and commitments that transcend differences" (p. 844).

It is Dewey (1916), then, who provides the justification for the inclusion of the key value *community*. He informs us that "we live in a community in virtue of things which they have in common" and this "in-common" then makes community possible. Such community is democratic, for it is constituted by "a mode of associate living – of conjoint communicated experience" (p. 87). And within the community is the spirit of expanded participation.

> [t]he extension in space of the number of individuals who participate in interest so that each has to refer to his own action to that of others, and to consider the action of others to give point and direction to his own, is equivalent to the breaking down of those barriers of class, race, and national territory which kept men from perceiving the full import of their activity. These more numerous and more varied points of contact denote a greater diversity of stimuli to which an individual has to respond; they consequently put a premium on variation in his action. They secure a *liberation* of powers which remain suppressed as long as the incitations to action are partial, as they must be in a group which in its exclusiveness shuts out many interests.   (p. 87)

Thus, it is most difficult to conceive of a democratic discourse that does not contain within it a reference to a collective self which hold beliefs in common. Davis (cit. in Pateman 1970: 21) writes that the theory of participatory democracy is ambitious in its attempt to educate "an entire people to the point where their intellectual, emotional, and moral capacities have reached their full potential and they are joined freely and actively in a genuine community" (p. 140). Thus, there may be community, but a genuine community is possible only if constituted by its democratic nature. And interestingly, the word community does not have, nor has it ever had a negative connotation: "What is most important, perhaps, is that unlike all other terms of social organization (*state, nation, society*, etc.) it seems never to be used unfavorably, and never to be given any positive opposing or distinguishing term" (Williams 1983: 76).

Concerning the word *democracy*, its meaning has not always been warmly felt. Williams writes, "the fact is that, with only occasional exceptions, dem-

ocracy, in the records we have, was until the C19 [nineteenth century] a strongly unfavorable term" (ibid.: 94). Abstracting from Williams (pp. 93–8), the word signified mass rule, popular class rule whereby power in the people by sheer numbers would lead to the multitude acting as a collective tyrant. The late eighteenth century witnessed a new meaning. Harbingers can be traced to the Greeks in the sense of people and *rule*, and to the New World as shown by Rhode Island, 1641, which first used the term *democracy*, defined as popular government in a political constitution with power invested in the "freemen orderly assembled, or a major part of them, to make or constitute just Lawes, by which they will be regulated" (ibid.). Yet, this form of direct democracy was not what the founders of the American Constitution had in mind. For Alexander Hamilton in 1771, to vest power in a collective body of people brings about the expectation of "error, confusion and instability" (p. 93). Rather, a representative democracy was necessary in which "the right of election is well secured and regulated, and the exercise of the legislative, executive and judicial authorities is vested in select persons" (ibid.). While it is this sense of democracy that seems to predominate modern understandings, the ideas of popular democracy, democracy as open agreement, of rights irrespective of institution, and of democratic manners free, or at least unconscious of, class distinctions also remain. Williams concludes that while the term remains confused, the pejorative meaning of democracy seems to have largely dissipated although some suspicion about the efficacy of popular democracy and public competence still exists.

As thorough as it is, Williams' analysis ignores the moral and personal values associated with democracy. Not so for John Dewey. According to Robert Westbrook (1991), while Dewey recognized democracy as the "most effective means of organizing consensus and preserving stability . . . to evaluate it simply in these instrumental terms . . . was to miss the more fundamental significance of democracy as an end, as an ethical ideal" (p. 41). This insertion of ethics into the discourse of democracy was made by Dewey over one hundred years ago when he wrote that "democracy is an ethical idea, the idea of a personality, with truly infinite capacities, incorporate with every man. Democracy and the one, the ultimate, ethical ideal of humanity are to my mind synonyms" (Dewey 1888: 248). Notice the power of Dewey's phrasing. Democracy, an "ethical idea" is at the same time an "idea of personality"; the ideal of democracy therefore exists in every person. At the same time, there is an extension beyond the individual to all humanity. For him, the person is sacrosanct, yet it is only in dialectical concert with others in community that individual self-realization and true freedom can occur.

These variations in understandings of the value democracy need to be taken into account. Since the complete and eventual interest was the democratic language orientation of the two studies, it seems reasonable, at first blush, that any text which reflects democracy would certainly, at the minimum, tend to use the word. Yet, to re-emphasize, care needs to be exercised in assuming that the use of the word democracy in and of itself portends differentiation in democratic discourse for the reasons given by Williams and Dewey. And further, as Foucault reminds us, different contexts give words different meanings. Both conservatives and socialists are apt to use the word, yet as they rank equality and freedom differently, democracy for each is clearly at variance. It is only when democracy is used in conjunction with words such as community, equality and freedom that confidence can be raised about any text's democratic orientation.

Furthermore, as was the case with equality and freedom, it became necessary to add several value categories to community and democracy. The categories chosen for community were unity, co-operation, participation and commonality and for democracy, justice and fairness. The justification for these sets of value categories awaits another time. It suffices to say that the logic for the community categories draws from Dewey's (1916) previously cited conceptualization of the connections among community, communication and the sharing of what is held in common. Value categories for democracy come from an analysis of its relationship to John Rawl's (1971) theory of "justice as fairness".

The idea of democratic value discourse, therefore, can be identified by the combination of the four key values below (again, with their categories in parentheses):

- Freedom (independence, free choice, liberty, individual autonomy)
- Equality (brotherhood, equal opportunity for all, egalitarian)
- Community (unity, cooperation, participation, commonalty)
- Democracy (justice, fairness).

The more these four words and categories appear in a text, the more that text represents a democratic discourse. The singular use of any one, or even two, of the words would provide only a limited analysis of a text's democratic nature. Using this standard, both texts were read and the number of times the words or the value categories appeared they were counted. For example, if autonomy was read, it was counted as freedom; commonalty counted for community, and so forth.

Findings

Table 16.1 shows the frequency, percentage response, and rank order (RO) for each of the four words from the two texts.

Table 16.1 Findings of the study

	Story of the Eight Year Study (EYS) (11,570 words)			Horace's Compromise (CES) (87,046 words)		
	F	%	RO	F	%	RO
Freedom	30	.3	1,2	51	.06	1
Equality	1	.009	4	4	.005	2,3
Community	31	.3	1,2	7	.008	4
Democracy	20	.2	3	42	.05	2,3

Note: F = Four Word Frequency, % = percentage response, RO = rank order

These frequencies and percentages from Table 16.1 are within the range found by Rokeach as indicated by Table 16.2 for the values of freedom and equality in his original study.

Table 16.2 Frequency and percentage response to Freedom and Equality from 25,000 word samples

	Socialists		Hitler[4]		Goldwater		Lenin	
	F	%	F	%	F	%	F	%
Freedom	66	.3	−48	.2	85	.3	−47	.2
Equality	62	.2	−72	.3	−10	.04	88	.4

Note: Frequencies taken from Rokeach 1973: 174, Table 6.2, percentage responses rounded

A comparison of Tables 16.1 and 16.2 demonstrate that the percentage use of the word "freedom" is similar regardless of the explicit textual discourse. Freedom's pattern is the same in political and education reform texts; it appears either positively or negatively at .2 per cent or .3 per cent. The word "equality" requires somewhat finer discrimination for it appears with greater percentage frequency in the political texts than it does in the educational texts, which might imply that educational writers are less interested in equality than are political writers.

With respect to the central concern of discourse comparisons between the two educational reform movements, Table 16.1 indicates that three of the values (freedom, community and democracy) are mentioned more in the *EYS* than in *Horace*, with freedom cited about five times as much, community 37.5 times and democracy four times. Only equality is mentioned more in *Horace* than in *EYS* at 1.8 times, yet it should be noted that for both *EYS* and *Horace*, equality is practically invisible.

To test further the validity of using the four key words as indicators of democratic discourse, three additional texts were examined. The criteria for selecting these works was two fold: (1) reasonable persons would agree that each probably speaks to democracy in a direct way and (2) if point (1) is true, then each will contain the four words in rough similarity to *The Story of the Eight Year Study* and *Horace's Compromise*.

The texts chosen for this subsequent analysis were Martin Luther King's *Letter From a Birmingham Jail (LB)* (King 1963), King's *I Have a Dream (DR)* (Chambers 1968) and Kozol's *Savage Inequalities (SI)* (1991). Table 16.3 shows the results of this analysis:

Table 16.3   Analysis of the additional texts

	LB (3,258 words)			DR (1,537 words)			SI (93,200 words)		
	F	%	RO	F	%	RO	F	%	RO
Freedom	3	.90	2	20	1.33	1	26	.03	4
Equality	1	.03	3	6	.39	3	161	.17	1
Community							30	.03	3
Democracy	25	.77	1	12	.76	2	69	.07	2

Note: F = Four Word Frequency, % = percentage response (rounded), RO = rank order

Table 16.3 demonstrates that King's rhetoric stressed the value of democracy (specifically the value category "justice") more than it did either equality or freedom in *LB*. In the case of *DR* however, freedom became the defining characteristic. Yet, in both of his texts, while freedom had higher importance than equality, freedom was cast in its positive sense of opportunity rather than in the negative free from restraint, *laissez faire* form, thus

linking it with equality. In combining the two sets of data for King, freedom equals .48, equality .15 and democracy .77. It appears, therefore, that King's value pattern is even more democratic than either *EYS* or *Horace* in terms of the percentage use of the values of freedom, equality and democracy. And, interestingly, his values of equality and freedom approximate those of the Socialists as indicated by Rokeach in Table 16.2 and are discrepant from those of the Communists. So much for the characterization of King as a Communist by late J. Edgar Hoover, former director of the Federal Bureau of Investigation, who apparently was unable to discern significant value distinctions between the two ideologies.

Concerning *SI*, it could be expected that a text titled as such would stress the value of equality and, as Table 16.3 demonstrates, this does seem to be the case. Kozol's use of the value equality is almost three times higher than his other values of freedom and community and over twice as much as for democracy. It is the value of equality that distinguishes *SI* from *EYS*, and it is the value that places Kozol in accord with King. However, in consideration of the three other values of freedom, community and democracy, *SI* seems to fall between *EYS* and *Horace*. Freedom is lower in *SI* than in the other two texts yet both community and democracy are higher than in *Horace* but lower than in *EYS*.

Based on the above analysis, the assumption of a rough correspondence among the King, Kozol, Aiken, and Horace texts seems to hold true with King's combined work having the more complete democratic orientation, with *Savage Inequalities* finding a place somewhere between *EYS* and *Horace*.

Discussion

With the information from Table 16.3 serving as a rough validity check on salience of the four word/ value approach to democratic discourse analysis only, this discussion is limited to the original comparison between *EYS* and *Horace*.

Based upon our conceptualization of democratic discourse as revealed by four core values, the historical work of the *EYS* is more democratic than the contemporary efforts as delineated in *Horace*. This in no way suggests that the CES, as indicated by *Horace*, is not democratic, for both movements clearly are in what can be called the tradition of liberal educational reform. A number of the principles of CES are semantically close to the objectives stated in *EYS*. Both reforms, when examined for the value categories of freedom and equality, as indicators, are closer to the Goldwater Capitalist (high on freedom, lower on equality) than they are to the Socialist (high on both) ideologies. This finding is particularly interesting with respect to the *EYS* with its Progressive Education Association lineage and its existence within a rather strong movement for school democracy in the 1930s and 1940s (O'Conner 1993). One might expect that a text which was quite forceful in its call for schools to rediscover their "chief reason for existence" (Aiken 1942: 18) makes virtually no mention of an *equality* value claim. In terms of historical context, the period from 1932 to 1942 did not have an explicit equality, civil rights agenda as has had the nation since the late 1950s, although the notion of equality, particularly in the economic realm, was certainly manifest. Nonetheless, the different social context of the 1930s and 1940s might help explain the lack of an equality finding in *EYS*. Given the historical accounting of O'Conner and shift in both rhetoric and practice concerning equality during the last forty years, the conservative – lack of equality – finding for CES is even stronger and more difficult to understand.

A case could be made that the notion of community which finds a much higher salience in *EYS* than in *Horace* speaks to *equality* in an indirect way. Recall that Davis (cit. in Pateman 1970: 21) called for a "genuine community". Intuitively, in what kind of genuine community would there not be a sense of equality whereby all members have an equal right of opportunity and of participation to achieve Dewey's notion of self-realization and the common good of democracy? Thus, when community is linked with equality, it adds support to a tentative conclusion that the *EYS* is democratically stronger at the language level than is CES, at least as revealed by *Horace*.[5]

This conclusion, however, must be tempered by a reminder that it applies only to textual material as found in *Horace* and *The Story of the Eight Year Study*. Clearly, a more complete analysis of both texts as discourses would have to include a much stronger look at the historical context in which they were written than is done herein. It is as Tye (1992) has forcefully stated: "Tell me this. How many of the thirty EYS schools were black . . . so whose community, whose equality, whose democracy?"

It could be argued quite rationally and perhaps convincingly that the meanings in *Horace* that led to the nine common principles of the CES are in themselves as democratic as those principles of the EYS (referring now to the larger study beyond the text itself) in spite of the relative lack of specific CES mention of them. In fairness to Ted Sizer, he would, in all probability, powerfully and cogently state that his major and most consistent objective centers on the school's responsibility which "without exception for all students, is intellectual development" (Brandt 1988: 31). He does link such development to democracy for "democracy depends on the use of that mind . . . and on wisdom of individual citizens" (p. 33). Additionally, his opposition to tracking (streaming), to different school goals for different classifications of students, and his plea for decency (fairness, generosity, and tolerance) are certainly democratic values in spirit. Further, he states that decency, his own definition notwithstanding, must be defined in context and that it "will emerge only when the students as well as the faculty want it, when its local definition is 'theirs', when they have 'ownership' of it" (Sizer 1984: 24).

Yet, what Sizer doesn't do is to use explicitly the direct value words of democracy to any significant degree. The EYS does a bit better, yet both, particularly on the values of freedom and equality, reflect a rather conservative discourse. When the values of community and democracy are included, then EYS does seem to be more democratic. For CES, the question still remains: If the ultimate intent for CES is the development of democracy, as inferred herein, then why not say it directly? By not doing so, Foucault's position seems to be reinforced. As was said in the introduction to this chapter, discourses constrain the possibilities of thought and they are constituted by exclusion as well as inclusion. By excluding much of what could be pronounced as a democratic agenda, the CES, to a greater degree than the EYS, limits its emancipatory potential by placing direct, democratic discourse out of bounds.[6]

In conclusion, Rokeach's position on the efficacy of determining political ideology from word/value analysis seems to be born out for educational as well as political texts. To his previously cited claim that beyond political documents "there seems to be no reason why the present method cannot be extended to extract the values in other kinds of documents – historical, literary, biographical and so on" (p. 186), the addition of the word *educational* appears now to be warranted.

Notes

1 With minor stylistic changes, this explanation is taken directly from the citation.

2 Political ideology, it is assumed, approximates a form of political discourse.

3 Of course, in a larger sense, there is acceptance that all educational documents and texts are eventually political, for all education is saturated with issues of power, control and domination. This is not only Foucault's point, but others as well (Freire 1985).

4 Negative frequencies were tabulated by Rokeach; he used both positive and negative mentions of freedom and equality. The frequency of the value was then the total number of positive minus the total number of negative mentions. In this current work, we found no negatives for the values freedom, equality, community or democracy.

5 There is much in CES language that is quite similar to that found in EYS. A number of the principles of CES are semantically close to the objectives stated in EYS. A common liberal discourse seems fundamental to both.

6 There is some recognition of the missing direct democratic discourse within those sympathetic to the CES principles (Sperry 1990). The Coalition added a tenth common principle on 5 November, 1997: The school should demonstrate non-discriminatory and inclusive policies, practices, and pedagogies. It should model democratic practices that involve all who are directly affected by the school. The school should honor diversity and build on the strengths of its communities, deliberately and explicitly challenging all forms of inequity.

References

Aiken, W. (1942) *The Story of the Eight Year Study*. New York: Harper and Brothers.

Ball, M. (ed.) (1990) *Foucault and Education: Disciplines and Knowledge*. London: Routledge.

Brandt, R. (1988) Interview with Ted Sizer: "On changing secondary schools: A conversation with Ted Sizer". *Educational Leadership*, February: 30–5.

Chambers, B. (ed.) (1968) *Chronicles of Black Protest*. New York: Mentor Books.

Coalition of Essential Schools (1984) *Prospectus 1984–1994*. Providence, R.I.: Education Department, Brown University.

Dewey, J. (1888) The ethics of democracy. In G. Axtelle et al. (eds) *The Early Works of John Dewey, 1882–98: Vol. 1*. Carbondale, IL: Southern Illinois Press: 227–49.

Dewey, J. (1916) *Democracy and Education*. New York: The Free Press.

Freire, P. (1985) *The Politics of Education: Culture, Power and Liberation*. South Hadley, MA: Bergin and Garvey.

Jaeger, M. (1943) *Liberty Versus Equality*. London: Thomas Nelson and Sons Ltd.

Kahne, J., King, S. H. and Westheimer, J. (1996) Visions of community and education in a diverse society. *Harvard Educational Review*, 66(4): 843–57.

King, M. (1963) *Why We Can't Wait*. New York: New American Library.

Kozol, H. (1991) *Savage Inequalities: Children in American Schools*. New York: Crown.

O'Conner, T. (1993) Looking back to look forward. *Democracy and Education*, 8(2): 9–16.

Pateman, C. (1970) *Participation and Democratic Theory*. Cambridge: Cambridge University Press.

Rawls, J. (1971) *A Theory of Justice*. Cambridge, MA: Harvard University Press.

Rokeach, M. (1973) *The Nature of Human Values*. New York: The Free Press.

Sizer, T. (1984) *Horace's Compromise: The Dilemma of the American High School*. Boston: Houghton Mifflin Company.

Sperry, C. (1990) Is Ted compromising on his principles or why not make democratic school government the tenth principle? Unpublished manuscript. Ithaca, New York: Alternative School.

Tye, B. (1992) Unpublished comments to the initial version of this chapter. School of Education, Chapman University, Orange, CA.

Westbrook, R. (1991) *John Dewey and American Democracy*. Ithaca, New York: Cornell University Press.

Williams, R. (1983) *Key Words: A Vocabulary of Culture and Society*. New York: Oxford University Press.

17 Citizenship and Nationhood
The Constructions of British and American Children

BRUCE CARRINGTON AND GEOFFREY SHORT

Introduction

Few would take issue with the claim that schooling in every society, whether modern or postmodern, plays a crucial part in the maintenance and reproduction of the dominant culture. The corollary, that all school curricula are necessarily imbued with assumptions, both tacit and explicit, about national identity, is likewise uncontentious. Yet despite the importance of this aspect of political socialization, relatively little is known about children's constructions of national identity and how they develop. As action-researchers with a long-standing commitment to anti-racist and multi-cultural education, we have voiced concern about this apparent lacuna in the literature. Clearly teachers need to have some idea about how children construe their national identity if exclusivist and ethnocentric assumptions about citizenship are to be deconstructed. Mindful of the adage that no teaching will be effective unless it makes contact with the learner's existing knowledge and understanding, we decided, in 1994, to embark upon a programme of ethnographic research in English primary schools (Carrington and Short 1995, Short and Carrington 1996). The research sought to explore the impact of age, geographical location and ethnicity on children's understanding of national identity. A further concern was the extent to which their thinking about identity bore the imprimatur of the 'new racism' (Barker 1981), an ideology that first surfaced during the late 1970s on the Right-wing of the Conservative Party. Eschewing ideas of either biological or cultural inferiority, the new racism, according to James Donald and Ali Rattansi (1992: 2):

presented itself as a worldly acknowledgement that different communities have different values and different ways of life which they have an instinct and a right to defend. There was an increasingly explicit articulation of a 'white ethnicity' linking discourses of family and community, national belonging, English patriotism, xenophobia and popular conservatism.

Within the new racism, national identity is defined in terms of cultural affiliation. The apparently unproblematic notion of a homogeneous 'British way of life' (as English and Christian) is central to such discourse that not only views ethnic minority groups as aliens, having different (and supposedly incompatible) traditions and values from the ethnic majority, but also depicts them as a potential threat to social cohesion. Norman Tebbit's widely-publicized proposal in 1990 for a 'cricket test' to assess the acceptability of South Asians and Afro-Caribbeans as British citizens may be regarded as exemplary of this type of thinking. The 'true' Briton, according to Tebbit, would always cheer for the English side rather than the Indian or the West Indian in an international match (*Sunday Times*, 19 April 1990). Three years later, another prominent Tory, Winston Churchill, was also to endorse an exclusivist and monolithic view of British identity, when he advocated calling a halt to 'immigration if the British way of life is to be preserved' (*The Times*, 29 May 1993).

With their concomitant emphasis on 'white ethnicity' and English patriotism, such neo-conservative constructions of national identity have not only served to undermine the position of ethnic minorities in British society but have also reinforced the marginality of the Scots, Welsh and Northern Irish. According to Tariq Modood (1992), the latter groups are expected 'to make some adjustments' and conform to English norms while the English, 'secure in their ethnic and national identity', need give 'little attention to what "Britishness" means' (1992: 80). With these observations in mind, we decided in 1995 to extend our study to include a sample of Scottish 9- to 11-year-olds, drawn from an Edinburgh primary school (Carrington and Short 1996).

We were also interested in other claims made by Modood, which suggested that it could be of theoretical interest to replicate the research in an American context. As well as arguing that the English are generally less reflexive about their national identity than other sections of the British population, Modood contends that Americans tend to operate with more inclusive, pluralistic constructions. Thus, he states:

> We have something to learn from the Americans, who have come to have a notion of *hyphenated identity*. They take pride not just in their Americaness but in asserting that they are Irish-American, Black-American, African-American, Greek-American and so on. . . . "British", by contrast, is virtually a quasi-ethnic term, so it is not surprising that descriptions such as British Black or British Pakistani are at present little more than courtesy titles and carry little conviction.   (1992: 78)

For these reasons (among others), we embarked upon a collaborative venture with Karen Wyche and Deborah Reaves,[1] undertaking a parallel investigation of children's constructions of American identity in a Massachusetts elementary school. We felt that a comparative dimension to our research was especially germane with the advent of 'globalization' and the accompanying declining political authority of the nation-state.

Researching in a British context has undoubtedly served to heighten our own awareness of the political effects of globalization at a national level. The movement towards a federal European Union has not only divided the Conservative Party but has also prompted some political commentators to claim that the hegemony of the New Right was coming to an end (Avis et al. 1996). Although its influence may now be waning, there can be little question that it has been the most potent force in British politics since Mrs Thatcher's election to office in 1979. However, until recently, the ideology of the New Right – an eclectic blend of nationalism, free-market liberalism and social authoritarianism – has permeated every sphere of policy-making. In education, for example, successive ministers have focused obsessively on improv-

ing the so-called 'basics' of English, mathematics and science in an attempt to upgrade the skills of Britain's workforce and, thereby, enhance the competitiveness of its industries in global markets. Education has not only been a linchpin in the New Right's strategy to curb the country's long-term economic decline, but has also figured prominently in its policies to address the nation's allegedly crumbling social and moral fabric. To cultivate a greater sense of common purpose and direction, the New Right's 'cultural restorationist' wing (Ball 1993) has sought to rid the school system of any vestige of cultural and moral relativism. Not surprisingly, pluralist measures, such as anti-racist and multi-cultural education, have been vigorously attacked as the cultural restorationists have endeavoured to impose their own assimilationist agenda and narrow construction of nationhood on the National Curriculum in England and Wales (see, for example, Gaine 1995, Gillborn 1995, Phillips 1995, Troyna 1993). Since the passing of the Education Reform Act in 1988, they have continued to lobby, often with considerable success, for curricular policies that give prominence to the teaching of British history, Christianity, standard English and the English literary heritage. Nick Tate, the government's chief adviser on the curriculum in England and Wales, has defended this ostensibly Anglocentric stance on the grounds that schools need to 'reinforce a common culture'. The National Curriculum, he claims, 'plays a key part in helping society maintain its identity' (Tate 1994).

There have been parallel developments in the United States, where issues relating to religion and language have also figured prominently in contemporary Right-wing polemics against liberalism. Not surprisingly, some minorities have felt threatened by a newly energized evangelistic movement that seeks openly to reintroduce prayer into the public schools and, somewhat less openly, to redefine America as an essentially Christian nation. The subtext is important, not least because it resonates with what high-profile Republicans like Newt Gingrich have in mind when they call for the reassertion of American culture. Consider, for example, his observations while addressing Congress during a debate on proposed legislation to make English the country's official language (1 August 1996). Responding to Census Bureau estimates that by the year 2010 the Hispanic population would exceed the Black, he voiced concern about the apparent ramifications of linguistic diversity, including Balkanization. He went on to make the following assimilationist (and, arguably, exclusivist) declaration: 'Part of becoming American involves English. . . . It is vital historically to assert and establish that English is the common language at the heart of our civilisation' (*Independent on Sunday*, 22 September 1996).

In this chapter, we will provide an appraisal of the main findings of the three case studies. As well as drawing international comparisons (giving particular attention to age-related and ethnic differences in response), we will also consider the influence of regional factors on British children's notions of national identity. We conclude by reflecting upon the curricular implications of the findings.

The research

The sample

265 children (136 boys and 129 girls), aged between 8 and 12, took part in the research. Almost all the children (95 per cent) were UK- or US-born. The sample was an opportunist one, selected primarily for reasons related to access. The English cohort, drawn from two schools in the North East and one in the South East, comprised 128 children, from a variety of social and ethnic backgrounds. More than two-thirds of these children were white (71 per cent); the remainder came from South Asian (25 per cent) or Afro-Caribbean/African (5 per cent) backgrounds. In contrast, the Scottish sample of 76 children was far more homogeneous. Most of them came from white collar and professional backgrounds and, with a single exception, all of the children were white. While similar to the Edinburgh sample in terms of its socio-economic composition (i.e. disproportionately middle class), the American cohort of 61 children was more ethnically diverse, with one in five belonging to so-called 'visible' minority groups.[2]

Methodology

Individual semi-structured interviews provided the principal means of data collection, which were conducted after the researchers had established rapport with the children in a classroom setting. All the participants were volunteers and were given an assurance that appropriate steps would be taken to maintain both their personal and institutional anonymity. They were also told that the interview should not be construed as a test of any kind and that they could terminate it at any time of their choosing. During the interviews, the researchers avoided commenting *directly* on the accuracy or validity of the children's responses. However, the children were encouraged to elaborate upon or qualify their comments. In addition, appropriate steps were taken to ensure that none of the participants were placed in a potentially embarrassing or threatening situation.

To broach the issue of national identity, the younger children in the two British cohorts were asked, 'Have you heard the term "British" before?'. The interviews with older children began with the statement, 'You have obviously heard the word "British"'. In contrast, the American children, were invited at the start of each interview to respond to the question, 'What is the name of the country you live in?'. A semi-structured format was then adopted for the remainder of the interviews (with each cohort) using the following schedule:

- Are you British/American or are you something else?
- What makes a person British/American?
- Is everyone who lives here in this country British/American?
- Is it possible to stop being British/American and become something else?
- What are the best and worst things about being British/American?[3]

In addition to these questions, the American cohort was also asked whether some people were more American than others, while their British counterparts were questioned about the perceived importance of their national identity.

The findings

The children's descriptions of their national identity

A number of differences – ethnic, national and regional – were evident in the children's responses to the question, 'Are you British/American or something else?'. Whereas almost all (94 per cent) of the white children in the English schools saw themselves as unequivocally 'British', only two-thirds of this ethnic group (65 per cent) in the

Massachusetts school referred to themselves as simply 'American'. In contrast, the responses of the 'visible' minority children in each setting were almost identical: about a third (i.e. 33 per cent in Massachusetts and 31 per cent in England) viewed their national identity in hyphenated terms: for example,

> My mom and dad are Chinese, but they were born in Taiwan and I was born here and my sister and brother were too – half Chinese and half American (Benjamin, 10 years)[4]

> Either Puerto Rican, Dominican, Spanish or American (Beatriz, 10 years)

> Mum was born in England and she's British and my dad was born in Kenya. He's Indian . . . I'm both – a bit British and a bit Kenyan (Prashant, 9 years)

> I'm half British and half Ugandan. I was born in Britain and my parents were born in Uganda (Sonalee, 10 years).

In general terms, the American children, irrespective of ethnicity, seemed much more aware of their ethnocultural heritage than their white English peers. In addition, they appeared to operate with more broadly-based and inclusive notions of their national culture. Living in a 'society of immigrants', the Americans repeatedly made reference to their family lineage when describing their national identity. Thus, Alexander (10 years) told the researcher that he was 'American and sort of German and some Italian', while Danny (10 years) said: 'On my mother's side of the family, I'm Italian; I'd say Italian-American – I think I'm a little of both'. Similarly, Kevin (10 years) described himself as 'American, Irish, French, and partly German', while Cindy (11 years) stated: 'I'm mostly Chinese [but] I consider myself American'. In contrast, Emily (10 years) – whose father had emigrated from Israel – thought of herself as 'mostly American' because she was born in the USA.

While less likely than their American peers to view national identity in hyphenated terms, the Scottish children appeared to operate with more fluid conceptions than their white English counterparts. Although three-quarters of the Edinburgh cohort said that they were 'British' when replying to the question, 'Are you British or something else?', the older children (particularly the girls), were more inclined to describe themselves as having either a dual national identity – 'Scottish and British' (Claire, 11 years); 'I'm half British and half

English' (Caroline, 10 years); 'I'm British and I'm Scottish' (James, 11 years) – or as having only a Scottish nationality. While their reasons for doing so varied, several (in common with their American peers) made reference to aspects of their family history: 'My mum's British but my dad's Italian – so you could say I was half and half' (Bruno, 11 years); 'I'm half English and half British . . . because my mum was born in England' (Rachel, 10 years).

The Scottish children's descriptions of their national identity (especially the 11-year-olds) bore a stronger resemblance to those of the 'visible' ethnic minority respondents in our English sample than those of the ethnic majority. The apparent rejection of the simple epithet 'British' by a quarter of the Scottish children appeared to lend support to Modood (1992). In contrast to their white counterparts in English schools, the Scottish children seemed to be rather less complacent about their national identity. It was evident that some of these children had reflected upon the meaning of 'Britishness' and were aware of the divide between Celtic and English Britain. As a result, they were prepared to take issue with the assumption that English norms and values should prevail in society. And while this questioning very rarely took the overtly political form, it surfaced in other ways. Eleven-year-old Ruth, for example, resented the fact that, in popular discourse, Britishness is often constructed in an Anglocentric manner: 'When people say you're British, they seem to think you're *English* – not Scottish. . . . A lot of people automatically assume that you're English and I don't really like that much, because *we're not English*'.

Constructions of nationhood

The concept of 'nationhood' is a complex and multi-faceted one which, as Jan Penrose (1993: 29) has pointed out, can be regarded as having three main components. The first assumes the existence of a distinctive group of people defined in terms of 'tangible characteristics such as language, religion, cultural practices or physical and/or behavioural traits'. Such characteristics are, on occasions, held to have origins 'which lie deeper in abstruse realities such as a "national soul", "national consciousness" or "national identity"'. The second is predicated upon the assumption that these groups occupy or lay claim to a distinctive territory or place. Finally, it is held that 'a mystical bond' is forged between people and place to form an 'immutable whole': the nation.

It came as no surprise to find that the vast majority of the participants in the study – on both sides of the Atlantic – focused on the 'tangible characteristics' of nationhood when responding to the question, 'What makes a person British/American?'. Although there was some variation by age, the children in both the English and Scottish cohorts (irrespective of ethnicity) believed that the *sine qua non* of Britishness was to be born in Britain (65 per cent), to speak English as a first language (32 per cent), to live or work in Britain (18 per cent) and to have British parents or grandparents (17 per cent). The following responses were typical:

> You're British . . . 'if you were born in Britain, or your mum and dad's British (David, white British, 9 years)

> A person who is British, comes from England; they're born in England and their Mum and Dad are born in England (Gita, British South Asian, 9 years)

> I'm British because . . . I was born [in Britain] and speak British (Chris, white British, 9 years)

> It's just the way they talk and where they were born (Douglas, white British, 9 years)

> You're British . . . if you're born in Britain, if you've lived in Britain all your life, if you've got a British passport (Syreeta, British South Asian, 10 years)

> To be British . . . you'd have to be born in Britain and you'd really have to speak the language (Colin, white British, 11 years)

> If they were born over here and if their birth certificates say that they were born in Britain (Ben, British Afro-Caribbean, 11 years).

The 11-year-olds appeared to attach greater significance than the younger children to place of birth as a key determinant of nationality and, concomitantly, somewhat less importance to issues relating to language, country of domicile and family background. Although a small minority of those interviewed (8 per cent) made reference to cultural habits or affiliation when defining their national identity (e.g. You're British 'when they do the same things as the British and have the British accent'), it

was noticeable that virtually no child actively embraced an overtly racist perspective, or viewed Britishness in ethnically-exclusivist terms.

The American children also tended to define their national identity in concrete terms: the majority (64 per cent) underlined the importance of being born in the USA, while others mentioned living or working in the country (31 per cent), having American citizenship (16 per cent), or parents or grandparents who were American (11 per cent). Only one or two individuals made reference to cultural practices when replying to the question, 'What makes a person American?': for example, '[You're American if you] live in America, [are] born in America, speak English, dress like the people do around you, act like the people around you' (Lesley, white American, 11 years); '[An American needs] to get along with other Americans and use the core values' (Jim, white American, 11 years). In common with the two British cohorts, there was little evidence of any ethnic difference in response and very few of the children were found to hold exclusivist or ethnocentric conceptions of American identity. These following comments are broadly illustrative of the children's constructions:

> [An American is someone who is] born here or [who has] lived here a long time (Louise, white American, 9 years)

> [A person who] was born here and, possibly, their mother was – otherwise people can come here (Doug, white American, 10 years)

> Born in the state of America (Michael, African American, 10 years)

> Lives here, born here, parents, grandparents or ancestors stayed here for a while – at least or someone who lived here for a long time (Emily, white American, 10 years)

> [You have] papers, if you've been here most of your life (Beatriz, Puerto Rican American, 10 years)

> Born in America or living here – not just taking your vacation here (Jane, white American, 11 years).

Although the replies of the Massachusetts cohort to the question 'What makes a person American?' were broadly comparable to those of their British peers, there were some notable differences. For example, whereas the American children made only the odd reference to linguistic issues when defining national identity, about a third of those interviewed in the United Kingdom believed that having English as a first language was part and parcel of quintessential Britishness. In contrast, the American children were rather more inclined than their British counterparts to draw attention to the formal (i.e. juridical) components of citizenship (see Beatriz's remarks above), or alternatively, to its phenomenological dimensions. As Karen, a 10-year-old African American, pointed out, an integral part of being an American is 'believing that you're American' – an issue we will return to later.

Immigration, emigration and naturalization

Other questions ('Is everybody who lives in this country British/American?', 'Is it possible to stop being British/American and become something else?', 'Are some people more American than others?') not only supplied additional data on how the children constructed their national identity, but also provided a further opportunity to assess the extent to which their conceptions were pluralistic or exclusivist. Moreover, the questions served to shed light upon the children's knowledge of the motives underlying international movements of labour and their understanding of complex juridical notions, such as naturalization and citizenship.

Once again, very few of the children – either British or American – were found to conceptualize their national identity in an exclusivist manner. There was, however, a handful of white respondents who made direct references to 'race' or ethnicity when replying to the question, 'Is everyone who lives in this country British/American?'. For example, Stuart, one of the 11-year-olds in Massachusetts, answered negatively, stating: 'I know people who aren't – they're Chinese and stuff'. Likewise, in the English cohort, a 10-year-old told the researcher that it was not possible for people of Chinese origins to be British simply because 'they don't look British'. The remarks of one of the white 9-year-olds in Edinburgh, as the following transcript shows, revealed a similar potential for cultural racism:

BC: Is everybody who lives in the country British?
Chris: No.

BC: What sorts of people are not British?
Chris: Some Pakistani people.
BC: Why are they not British?
Chris: Because they have different lives.
BC: Can you explain a bit more? In what way is their life different?
Chris: They come from different places.
BC: So they come from other countries? What about people who come say from France?
Chris: They can usually speak the language.

However, the vast majority of those interviewed (irrespective of age, ethnicity, or geographical location) responded to the question in a seemingly innocuous fashion, stating simply that there were people living in Britain or the United States who were born in other countries, or that they were tourists, students or workers from overseas. In the English cohort, for example, 9-year-old Andrew (white British) noted that 'people come from all over the world to visit [the UK], or they come to some of the British universities', while Sangita (British South Asian, 9 years) and David (white British, 10 years) said, respectively: 'Some people come from different countries and come to live in England'; 'Some people come from different countries and move over here . . . for jobs'. Similarly, in the Scottish cohort, 9-year-old Emily (white British) told the researcher that there were people living in Britain who 'have been born somewhere else, like in Japan. [Or] . . . they're on holiday', while Nicholas (white British, 10 years) replied: 'No – some are tourists and come to see the sights'. Other Edinburgh children (in common with David) referred to the economic reasons for international migration in their responses: for example, 'sometimes it's for jobs, sometimes it's [because] the country they are living in isn't up to standard or something' (Stuart, white British, 11 years). One or two of the Scottish children were also found to have a grasp of the notion of 'naturalization', though, not surprisingly, no one actually employed the term during interview:

Ruth (11): Well people emigrate from places like America or whatever: They're not British.
BC: If they want to become British, can they be?
Ruth: I think so, but you have to change your passport and everything. . . .
BC: Do you have to do anything else to become British?

Ruth: If you go to America, you have to have a Green Card or something.

Predictably, the American children – living in a 'society of immigrants' – not only appeared to have a better understanding than their British counterparts of the motives underlying international migration, but also seemed to have a firmer grasp of its wider social, legal and political ramifications. Thus, when replying to the question 'Is everyone who lives in this country American?', 9-year-old Alexander (white American) stated: 'No – they could be immigrants from other countries. They can become citizens, but they were still born in America'. In a similar vein, 9-year-old Louise (white American) remarked, 'If you were born in another country and lived here a long time you could be American', while 10-year-olds, Mustafa (an Asian American), José-Luis (a Puerto Rican American) and Matthew (white American) noted, respectively: 'No – they might come from other places and maybe they are just living here for a while'; 'No – an immigrant isn't American'; 'No – some people are immigrants, they're not citizens'. It should be emphasized that not all of the American participants in the research were to broach the matter of citizenship in such a formal or legalistic manner. Indeed, a few of them (like Karen cited earlier) went to some lengths to emphasize that there is a subjective or phenomenological dimension to national identity, arguing that Americans are essentially individuals who regard themselves as being American:

> They were born here, or came over here when they were young, and think of themselves as American (Michael, white American, 11 years)

> It could be either way. There could be people who consider themselves American even if they're not – and there could be people who are American, but they don't consider themselves American (Jim, white American, 11 years).

National identity – achieved or ascribed?

The question, 'Is it possible to stop being British/American and become something else?', enabled us to probe the children's understanding of issues relating to migration more directly. Although the children – on both sides of the Atlantic – were divided in their views, a majority answered affirmatively. And since taking up residence in another country was one of the principal reasons given for a positive reply, we might reasonably infer that a number of the children recognized that national identity need not be wholly ascribed: that is, determined solely by a person's country of origin. For example, Barbara, a white American 11-year-old, told the researcher: 'If you move to another country and live there for a long time, you become that [nationality]'. In a similar vein, Charlie (a white British 9-year-old), stated that a change of nationality would be possible 'if you went abroad and got a new passport or something', while Debbie (an 11-year-old Native American/African American) noted: 'if you don't want to be an American anymore you could cancel your citizenship'. Others, responding in a more equivocal manner, sometimes appeared to recognize that a person's national identity may be determined – albeit in varying degrees – by his or her country of domicile, as well as country of origin. Consider, for example, the following comments of Mark (an 11-year-old, British Afro-Caribbean): 'If you're born British, then you'll always be British. But if you are born in another country and you travel to Britain, . . . you're partly British because you live there'.

We would like to draw attention to two principal differences between the British and American children (which were also evident in their replies to the question, 'What makes a person British/American?'). When asked whether it was possible for a person to change their national identity, those British children who responded affirmatively, were far more likely than their American counterparts to underline the importance of linguistic factors. Whereas only one or two of the Americans (3 per cent) felt that learning the language of the country concerned would be a necessary prerequisite of such a change, the corresponding proportion in both the English and Scottish samples was appreciably higher (i.e. 25 per cent and 18 per cent respectively). The second difference between the American and British children concerns the importance attached to place of birth. Whereas nearly a third of the British children said it was impossible to change one's nationality because birthplace was crucial, such responses were comparatively rare among the Americans. The following examples are illustrative of these differences:

> Not really, because you were born in America. You can become a citizen of another place, but you are still American (Alexander, white American, 9 years)

Yes . . . you need to go abroad . . . [and] learn their speech (Kirsty, white British, 10 years)

You could just learn their language and go and live there but you can't change from [being] British (Katie, white British, 10 years)

No . . . if you're born British, you stay British (Lee, white British, 10 years)

You've always got the British in you – because you were born in Britain (Jitendra, British Asian, 11 years).

Although many of the children – British and American alike – made reference to the juridical components of citizenship when replying to the question, 'Is it possible to stop being British/American and become something else?', on this occasion, as on others, the Americans were more inclined to focus on its phenomenological or subjective dimensions. And whatever new national identity an individual might acquire as a result of migration – and subsequent naturalization – an affiliation to their country of origin would remain with them throughout their lives. Cognizant of the crucial role played by this form of initial socialization on the formation of national identity, Mary, a 10-year-old white American, told the researcher that it would be possible to 'live in another country but [you'd] still be American, if you were originally from America'. She went on to explain: 'Being an American, being born here, or raised here and then you decide to go to another country. America is still part of your child[hood], or your adult[hood] – whenever you lived in America'.

Similarly, Cindy, an 11-year-old Chinese American, said that it would be necessary 'to go somewhere else and become something else – and stop thinking you're American', while Fatima, an East Indian American of the same age, said that people could change their national identity 'if they really hated it here, or were forced to live here and didn't want to be American'. Others, in common with British respondents such as Mark (see p. 189), alluded to the issue of hyphenated identity in their replies. Consider, for example, the respective responses of Ildi and Josef (both white 10-year-old immigrants), or Liz (white American, 11 years) and Danny (white American, 10 years): 'Yes – they could be something else, but still be American'; 'You can't stop being American – but you can also become something else'; 'No, you could never stop

being American, but you could become part something else'; 'If you went to Canada or Japan, you could still be American – but you could also be Chinese or African'.

Neo-conservative versus pluralist constructions of nationhood

As we noted in our opening remarks, neo-conservative constructions of nationhood (both in the United Kingdom and the United States) are predicated upon assimilationist and exclusivist assumptions. The question, 'Are some people more American than others?', provided a further opportunity to assess the extent to which those in the Massachusetts cohort may have been influenced by such constructions. The British children, as we have indicated, were not invited to explore an equivalent question.

The most common affirmative response – albeit largely confined to the 8- to 10-year-olds – was that those born in the United States were more American than those born elsewhere. The respective comments of Alexander (a white American 9-year-old) and Michael (an African American, 10-year-old) exemplify such thinking: 'If your parents were born in the US, you are more American than a person whose parents were born in China'; 'If you are born in America, you are more American than people who came to the country'. The 11-year-olds in the Massachusetts sample were more inclined than their younger peers to respond to the question negatively. Nearly three-quarters of them (73 per cent) answered in this manner; the corresponding proportions for the 8- and 9-year-olds were 10 per cent and 27 per cent respectively. Often the 11-year-olds went to considerable lengths to justify an avowedly pluralist stance. The following comments, for example, come from two white children. 'If you're American, you're American – there is no higher stage'; 'Everyone who lives here is the same amount of American'. Lesley, another white child, voiced the same liberal sentiments when she stated: 'We're all basically the same – Native Americans can be called more American because their family originated from America'. In a similar vein, Cindy, a Chinese American, stressed that 'you can't be more or less [American]' while Carol (who was Chinese and Burmese in origin) opined, 'Americans are all equal – no one's more important than another'.

Despite such daily rituals as pledging allegiance

to the flag, none of the children expressed nationalistic views when responding to this question and very few depicted national identity in terms of cultural affiliation. The following isolated, assimilationist (and, arguably, ethnocentric) references were made:

> Someone could be all American and somebody could be from a different country. And people who celebrate Christmas may be more American than people who celebrate Chanukah (José-Luis, Puerto Rican American, 10 years)

> Yes if they really like their original clothing and are in communication with their other country, they would be less American (Jim, white American, 11 years).

The symbolic significance of national identity

In contrast to the American children, those in the English and Scottish cohorts were asked directly about the symbolic significance of national identity, when they were invited to address the question, 'Is being British important to you?'. Although the children were almost evenly divided in their replies, with just over a half of both cohorts answering affirmatively (i.e. English 52 per cent, Scottish 53 per cent), there were a number of regional variations in response, along with age-related and ethnic differences. Whereas about a half of the 11-year-olds (53 per cent) in the Scottish cohort answered affirmatively, the corresponding proportion for the 9-year-olds was nearly three-quarters (70 per cent). As we have already noted, the older Scottish children were more likely than the younger ones to take issue with populist, Anglocentric constructions of Britishness. With our English sample, the situation was reversed: nearly two-thirds of the 11-year-olds regarded being British as important (65 per cent) compared to a half of the 8- and 9-year-olds.

For the large part, those responding affirmatively – on both sides of the border – chose (once again) to focus on the more tangible aspects of their national identity, referring variously to place of birth, familial and other ties, language and a sense of belonging. The following comments, from the Scottish cohort, are representative: 'Britain is the place I was born and also all my family are in Britain and all my friends as well' (Melanie, white British, 9

years); 'When anyone asks me where I come from and what language I speak, I have to say British' (Caroline, white British, 10 years); 'I was born there and like it' (Adam, white British, 10 years). Although there were the odd occasions when the children's remarks were patriotic in tenor ('You should be proud of your country – it's the place you've been brought up in') few if any, in either cohort, came across as being xenophobic.

Less than half of the visible minority children were asked whether being British was important to them. In the many cases, the question had been rendered redundant by comments already made by the individual concerned about her or his preferred national identity (or identities). As we have already noted, more than a third had indicated that they perceived themselves as having hyphenated identities. We were also aware of the possibility that some of the children might regard the question as a controversial and sensitive one – especially in view of the construction placed upon 'Britishness' in the discourse of the New Right. Understandably, the minority children in the study who described themselves as British appeared more blasé about their national identity than their white counterparts. Krishna (British South Asian, 11 years), for example, stated unequivocally: 'I don't really mind [what I am]. I don't really make a big fuss about it; I don't even think about it'.

Conclusion

The findings of this research suggest grounds for optimism. There was little evidence to suggest that the children's constructions of national identity – on either side of the Atlantic – bore the imprimatur of neo-conservative discourse on nationhood. There was a dearth of comments that were self-evidently racist, ethnocentric, xenophobic or nationalist and very few of those interviewed appeared to be committed to the doctrine of assimilation. Despite this, some caution should be exercised when generalizing from the research. Although the sample is not insubstantial for a study of this type, it cannot be regarded as representative. Not only was the sample an opportunist one, but a disproportionate number of those interviewed came from white collar and professional backgrounds. In addition, we also acknowledge that the findings might have been very different had the research been undertaken in other geographical settings, for example, in other parts of the United Kingdom (such as rural Wales or the Scottish Highlands) where support for nationalism may be more firmly entrenched. Likewise, had the research been carried out elsewhere in the United States (e.g. where issues relating to immigration figure more prominently in local political debates, or where the influence of the Far Right is particularly marked) the findings may have been very different. We not only recognize the limitations of our sampling procedures, but also acknowledge the attendant risks of accepting – at face value – the children's reflections on a number of vexed and complex issues. For example, we cannot say whether our line of questioning encouraged the children to think of their British or American citizenship in 'minimalist' rather than 'maximalist' terms (McLaughlin 1992): that is, to dwell largely upon its formal (i.e. juridical) dimensions rather than phenomenological ones. Furthermore, the relative absence of remarks that were self-evidently racist or xenophobic, could have reflected a reluctance on the part of the children to articulate views which in postmodern, liberal democracies are not only to be publicly disavowed, but are also regarded as lying beyond the bounds of respectability (Billig et al. 1988).

Leaving aside these limitations, our findings suggest that we may have identified some of the 'central organising principles' (Damon 1977) of the children's thinking about national identity. Although there were some regional and national differences, the pattern of response within each of the cohorts was broadly comparable. Quite apart from the similarities referred to above, others were also evident. For example, the majority of children, both British and American, were found to construe their national identity in largely concrete terms, referring mostly to its surface features, such as: place of birth, living or working in the country, or ties of consanguinity. Another similarity was the small proportion of children who viewed their national identity primarily as a form of cultural affiliation.

Despite this, the tendency for a minority to draw attention to the salience of cultural differences in the construction of national identity is a matter for concern, for our data suggest that children as young as 8 or 9 may be vulnerable to the spurious 'logic' of the new racism. Thus, it is important that teachers (in the primary or elementary school) attempt to engage with the view that cultural homogeneity is the defining feature of nationhood

and, its corollary, that social cohesion is dependent upon assimilation. Monolithic constructions of either British or American identity can be challenged in a variety of ways. As well as underlining the multifarious ways in which various migrant groups have helped to shape both British and American 'culture' over the centuries, teachers might also encourage children to reflect directly upon their taken-for-granted assumptions about nationhood. Certainly, notions – which abound in popular discourse – such as '*the* British way of life' – need to be deconstructed. In respect of this, we see no reason why questions of the type employed in this study could not be used by teachers as a basis for class discussion. As well as making children (such as the ethnic majority in the English cohort) less complacent about their national identity, such discussion could also serve to highlight the inadequacy of exclusivist constructions. To some degree, the value of such an approach has already received some official recognition in Wales, where teachers have been invited to encourage children 'to think critically about the nature and significance of nationality', by addressing questions such as:

- Does nationality depend on where you were born?
- Do you take your nationality from your parents?
- What if your parents have different nationalities?
- Is a Welsh speaker more Welsh?
- Can we change our nationality?
                    (Curriculum Council for Wales 1993: 34)

This approach has other potential advantages. As well as providing a context for deepening the children's understanding of racism, xenophobia and nationalism and for raising various issues relating to the formal aspects of citizenship, the approach could also provide a starting point for a discussion of its subjective dimensions. If children are to develop inclusivist notions of citizenship, they will first need to grasp that it is 'a richer thing than (say) the possession by a person of a passport, the right to vote and an unreflective "nationality"?':

the citizen must have a consciousness of him or herself as a member of a living community with a shared democratic culture involving obligations and responsibilities as well as rights, a sense of common good, fraternity and so on. (McLaughlin 1992: 236)

It is, of course, this shared commitment to

democratic values that provides the basis for social cohesion in the postmodern state and not, as the protagonists of the new racism argue, the existence of 'common culture'.

Acknowledgement

We would like to record our thanks to Karen Wyche and Deborah Reaves for allowing us to draw freely upon their data.

Notes

1 At the time (1995) Karen Wyche was at Brown University; she is now based at New York University. The interviews were conducted by Deborah Reaves, a school psychologist.
2 African American, 2; Chinese American, 3; Other Asian American, 2; Iranian, 2; Puerto Rican American, 2; Haitian, 1; Native/African American, 1.
3 Space does not permit us to discuss responses to this question.
4 Pseudonyms are used throughout this chapter.

References

Avis, J., Bloomer, M., Esland, G., Gleeson, D. and Hodkinson, P. (1996) *Knowledge and Nationhood*. London: Cassell.

Ball, S. (1993) Education, Majorism and "the curriculum of the dead". *Curriculum Studies*, **1**(2): 195–213.

Barker, M. (1981) *The New Racism*. London: Junction Books.

Billig, M., Condor, S., Edwards, D., Gane, M., Middleton, D. and Radley, A. (1988) *Ideological Dilemmas: a Social Psychology of Everyday Thinking*. London: Sage.

Carrington, B. and Short, G. (1995) What makes a person British? Children's conceptions of their national culture and identity. *Educational Studies*, **21**(2): 217–38.

Carrington, B. and Short, G. (1996) Who counts; who cares? Scottish children's notions of national identity. *Educational Studies*, **22**(2): 203–24.

Curriculum Council for Wales (CCW) (1993) *Advisory Paper 18 – Developing a Curriculum Cymreig*. Cardiff: CCW.

Damon, W. (1977) *The Social World of the Child*. San Francisco, CA: Jossey-Bass.

Donald, J. and Rattansi, A. (eds) (1992) *'Race', Culture and Difference*. London: Sage.

Gaine, C. (1995) *Still No Problem Here*. Stoke: Trentham Books.

Gillborn, D. (1995) *Racism and Antiracism in Real Schools*. Buckingham: Open University Press.

McLaughlin, T. (1992) Citizenship, diversity and education. *Journal of Moral Education*, **21**(3): 235–51.

Modood, T. (1992) On not being white in Britain: discrimination, diversity and commonality. In M. Leicester and M. Taylor (eds) *Ethics, Ethnicity and Education*. London: Kogan Page.

Penrose, J. (1993) Reification in the name of change: the impact of nationalism on social constructions of nation, people and place in Scotland and the United Kingdom. In P. Jackson and J. Penrose (eds) *Constructions of Race, Place and Nation*. London: UCL Press.

Phillips, R. (1995) The creation of history in the National Curriculum in England and Wales: some implications of cultural restorationism for cultural identity and national awareness. Paper presented to the European Conference on Education Research, University of Bath, 14–17 September.

Short, G. and Carrington, B. (1996) Anti-racist education, multiculturalism and the new racism. *Educational Review*, **48**(1): 65–77.

Tate, N. (1994) Off the fence on common culture. *Times Educational Supplement*, 29 July.

Troyna, B. (1993) *Racism and Education: A Research Perspective*. Milton Keynes: Open University Press.

18 Value Pluralism, Democracy and Education for Citizenship[1]

DON ROWE

Introduction – citizenship education as a controversial subject in democratic societies

Across the education systems of Western Europe, a resurgence of interest in citizenship education[2] is taking place. A number of factors are seen to be contributing to the urgency of the matter, including disillusionment with democracy, the threat to democracy from the mass media, the rapid pace of social and political change, the alienation of young people, rising crime rates, and increasing ethnic intolerance (Newton 1994). In Eastern Europe, too, many similar concerns are being expressed and are compounded by the need to introduce new approaches to civic education in response to the introduction of ideological pluralism and market economics (Valchev 1992, Rachmanova and Severukhin 1994). A recent report (UNESCO 1993) emphasizes the critical role played by schools in promoting stable pluralist societies where coherence within the community is not threatened by value diversity. It suggests that schools must be places where 'peace, human rights, tolerance, international and intercultural understanding, solidarity and cooperation, peaceful conflict resolution and democratic organisation are fostered'.

Aims such as these are easy to express but they present considerable challenges to classroom teachers faced with children of different ages, abilities, attitudes and values. And the task is made more complex by the politically controversial nature of the subject matter (for an Austrian example, see Dachs 1995). There is no single view of what 'society' and 'citizenship' should mean such that the content of the citizenship curriculum has often been a matter of heated debate between teachers, parents, politicians, church leaders and other interest groups. For this reason, it has been easier to implement programmes in non-democratic societies. Ironically, the very existence of value pluralism in society has tended to prevent liberal democracies from developing what I would call mature (i.e. pluralist) programmes of civic education because of the fear that such arrangements would be used by one group to indoctrinate the young in partisan values. The principle focus of this chapter is the wide variety of approaches towards citizenship education that have arisen in democratic societies in direct response to the presence of value pluralism. As we shall see, some models have attempted to ignore or suppress this pluralism, though in different ways and for a variety of reasons, whilst a minority have attempted what I argue is the necessary, but more challenging, task of facing up to the reality of pluralism and developing educational models that prepare young people for the essential role it plays in democratic systems (Dachs ibid.).

Many assumptions appear to underlie the teaching of social and moral values which often amount to working theories or models of citizenship education. These models are not necessarily clearly articulated or empirically validated and yet, I suggest, they influence the development of curricula in highly significant ways. For this reason, I believe it is important to be as clear as possible about the differences between these theoretical models, their functions and their implications. Because a principle claim of this chapter is that all democratic societies face these inherent difficulties, I shall support my arguments with references to civic education practices across Europe.

Broadly speaking, there are three main categories of citizenship learning that relate to the three domains in which social and moral development takes place – the cognitive, the affective and the active or experiential. However, within these broad categories a number of different models can be discerned and it is to these I now turn.

Cognitive models

Constitutional knowledge model

This model adopts a descriptive approach to public institutions such as the constitution and the mechanics of local and national government. It recognizes the need for citizenship education to foster social cohesion and civic virtue but tends to regard value pluralism as a potential source of confusion for children and young people. Therefore, it avoids or minimizes controversy and concentrates on 'safe' or consensus areas where pupils will encounter little or no value conflict. This model is more likely to be observed in secondary schools because of its relatively complex content but simplified forms are not unknown in primary schools, as in the French example described by Starkey (1992). Citizenship on this model is seen much more as a future political status than a dynamic set of rights and obligations encountered within one's daily life.

Because it avoids controversial issues, this model tends to lack relevance and interest for students. The methodology adopted by this approach is often formal and didactic, dominated by the one way flow of information from teacher to pupil. Because there is little scope for discussion the model is weak as far as the development of democratic skills and attitudes are concerned. Its failure to address the affective domain of learning is also significant.

However, despite its grave limitations, this model does have some practical advantages which may account for the fact that it has been the single most common approach to be found in operation. For example, it is easier to implement than value laden approaches and there is some evidence that, because of this, it is reverted to by inexperienced or non-specialist teachers (Stradling and Bennett 1981). Where citizenship courses are taught by non-specialists – which is not uncommon for example, in the UK and Flanders (Ministry of Flemish Community 1994) – this model is more likely to be officially commended because of its relatively undemanding pedagogy. In addition, it has the advantage that it is less likely to bring the school

into conflict with outside bodies such as parents or government.

At a national level this constitutional model is likely to be favoured because of its non-controversial nature and its consequent ability to gain support across the political parties. The battle between the political right and left over the content of citizenship education is evident in many countries, with the religious authorities often being additional players (see, for example, Stradling and Bennett's account of the political struggle over citizenship education in the former West Germany and Dachs on the Austrian experience).

An obvious objective of the constitutional model is to present a positive and clear account of society for young people but ironically, this whole approach has the potential to become counter-productive, since some commentators (Rowe 1992) have claimed that the 'sanitized', problem-free view of society only leads to disillusionment when students begin to see for themselves that 'the world is not like that'. The failure of the school to offer students an adequate model of social conflict may leave confusion where there should have been understanding.

One further characteristic of this model can be observed. It appears to be favoured in circumstances where pupils are believed to be less capable of handling value conflict, as with younger and less able pupils. As already noted, primary school children are less likely to be presented with value conflicts and more likely to be offered a world view where social cohesion predominates and adults work harmoniously together for the common good. Even in Holland when a value conflict model was recommended in secondary schools (Hooghof 1987) there was no apparent attempt to introduce it into the primary curriculum. A paternalistic desire to protect innocence may be at work here, despite much evidence that primary pupils experience moral uncertainty (Cullingford 1992) and that the development of social and moral understanding is a continuous process throughout childhood (e.g. Dunn 1988).

Patriotic model

This model regards the promotion of loyalty to the state or the community as the central concern of citizenship education. As such it stands in a very long tradition (Lister 1988). In its militant or strong form this model becomes overtly propagandist, supporting the ideology of the ruling élite, as was the case in Franco's Spain (Buxarrais et al. 1994), the former Soviet bloc (e.g. Vari-Szilagyi 1994) and Austria/Germany under the Nazis (Dachs op. cit.). Dissent or criticism is suppressed and represented as socially unacceptable or subversive. Social control, as opposed to influence, is the central aim of the strong patriotic model. As such it fails to recognize the reality of pluralism, is anti-democratic and denies the fundamental human right to freedom of belief and expression. Yet it cannot be said that those who favour this model always do so for the cynical purpose of promoting state ideologies. It has been justified on the grounds that those being 'educated' will also benefit from it, although this can be seen as an extension of state control beyond the political into the field of culture. For example, Lister (op. cit.) quotes Lord Macaulay who, in 1835, expressed the view that Indian education under the British should create people who were 'Indian in blood and colour, but English in taste, morals and intellect'.

The more subtle form of the patriotic model aims to promote civic cohesion by under-emphasizing, or sanitizing, issues that reflect badly on the good image of the state. For example, this model was influential in British civic and history textbooks in their treatment of the British Empire. In a secondary school civics textbook, Larkin (1951) describes the British Empire in terms of a united family, with no reference at all to colonization, exploitation or the suppression of human rights. The image of the family subtly implies a commonality of interests and perhaps even suggests a picture of Britain, as the parent, doing what it thinks to be in the best interests of its sometimes rebellious and ungrateful children.

It is probably fair to say that some aspects of this model are never entirely absent from citizenship education, though some teachers will be more prepared than others to acknowledge its subtle influence. Some observers believe strongly that the patriotic model is essential for the development of a sense of national identity. This is particularly likely to be prominent in the curricula of new nations, especially those emerging from a diversity of ethnic groups. As Osborne (1994) says of the Canadian experience, 'history was the major vehicle for the creation of national identity and patriotism. It told the national myth'. On the whole this model is now regarded with suspicion in post-colonial, multi-

cultural Britain. Starkey (1995), however, compares the English approach unfavourably with the more patriotic French on grounds that, whereas the French civic education guidelines emphasize 'all that unites a nation, from symbols and mottos to President and Parliament', the English recommendations (NCC 1990) make no mention at all of national symbols such as the monarchy, the flag or the National Anthem. Unfortunately, national symbols all too easily encourage attitudes of national superiority and xenophobia in the psychologically immature. The problem is that the patriotic model tends to place national allegiance above respect for justice, truth or universal human rights (Lister op. cit.). It too readily encourages an uncritical view of the *status quo* and in this respect has much in common with the constitutional model.

Parental model

Parents quite properly have a desire and a right, under the European Convention of Human Rights, to raise children according to their own beliefs. This model openly acknowledges the difficulties of transmitting civic values that are in conflict with those of parents. This is one of the very clear points of tension between family values and those of the democratic state, and for teachers there may be no easy way to resolve the conflict this creates. This parental right to 'freedom of instruction' for children has, for example, been enshrined in the Spanish Constitution (Buxarrais et al. op. cit.) making possible schools with a distinctive religious or ideological character where contact with democratic pluralism is minimized. This issue affects families in many different ways but is often acutely felt by parents for whom the maintenance of a distinctive culture is important. In Britain, the Muslim minority has long campaigned for state-supported separate schools (on a par with existing arrangements for Roman Catholic and Jewish schools) where their own cultural and religious traditions can be nurtured and respected. The British government, however, has long been reluctant to allow such schools, probably out of a fear of Islamic separatism or fundamentalism.

In her survey of teaching for conflict resolution in Europe, Walker (1989) quotes several instances, including in Northern Ireland, where teachers expressed reluctance to engage in activities that would encourage inter-community understanding (in this case between Catholics and Protestants) because they knew many parents would strongly object to any activity that appeared to erode their own strongly-held beliefs.

Again, as in the constitutional and the patriotic models, the wish to protect children from contaminating ideas is present, though this model sees the school, and not society, as the main agent of contamination. The reality is, of course, that children in a plural society and in the age of the mass media are bombarded with a multiplicity of values from a very young age from which it is virtually impossible to protect them. Parents and teachers who fail to acknowledge the confusion experienced by children arguably make it more difficult for them, in the long run, to cope with it constructively.

A major difficulty with the parental model is, of course, that it leaves no role for the school in the development of democratic dispositions and fails to help young people deal with the fact that, outside of their own family culture, they will need to engage one way or another with a multiplicity of value positions. The kind of monocultural morality learned within the primary relationships of family and kin needs to be augmented by a secondary, but equally important, public morality, based on notions of rights and obligations rather than affection and loyalty. Quite obviously, schools are primary locations for the development of this public morality.

Religious model

The religious model of civic education reflects the widely-held view that the best means by which to teach civic virtue is through religious education. No doubt the appeal for many is that religious beliefs are generally identified with clear and authoritative moral standards and it seems that many adults (even agnostics and atheists) believe religious teaching to be among the most effective means of inculcating moral values in children. Historically, this model was very strong with English pioneers of mass education, the first civic education textbook being the Bible. There is little doubt that where this model is firmly established it can obstruct the emergence of pluralist civic education. In England during the early 1990s, for example, whilst citizenship education languished on the margins of government concerns, the Secretary of

State for Education suggested that religious education was the most effective vehicle for the promotion of values such as honesty and concern for others (NCC 1993).

This model has a long history and dates from times when there was little or no distinction between the values of church and state and the dichotomy between public values and private beliefs was hardly recognized. It is an approach very deeply embedded in many cultural traditions and therefore is still highly influential, particularly in societies where the association between the state and the established religion remains relatively non-problematic, for example, in the Irish Republic and Spain. In Franco's Spain, according to Buxarrais et al. (op. cit.) the state ethic *was* that of the Roman Catholic Church, and teachers were forbidden to promote moral views counter to those of Rome. Since the democratization of Spain and the embracing of pluralism, the legacy still remains and in only one region of Spain (Catalonia) has a secular form of moral education been introduced as an alternative to religious education.

Teaching 'good citizenship' by means of religious education is, of course, problematic. First, the model is philosophically flawed because, as White (1994) points out, the identification of the *moral* with the *religious* is untenable. Citizens should understand that the religious may not always be 'good' and the 'good' need not be religious. Second, the religious model fails to address many value issues that arise in secular societies. Its chief weakness is, perhaps, its lack of relevance or authority for those who hold a minority faith or no faith at all. For example, in England, the identification of British civic values with Christianity subtly promotes the view that to be, for example, a Sikh or a Buddhist is to be less than fully British. This does nothing to assist young people of minority faiths to come to terms with the problem of divided loyalties – and identification with the community is crucial to the development of positive, participative citizenship (Rowe 1993).

There is a strong case for arguing that all state systems should teach citizenship education irrespective of the presence of religious education in the curriculum. This would provide a forum for the discussion of public issues (such as the death penalty or the role of women in society) in which religious and secular perspectives can be put forward with equal weight. In this way, classroom discussion becomes genuine 'democratic dialogue' where opinions and propositions are judged, not on the basis of the authority claimed for them, (which would be disputed outside of the faith community) but on their intrinsic merits (Haydon 1995). This brings me to my final cognitive model of citizenship education.

Value conflict or pluralist model

This model openly acknowledges that humans experience many conflicts of value – both within themselves and in their relations with others – with the result that they take up widely differing positions on public issues. It bases its philosophical justification on the idea that each person has an inalienable right to freedom of belief and expression. On this view, the over-riding aim of citizenship education is to develop morally autonomous citizens who can think critically and contribute positively to public discourse. It places value on personal development and individual integrity and recognizes that the highest form of civic motivation is that which arises from principled commitment rather than coercion or persuasion. This is exactly the rationale underlying the Dutch social and political curriculum developed in the mid-1980s (Hooghof op. cit.) and is implicit within the British government's guidance of 1990 (NCC 1990). This model not only accepts, but is able to utilize, value conflict because, as Kohlberg has shown, this contributes to more mature moral reasoning (Kohlberg 1984). It also develops better informed, more politically aware and tolerant citizens (Lipman 1991). Further, as Tappan and Brown (1996) point out, acceptance of value pluralism is precisely what is demanded by a 'post-modern moral pedagogy'. This is to affirm the existence of many diverse sociopolitical perspectives, including those of the alienated and the oppressed of society. It is to argue that teachers need to acknowledge the authentic nature of each individual's perspective, which may be very different from that of the dominant ideology, and that such acknowledgement is potentially liberating.

Unlike the constitutional knowledge model, this approach is equally relevant to pupils of all ages. Even primary school pupils experience value conflict as they strive to understand their social world. The following example is taken from a discussion of fair and unfair rules with a class of English 7-year-olds (Rose 1994).

Aaron:	I know a school rule that isn't fair.
Teacher:	Which one is that, Aaron?
Aaron:	The one that says if somebody hits you, you are not allowed to hit them back.
Teacher:	Why do you think that is unfair?
Aaron:	Well, if you hit them back they leave you alone.
Teacher:	What happens when you hit them?
Aaron:	They hit you back.
Teacher:	What happens then?
Aaron:	You hit them again.
Teacher:	And what have you got then?
Aaron:	A fight.
Teacher:	What would happen if everyone did that?
William:	It would be chaos. Everyone would join in.
Aaron:	[After thinking for a few seconds] It might not be a fair rule but it's probably a good one because teachers have to look after you and teach you.

This example demonstrates how Aaron's egocentric perception of justice is in conflict with the values underlying the school rule. If the teacher had not acknowledged the possibility of value conflict and encouraged her pupils to express their own ideas it would not have been possible to challenge Aaron's views with a broader perspective. The pedagogical requirement is to create a situation in which children's existing ideas come up against other perspectives and are modified. This is the importance of so-called 'active learning' techniques. Contrary to popular belief, pupils can be enabled to take part in discussions of this kind as soon as they begin school and research indicates that a weekly session can measurably raise the quality of children's sociomoral reasoning within a short space of time (Medrano and De La Caba 1994).

However, the value conflict model creates significant problems for teachers concerning which values to encourage, which to discourage and on which to remain neutral. How, for example, is a teacher to react when a child expresses a racist attitude and reveals that this attitude is shared by its parents? There are two problems here. First, to what extent does the teacher have the right to undermine the parents' authority in the eyes of the child? Second, how far should teachers, in line with the free speech espoused by the value conflict model, encourage a classroom climate where harmful or anti-social views are permitted? Arguably, unless offensive opinions are expressed they cannot be challenged, but this position could deteriorate into a fully relativist approach where no opinions are held to be better or worse than any others. This is clearly not the case. Part of the function of this model must be to encourage students to understand that in democratic societies there is a core of essential beliefs to which prejudicial views do not conform, and yet, at the same time, there are many other ideas that are quite properly contested.

In fact, these contested ideas can provide a framework of concepts around which teachers can construct the content of the citizenship curriculum. Whilst being strong on process, this model should not be light on content, and should include issues that draw on curriculum areas such as moral education, social education, human rights education, law-related education and political education. The curriculum should help children develop an understanding of concepts such as justice, fairness, rights, responsibilities, rules, laws, power, authority, equality, diversity and community (Rowe 1995) all of which are open to many different interpretations. These ideas permeate mature political debates but are also of keen interest to young children (Dunn 1988). In my view, each of these concepts can and should be explored within the curriculum at a level appropriate to the children's age and maturity. I have directed a project (Rowe and Newton 1994) that uses stories specially written to enable pupils from the age of five or six to explore the above key ideas in what Lipman (1991) calls a community of enquiry.

This value conflict model is highly demanding of teacher skill and requires the creation of a classroom atmosphere where pupils can feel free to express themselves and engage constructively with the views of others. However, there is much research to suggest that teachers, albeit unwittingly, tend to suppress pupils' own views and inhibit their ability to take the initiative in discussion. For example, Wood (1991) reports that the more questions teachers ask, the shorter are pupils' replies. Further, teachers rarely allow sufficient time for children to think before replying. In one study, when the teachers increased the pause after a question from an average one to three seconds, the responses of the children lengthened significantly. The teacher's style of language also influences that of the class – when she adopts a more reflective style of language herself (using fewer questions and more statements) then the children's discourse also

becomes more reflective. In discussing social and moral issues, teachers need to use questions that encourage judgement rather than recall. They should elicit higher order thinking such as analysis, comparison and justificatory reasoning. Other techniques can also help, such as asking the whole class to vote on a pupil's statement and then analysing the reasons underlying the different positions generated.

Naturally, this conflict model is not without its critics. Indeed, all the previous models, with their emphasis on unitary values, implicitly criticize this approach. Watts, for example, quoted in Lister (op. cit.), argues that acknowledging value conflict undermines civic loyalty in the young and O'Hear (1991) claims that its emphasis on critical thinking places insufficient importance on respect for the received wisdom of older generations. O'Hear, however, ignores the fact that value conflict is observable among earlier generations too, and that, in any case, successive generations cannot uncritically apply old ideas to novel situations. Even where a general precept is held to be true for all generations, for example that killing is wrong, there will be conflict generated by the different ways this rule is interpreted in any given set of circumstances.

Finally, the importance of the value conflict model in developing inter-community tolerance and understanding cannot be over-emphasized. The more young people learn to see value pluralism as normal, ubiquitous, and not simply ethnically or culturally based, then the less it will be seen as threatening or divisive.

Affective models

So far in this discussion we have dealt with cognitive models of citizenship education. These develop social understanding, clarify values and create an awareness of rights, duties and obligations. These perceptions are very important in motivating citizens to take public action. Yet, as Gibbs (1991) argues, humans experience two quite distinct sources of moral motivation, the second being an empathic concern for others. Empathy has been defined (Damon 1988) as the ability to recognize the feelings of others, the ability to take another's point of view and to vicariously share in another's emotional state. Empathy has both cognitive and affective components. Whilst the cognitive informs and activates the affective domain, the latter undoubtedly motivates and enriches cognition. Without the ability to empathize with others, moral decision-making would be severely impaired and, according to Damon, higher empathizers are more likely to engage in pro-social actions. Citizenship education has therefore to address the question of educating the feeling, as well as the thinking, self. Students should be helped to see that citizenship education is ultimately about people and the quality of their lives in society. At all stages, therefore, pupils should be encouraged, through the use of case studies, narrative, video and other means, to enter imaginatively the experience of others as well as to consider and articulate their own feelings. So, in promoting empathic reasoning, the teacher will use questions such as 'why do you think X believed that?' or 'how do you think Y was feeling in that situation'?

Teachers are trained primarily to impart knowledge and consequently many find it difficult to address the demands of the affective curriculum. Its importance in the study of the arts and literature is clear but social studies and civic education have not wholly embraced affective approaches, being influenced, instead, by more empirical sociological and political models. Walker (op. cit.) reports that during the 1970s the Luxembourg authorities considered the affective side of the curriculum so important that affective goals were included in a new curriculum planning model. Unfortunately, according to a government official, these goals were seldom realized.

Experiential models

Experiential approaches to citizenship education emphasize the importance of delivering an holistic citizenship education in which both cognition and affect are fully involved, and in which citizenship skills are put into practice. I would identify two common models in this category – the school ethos model and the community action model. These are of relevance to this particular review because they also need to take account of value pluralism in different ways. I suggest that the controversial nature of civic education curricula has sometimes encouraged teachers to rely on these less contentious experiential models, rather than bite the bullet and deal with controversial issues. In the UK, this approach has been particularly true of primary schools (Rose op. cit.).

School ethos model

In democratic societies, schools should ensure that their organization and ethos take account of value pluralism and respect the right of all members to be consulted on issues of concern to them. Power should be exercised responsibly, not in an authoritarian or despotic fashion. Values such as respect for persons and for justice are undoubtedly learned experientially and therefore they should permeate the whole of school life. Teachers encouraging respect for human rights in the classroom should, of course, act in a consistent manner (Best 1992). Rules should be seen to be fair and should be enforced humanely. As Lister (op. cit.) succinctly puts it, civic educators 'need to shape institutions and not just plan curricula'.

Many schools have worked hard on their democratic or consultative structures on the view that pupils need to experience democracy, not simply be taught about it (Best op. cit., Trafford 1993). In the United Kingdom, for example, a survey undertaken in 1993 showed that about half of all state secondary schools and one-seventh of primary schools had pupil councils for the discussion of issues raised by pupils themselves (Ashworth 1995), though this survey indicated that consultations often take place by other means, such as questionnaires. Walker (1989) refers to consultative procedures in Germany, Denmark and Italy where pupils can comment on curriculum matters, discipline, textbooks and the organization of learning. Harber (1995) quotes examples from The Netherlands and the UK where, even in primary schools, pupil participation in decision-making has genuinely enriched the quality of community life and contributed to more positive attitudes of respect and understanding between staff and pupils. In addition, pupil councils provide experience of important aspects of the democratic processes such as standing for elections, representing the opinions of others, campaigning for change, participating in formal meetings and reporting back (Rowe 1997). A trend towards involving young people in municipal decision-making is also discernible in a number of countries, including the UK and France (see for example, Rossini and Vulbeau 1994, Starkey 1992).

There are, of course, limits in the extent to which state schools can democratize. Indeed, some teachers are uncomfortable with the language of democracy in schools (Rowe 1997) and others have preferred to think in terms of creating schools characterized by the more comprehensive values of justice or human rights. Kohlberg's 'just community' schools are the best known example of this trend, though Kohlberg's own experiments were carried out with specially selected groups of pupils, creating highly democratic, self-regulating 'schools within schools' (Power et al. 1989) A radical approach of this nature is very difficult to replicate in large mainstream schools. However, Walker (op. cit.) describes the Loretto Catholic Girls' Schools in Ireland as basing their ethos on the 'specific philosophy of justice and peace', emphasizing the quality of relationships, structures and processes throughout the school. On this model even school discipline should take account of the high standards demanded by the justice concept (see, for example, Cunningham 1992). In similar work, Rogers (1994), has developed a highly sophisticated approach to classroom control that is effective yet always maintains respect for the rights and responsibilities of students.

Community action model

Many schools encourage citizenship learning through community action programmes in which pupils are encouraged to identify a local or national issue and take appropriate action. Typical projects would include working to improve the environment, helping old people or supporting national and international charities (Best 1992 refers to typical examples in Denmark, Portugal and France). Community action can be part of a structured learning programme or a voluntary activity undertaken in pupils' own time.

Another example of this action model can be seen when, during the study of a particular issue, such as environmental pollution or human rights abuse, the teacher requires each pupil, as classwork, to write a letter to a politician expressing concern and demanding action. However, if pupils are not given a free choice about the views to be expressed, there is a danger that work of this kind could become indoctrinatory. Where such activities are voluntary, as when they arise out of membership of a school society, this problem is avoided.

Conclusion

The central theme of this chapter has been that the very nature of democracy and pluralism poses complex problems for citizenship education. I am of the belief that some of the models described above are philosophically and educationally better than others, and I have therefore not presented this framework as a neutral observer. I have argued, in effect, that nothing that is controversial outside of the school, should be presented to pupils in any other light. Clearly, these models are not mutually exclusive – many of them certainly interact and overlap. Within a single course, several models might justifiably be present. For example, it will be important to ensure that a proper balance between cognitive, affective and experiential learning is maintained. However, it is important to emphasize that a number of these models are incompatible with pluralism. Models that emphasize consensus or unitary values, ultimately fail to prepare young people for full democratic citizenship, though I believe that teachers are not always aware of the implications of the pedagogies they adopt. In this respect, the analysis offered here may encourage curriculum planners at school, local and national levels to be more clear about which models of citizenship education are present within their own curricula, and to ensure they are there as the result of careful planning and not by default or accident.

At the present time, there is a resurgence of interest in citizenship education as the importance of schools in the socialization process, and not merely as producers of technologically competent workers, is rediscovered. As Skilbeck (1989) points out in his review of major international trends, 'education as a means of nation building or rebuilding is once again high on the agenda'. However, the potential pitfalls for such a project are many and, ironically, the gap between national and international rhetoric and the quality of delivery in the classroom is nowhere greater than in this field. In many countries citizenship education remains optional, fragmented, poorly resourced, lacking a sound theoretical base and taught by reluctant or poorly trained teachers. This is a situation that needs urgent and concerted attention at all possible levels.

Notes

1 An earlier version of this paper appeared in Gordon H. Bell (ed.) (1995) *Educating European Citizens: Citizenship Values and the European Dimension.* London: David Fulton Publishers.
2 In this chapter, I use the terms citizenship education and civic education interchangeably.

References

Ashworth, L. (1995) *Children's Voices in School Matters.* London: Advisory Centre for Education.

Best, F. (1992) *Human Rights Education, Summary Work on the Council of Europe.* Strasbourg: Council of Europe.

Buxarrais, M. R., Martinez, M., Puig, J. M. and Trilla, J. (1994) Moral education in the Spanish education system. *Journal of Moral Education,* **23** (1): 39.

Cullingford, C. (1992) *Children and Society: Children's Attitudes to Politics and Power.* London: Cassell.

Cunningham, J. (1992) Rights, responsibilities and school ethos. In E. Baglin Jones and N. Jones (eds) *Education for Citizenship: Ideas and Perspectives for Cross-Curricular Study.* London: Kogan Page.

Dachs, H. (1995) Civic education in Austria – a controversial issue. Paper presented to the European Conference on Curriculum Development: Civic Education in Central and Eastern Europe. Vienna, October 1995.

Damon, W. (1988) *The Moral Child: Nurturing Children's Natural Moral Growth.* New York: Free Press.

Dunn, J. (1988) *The Beginnings of Social Understanding.* Oxford: Blackwell.

Gibbs, J. (1991) Toward an integration of Kohlberg's and Hoffman's moral development theories. *Human Development,* **34**: 88–104.

Harber, C. (ed.) (1995) *Developing Democratic Education.* Ticknall, Derbyshire: Education Now Publishing Cooperative.

Haydon, G. (1995) Thick or thin? The cognitive content of moral education in a plural democracy. *Journal of Moral Education,* **24** (1): 53–64.

Hooghof, H. (1987) Curriculum development for political education in The Netherlands. Paper delivered to International Round Table Conference on Political Socialisation on the Young in East and West, National Institute for Curriculum Development, Enschede, Holland.

Kohlberg, L. (1984) *The Psychology of Moral Development.* New York: Harper and Row.

Larkin, P. (1951) *Know Your World.* London: John Murray.

Lipman, M. (1991) *Thinking in Education.* New York: Cambridge University Press.

Lister, I. (1988) Civic education for positive pluralism. Working paper presented to the Conference on Education for Citizenship in Multi-Ethnic Societies, Rutgers University, New Jersey, USA. England: University of York.

Medrano, C. and De La Caba, M. A. (1994) A model of intervention for improving moral reasoning: an experiment in the Basque Country. *Journal of Moral Education,* **23** (4): 427–37.

Ministry of the Flemish Community (1994) *Proposal for Final Objectives for Secondary Education – First Grade.* Brussels: Department for Education.

National Curriculum Council (1990) *Curriculum Guidance 8: Education for Citizenship.* York: National Curriculum Council.

National Curriculum Council (1993) *Spiritual and Moral Development – A Discussion Paper.* York: National Curriculum Council.

Newton, K. (1994) The causes of declining interest in public affairs and politics in the old established democracies of Western Europe and in the new democracies of Eastern and Central Europe. In *Dissillusionment with Democracy: Political Parties, Participation and Non-participation in Democratic Institutions in Europe.* Strasbourg: Council of Europe.

O'Hear, A. (1991) *Education and Democracy – the Posturing of the Left Establishment.* London: The Claridge Press.

Osborne, K. (1994) Democratic citizenship and the teaching of history. *Citizenship,* **3** (2). London: The Citizenship Foundation.

Power, F. C., Higgins, A. and Kohlberg, L. (1989) *Lawrence Kohlberg's Approach to Moral Education.* New York: Columbia University Press.

Rachmanova, E. and Severukhin, V. (1994) Teaching human rights as the main trend in educational reform in Russia. *Citizenship,* **3** (2). London: The Citizenship Foundation.

Rogers, B. (1994) *The Language of Discipline.* Plymouth: Northcote House Publishers.

Rose, G. (1994) (unpublished) *A Consideration of the Primary Project of the Citizenship Foundation in the Light of Curricular Demands for Citizenship Education.*

Rossini, N. and Vulbeau, A. (1994) Children and young people's city councils: an evaluation report prepared for the National Association of Children and Youth Boards (L'Anacej). In Gordon H. Bell (ed.) *Educating European Citizens: Citizenship Values and the European Dimension.* London: David Fulton Publishers.

Rowe, D. (1992) Law-related education, an overview. In J. Lynch, C. Modgil and S. Modgil (eds) *Cultural Diversity and the Schools, Vol. 4: Human Rights, Education and Global Responsibilities.* London: Falmer Press.

Rowe, D. (1993) The citizen as a moral agent – the development of a continuous and progressive conflict-based citizenship curriculum. *Curriculum,* **13** (3).

Rowe, D. (1995) Developing spiritual, moral and social values through a citizenship programme for primary schools. In R. Best (ed.) *Education, Spirituality and the Whole Child.* London: Cassell.

Rowe, D. (1997) *The Business of School Councils: A Study*

of Democracy in Schools. Report available from the Citizenship Foundation, London.

Rowe, D. and Newton, J. (1994) *You, Me, Us!: Social and Moral Responsibility for Primary Schools.* London: The Home Office. (Available from The Citizenship Foundation.)

Skilbeck, M. (1989) A changing social and educational context. In B. Moon, P. Murphy and J. Raynor (eds) *Policies for the Curriculum.* London: Hodder and Stoughton.

Starkey, H. (1992) Education for citizenship in France. In E. Baglin Jones and N. Jones (eds) *Education for Citizenship: Ideas and Perspectives for Cross-Curricular Study.* London: Kogan Page

Starkey, H. (1995) From rhetoric to reality: starting to implement education for European values. In G. H. Bell (ed.) *Educating European Citizens – Citizenship Values and the European Dimension.* London: David Fulton Publishers.

Stradling, R. and Bennett, E. (1981) *Political Education in West Germany: A Pilot Study of Curriculum Policy.* London: Curriculum Review Unit, Institute of Education, London University.

Tappan, M. and Brown, L. M. (1996) Envisioning a post-modern moral pedagogy. *Journal of Moral Education,* **25** (1): 101–9.

Trafford, B. (1993) *Sharing Power in Schools: Raising Standards.* Ticknall, Derbyshire: Education Now Publishing Cooperative.

UNESCO/CIDREE (1993) *A Sense of Belonging: Guidelines for Values for the Humanistic and International Dimension of Education.* Paris: UNESCO.

Valchev, R. (1992) The civic education experiment: ideas, problems and prospects for Bulgaria. *Citizenship,* **2** (2). London: The Citizenship Foundation.

Vari-Szilagyi, I. (1994) Values education in Hungary. In M. Taylor (ed.) *Values Education in Europe: A Comparative Overview of a Survey of 26 countries in 1993.* Paris: Consortium of Institutions for Development and Research in Education in Europe and UNESCO.

Walker, J. (1989; reprinted 1992) *Violence and Conflict Resolution in Schools.* Strasbourg: Council of Europe.

Wood, D. (1991) Aspects of teaching and learning. In P. Light, S. Sheldon and M. Woodhead (eds) *Learning to Think.* London: Routledge.

White, P. (1994) Citizenship and 'spiritual and moral development'. *Citizenship,* **3** (2). London: The Citizenship Foundation.

19 Religious Education as Democratic Education

FERNAND OUELLET

Introduction

The cultural and religious diversity and the secularization of public institutions in contemporary democratic societies have led to a reappraisal of religious education in public schools. In some countries, like France and the United States, RE has been removed from the curriculum, whereas in other countries, it has been maintained, but not without deep changes as to its traditional aims and objectives. In Great Britain, for instance, RE has been redefined in educational terms and is now part of civic and democratic education. This paper will attempt to see what it means to define RE as democratic education. Amy Gutmann's theory of democratic education will be discussed in the context of the ongoing debate between conflicting views of democracy and civic education: democratic individualism versus liberal democracy; 'comprehensive' versus 'political' liberalism. In light of this discussion, some facets of the transformation of RE in the United Kingdom during the last two decades will be presented. It will be shown that the British experience is a concrete illustration of the significant contribution that RE can bring to civic education in a democratic society.

Is there a place for religious education in the public schools curriculum of a modern democratic society? This question is currently generating much debate among educators in Quebec. The debate centres around the position of the Centrale de l'enseignement du Québec (CEQ) which is in favour of an 'open secularism' where the present curriculum of confessional religious education would be replaced by moral education and a 'cultural' study of world religions. Religious education would then no longer serve the interests of a particular religious confession, but would rather contribute to the development of 'values of mutual aid, cooperation, freedom and justice which inspire democracies' (CEQ 1995: 16). This position of the CEQ reflects the views of the 'Société québécoise pour l'étude de la religion' which, in 1994, sought 'the elaboration of a syllabus in which the religious phenomenon would be explored in an educative perspective, independent of any form of confessional control . . . as a part of civic and democratic training' (SQER 1994: 18–19).

In my opinion, this is a basically sound and promising position. In a society where there is a growing diversity of religions and religious practices, it is the only practical way to take into account both the legitimate expectations of parents concerning religious education in schools, and the necessity of creating a common ground where pupils learn how to deliberate on diverging conceptions of the good life and how to live and work in cooperation with people who share religious convictions differing from their own.

However, there is no consensus on this view of religious education. In countries where RE is part of the public school curriculum, teaching is generally under the control of churches and has a confessional orientation.[1] In a country like the United States, where religious education in public schools is prohibited by the Constitution because of the principle of the separation of church and state, initiatives to introduce the comparative study of religions in schools have not succeeded (Ouellet 1985a: 3–91). In Quebec, partisans of confessional religious education in schools defend the *status quo* by calling upon the principles of democracy and the rights of parents to a religious education that corresponds to their convictions. Many polls have indeed revealed that a great majority of parents want some form of religious education at school for their children, even if they themselves no longer practise their religion. The question is, can there be an alternative to confessional religious education that would be acceptable to the majority of parents and in harmony with the principles of democracy? I will support the view that such an alternative exists and has been implemented successfully in many schools in Great Britain.

However, first it is necessary to discuss the notion of democracy itself, since this word does not mean the same thing for everyone. Liberals, republicans or communitarians often have very different ideas about democratic and civic education (Kymlicka 1992). According to Thériault (1997), their diverging views can be reduced to two: *democratic individualism* and *liberal democracy*. Democratic individualism is based on an abstract conception of equality: because they share a common humanity individuals have equal rights to share political power. But this implies a move beyond the limited horizon of ethnicity:

> Democratic individualism operates at two levels: it severs the individual from the ancestral hierarchical links which, in pre-democratic times, tied him to society like the tree to its trunk, and it restructures the social link 'from upside', through republican virtue. In such a perspective, democracy is born when people begin to substitute the status of citizens for the 'natural' sociological statuses of women, peasants, workers, ethnics, etc. . . . On the one hand, the violent rejection of tradition and of cultural and religious traditions; on the other, the consecration of the civic virtues, of attachment to the Republic. (Thériault 1997: 21–2)

In contrast, liberal democracy sees the person as a concrete individual and as a member of a concrete human community. It insists on self-government while preserving individual freedom. Theriault quotes Lasch (1991) for whom 'the American practice of democracy owes much to a communitarian populism very far from republican virtue. For him, American democratic virtue has its roots in a concrete world, communitarian and religious, rather than in the republican abstraction' (Thériault op. cit.: 26).

Thériault sees problems in each of these two models of democracy. The republican model produces discriminations towards those unable to reach the common norm:

> By making equality compulsory, it creates, as we

have shown, new discriminations based on the gaps in relation with a normativity which presents itself as universal. Any gap is unacceptable from the universal point of view of the State which will quickly single out the deviant population. (p. 23)

And its universalism is a false universalism that 'cannot take into account the pluralism inherent in contemporary societies' (p. 24). As for the liberal model, its main problem is the fragmentation of social space because of the pressure from particular claims. 'Left to itself, liberal democracy disrupts the common ground which is necessary for democracy to function properly, by dividing citizenship into as many spaces as there are areas of identity' (p. 30).

Thériault does not believe that we must choose between these two models. Rather, we should try to find a mediation between the two trends, abstraction and fragmentation, that have recently become more and more visible in many societies, due to the combined impact of growing individualism and of globalization. According to him, the only 'happy democracies' are those where republican egalitarism is combined with liberal differentialism, in a creative tension:

> Today, we have to politically recreate what the Western traditions produced spontaneously: a place on earth which would simultaneously be a world open to all (and so, uprooted), and a world where I can say We (and so, historically situated). However, this synthesis can only be the result of gathering differences around a common culture or a common trunk. (Thériault op. cit.: 32)

This kind of typology can be very helpful in finding one's way among the complex and various views of democracy and citizenship which prevail today and make it difficult to have a clear perception of the issues underlying the contemporary debates on civic education. It will be used here to test the validity of one theory on democratic education, developed ten years ago by Amy Gutmann, an American political philosopher. The main points of her theory of democratic education will be presented, and its implications for various educational issues will briefly be examined. Special attention will be given to her approach to moral education. In light of this discussion, I hope to show that, contrary to the claim of some partisans of 'political liberalism' (Macedo 1995), her theory does not represent a subtle form of indoctrination into liberal values. It maintains the fragile balance between individualism and communitarianism, and escape the risks of abstraction and of fragmentation. In the last section, I will discuss some recent developments in the field of religious education in light of that theory.

Amy Gutmann's theory of democratic education

Any discussion about the place of religious education in public schools raises a fundamental question: in a democratic society where many groups with different conceptions of the good life must coexist, which one would have the authority to determine the orientations of the educational project in public schools? Is this authority in the hands of the state, of parents, or professional educators? Gutmann rejects the three educational theories that would give exclusive authority to one of these three: the Platonic theory of the *family state* where the philosopher-king (or queen) can impose his or her conception of the good life; the theory of the *state of families* where only parents have the authority to 'predispose their children, through education, to choose a way of life consistent with their familial heritage' (Gutmann 1987: 28); and the theory of the *state of individuals* where authority is in the hands of professional educators whose mission is to promote the liberal values of neutrality and freedom of choice.

Gutmann's theory of democratic education recognizes the educative contribution of parents, and of the communities to which they belong, as they try to transmit and perpetuate a particular conception of the good life. This distinguishes it from the theory of the 'family state' which tries to cut the child off from his or her family in order to inculcate 'the true' conception of the good life. And, in contrast to the theory of the 'state of individuals', it does not reject the responsibility of the state and 'recognizes the value of political education in predisposing children to accept those ways of life that are consistent with sharing the rights and responsibilities of citizenship in a democratic society' (p. 42). Finally, in contrast to the theory of the 'state of families', it recognizes the professional authority of educators who train children to appreciate and evaluate ways of life that differ from those of their families.

According to Gutmann's theory of democratic education, the state, families and educators must share the responsibility of defining the orientations of the educational project and contribute to promoting of the central value of democracy: 'conscious social reproduction in its most inclusive form' (p. 42). Promoting this value requires that children be prepared to participate in constructing society: 'A society that supports conscious social reproduction must educate all educable children to be capable of participating in collectively shaping their society' (p. 39). This participation presupposes that they are able to understand and evaluate the various conceptions of the good life which compete in that society: 'A necessary (but not sufficient) condition of conscious social reproduction is that citizens have the capacity to deliberate among alternative ways of personal and political life' (p. 40).

Training children for critical deliberation is a primary concern in Gutmann's theory of democratic education. But this insistence on critical deliberation goes against the grain of the 'family state' and 'state of families' educational theories that try to inculcate a particular conception of the good life, instead of developing the capacity to understand and evaluate competing conceptions of the good life and of the good society: 'The value of critical deliberation among good lives and good societies would be neglected by a society that inculcated in children uncritical acceptance of any particular way or ways of (personal and political) life' (p. 44). So, a society where sexist values would be inculcated in schools and where it would be thought that the only acceptable role for women is to serve men and to raise children would not be a democratic society, 'not because these values are false (which they certainly are in American society), but because that society failed to secure any space for educating children to deliberate critically among a range of good lives and good societies' (ibid.).

But such a 'space of deliberation' cannot exist unless parents accept that their children will eventually be exposed to ideas and practices that might differ from those they encounter in the family circle:

> It is one thing to recognize the right (and responsibility) of parents to educate their children as members of a family, quite another to claim that this right of familial education extends to a right of parents to insulate their children from exposure to ways of life or thinking that conflict with their own. (p. 29)

This limitation of parental authority over education in democratic societies rests on two principles: non-repression and non-discrimination. 'The principle of non-repression prevents the state, and any group within it, from using education to restrict rational deliberation of competing conceptions of the good life and the good society' (p. 44). However, this principle does not exclude the possibility of using education to 'inculcate those character traits, such as honesty, religious toleration and mutual respect for persons that serve as foundations for rational deliberation of differing ways of life' (ibid.).

The principle of non-discrimination is an extension of the principle of non-repression. It prevents states or families from 'being selectively repressive by excluding entire groups of children from schooling or by denying them an education conducive to deliberation among conceptions of the good life and the good society' (p. 45). According to this principle, 'no educable child may be excluded from an education adequate to participating in the political processes that structure choice among good lives' (ibid.).

A theory of education based on these two principles can be considered democratic because it allows citizens to explore critically conceptions of the good life that are not limited to those of the subcommunities to which they belong, and because it gives them 'a chance to share in self-consciously shaping the structure of their society' (p. 46). This theory does not defend neutrality with regard to conceptions of the good life. Even if it does not restrict deliberation about these conceptions, it restricts the pursuit of 'ways of life dependent on the suppression of politically relevant knowledge. Democratic education supports choice among those ways of life that are compatible with conscious social reproduction' (ibid.).

Gutmann adds interesting indications on the responsibility of the family and the school in training children for democratic deliberation. According to her, the contribution of schools in this training increases with age:

> For most children, the family plays a large role in building character and in teaching basic skills for many years. But early in the lives of most children, their parents begin to share these primary educational functions with other associations: day-care centers, elementary (and then secondary) schools, churches and synagogues, civic organizations, friendship circles, and work groups. (p. 50)

This gradual delegation by the family of its responsibility for the education of a child parallels a decrease in the importance of discipline and example, and an increase of rational deliberation:

> Nor can we assume that children are born ready for rational deliberation. The earliest education of children is not and cannot be by precept or reasoning; it must be by discipline and by example. Children are first educated by their parents, and so must they continue to be as long as raising children constitutes one of our most valued personal liberties . . . As children move outside their original families, their character and their skills are shaped by the examples of those whom they love and respect and by the rules regulating the associations to which they belong.

> But training of this 'exemplary' sort is only one kind of education, undoubtedly most effective during our childhood. At some fairly early stage in their development, children also become responsive to another kind of education, one that is more intellectual in its effect and rationalist in its method. They learn the three R's largely by direct instruction. They also develop capacities for criticism, rational argument, and decision making by being taught how to think logically, to argue coherently and fairly, and to consider the relevant alternatives before coming to conclusions. (ibid.)

Even if educators' influence over the development of students by the example of their personal and professional behaviour is not to be excluded, it is mainly by their contribution to the development of critical thinking that they bring an essential contribution to the development of 'democratic virtue':

> Training of this 'didactic' sort is democratically desirable because it enables citizens to understand, to communicate, and in some cases to resolve their disagreements. Without this sort of mutual understanding, we could not expect to achieve widespread toleration of dissent and respect for differing ways of life . . . But quite apart from its political function, children will eventually need the capacity for rational deliberation to make hard choices in situations where habits and authorities do not supply clear and consistent guidance . . . Children must learn not just to *behave* in accordance with authority but to *think* critically about authority if they are to live up to the democratic ideal of sharing political sovereignty as citizens. (p. 50–1)

Teachers have a central role to play in Gutmann's conception of democratic education. In this conception, the basic mission of public schools is to help all students master the skills of critical thinking and democratic deliberation. And when it comes to the education of children, this mission can only be accomplished if both parents and the state cede some of their authority to professional educators. Without such a partial delegation of authority, schools could not create this space of democratic deliberation where the diverse conceptions of the good life that students bring with them, and which compete in society, will be critically analysed and evaluated.

Gutmann's perspective on some controversial issues in education

If 'a primary purpose of schools is to cultivate common democratic values among children, regardless of their academic ability, class, race, religion or sex', is it legitimate to allow parents to send their children to private schools 'which claim a right to cultivate particular values and select students according to their ability, class, religion, race and sex' (p. 116)? The supporters of the 'state of families' ideology claim that the right to private schools is based on a 'natural right' of parents to control the education of their children. While rejecting this argumentation, Gutmann recognizes the legitimacy of private schools. She does not believe that the abolition of these schools would produce an improvement of the public school. A democratic society can accept that parents 'who are intensely dissatisfied with the lack of religious or other forms of education in public schools' (p. 117) send their children to private schools, but on one condition: like public schools, private schools must teach a common set of democratic values. Gutmann recognizes that the implementation of this type of teaching might raise difficulties in some cases, but she does not believe that these difficulties justify the elimination of private schools.

The right of parents to withhold their children from a school activity that conflicts with their religious convictions is another controversial issue which Gutmann resolves on the basis of her theory of democratic education. For instance, a school does not violate the principle of non-repression and of non-discrimination when it exempts the children of Jehovah's Witnesses from the obligation to salute the flag. By granting this exemption, schools do not limit the chances of these students to have a good education, nor do they interfere with the democratic education of the other students. But it would be a completely different matter if sympathizers of the Ku-Klux-Klan refused to allow their children to sit near black children or if Amish parents claimed the right for the adolescents of their community to leave school after the ninth grade, because it would 'result in a significant shortening of the time that Amish[2] adolescents were exposed to knowledge and ways of thinking essential to democratic deliberation' (p. 123).

The choice of books and textbooks for the school library is another question where the principles of democratic education are not always applied in a satisfying manner. Gutmann recognizes that books which encourage students to adopt ways of life that are socially unacceptable must be banned from schools. But she criticizes the way that notion is sometimes abused, leading to a form of censorship that deprives students of the opportunity to think about other forms of behaviour and political points of view. According to her, it is not legitimate to protect students from all controversies. She also criticizes, in the name of the principle of non-repression, the undemocratic nature of the kind of procedures which lead to the banishment of some kinds of book from the library. The procedure of textbook selection is not legitimate unless it allows citizens to participate and gives more room to 'the opinions of teachers and historians than to those . . . of their constituents' (p. 101).

Sex education is another controversial matter that causes heated debates among parents. Most of them are in favour of sex education in schools, but some parents believe that sex is too intimate a subject matter to be taught in schools. According to Gutmann, the principles of democratic education do not allow for a clear-cut judgement in favour or against sex education in schools. However, since the vast majority of parents are in favour and since the social consequences of sexual activity among adolescents are very serious, she believes that sex education has its place in the school curriculum. But according to her, it would be wise to allow parents who believe in the sanctity of sex and for whom mandatory sex education is as offensive as 'mandatory prayer is to parents who do not believe in God' to exempt their children from taking such courses and rely upon the informal teaching of friends to educate those adolescents who are not themselves committed to their parents' point of view (p. 110).

The principles of democratic education are more helpful in the case of another controversy which raises much passion in United States, the debate between the creationists and the evolutionists:

> Teaching creationism as science – even as one among several reasonable scientific theories – violates the principle of non-repression in indirectly imposing a sectarian religious view on all children in the guise of science. Teaching creationism as a scientific theory entails teaching children to accept a religious view that takes the words of the Bible to be the literal God-given truth as a scientific explanation of the origins of species. Teaching creationism as a religious rather than a scientific doctrine, on the other hand, is as out of place in a biology classroom as is teaching the Lord Prayer. . . .
>
> The rationale for teaching any particular religious doctrine in public schools – either as science or as a reasonable alternative to science – conflicts with the rationale for cultivating common, secular standards of reasoning among citizens. To teach creationism as a science entails not teaching science (which consists of secular standards of inquiry and knowledge). To teach creationism as an alternative to science entails allowing public schools to give equal time to every religious belief firmly held by citizens, even if the belief is unreasonable (as in the case of creationism) or incompatible with basic democratic principles (as in the case of racist doctrines). (pp. 103–4)

Therefore, it is because the teaching of creationism in school appears to her as fundamentally incompatible with the non-confessional character of the public school that Gutmann is so firm[3] in her rejection of it:

> the indirect, if not the direct, result of establishing religion in public schools would be to restrict rational deliberation among competing ways of life. . . . If democratic majorities in a religiously diverse society refuse to differentiate between a sectarian and a secular curriculum, they will unintentionally thwart the development of shared intellectual standards among citizens, and discredit public schools in the eyes of citizens whose religious beliefs are not reflected in the established curriculum. A religiously diverse democracy must therefore choose between the disestablishment of religion within public schools and the *de facto*, if not *de jure*, disestablishment of democratic schools. (p. 104)

Thus, a confessional school cannot be a democratic school in Gutmann's perspective, but that does not mean that the principle of non-repression excludes the possibility of a form of civic education in the school curriculum that would aim at the development of common values:

> But public schools need not therefore sacrifice a common moral education for the sake of avoiding repression. Public schools can avoid even indirect repression and still foster what one might call a democratic civil religion: a set of secular beliefs, habits, and ways of thinking that support democratic deliberation and are compatible with a wide variety of religious commitments. (ibid.)

This democratic civil religion could be promoted through a renewed teaching of civic education and history, where one of the major goals of teachers would be to 'challenge their students to think critically about history or politics' (p. 106). According to her, there has not been enough stress on the development of critical thinking in civic education:

> The ability is so essential to democratic education that one might question whether civics courses that succeeded in increasing political trust, efficacy, and knowledge but failed to increase the ability of students to reason about politics were indirectly repressive. How can a civics course legitimately teach teenagers to trust their government more without also teaching them to think about what kind of government is worth trusting? (pp. 106–7)

Democratic deliberation and moral education

Civic education and moral education appear, then, as privileged areas for teaching democratic virtue, the capacity of critical deliberation on different conceptions of history and politics. Moral education should then be a major concern in democratic schools. But this is not the view of those who believe that schools should concentrate on 'core subjects': 'You teach them English, history, mathematics, and science, and we will . . . look after their souls' (*Washington Post*, 21 October 1984: H 1. Cit. in Gutmann 1987: 53). This view must be rejected, since the school has a major influence on the moral character of the students:

> Schools develop moral character at the same time as they try to teach basic cognitive skills, by insisting that students sit in their seats (next to students of different races and religions), raise their hands

before speaking, hand in their homework on time, not loiter in the halls, be good sports on the playing field, and abide by many other rules that help define a school character.   (ibid.)

It is impossible for the school not to be involved in moral education and in building the moral character. However, there is no consensus as to how it should be done. Should schools let students choose their own values? This is the position of the partisans, the supporters of value clarification who claim that the school should help students to understand and develop their own values and to respect those of other people. Gutmann rejects this approach, which she feels gives individuals exclusive authority on education and leads to a form of subjectivism: 'I have my opinion and you have yours; who can say who is right?' The school cannot promote an indiscriminate respect of all the values that children bring with them:

> If children come to school believing that blacks, Jews, Catholics, and/or homosexuals are inferior beings who shouldn't have the same rights as the rest of us, then it is criticism, not just clarification of children's values that is needed. . . . Indiscriminate respect for children's values cannot be defended either as an ultimate end or as a tenable means of cultivating good character.   (p. 56)

Gutmann also rejects the moralistic position of the supporters of the 'family state' and the 'state of individuals' who limit the choices children can make to those worth pursuing according to their own partisan view. The supporters of conservative moralism try to protect children from false political and religious beliefs, rather than providing them with reasons to criticize and reject these views of their own accord. They insist on the importance of patriotic rituals, dress codes and respect for authority and discipline in the classroom.

The supporters of liberal neutrality reject conservative educational programmes as indoctrination, or at least as too restrictive of individual freedom, and promote the development of moral autonomy. Under the influence of Rawls and Kohlberg, they distinguish three stages of moral development:

1 the *morality of authority*, 'an improvement over the anarchy of desire';
2 the *morality of association*, 'characterized by an acceptance of rules because they are appropriate to fulfilling the roles that individuals play within various associations. . . . The morality of associ-

ation is an improvement over the morality of authority because children learn to alter their habits and to criticize established authorities out of empathy for others and a concern for fairness';
3 the *morality of principle*, 'characterized by a direct attachment to moral principles themselves' (Gutmann 1987: 60).

The liberal moralists have tried to define what the schools must do in order to take students up to the third stage, but research shows that they have not succeeded. According to Gutmann, it is because they put the mark too high, in contrast to the conservative moralists, who put it too low. In doing so, they run the risk of inducing moral cynicism. Schools, therefore, should rather concentrate on the morality of association, 'the willingness and ability to contribute and to claim one's fair share in cooperative associations' (p. 61). This represents an ideal that is politically primordial, even if it is philosophically subordinate. Promoting the morality of association means cultivating values like empathy, trust, fairness and benevolence (p. 62) and teaching respect among races, religious toleration, patriotism, and political judgement. For Gutmann, the role of the school is not limited to teaching moral autonomy; it includes the development of democratic virtue understood in a very wide sense:

> If by virtue we mean moral autonomy, then the role of schools in moral education is necessarily a limited one. We have little reason to believe that schools, or anyone else, can teach virtue in this sense. We have, on the other hand, considerable evidence that *democratic* virtue can be taught in many ways – by teaching male and female, Protestant and Catholic, black and white students together from an early age in the same classrooms; by bringing all educable children up to a high minimum standard of learning, by respecting religious and ethnic differences; by teaching American history not just as a series of elections, laws, treaties, and battles, but as lessons in the practice (sometimes successful, sometimes not) of political virtue, lessons that require students to develop and to exercise intellectually disciplined judgment.   (p. 63)

According to Gutmann, schools have an important responsibility in the moral development of children in order to prepare them to participate in 'conscious social reproduction' in a democratic society. Their mission does not consist of promoting particular conservative or liberal values, but of the development of democratic virtue. They cannot accomplish this difficult task without providing children with a space of rational deliberation on divergent conceptions of the good life. Schools share this responsibility of forming the moral character of children with parents and the state, but democracy implies that both parents and the state accept that their influence is limited by the principles of non-repression and of non-discrimination. Schools would not respect these principles if it did not provide all students with a space of rational deliberation that neither parents nor the state could try to restrict without threatening the very foundation of democracy.

This conception of democratic education has been contested by fundamentalist groups in the United States. Many parents, whose beliefs are based on the Word of God as found in the Bible, and who want to protect their children from diverging points of view, claim that this type of liberal education represents a subtle form of indoctrination to liberal values, like individualism and moral autonomy, whose ultimate foundations can be contested by reasonable people. According to Macedo, if they want to escape this accusation, the supporters of liberal education must reject 'comprehensive liberalism' (Raz 1990) and opt for the form of liberalism recently elaborated by Rawls (1993) – political liberalism – which requires that we put aside some of our beliefs when we have to establish the basis of common political institutions: 'What political liberalism asks of us is not to renounce what we believe to be true but to acknowledge the difficulty of publicly establishing any single account of the whole truth' (p. 474).[4]

Gutmann (1995) holds the view that this distinction has little validity when it comes to defining the goals and objectives of moral and civic education. Her detailed analysis of the views of comprehensive and political liberals on civic education shows a remarkable convergence of the two positions. And she makes clear that her own conception of democratic education does not rely on controversial opinions regarding metaphysical questions. In contrast to what Macedo seems to suggest, she demonstrates that the promotion of rational deliberation on divergent conceptions of the good life is not a subtle form of indoctrination to liberal values, but an essential component of education in a democratic society.

But one might ask whether or not Gutmann's theory gives too much importance to critical delib-

eration at the expense of participation in a concrete human community, breaking the delicate balance between abstract individualism and communitarian liberalism. We have seen that in her view, democratic education rests on a balance between the legitimate interests of parents and communities and those of the state, who both accept the need to delegate some of their authority on the education of children to professional educators. It is clear, therefore, that Gutmann's theory of democratic education is not a kind of republican individualism. Her position is closer to the classical liberalism of Locke and Montesquieu than to the modern versions of Dworkin and Rawls. Classical liberalism does not try to convert everyone to the liberal point of view, but asks rather for a 'space of freedom' in an hostile environment where the partisans of virtue (the republicans) and the partisans of equality (the democrats) have a much larger constituency than the partisans of freedom (the liberals).

> Moderation often requires that liberals rest content with toleration or 'permission', and do not seek additional 'praise' or respect, for their private ways of life. Often enough, democrats and republicans are willing to abide liberal individualists in the community, so long as their heterodoxy remains obscure, and, consequently unthreatening. But the liberal who seeks not only permission but also praise, or who asks to be treated with 'equal concern and respect', sometimes over-reaches. In seeking the 'respect' of the community, the dissenter implicitly admits that private choices are indeed the 'business' of the community; such an anxious liberal is not happy to be left alone, and is not willing to leave others alone. He does not mind his own business. (Kautz 1995: 63)

Gutmann agrees with Kautz and classical liberals that democratic education does not rely on the promotion of liberal values. However, she seems to believe that the liberal plea for moderation must not be pushed too far. In modern pluralistic societies, civic education cannot be limited to the promotion of liberal tolerance. It must try to develop understanding and 'respect' for ways of life that differ from the mainstream, in so far as they are not hostile to the democratic principles of non-repression and non-discrimination. What we have here is a compromise between the interests of the partisans of freedom and those of equality, which resembles the strategy put forward by Kautz to defend liberalism.

The problem with Gutmann is that she neither

gives a detailed plan as to how schools can best contribute to moral education, nor does she state whether moral education should be recognized as a distinct discipline within the school curriculum, or whether it could be dealt with as a part of civic education.[5] Nor does she provide any explicit theory on the place of the study of religion in public schools, on the questions it raises in the context of a secular educational system and of religious pluralism in society. This is not too surprising since there have been very few initiatives in this field in the United States; the American Constitution forbids any form of confessional religious education in public schools in the name of the separation of church and state. Even if the 'scientific' study of religion is not against the Constitution, American educators have been reluctant to promote it, fearing legal suits against teachers who might be accused of using the classroom to promote or depreciate specific religious options.

The 'new' religious education in Great Britain

The situation is quite different in Great Britain and also in Quebec, where religious education is an officially recognized subject in the school curriculum. Thirty years ago, there was little difference in the orientation and practice of RE in Great Britain and Quebec. Religious 'instruction' had an explicit confessional orientation and its aim was to 'nurture' the Christian faith. But during the last thirty years there has been a triple 'revolution' in the orientation of RE in Great Britain:

1   since the middle of the 1960s, RE has become less 'Bible centred' and more 'child centred';
2   since the 1970s, RE has moved from religious instruction and the nurturing of the Christian faith to 'education';
3   and since the 1980s, the content of RE has been broadened to include an exploration of World religions and of non religious life stances.

This triple revolution radically changed the landscape of RE in Great Britain, whereas in Quebec there has been a reinforcement of the confessional orientation;[6] there the debate has been polarized between the supporters of confessional RE and the supporters of a secular education, where RE would have no place in the curriculum of public schools. Until now, the former have won the battle, even if a

large majority of teachers are against the present orientation of the RE programmes. For more than twenty years, I have been supporting the view that there is a third option, 'cultural RE', which would be acceptable to the majority of parents and teachers (Ouellet 1977, 1980a, 1980b, 1983a 1983b, 1985a, 1985b, 1992, 1997). This 'new religious education,' which is currently called 'multi-faith RE' in Great Britain, could bring an important contribution to civic education in a society where religious and cultural diversity has become a reality. However, would it be compatible with the principle of democratic education? To answer this question, it is necessary to have a closer look to the British experiment.

Two important events constitute landmarks in the development of multi-faith RE in Great Britain: the publication of the Birmingham Syllabus in 1975 and the introduction of the National Curriculum in 1988. The first is more important because it marked the passage from confessional RE to multi-faith RE. The underlying principles of this syllabus have been very well formulated by John Hull (1978), an Anglican theologian who has played a major role in the implementation of this reform and in the discussion of the objections raised by its opponents in the Christian churches, the non-Christian religious traditions and those who had moved away from religion altogether. During the Parliamentary debate that preceded the adoption of the National Curriculum, many of these principles were contested by representatives of various groups, especially by the lobby of the Christian Institute which was very critical of multi-faith RE. Robert Jackson from the Faculty of Education at the University of Warwick, who has devoted his academic career to research, teacher training and curriculum material development in RE (Jackson 1989, 1990, 1995, 1996, 1997b), has recently made a detailed analysis of that debate (Jackson 1997a). It is mainly in the light of this analysis that the six principles of the Birmingham Syllabus identified by Hull will be discussed here.

1   A clear distinction was made between 'nurture' and 'education'. The intention of nurturing Christian faith or of promoting any form of religious commitment was abandoned.

The distinction between nurture and education was not easily accepted by some Christian groups and Humanists. Hull believes that 'no child should be placed in a position where he has to be withdrawn from the public, official curriculum of his school . . . Nurture is for some, but education is for all' (p. 141). He gives theological arguments in favour of this distinction and of a policy where schools receive public money only for their educative mission and not for any form of nurture:

> This situation, where the public schools ought not to intend to nurture faith at all, depends, for its continuing acceptance by Christians upon maintaining this intimacy between Christian faith and education, which means enabling education to become itself. For while the school ought to give no more help to the pupil moving in the direction of religious faith than it should give to one moving in the opposite direction, it ought also to give no *less*. This means that we are opposed to schools being dominated by non-Christian or anti-Christian viewpoints just as sharply as we oppose the wish of some Christians to have schools dominated by Christian evangelistic interests. The churches' mission in education is to safeguard the open secularity of education and to preserve genuine pluralism. (Hull op. cit.: 138–9)

The National Curriculum debate provided those who opposed this radical reorientation of RE with the opportunity of contesting it. According to Jackson, that debate was dominated by the attempts of the radical right and of the members of the Christian Institute to restore the confessional orientation of RE. In spite of all their intrigues, they have not succeeded:

> The most positive feature of the 1988 legislation, although a compromise, was that it confirmed the educational nature of RE and ensured that all the principal religions in Britain would be studied as part of the programme of all students in state funded county schools.   (Jackson 1997: 58)

The importance of this replacement of nurture by education in British RE cannot be exaggerated, since it implied a substantial redefinition of the goals of this discipline.

2   Three subsidiary purposes for RE barely mentioned in earlier Agreed Syllabuses become prominent:

1   contributing to community life in a plural society;
2   developing a better understanding of religion;
3   'enabling pupils to formulate their own personal philosophies and outlooks as a result of

their encounter with the world religions'. (Hull op. cit.: 127).

Concering the first of these subsidiary purposes, it seems that the National Curriculum debate has led some of the promoters of RE to keep in a low profile its potential contribution to intercultural and inter-religious understanding. For instance, in her defence of the Model Syllabuses, Wintersgill (1995: 10) suggests that RE should concentrate on what it alone can offer, the study of religion, and resist any attempt to transform it into multi-cultural education.

The view adopted on the second purpose can have important implications for the teacher's responsibility towards his pupils. Hull adds interesting comments on this issue:

> All pupils, whatever their family background, ethnic, cultural, social class or religious origins or life, are entitled to expect that their teacher will help them to understand, to grow both in their own tradition and in the wider values of the educated life. But this basic truth about teacher–pupil relations immediately requires the teacher to teach each religion represented in his or her class-room, or school (or world?) with the same spirit of thoughtful, courteous appreciation and inquiry. (p. 131)

After the publication of the Birmingham Syllabus, a trend of thought has emerged (Hulmes 1979) which insists that the teacher cannot be faithful to the nature of religion unless he or she approaches it from the standpoint of a specific religious commitment. This point of view has been challenged (Ouellet 1983b: 8–13), and there is a broad consensus among professional educators in this discipline that what is required from the teacher is neither commitment nor neutrality, but impartiality (Jackson 1989: 5). The educational revolution in RE implies that there is no longer any link between the teacher's religious or non-religious commitment and the content of his or her teaching:

> Being impartial does not require the teacher to deny his or her faith but demands the professional integrity of balancing it with the views of others, of managing open discussion of the issues raised and expecting pupils to arrive at a range of conclusions. (ibid.)

As for the third purpose, it has been one of the characteristic features of the British approach to the new RE that it has not limited itself to giving students 'objective' notions about world religions.[7] The pupils are not only asked to learn about 'religions', but they are also invited to learn 'from' the various religious traditions to which they are introduced. They are encouraged to 'examine or re-examine aspects of their own lives and thinking in the light of questions, issues, or experiences which are encountered in particular religious traditions, but which also have universal significance' (Jackson 1997a: 216). RE cannot be restricted to the 'objective' study of religions and should always involve that possibility of 'edification', which Jackson describes as a process whereby pupils are led to reassess and deepen their understanding of their own way of life.

3 Religious traditions should be understood in the context of secular ideologies, like Humanism and Communism. Even if they are studied for their contribution to the pupil's *religious* education, they must be approached in themselves, 'with fairness, objectivity and balance' (Hull op. cit.: 128).

This principle seems to have been abandoned in the recent developments of RE in Great Britain. I have seen no mention of it in the National Curriculum debates and in the discussions about the Model Syllabuses.

4 Any description of a system of beliefs, whether religious or secular, must be done in a manner with which believers would agree.

The believer is the final authority on what he or she believes. Everything is to be thought as if in the presence of those whose life-faith it is. Both criticisms and appreciations are offered of all ways of life, although it is also true that it was generally thought best to allow a religion to unfold without constant critical interruption, and pupils are expected to be respectful and thoughtful in their approach (Hull: 128–9).

This principle would be unacceptable to any social scientist if it meant that the final authority on what we can say about someone's beliefs is the believer himself. It is impossible to imagine a study of a religious tradition that would not be rejected in part by some believers in that tradition. However, this inevitable tension between the scientific and the religious perspective need not always be at the centre of the educative process and criticisms and appreciations should come only after serious efforts

to see things from the believer's perspective. It seems to be the strategy adopted by Jackson and his team, who have developed curriculum material based on ethnographic material collected among children and their families from various religious traditions living in Britain. In this project, an interpretative approach was used to describe what it means to be religious for these young people with whom pupils from the same age can easily identify (Jackson 1997a: 196–217, 1997b).

5 The Birmingham Syllabus was the outcome of an agreement not on the truth of what should be taught, but on its educative value in a given context. So, it is because some knowledge of Christianity is necessary for all British citizens that its study should be required for every pupil. And because there was no significant presence of – for example – Buddhists in the community, Buddhism was not recommended for study.

This is an application of the first principle; the replacement of a confessional by an educative perspective. The 1988 Education Act requires that a 'predominant' place be given to study of Christianity. This has been understood by some spokesmen of the radical right as a return to nurture. But the professionals of the new RE have shown that it is far from being the case:

> Christianity is 'taught' as part of a programme of religious education. Nothing of the gains of the past twenty-five years have been lost in this part of the legislation. RE remains firmly an educationally justifiable exercise; it contributes to a child's development – in intellect, imagination and spirit. RE fosters an understanding of the world in its diversity and richness; it helps to face difference, conflict, doubt. RE's aims has been expressed in many different ways, but there is a wide agreement that it has to do with helping a child grow by encountering and increasingly understanding the religious traditions of mankind.   (Doble 1989: 1)

This quotation is a clear indication that the attempts to restore confessional RE have failed, and the gains of the educational revolution of the 1970s were not lost in 1988.

6 Whereas 'in previous Agreed Syllabuses world religions had not generally been studied before the Sixth Form, in the Birmingham approach, pluralism in religion is presented to the child from his first year in school' (Hull 1978: 129–30), although it is still only at the end of second-

ary school that pupils study systems of beliefs seen as coherent and distinct from one another.

This principle has not been challenged in the 1988 National Curriculum debate. In light of the quality of the world religions curriculum material, which has been developed and implemented with relative success in elementary schools, the objections of those who claimed pupils should not be introduced to other religious traditions before they are 14 or 15 appears to have been invalidated.

Conclusion

In this brief review of some of the debates surrounding the recent transformation of RE in Great Britain, it has not been possible to do justice to the great amount of documentation, both theoretical and practical, that has contributed to the establishment of multi-faith RE as a recognized subject in the school curriculum. In spite of this limitation, this discussion suggests that this type of educational RE could bring an important contribution to civic and democratic education. With all its ambiguities and struggles, the British experience in this area represents a concrete illustration of the conception of democracy put forward by Thériault in which the demands of democratic individualism are braced in a creative tension with those of communitarian liberalism. In the context of Quebec at least, this type of radical transformation of the orientations of RE appears more promising than the prudent American abstentionism reflected in Gutmann's writing, and of the anachronistic clinging to a confessional approach of the bishops of Quebec who recently invited the Catholics to 'use all means' in order to save the Catholic school.

Notes

1 We will see that Great Britain is an exception on this point. Religious education is part of the curriculum of public schools, but its content has been largely redefined on an educational, rather than a confessional basis.

2 Spinner (1994) believes that this exemption could be justified in the case of Amish who live at the margin of mainstream society and who have chosen to be what he calls 'partial citizens'. According to him, it can be reluctantly 'tolerated' that they inculcate their children with values antagonistic to liberal values, such as the subordination of women, since they would lose the possibility of perpetuat-

ing their particular lifestyle if their children were forced to go to school until the end of the secondary course. This tolerance relies also on the fact that it is possible to leave the community and that a significant proportion of members do actually leave every year.

3 Macedo (1995) is much less categorical concerning the question of whether creationism is reasonable or not. He supports the view of Judge Chamblis who defends the place in public schools of widely accepted scientific evidence as criteria, while not taking sides on the question of how, or whether, God fits into the whole business (p. 476).

4 For a criticism of Rawls' theory of political liberalism, see Kautz 1995: 177–9.

5 This is a complex issue which it is impossible to explore here. For an interesting discussion on some aspects of it, see Chazan 1985.

6 There is no space here to substantiate this affirmation which is valid for the Roman Catholic network. The Protestants have their own educational network and have been largely influenced by the developments in Great Britain. See Aubert 1997: 35–50, and Milot 1997: 127–50.

7 Opponents of the introduction of 'cultural RE' in Quebec often caricature it as an 'objective' presentation of factual data on world religions that have no relevance to the students and claim it does not answer their existential questions (Côté 1995: 16, Comité catholique 1995: 11–12). For a criticism of this view see Ouellet 1996: 223–54.

References

Aubert, M. (1997) Conceptions des droits en matière de transmission de la religion. In M. Milot and F. Ouellet (eds) (1997) *Religion, Éducation et Démocratie. Un Enseignement Culturel de la Religion est-il Possible?* Montréal: Harmattan: 35–50.

Centrale de l'enseignement du Québec (CEQ) (1995) Le débat est lancé. L'école doit-elle être laïque? *Nouvelles CEQ,* Janvier–Février: 21–6.

Chazan, B. (1985) *Contemporary Approaches to Moral Education. Analyzing Alternative Theories.* New York: Teachers College Press.

Comité Catholique (1995) *Le Point sur L'école Catholique.* Québec: Gouvernement du Québec.

Côté, G. (1995) L'enseignement religieux et la pastorale à l'école. In *L'Église Canadienne,* **28** (1–3): 13–16, 52–4, 78–80.

Doble, P. (1989) Approaching Christianity in the classroom. *Resource,* **11**(3): 1–3.

Grimmitt, M. (1978) *What can I do in R.E.?* Great Working: Mayhew-McCrimmon.

Gutmann, A. (1995) Civic education and social diversity. *Ethics,* **105**: 557–79.

Gutmann, A. (1987) *Democratic Education.* Princeton: Princeton University Press.

Hull, J. (1978) Keynote Address: From christian nurture to religious education: the British experience. *Religious Education*, 73(2): 127.

Hull, J. (1991) Agreed Syllabuses and the law. *Resource*, 14(1): 1–3.

Hulmes, E. (1979) *Commitment and Neutrality in Religious Education*. London: Geoffrey Chapman/New York: Macmillan.

Jackson, R. (1989) Fortifying religious education. *Resource*, 11(3): 5–6.

Jackson, R. (1990) Religious studies and developments in religious education in England and Wales. In U. King (ed.) *Turning Points in Religious Studies*. Edinburgh: T. and T. Clark: 102–16.

Jackson, R. (1995) Religious education's representation of religions and cultures. *British Journal of Educational Studies*, 43(3) September: 272–89.

Jackson, R. (1996) Ethnographic research and curriculum development. In L. Francis, W. Kay and W. Campbell (eds) *Research in Religious Education*. Leominster: Gracewing.

Jackson, R. (1997a) La 'nouvelle éducation religieuse' en Grande-Bretagne. Bilan partiel de trente années de recherches. In M. Milot and F. Ouellet (eds) (1997) *Religion, Éducation et Démocratie. Un Enseignement Culturel de la Religion est-il Possible?* Montréal: Harmattan: 183–222.

Jackson, R. (1997b) *Religious Education: An Interpretive Approach*. London: Hodder and Stoughton.

Kautz, S. (1995) *Liberalism and Community*. Ithaca and London: Cornell University Press.

Kymlicka, W. (1992) *Théories Récentes sur la Citoyenneté*. Ottawa: Multiculturalisme et citoyenneté Canada.

Lasch, C. (1991) *The True and Only Heaven*. New York: Norton.

Macedo, S. (1995) Liberal civic education and religious fundamentalism: the case of God v. John Rawls. *Ethics*, 105: 468–96.

Milot, M. (1997) L'école face aux particularismes religieux: deux plaidoyers. In M. Milot and F. Ouellet (eds) (1997) *Religion, Éducation et Démocratie. Un Enseignement Culturel de la Religion est-il Possible?* Montréal: Harmattan: 127–50.

Ouellet, F. (1977) L'étude des religions dans les écoles du Québec: la question du 'Pourquoi'. *Medium*: 13–30.

Ouellet, F. (1980a) L'étude des religions dans les écoles: essai de problématique. *Studies in Religion/Sciences Religieuses*, 9 (1): 69–86.

Ouellet, F. (1980b) Étude scientifique des religions et monopole confessionnaliste dans les écoles du Québec. In J. P. Rouleau (ed.) *Sciences Sociales et Églises: Questions sur l'évolution religieuse du Québec*. Montréal: Bellarmin: 183–96.

Ouellet, F. (1983a) L'étude des religions et l'éducation religieuse à l'école: l'expérience anglaise et sa pertinence pour le Québec. *Cahier de l'ACFAS*, 15 'Confessionnalité et pluralisme dans les écoles du Québec, les principaux enjeux du débat': 175–90.

Ouellet, F. (1983b) Religious understanding: an obsolete concept in the public school context? *British Journal of Religious Education*, 6(1): 8–13.

Ouellet, F. (1985a) *L'étude des religions dens les écoles: l'expérience américaine, anglaise et canadienne*. Éditions SR. Waterloo Ont.: Wilfrid Laurier University Press.

Ouellet, F. (1985b) Religious education and the challenges of intercultural communication. *British Journal of Religious Education*, 7(2): 81–6.

Ouellet, F. (1992) Religious values and education in plural societies. In J. Lynch, C. Modgil and S. Modgil (eds) *Cultural Diversity and the Schools. Vol. 1: Education for Cultural Diversity Convergence and Divergence*. London and Washington DC: The Falmer Press: 233–43.

Ouellet, F. (1996) L'enseignement religieux à l'école face aux défis du pluralisme ethnoculturel. In K. Fall, R. Hadj-Moussa and D. Simeoni (eds) *Les Convergences dans les Sociétés Pluriethnìques* Ste-Foy: Presses de l'Université du Québec: 219–37.

Ouellet, F. (1997) L'enseignement religieux culturel: une alternative valable à l'enseignement confessionnel? In M. Milot and F. Ouellet (eds) (1997) *Religion, Éducation et Démocratie. Un Enseignement Culturel de la Religion est-il Possible?* Montréal: Harmattan: 151–82.

Rawls, J. (1993) *Political Liberalism*. New York: Columbia University Press.

Raz, J. (1990) Facing diversity: the case of epistemic abstinence. *Philosophy and Public Affairs*, 19: 3–47.

SCAA (1994) *Model Syllabuses*. London: School Curriculum and Assessment Authority.

Société québécoise pour l'étude de la religion (SQÉR) (1994) L'enseignement religieux et la confessionnalité des structures scolaires au Québec. Position de la Société québécoise pour l'étude de la religion. *Bulletin*, 9: 17–20.

Spinner, J. (1994) *Boundries of Citizenship. Race, Ethnicity and Nationality in the Liberal State*. Baltimore and London: Johns Hopkins University Press.

Thériault, J. Y. (1997) Les deux écoles de la démocratie. In M. Milot and F. Ouellet (eds) *Religion, Éducation et Démocratie. Un Enseignement Culturel de la Religion est-il Possible?* Montréal: Harmattan: 19–34.

Wintersgill, B. (1995) The case of the missing models: exploring the myths. *Resource*, 18(1): 6–11.

20 'The Good Citizen': Cultural Understandings of Citizenship and Gender Amongst a New Generation of Teachers

MADELEINE ARNOT, HELENA ARAÚJO, KIKI DELIYANNI-KOUIMTZIS, GABRIELLE IVINSON AND AMPARO TOMÉ

This exploratory chapter makes tentative comparisons of how national-cultural traditions might affect teachers' values in relation to citizenship, gender relations and the goals of education. It draws on some of the findings of a sociological research project entitled *Promoting Equality Awareness: women as citizens*, which investigated the knowledge and discourses of citizenship used by student teachers in Greece, Spain, Portugal, England and Wales in relation to men and women's position in society.[1]

This chapter focuses specifically on the ways in which the values of citizenship are discussed in relation to gender. Qualitative data were collected from single-sex focus groups conducted with secondary student teachers in Greece, Spain and the UK; from semi-structured interviews with a sample of their trainers in all five countries, and from open-ended questions in the survey and interviews with student teachers and their trainers in Portugal.[2]

The first part of the chapter begins by considering current theoretical debates in sociology of education concerning the nature of citizenship and its implications for citizens' identities. We then consider the ways in which student teachers describe citizenship values and what constitutes the ethical virtues of 'a good citizen'.

The data suggest ways in which a new generation of teachers currently understand the relationship between individuals, the collective or 'common good', and the role of the state. The language and values of citizenship are shown to be sustained by past legacies, by government strategies, and by the subtle ways in which they are continually being restructured, particularly by women. Our analysis speculates about the possible implications of student teachers' values for women's position and participation in advanced industrial societies/ postmodern societies.

The social construction of citizenship

Derek Heater's seminal account of the concept of citizenship as a civic ideal in world history gives a new slant to our understanding of education as the 'modernist project *par excellence*' (Gilbert 1992: 56). Citizenship education, in whatever form, is portrayed as buffeted by the impact of three major political doctrines: *nationalism* which requires a citizenry schooled to display enthusiastic loyalty; *liberal democracy*, requiring a citizenry to cast its vote with understanding and due deference to their betters; and *socialism*, where it could potentially destabilize middle class, capitalist establishments (Heater 1990: 76–88).

Heater (ibid.) argues that nationalism is likely to favour civic education, raising mass consciousness of national identity with the aid of flags, patriotic songs and the celebration of national anniversaries. Central control over education combined with overt teaching strategies, particularly in history and languages, helps homogenize society and overcome differences. Socialism requires education systems to equip individuals with a basic understanding of political structures and some understanding of Left-wing theoretical analyses, so as to encourage active political participation in the name of social justice. Liberal democracy, on the other hand, requires a different agenda for the education of its citizens. Here, all citizens would be encouraged to develop their talents and to achieve individual autonomy through a broad and balanced education.

If the Enlightenment was the 'best hour' (Wexler

1990) for modern concepts of citizenship, citizenship was 'an emblem of modernity', of equal freedoms, of the bond between people across often hierarchically structured and ethnically diverse societies. The concept of citizenship offered liberal democracies, 'a direct sense of community membership based on loyalty to a civilisation which is a common possession' (Marshall 1965: 101).

With shifting economic and political conditions, such modernist narratives and such concepts of citizenship were contested again and again (c.f. Heater 1990). New forms of solidarity and 'rationalities' were formed and reformed, impinging more or less upon state educational systems. In the following sections, we illustrate the extent to which the concept of citizenship is problematic as a set of values and as the basis for a modern social identity.

Gender and citizenship

Contemporary debates within the women's movement[3] about equality and difference, especially in the context of Europe and of European political/ philosophical traditions have highlighted the extent to which citizenship as a concept signifies not rights of inclusion, but rather of exclusion.

For example, when considering women as citizens within Europe, Yuval-Davis (1992), like other feminist political theorists, challenges evolutionary theories of the development of rights. She argues that the processes of inclusion and exclusion are contained within national political histories. The politics of difference was subsumed into the notion of a 'given collectivity' and was not usually presented as an ideological or material construction. Boundaries, structures and norms are the result of a 'constant process of struggles, negotiation and general social developments'. Of great importance, therefore, is an understanding of the processes by which such arbitrary notions of collectivity are constructed especially in so far as they define membership, identities, cultural 'needs', and national self determination. Yuval-Davis argues that, although citizenship rights are represented as 'universalistic', they are not 'universal discourses'.

The boundaries of community (or as some now call 'nation space') also define *de facto* those who are excluded from membership. The construction of a new community in Europe provides examples of the different status being awarded to different groups of people. As Yuval-Davis points out, while some women gain the right of free movement, others (15 million minorities) have restricted movement. The concept of 'Fortress Europe' signifies the centrality of religion – in this case Christianity, but also of xenophobia and racism. As Sultana (1995) argued, the project of creating a 'uniting Europe' is characterized as much by the tensions created by difference as it is by the goal of solidarity. Multi-culturalism in this context suggests the importance of understanding not just differences within nations, but also cultural differences between European nations and the significance this has for those within.

The implications of the various social constructions of public/private spheres and male/female worlds for discourses of citizenship are also important. Privacy, for example, is both publicly determined and gendered. Thus, the supposed 'femaleness' of private spheres does not have a natural basis. Similarly, in some countries, the concept of 'public life' does not exist. The dichotomy between public and private spheres is both culturally and historically specific. Carole Pateman (1988), who set in train feminist critiques of the gendered nature of European political/ philosophical thought, focused both on the masculinized basis of citizenship in such traditions and the dilemmas it poses for women wishing to participate more equally in democratic societies. Pateman's analysis of the 'fraternal pact' that underlies liberal democratic thought, as well as her exposure of the gender assumptions that shape the citizen as male, are challenging critiques of the ways in which women have, by definition, been included as a negative reference point in theories of democracy and citizenship. At the same time, she recalls what she refers to as 'Woolstonecraft's dilemma' – whether women should fight for equal/identical rights with men or whether they should fight for recognition of women's particular contribution to citizenship and society. Should motherhood, for example, provide the basis of citizenship for women or should one sustain the notion that men and women deserve identical treatment? She has pointed out that all too often: 'Motherhood and citizenship are . . . set apart' (Pateman 1992).

Using such theoretical frameworks two of the key questions we addressed in our research were:

1 To what extent is citizenship associated with male public spheres?

2 Are women attempting to construct alternative models and values of citizenship?

In the next four sections, we explore the meaning and relevance of citizenship to values of social justice and the gendered aspects of citizenship, first at a general level and second in relation to three discursive frameworks.

Citizenship in everyday life

Reading the responses of student teachers for the first time, it seemed as if citizenship had little meaning in everyday life and was not the basis for a political identity. It seemed that the concept of citizenship meant little to student teachers and their trainers in all five countries.

In England and Wales, despite having an appropriate word, student teachers initially appeared to have difficulty in defining and using the term. One male student teacher, who seemed to speak for many of the British student teachers, suggested that he had no idea what a citizen was. Typical responses were:

> I don't know. I think there is such a thing as citizenship.   (English male student teacher)

> I think I'm a citizen but I mean I'd have to delve into a dictionary really.   (English male student teacher)

A group of English female student teachers also struggled for meaning:

> Does it mean anything to you to say that I am a citizen?
> No.
> Nothing at all.
> From what people say, yes, I feel that way but I would feel nothing today . . . Oh I am a citizen.
> That doesn't mean anything to me really.
> I can't really relate to the actual word citizen.

Yet discussions with student teachers revealed that, although citizenship had little currency in everyday discourse in all five countries, it was possible to identify the different metaphors, associations and values that they called into play in trying to make sense of the term. Student teachers articulated complex relations between their moral stances and their critical interpretations of modern society. Below, we attempt to unravel some of the common threads, distinctions and tensions associated with the concept of citizenship.

Space and 'belonging'

The spatial dimension of the concept of citizenship refers to the way it was used to signal membership of geographic, cultural or political communities. Citizenship can be brought into relation with localities of different size and scale, such as villages, regions, nation states, international orders, the European context and the global village. At times, it was possible to detect strong, individual, political identities in respondents' descriptions of the community boundaries and the criteria for membership.

In the UK alone, a range of geo-political communities was mentioned, including the UK, Great Britain, England, Scotland, Wales and Northern Ireland, Europe, the international community and the global community. A range of criteria for membership was also used, such as being resident, having been born in the country, having been educated in the country, cultural membership and member of racial groups. As the following set of quotations suggest, the expression 'being part of' begged the question of what membership actually referred to in practice.

> Well, um, I'm a bit confused about this citizenship. Is it citizenship as in general or a community, . . . or is citizenship as in part of a country? (English female student teacher)

> Well I see the word citizen to me means part of the country, in fact I suppose it means more part of the community, more European community. So the word citizen I would equate with being part of Europe.   (English female student teacher)

> No, it's being part of a member of a town, somebody who lives in an urban community.   (English female student teacher)

For some student teachers, membership of a regional or national community had more emotive than physical/residential connotations. Male student teachers, in particular, spoke of concepts such as pride in being part of a particular country/nation or sharing a national cultural heritage.

> I think there is an element of pride that comes out to me, proud to be a citizen of this country. (English male student teacher)

> Yes, in a way, an air of pride, a country pride I suppose it goes along certain different levels, depending on who you'd be discussing citizenship with . . .

You'd be proud of being Welsh I suppose. (English male student teacher)

On the other hand, national pride can be constructed as a reaction to difference. The concept of citizenship could be the vehicle by means of which the individual is constructed in opposition to those who are excluded by the category. The following quotation gives some hint of this dialectic between self and 'otherness':

> the only time you really think of citizenship is when you are introduced with another culture and you find yourself alienated, especially going abroad. I think in Britain when I meet people from other countries that come over here, I'm very conscious of just doing what is right so these people do have a good impression. I think that's the only time I'm aware of being a citizen. (English male student teacher)

Students also constructed citizenship as an abstract, but nevertheless inclusive category. They described a sense of belonging somewhere even if 'somewhere' was vaguely defined. We found rather abstract references to belonging to 'a group', 'a culture' or 'society'. These descriptions implied more than formal criteria of membership such as place of residence, place of work or place of birth. They appeared to stress the 'feeling of belonging' rather than any explicit political identity. One Portuguese science educator, for example, spoke of 'habits', 'principles' and 'visions', concepts closer perhaps to Bourdieu and Passeron's (1977) notion of habitus. He stated: 'We understand a citizen of a nation state as someone who belongs to a culture, who has certain habits, certain principles, certain visions of the world' (Portuguese teacher trainer).

A related critical tension identified in the discussions with student teachers was that between *ascribed* and *achieved* citizenship. The question of whether citizenship was something that could be earned touched on whether women, minority ethnic groups and those with disabilities could apply. If the concept of citizenship was seen as a 'cultural arbitrary' rather than a 'natural' category, then there was always the possibility that it could be restructured, or its membership redefined.

Student teachers in Greece however, used other benchmarks in their discussions of citizenship – namely the relationship between the individual and society. They referred less to a cultural concept of citizenship or nation and more to a political entity represented by the state. Being a citizen offered this

female teacher trainer: 'a sense that you belong somewhere, that you are a member of an organized society in which you have the right to act and which offers you an entity'.

'Organized society' provided a framework of legally defined benefits for the individual. One student described citizenship as: 'a concept of living in the context of an organized state, according to the range of laws that have, as a precondition the benefit of the citizen within the same organization' (Greek male student teacher). However, tensions between 'the benefits' of citizenship in these definitions and the potential loss of individual freedom were referred to frequently. In Greece, the contradictions between a protective organized state and the unprotected citizen were clearly at the forefront of student teachers' understanding of citizenship.

In the Portuguese and Greek groups, tensions were found between the need for respect for, and perhaps conformity to, the state and the need for civic activism and political reform. In some instances, what McLaughlin (1992: 236) has referred to as *minimal* views of citizenship were used to define the good citizen. Reference was made to citizenship that involved civil status and the associated rights based on the rule of law. In these discussions, stress was laid on conformity to core values, community-based voluntarism and limited political engagement. In other groups however, the 'thicker' *maximal* version of citizenship were found which McLaughlin described as 'a richer thing than, say, the possession by a person of a passport, the right to vote and an unreflective 'nationality' (ibid.). These maximal views of citizenship tend to define the citizen in social, cultural and psychological terms, somewhat in line with McLaughlin's description.

> the citizen must have a consciousness of him or her self as a member of a living community with a shared democratic culture involving obligations and responsibilities as well as rights, a sense of the common good, fraternity [sic] and so one. This latter, maximal, interpretation of the identity required by a citizen is dynamic rather than static in that it is seen as a matter of continuing debate and redefinition. (ibid)

As McLaughlin pointed out, maximal views of citizenship presuppose a considerable degree of explicit understanding of democratic principles, values and procedures and require individuals to have the necessary dispositions and capacities for the conceived level of democratic participation. It was possible to identify student teachers who did indeed expect critical engagement with, and participation in, political and social life. This suggests that unquestioning conformity *per se* was considered unacceptable by these student teachers and may also be a matter of concern in a democratic society. These generic tensions in defining the boundaries of citizenship were differently expressed in the focus group discussions in each country.

In the following three sections we explore these tensions further in the context of three discursive frameworks which, from a reading of our collective data, appear to have shaped the meanings attached to the word 'citizenship'. Such discursive frameworks suggest that not one but a number of different languages are drawn upon to make sense of contemporary values in relation to citizenship; languages that each allow for maximal or minimal concepts, and which each have gendered dimensions. Even from such a small set of discussions one can glimpse the tensions between identity and the ideals of social justice. We focus here on

1 Discourses of duty
2 Morality, caring and common values
3 Social rights and egalitarianism.

Discourses of duty

Political discourses appear to be active in countries that construct notions of political duty, both in relation to the individual to society and of the state to the individual. All schools in Greece teach traditions of ancient Greece and provide civic education on the *Principles of a Democratic Regime*. It would appear that lessons learned from the dictatorship of the colonels, which ended in the 1970s, have deeply influenced student teachers' understandings of citizenship. It was significant that they used the notion of the citizen as a vantage point from which to define membership of the *polis*, used in its original sense as the city. In one group discussion, male student teachers mentioned:

'Citizenship is a person that is integrated into a "city" with the ancient meaning'.
'A democracy'.
'Specific community with a specific legislature'.
'I mean in a political organization'.
'A citizen is one who participates in the election'.

These notions of citizenship signalled a complex interaction between the rights of individuals to know and be aware of political choices and the right to be informed about choices, opportunities, rights and responsibilities. They also involved the right to be elected and to elect those who would govern. Political representation and participation were presented as key symbols of the freedom enjoyed by all citizens.

Without the freedom to participate in 'every aspect of work relations, in every aspect of life, financial, cultural, social, everything' (Greek male student teacher) the citizen would not be able to exercise his/her rights and duty to control the direction of events in society. Citizenship was described as the need to make decisions to protect one's own life, choices (liberty and autonomy) and also to sustain solidarity with others. As one Portuguese education lecturer commented:

> The intervention of man in the **polis**, in the city is the capacity of interfering in the life of the polis. It is the intervention of the subject on the city, he [sic] has the capacity to intervene, to take and share decisions. I have always thought that power must be shared by all. That capacity of people to feel that they have an obligation to intervene, that they have the right to intervene, to understand that citizenship will necessarily give them a set of rights and duties.

These kinds of values were elaborated further in some of the Portuguese discussion groups. One teacher trainer referred to 'collective edification' and described it as the need to seek improvement in the rights for others, their social benefits and the promotion of the social good.

The critical citizen

In the context of this political discourse, a good citizen was not necessarily constructed as one who obeys. Indeed, in countries that have experienced Right-wing dictatorships such as Greece, Portugal and Spain, conformity may threaten the rights of citizens.

In Greece, it was precisely the 'cultural arbitrariness' of the state that raised doubts about the desirability of conformity and justified the role of the good citizen as social critic. As one female student teacher commented:

> I don't agree with the term [a good citizen]. As things are today, I don't know what it means to

discuss the good citizen. I mean, even if somebody is a good citizen, he becomes a bad one, the reality transforms him.

The good citizen, for some Greek student teachers, was someone who had a duty to act, and to change the established order, to mobilize and fight for rights. The comments that follow illustrate the way in which this 'maximal' view was discussed as positive but also as a potentially dangerous task:

> To be a good citizen does not mean you must always obey what the state lays down because if so, the citizens would be considered a weak willed, undecided people. Citizens must be fighting, socialized, in order to be able, when the time comes, to overthrow everything that is going wrong in Greece, or even in the international order.

The debate amongst predominantly male student teachers about self-protection, mobilization and participation in decision-making in political life presented an image of the citizen fighting to keep control of a potentially dangerous state. The memory and experience of dictatorship, particularly for the older student teachers seemed to be present in their constructions of a politicized citizenry. As one male student teacher emphasized:

> We should never, as citizens, stop caring about who is governing, about the methods, etc. We should try to intervene, to be politicized, to be active. This is the only way to control. This is the citizen's right. Otherwise, I mean if the citizens don't care one day they realize that things have happened and they have not been informed. (Greek male student teacher)

There seemed to be a similar concern in the Portuguese student teachers' discourse about sustaining critical participation. They expressed a need for social commitment as well as a capacity to act and take decisions. They justified this with reference to about 50 years of Right-wing dictatorship (Salazarism from the 1930s to late 1960s). To them, individual participation implied critical collective participation and distancing one's self from the historical past of the 'New State' in which people's conformity to the government and its laws was not only expected but also built into educational institutions. The new mission was described as 'additive amelioration'.

> It is the capacity of participating in the life of the 'polis' in the city to which he [sic] belongs, the capacity to take and share decisions . . . It is the

people's capacity to feel that it is their duty to intervene, that they have the right to participate, to understand that citizenship will necessarily give them a set of rights and a set of duties. (Portuguese student teacher)

Despite a history of dictatorship under Franco, student teachers in Spain appeared less likely to articulate critical political discourses. Spanish male student teachers, in contrast with female colleagues, referred to a new democratic state and highlighted the ideals of the French Revolution:

> Citizenship means a group of people who live and relate to each other in an *estado de derecho* [constitutional state] and have the same duties and rights. (Spanish male student teacher)

> The idea of citizenship to me is related to the French Revolution, and since then, everyone has the right to be a citizen. (Spanish male student teacher)

However, their references to the political sphere appeared to be improvised and abstract, with few mentions of actual political roles *vis à vis* the state. Female student teachers tended to draw upon moral discourses to highlight the critical role of the 'caring citizen' (see below).

The sceptical citizen

In Britain, discussions with student teachers tended not to highlight the role of citizens in maintaining democratic regimes and their principles or practices. Interventionist and critical political discourse were rarely present. However, student teachers in Britain seemed aware of the arbitrariness of the state and were critical of the moral behaviour, intentions and actions of politicians. They did not, however, offer an equivalent image of the critical citizen. Some of their representations of the good citizen suggested a 'sceptical citizen', ever on the alert, but not necessarily active in promoting democracy. The European traditions of Greek political philosophy or the French Revolution appeared not to have shaped their understandings of the concept of citizenship. This may be a reflection of a different political history incorporating the British monarchy and a recognition of the different status of a *subject* from that of a citizen. It may also be due to the lack of civic education in most schools.

The following extracts demonstrate British student teachers' sensitivity to the problems of defining citizenship as a status as well as a recognition of the politically contested nature of the concept:

> If you look at it [citizenship] in a very modern way, some people would say it is a bit funny to be a citizen in Britain because we have still got a queen, so that we're subjects rather than citizens. So it's a bit of a conflict there, calling yourself a citizen in a monarchy.   (Welsh female student teacher)

> You think of the word citizen as being part of citizen of what? The state . . . Whenever I hear the word citizenship I always think of, the relevant stuff coming out of the . . . The Citizen's Charter, I can't separate the two. I think a Citizen Charter doesn't really seem to have much concrete meaning to me.   (Welsh female student teacher)

> The current government is seen to be promoting citizenship for political reasons – as much as for social reasons, which isn't necessarily the best way to go about it.   (Welsh female student teacher)

Descriptions of the role of the citizen in a multi-racial metropolis revealed the importance of recognizing difference, particularly cultural and ethnic difference. It may well be that awareness of social discrimination has affected British student teachers' political discourses. Their language suggested more about their 'politicization' than their conceptualization of polity. What follows is a typical discussion about the dilemmas involved in defining a political identity. The context of race, gender and class inequalities provide frameworks for those who appear to engage with more 'maximal' or 'empowering' definitions of political life. A group of English female student teachers training in a multi-racial inner-city area commented that citizenship meant:

> Having a voice and a right to changing anything.

> It's a lovely ideal, isn't it?

> Because it doesn't happen. You don't all have an equal voice in society. I don't just mean colour or sex – the man in the street doesn't have the same.

> I think to a certain extent it is a sense of belonging to something. That may be why I have no concept of it because I was born here, but I don't feel British.

> But you've got a right to be here.

You could argue that I have the right to be here but that's by the by. I'm here till whatever happens but it doesn't mean that I'm happy to be here in some respects but I can see that there are certain things that are working against me, because I'm here and because I'm black.

> If you are a black person and you are a citizen here it means a totally different thing from someone who is white.

The references have more to do with the structuring of discrimination than the power of the electorate. In politicized discourses such as this, student teachers appeared to be alert to the different experiences of particular groups and the inequalities they may face within a democracy. However, apart from 'having a voice', little emphasis was placed on sharing decision-making or critical action at state level or in the public sphere. This is characteristic of the scepticism referred to earlier. Only one English female student teacher talked about having a 'political voice' or of taking an active role in a democratic crisis while being informed and free to say what she thought. Often the most that came across from student teachers' comments was a suspicion that all was not well: 'I think the country's in real trouble to be honest' (Welsh male student teacher) or 'the non-Europeans have trouble, possibly with Western values. Asians and that, they probably have less rights, whether they should have or whether they shouldn't' (Welsh male student teacher).

Although there was a critical awareness amongst British student teachers, it appeared to have little to do with exercising their duties, especially in terms of intervening in the actions of the state. Although these comments demonstrate aspects of a 'maximal' view of citizenship, they appear to focus on the effects of state policies on people's lives rather than on the possibilities of 'civic action' described by their Greek and Portuguese counterparts.

Morality, caring and common values

Moral discourses bring together concepts of culture, community and 'the common good'. The focus here was less on state membership described as a legal status and more on the 'feeling' of belonging to a community. Individuals were discussed in relation to shared values, especially those that relate to Judaeo-Christian traditions of 'good neighbourliness', moral behaviour and caring.

The caring citizen

These moral discourses are especially well articulated by women in Catholic countries such as Spain and Portugal. There appeared to be considerable emphasis on conformity and respect for social values and rules. The person at the heart of this discourse would live in society without exceeding the limits of unsociable behaviour and would also sustain the virtues of loyalty, honesty and sensitivity to the problems faced by others. The good citizen could be summarized as: 'one who takes part in things . . . who rules himself by moral and ethical principles' (Portuguese teacher trainer).

Social order and caring for others were valued because they provided a check to excessive individualism. Responsibilities to the community rather than to the state appeared to be valued above rights. Descriptions of solidarity connoted universal rather than culturally-specific notions of the common interest. Fraternity rather than freedom was also central to the discourse.

Solidarity was associated with a range of groups that did not involve the state, for example, with neighbours, the community and within personal relations. When solidarity was mentioned in relation to a country or the global village, the references still tended to be made to an abstract concept of 'society'.

> I am a good citizen when I have the feeling that I must contribute as far as I can with love for the society and for my fatherland, with respect for the laws and to the governors and having always in mind that the common interest is much more important than my personal interest.   (Greek male teacher trainer)

In Spain, female student teachers in particular drew upon the language of Christianity to construct the good citizen as caring and self-sacrificing. Descriptions of the need to respect, to tolerate difference and to serve were sometimes vocational in tone. A group of Spanish female student teachers commented:

'Citizenship means service to the community'.
'Citizenship means respect for different cultures'.
'Citizenship should mean to educate people for the good of the rest'.

Service to the community and respect for others were mentioned more often than political principles. At the centre of moral discourse was the 'good person': 'I never think of people as citizens, but I talk about people as good or bad' (Spanish female student teacher) or 'Good people are good citizens. It is impossible to think of an example of a bad person being a good citizen' (Spanish female student teacher).

Dangers are also recognized. One female Portuguese student teacher felt that traditional Christian moralities and 'mentalities' could be responsible for perpetuating gender differences:

> In the Portuguese context, there is still a traditional mentality, a separation of the place of men and women, due to our Christian mentality. Therefore, there's the idea of women as secondary to men, they are here to serve men. It's a process that will take a very long time, all this question of women's liberation in the 1960s and 1970s, people think that the differences have already gone.

Christian principles were often described as a form of surveillance, used to inform and judge the behaviour of individuals within a community. In some of these descriptions the notion of rights was presented as a means of enforcing Christian values. Some Portuguese spoke of the rights to health as *mens sana, in corpore sano* (austerity, strength of mind), the rights to housing (in the sense of a home which was warm inside and gave a sense of community sharing) and the rights to education (a way of giving something of oneself to another, of teaching the poor and the weak).

However, even though the concept of 'the caring citizen' might mean being involved in charity work at the community level, in voluntary associations and in caring roles within the family, it was noticeable how difficult some student teachers found it to apply the term 'citizenship' to family life. For example, a male Portuguese student teacher commented:

> I never thought about the idea of a citizen within the family. Within the family, I tend to think more about a father, a husband, a son, a brother. There are concepts that I associate with family life and that of citizen is not one of them.   (Portuguese male student teacher)

Some student teachers in Britain struggled to recognize the relationship of community spirit and community activism to citizenship. It would seem that the image of the good citizen was not equated with the caring professions or charity work. For one male student teacher, charity work represented 'a failure on the part of the state to do its job properly' and was therefore not considered to be exercise of moral responsibility. In the following remarks, these two male student teachers appeared to be searching for a more meaningful definition of community activism than just 'good works'.

> You say what do you think is a good citizen, then instantly in your mind you get things like charity work and group work. There are a lot of people who are in very caring professions – that doesn't mean they are a good citizen. (English male student teacher)

> For me I can't think of something called citizenship, but things that make me feel, that's being a good citizen. For instance, there's all sorts of things such as charity work, that strike me as good citizenship but that's very tangible, people on committees, or running church fetes and all sorts of things like that and it goes much further and deeper and people work a lot harder, but that must stem from something a little bit deeper in psychological terms. . . . Perhaps something like a sense of community. (English male student teacher)

Other English and Welsh students recognized the value of the suppression of individualism in relation to collective values. One described a citizen as 'Someone who thinks a little bit beyond themselves – less selfish' (English male student teacher).

Although British politicians have emphasized individual advancement and materialism, these student teachers were at pains to stress the importance of maintaining concern for the community. The tension between individuals and the collectivity was a thread that ran through much of this particular discussion. Tolerance was high on their agenda: 'Being able to accept other people's views as well as your own' (Welsh female student teacher) and 'Admitting that people are not always going to be the same as you contributing to society' (Welsh female student teacher). These student teachers' views appeared to value diversity rather than homogeneity of communities.

The good citizen and social class

Notions of 'goodness' and the 'good citizen' constructed within moral discourses again were not unproblematic, especially if they implied social and moral conformity. For those student teachers who

seemed to be using a maximal version of citizenship (McLaughlin 1992), the 'good citizens' by the very nature of their being 'good' were in danger of undermining the goal of creating challenging, inquiring citizens. In Portugal, conformity to dominant values signalled for some, 'dangerous shades'. For some English student teachers, the 'good citizen' was presented as limited and thus 'exceptionally boring'. Indeed, if dominant cultures were perceived to be class dominated or oppressive, then the model of the caring and thus conforming citizen offered little that was positive:

> All the connotations to citizenship we have in society are very middle class. . . . I'll be a good citizen and play cricket, that type of thing . . . it has no relevance to most people . . . the average man in the street. (English male student teacher)

Among the English and Welsh student teachers, the class imagery that was used to describe the 'good citizen' was particularly striking. We found a surprisingly dated image of the respectable 'bowler hatted gentleman' of the 1950s. This image of male respectability in the public sphere provided a sharp contrast to the critical citizen described in political discourses.

> A middle-aged balding fellow with a nice garden and semi-detached house. (Welsh male student teacher)

> The citizen is a necessarily nice man in a bowler hat who had got a job . . . in the city and then comes back to his nice semi-detached house with a wife and 2.5 kids. (Welsh male student teacher)

> The first thing that springs to my mind about a citizen is that I get an image of a man in a bowler hat and a suit. (Welsh male student teacher)

Concern about class, gender and ethnic biases amongst student teachers who described Britain as multi-cultural and pluralist suggested that any concept of 'the common good' was highly problematic. Some student teachers appeared to be affected by concerns about imposing social values that would limit rather than extend social justice. They were unwilling to support values that they suggested might limit the opportunities of children to express themselves freely and develop their abilities. On the other hand, they were also concerned that imposing one set of values (even if they were egalitarian) might conflict with those of the children's families and their ways of life. Teaching values was not something they considered to be neutral and they were particularly concerned about being seen to indoctrinate.

These class-laden images of citizenship were described in terms that were not appealing, and student teachers were clearly struggling to find ways to imagine and articulate modern versions of citizenship which could accommodate cultural pluralism and economic change. For those who had already engaged in practice teaching in inner cities, and had witnessed at first hand conflictual community relations and diverse family structures and values, the framing of coherent and egalitarian-moral discourse, of a maximal kind, was a complex affair. The English and Welsh students reported that the likelihood of parental resistance to any one egalitarian-moral perspective provided an added anxiety.

In Greece, the good modern citizen was described as someone who overcomes self-interest and contributes to the common good, through economic rather than caring activities. The good citizen can be defined as the 'productive citizen', somebody who works for the good of society by contributing to the wealth of the nation. Fraternity in this context would mean working hard, paying taxes and encouraging greater national productivity. The shift in the construction of the modern Greek citizen is away from the ideal of ancient Greek and Christian cultures towards an economic role. The legacies of previous traditions are however evident in student teachers' concerns for the rights and dignity of others. What is not clear is how far the notion of the 'productive citizen' includes women's contribution to economic progress. Indeed this kind of framework may well render domestic labour invisible, further damaging women's status (Arnot et al. 1997).

Mother as reformer

In contrast, it would seem that by mobilizing moral discourses, women student teachers in Catholic countries such as Portugal and Spain were able to focus on feminist political empowerment. They argued that if ethical virtues are the basis of good citizenship, then those with sensitive or caring dispositions who are committed to solidarity and cooperation, will make good citizens. Here a Portuguese student teacher highlights the way women may be constructed as effective citizens within such a discourse:

A person who in principle is more sensitive to the problems of others, I think, women are more sensitive to what surrounds them. I think my grandmother is a good citizen, she has those dispositions . . . in men it is harder to find. (Portuguese female student teacher)

The theme of 'mother as reformer' also emerged in some Greek female student teachers' discussions. They described how women could potentially make up for a lack of public political power by mobilizing power within the family. These women did not engage with abstract ideals of the critical citizen but described women changing society by raising a new generation of children. In this way, young Greek female student teachers were able to define a position for themselves within a moral discourse.

Alternative feminist models of citizenship were also offered by female groups in Portugal, Spain, England and Wales. Some student teachers found ways to value female contributions to society by drawing on traditional gender roles. There was some suggestion that society could sustain complementary concepts of the good citizen. They suggested that women could be constructed as 'home citizens' and 'family builder citizens':

Traditionally it is expected that men do it by working, building up power structures while women do it in a more nurturing sense within the family. So men do it organizationally and women do it, at a more personal level. (English female student teacher)

I think we are able to do everything a man does, considering specific situations, children. All issues are masculine. I think few women know what they should or should not do as citizens . . . women exercise more citizenship in the family, in private life, they are not yet accustomed to being citizens. (Portuguese female teacher trainer)

Citizenship has to be dealt with within the family, parents, children and schools as a reflection of the family. (Spanish female student teacher)

Social rights and egalitarianism

The egalitarian discourses of the post-war period in the UK have been associated, on the whole, with the provision of what Marshall (1965) called social rights through state welfare provision. The predominant notion here is redistributive justice (cf.

Rawls 1972) where individuals are perceived to be entitled to basic human rights such as health care, education, housing, the right to work without discrimination, protection by legislation, social and family policies and state provision of services. The extent to which these rights and services are provided and protected by the state will differ between countries. The extent to which rights are equally shared by all citizens and over which range of public/private, male/female spheres are culturally and historically specific.

Thus in Portugal and in Spain, discussion about rights in relation to full citizenship is a relatively new phenomena in the new discourses of recent socialist governments. These egalitarian discourses tend to be superimposed on existing discourses and therefore do not entirely replace previous understandings of the social order and gender hierarchies. Alternatively, discourses become active at formal constitutional levels, without reference to everyday practice. Not surprisingly, a number of student teachers were aware of the formal provision of citizenship rights in relation to the state, but were not satisfied that all citizens had the same knowledge about such rights or how to claim them.

In Portugal, for example, men and women have only recently acquired rights under the new constitution established on 25 April 1974. The constitution was concerned with the creation of a 'social equilibrium', where individuals, particularly men and women, would work in complementary fashions. The discursive logic of these egalitarian discourses tends to evoke the new constitution as consensual, and rights as if they have already been acquired.

In contrast, in Greece contemporary discussion about rights dates back to the early 1930s, before the first dictatorship when the Communist Party was becoming stronger. Within the associated socialist discourses, attention was focused on the relation of individual rights to the organized state. The range of rights referred to in these discourses were not only those of justice, peace and equality, but the right to work, to be educated, to health provision as well as to corporal, psychological and intellectual rights.

The protesting citizen

Although the state was portrayed as the provider of benefits in the form of individual rights, it was also assumed that individuals would have to fight for them. We found that in line with strong national political discourses, Greek female teachers constructed the notion of the 'protesting citizen'. They voiced their concerns that the state might infringe individual rights and freedoms:

the term of citizen means to claim your rights, I believe we don't claim our rights enough. Take me, for example, in some cases, although I had the law with me, I was treated very badly. I could claim legally some things, but I didn't succeed. Maybe because I am a woman . . . or maybe I was not able enough . . . (Greek female student teacher)

The notion of citizen makes me think of the insecurity I feel all the times I want to claim these. What are considered legal rights of the citizen, which as a citizen in the Greek state I tried to claim. I felt unprotected. (Greek female student teacher)

However, most Greek student teachers appeared to speak with indifference about the social rights and benefits provided by the state. For many years, welfare services were poor and many people had learned to supplement them with private initiatives (such as extra teaching help at home). To some extent rights were more important in abstract than in relation to the implementation of legislation. Individuals were seen to need such rights as a precondition for their full political participation. One Greek female trainer considered the most important right to be the right to: 'create within the society within which he or she lives, according to his or her personality and abilities'.

The threat of an authoritarian government appears to have left a legacy of suspicion about the role of the state in Greece, and egalitarian developments could have been kept in check by this undercurrent. Concerns therefore were different to those expressed by English and Welsh student teachers. In Britain the lack of a written constitution and tradition of struggle over rights might have influenced student teachers' discourses.

I think there is a cult of ignorance because we have never had them defined. In the absence of a Bill of Rights, freedom, proper Freedom of Information Acts, . . . The concept of us having rights is one, we had a revolution 400 odd years ago which fizzled out and we got the old regime back again and there has never been a strong democratic movement. It is something that has evolved so gradually over a period of years that has always had the same sort of people behind it, keeping things like the House of Lords. The idea of a right . . . I think is something that hit us rather suddenly – things like Gay rights, women's rights, ethnic rights, all these sorts of things have happened very very suddenly. There is a worrying lack of legal definition for them. We think we'd all like to say yes, I treat everyone equally and that's great and there are very few people who would probably say differently. I don't think there is sufficient reinforcement, such as a state fall back.   (English male student teacher)

This student teacher described the British historical legacy as a slow evolution that tended to engender complacency and ignorance about individual rights but which has recently attracted renewed interest. Some English and Welsh student teachers date this new 'rights debate' to the 1980s, although discussion of children's rights were said to have been more recent. One of the main problems discussed was whether to use the law to ensure rights and to sustain, for example, freedom of speech in context of the scepticism referred to above. Some student teachers considered removing censorship at the same time as allowing those such as the 'moral majority' in the United States. If freedom of speech is guaranteed for all, oppressive views might be promoted by those in power.

We considered it worth exploring whether student teachers found any meaning in the language of rights and if so, how they might apply to different contexts. We found differing degrees of awareness of rights amongst student teachers in different countries and different perspectives about the most salient rights. The list from which to draw was extensive. Student teachers referred for example, to those who did not receive full rights of citizenship. They mentioned ethnic groups, racial groups, migrants, immigrants, those who were poor, those who were ignorant, AIDS victims, language groups, social class groups, and particular age groups amongst others. Even so the language of rights in relation to the 'good citizen' was problematic. For some, if applied to the private sphere, it could be seen as oppressive and potentially destructive (Arnot et al. 1997).

For some student teachers, an air of optimism characterized their responses: 'What is not your right today, can become it tomorrow if you mobilize' (Greek male student teacher). In Spain, society was represented as 'running a course', as if moving forward away from its historical past. There was a view that rights could be achieved without tension

through positive intervention by the state or other agencies: 'Equality seems to grow . . . we are living in a transition, so we all will be equals in the near future' (Spanish male student teacher).

However, there were many who could not see equal opportunities or equality as a natural phenomena that would be achieved without political intervention, particularly through educational reform. Spanish female student teachers' appeared far more critical and more pessimistic about the new society. Women teachers did not see themselves as part of the 'transition' narrative set up by the socialist government. They did not position themselves as feminists, nor did they relate to the strong egalitarian discourses supported by men. Instead as we have shown, they mobilized a moral discourse around femininity, caring and community-based cultures.

This struggle for women's rights is reminiscent of that found in Greece. Some female student teachers also expressed insecurity about the assumption that all individuals would be included within the framework of citizenship and would achieve full rights. They, too, stated that women needed to fight for their rights.

Some Portuguese women student teachers expressed concern about using the distinction between the public and private spheres. They pointed to the importance of linking the rights of citizenship to the private and not just the public sphere.

> If a woman is subject to violence within the family, with the strictly private, what can she do to stop this violence? She has to resort to the courts . . . She has to come out of the private sphere and come out to the public . . . there is a connection in my point of view. Citizenship has also to do with the private world of the family.

Portuguese student teachers also grappled with the difficult relationship between the discourse of rights and that of biological difference. Male and female student teachers' discussions suggested that they took the formal equality between the sexes as written in the 1976 constitution for granted. But, surprisingly, female student teachers used biological differences as the basis for arguing that women could play a different contributory role in contemporary society as mothers and carers. They suggested that if women were able to use biological differences constructively in public life, working in education and caring professions, they would be more likely to be valued themselves as citizens.

National contexts and the values of citizenship

Discussions with student teachers have illustrated how different concepts of citizenship are constructed around political, moral and egalitarian discourses. Within each, gender relations were considered. Male and female student teachers in the different countries gave us insights into the complex ways in which gender difference shapes their representations of the citizen and in particular the 'good citizen'.

Two major concerns can be identified in the data. The first involves the gendering of different spheres in relation to the values of citizenship. The data indicate the continuing identification of gendered spheres, and especially the dominance of what Connell (1990) referred to as the European equation between authority and a dominating masculinity. The image and language of discourses associated with citizenship were largely male. Even concepts of community were associated more with male notions of responsibilities rather than female contributions within the family and neighbourhood. Political and egalitarian discourses, especially, appeared to apply to public spheres and to assume both a relevance to men and a role for men in terms of 'civic action'.

In the five countries in our study, in which under 15 per cent of representatives in national assemblies were women, references to the rights and duties of citizens centred on the state or government. As male dominated institutions, such references reinforced women's position outside the discourses of citizenship. Indeed, modes of civic action described within political or egalitarian discourses emphasized public rather than private action. We gained the impression in our discussions with student teachers in Spain and Greece that political struggles over rights and duties had been delegated to men. The more recent transition in Spain from nationalist to socialist government and the new focus on rights seemed to have less relevance for women than for men.

Moral values in contrast, were described in ways that appeared initially to override the distinction between public and private. This was achieved through references to the common good and common values. Yet such discourses, in the various national forms, were often premised on a concept of good public works. Citizenship in this context had little to do with parenting roles, caring for the aged or the sick within the home. While male student teachers worried about the nature of social values, conformity and the possibility of encouraging a productive law-abiding member of society, female student teachers indicated the importance of the family as a relevant site for discovering the 'good citizen'. Indeed, in some countries, women's roles as mothers and as carers were highlighted and appeared to be celebrated as alternative sources of critical, civic action. The artificiality of the boundary between public and private was most apparent in the context of moral discourses.

In the first section of this chapter we referred to Heater's suggestion that within modernist narratives, concepts of citizenship can be contested again and again. New forms of solidarity and new 'rationalities' can be formed and reformed, impinging more or less upon state educational systems. This perspective makes it possible to understand the national tensions between political, moral and egalitarian discourses found amongst the new generation of student teachers, as well as the differences between national contexts. Student teachers today carry with them the legacies of nationalism, of liberal democracy and of socialism. For the older Greek student teachers, the legacies of the 1970s can be identified in their fears concerning the power of the 'organized state' and the need to forge ahead in what they referred to as a struggle for democracy. Their comments portrayed them as engaging in contemporary efforts to forge new political projects.

In contrast, Spanish teachers' representations of citizenship reflected the work of the Spanish central government, which has been trying for the last twelve years to define a new sense of national membership over and above regional and ethnic identities. After forty years of dictatorship (1939–1975), Spain established a new constitution in 1978. The struggle for democratic and human rights was described as a process of learning and an understandable level of insecurity about the nature and exercise of rights and duties could be detected in discussions.

A new version of what it meant to 'be Spanish' was described by many groups and can be seen as a necessary prerequisite for a break from Francoist Nationalist discourses. Symbolic as well as economic and political strategies were being employed to disconnect the past. Civic education in this new political context is being designed to promote a new system of values in an educational structure that is not truly democratic. The references we found to community values and the tentative egalitarian and political discourses therefore should not surprise us.

Within such national transformations, too, lie shifting definitions of political, economic, civil, social and reproductive rights. As Phillips (1991) points out, there is no necessary progression from say, civic to political to social rights (c.f. Marshall 1965). Different nations construct the notion of rights differently and at different periods. In Britain the establishment of the welfare state in the 1940s laid the ground for a floor of entitlements including social rights in housing, education and welfare. Such modern versions of social rights have only recently been introduced in the new egalitarianism of post-Salazar Portugal.

In sharp contrast, student teachers in Britain were brought up as 'Thatcher's children' – a generation that was told that 'the age of egalitarianism is over'(quoted in Arnot 1992). These relatively younger student teachers expressed concern over protecting individual freedom while at the same time valuing tolerance, suggesting a sensitivity to social diversity. Some have come through the period of their youth realizing the emphasis on market philosophies and materialistic values. They expressed concern about the lack of 'belonging' to a community. Their benchmarks in terms of citizenship values were not as clearly demarcated as those of their counterparts in the other countries. Working with concepts of diverse heterogeneous communities, they appear to be grappling both with egalitarian discourses and social movements of the past, as well as with current alienations from the present. There was little evidence from this small sample of the ability to articulate discourses of citizenship that were either personally meaningful or liberatory.

Without a programme of civic education similar to that provided in the other three countries studied, each new generation of student teachers in Britain is likely to come into the profession with insufficient training to articulate an intellectual, political framework for their social and moral concerns. The tensions between individual and collectivity were not easily articulated nor resolved. Our study revealed the weakness of political discursive frameworks among student teachers in Britain, suggesting that there might not be an adequate platform on which to build either a moral or an egalitarian project (whether feminist, multi-cultural or anti-racist).

Our data portrayed the relationship between the individual and the state as a permanent dynamic which remains at the core of the concept of citizenship. As feminist political theorists are all too aware, the traditions of Western European political thought have constructed an abstract individual in relation to abstracted sets of social relations, in particular the state. Perhaps because of the illusion of universalism implied by civil, political and social rights, the gendered nature of the concept of the individual and the gendered basis of the state (Connell 1990) are not generally exposed. For some female student teachers, such illusions are not sustained; for others, the abstraction allows them to ignore gender dynamics.

One of the key issues in the project was whether women could transform political life, whether women could offer alternative models for fulfilling the responsibilities of a citizen, or whether women should outline a role for themselves as citizens to ensure they achieve the rights owed to them. Our evidence suggests that feminist debates are still current and can be articulated in certain contexts. Some female student teachers attempted to extend the concept of citizenship to family life. The concept of a 'caring citizen' or a 'family builder' citizen was offered as the way forward. Yet, as we have seen, these concepts have tended to be sustained by a moral discourse that can fail to recognize exclusionary and oppressive practices in the state. Morality can emphasize the caring role of women, but without a transformation of the values of citizenship within political or egalitarian discourses, women are unlikely to achieve equal status and equal levels of participation to men.

Whether male ordered democratic discourses can be transformed by women successfully is a matter for debate. The moral, political and egalitarian values described by student teachers in relation to citizenship and the good citizen have major consequences for those who are seen to be outside the realm of citizenship – those who are constructed as 'other'.

Acknowledgements

This is an amended version of 'Teachers, gender

and the discourses of citizenship' published in *International Studies in Sociology of Education*, 6(1), 1996, pp. 3–35. Permission given with thanks.

The project was funded by the Human Resources, Education and Training Division of the European Commission (Stage 1 in 1994–5 and Stage 2 in 1995–6) under the 3rd Medium Term Community Action programme. We are grateful to the EC for their financial support and to the Leverhulme Trust for offering a research fellowship to M. Arnot to continue working on this theme.

We would like to thank in particular, Amanda Coffrey, Maria Dikalou, Pat Mahony, Sneh Shah, Daniella Tilbury, Xavier Ramblas, Xavier Bonal, Roula Ziogou, Christina Athanasiadou and Eleni Mavrogiorgou, Joanne Dillabough for her comments. The views represented here are entirely those of the authors.

Notes

1 The research is based on questionnaires of approximately 300 secondary student teachers in Greece, 375 in England and Wales, 103 in Catalonia, Spain and 180 in Portugal. Interviews were conducted with 14 teacher trainers in Greece and 40 in England and Wales, and with 9 Spanish and 10 Portuguese teacher trainers. In this report, the English and Welsh are referred to as British, and the Catalan as Spanish. The report of this research and its methodology is described in Arnot et al. (1995) and Tomé, Bonal and Araújo (1995). The original version of this chapter is Arnot et al. 1996.

2 Eight single-sex focus groups were conducted with male and female student teachers in England, five groups in Greece (two male, three female) and two groups in Spain. Each focus group had approximately five student teachers. The majority (75 per cent) of Greek male student teachers were between 30–40 years; the majority of female teachers were between 22–30 years. English and Welsh student teachers' average age was 24 years old.

3 See Pateman 1992, Phillips 1991, Dietz 1985, Rowbothan 1986 and Walby 1994.

References

Arnot, M. (1992) Feminism, education and the New Right. In M. Arnot and L. Barton (eds) *Voicing Concerns: Socio-*

Arnot, M., Deliyanni-Kouimtzis, K. and Ziogou, R. with Rowe, G. (1995) *Promoting Equality Awareness: Women as Citizens*. Final Report, June. Brussels: Equal Opportunities Unit, European Commission.

logical Perspectives on Educational Reforms. Oxford: Triangle Books.

Arnot, M., Araújo, H., Deliyanni, K., Rowe, G. and Tomé, A. (1996) Teachers, gender and the discourses of citizenship. *International Studies in Sociology of Education*, 6(1): 3–35.

Arnot, M., Araújo, H., Deliyanni, K., Ivinson, G. and Tomé, A. (1997) *Changing Femininity, Changing Citizenship*. Paper presented at the European Feminist Research Conference, Coimbra, Portugal.

Bourdieu, P. and Passeron, C. (1977) *Reproduction in Education, Society and Culture*. London: Sage.

Connell, R. W. (1990) The state, gender and sexual politics. *Theory and Society*, 19: 507–44.

Dietz, M. G. (1985) Citizenship with a feminist face: the problem of maternal thinking. *Political Theory*, 13: 19–37.

Gilbert, R. (1992) Citizenship, education and postmodernity. *British Journal of Sociology of Education*, 13: 51–68.

Heater, D. (1990) *Citizenship: The Civic Ideal in World History, Politics and Education*. London: Longman.

Marshall, T. H. (1965) Citizenship and social class. In T. H. Marshall *Class, Citizenship and Social Development*. New York: Anchor Books.

McLaughlin, T. H. (1992) Citizenship, diversity and education; a philosophical perspective. *Journal of Moral Education*, 21: 235–50.

Pateman, C. (1988) *The Sexual Contract*. Cambridge: Polity Press.

Pateman, C. (1992) Equality, difference, subordination: the politics of motherhood and women's citizenship. In G. Bock and B. James (eds) *Beyond Equality and Difference: Citizenship, Feminist Politics and Female Subjectivity*. London: Routledge.

Phillips, A. (1991) Citizenship and feminist theory. In G. Andrews (ed.) *Citizenship*. London: Lawrence and Wishart.

Rawls, J. (1972) *A Theory of Justice*. Oxford: Oxford University Press.

Rowbothan, S. (1986) Feminism and democracy. In D. Held and C. Pollitt (eds) *New Forms of Democracy*. London: Sage.

Sultana, R. G. (1995) A uniting Europe, a dividing education? Supranationalism, Euro-centrism and the curriculum. *International Studies in Sociology of Education*, 5: 3–23.

Tomé, A., Bonal, X. and Araújo, H. (1995) *Promoting Equality Awareness; Women as Citizens*. Final Report. Brussels: European Commission.

Walby, S. (1994) Is citizenship gendered? *Sociology*, 28: 379–95.

Wexler, P. (1990) Citizenship in the semiotic society. In B. Turner (ed.) *Theories of Modernity and Postmodernity*. London: Sage.

Yuval-Davis, N. (1992) Women as citizens. In A. Ward, J. Gregory and N. Yuval-Davis (eds) *Women and Citizenship in Europe*. London: Trentham.

21 Gender and Education for Citizenship: Promoting Educational Values and Values Education in Greece

KIKI DELIYANNI-KOUIMTZIS

Introduction

During the last decade a new interest in the notion of citizenship has emerged among academics: in international writings political scientists, sociologists, psychologists and, more recently, educators discuss, analyse and reconceptualize the meanings of citizenship. Beyond the theoretical discussions, new perspectives and approaches are proposed, especially in the field of education, with the aim of socializing new citizens in a way that will enable them to live and act according to the requirements of democratic societies.

In these recent analyses, there are attempts to redefine the notion of citizenship. Many return to Marshall's definition (1950: 28–9), who saw citizenship as a 'status bestowed on those who are full members of a community'. All who possess the status are equal and enjoy civil, political and social rights. On the other hand, Heater (1990) argues the need for a comprehensive definition of the term and proposes the concept of multiple citizenship, which includes the elements of identity and virtue in addition to the legal, political and social aspects of the status. Education is an integral part of the concept, since it is considered to be indispensable for the preparation of the young citizen.

Inclusion and a sense of togetherness and of belonging are the feelings mostly associated with the identity of citizenship (Heater 1990), whereas the real citizen is defined by his or her possibilities for active social and political participation. In this frame, whereas much of the citizenship literature has traditionally focused on inclusion, more radical contemporary writings tend to portray citizenship as a force for exclusion, which creates non- or partial citizens (Lister 1995).

Feminist analyses of citizenship, focusing on the downgraded position of women in all societies and their obvious under-representation in the important decision-making processes of contemporary democracies, point out that these exclusionary tendencies are inherently gendered (Phillips 1993). Furthermore, it is argued that the existing approaches and forms of citizenship could function as constraints to democracy's attempts to include women (Phillips 1993, Pateman 1989). As Arnot (1995) points out, if one considers the position of the female population in different aspects of life in contemporary democratic societies, it becomes evident that there is still much to be done for women to achieve full citizenship. Full democratic participation and social justice for instance, are goals yet to be achieved in the advanced modern economies. Therefore, it can be argued that until European democracies achieve full economic and political equality for men and women, they will be considered as 'partial' or 'immature' democracies (Phillips 1993, Arnot 1995).

According to feminist writers, for women to achieve full citizenship, the concept of democracy itself needs to be re-examined (Arnot 1994, Arnot et al. 1995). For some, change calls for democratic principles and practices to be extended to the family and the private sphere of personal and intimate relations, whereas for some others 'it would involve rethinking the ethical basis of western liberal democratic values and the "abstract individualism" which sustained it' (Arnot et al. 1995: 26).

Schooling is thought to be among the most powerful agencies to produce social change, in the sense that one of its goals is to educate citizens with a democratic conscience. Education for citizenship therefore becomes a key issue for the development and the promotion of values that have to do with gender equality in contemporary democratic societies.

Gender and education for citizenship

Education for citizenship is the basic societal means whereby each new generation of youth is expected to acquire the knowledge, skills and values needed for its members to become democratic citizens (Dynneson and Gross 1991). Buck and Inman (1995), having in mind McLaughlin's (1992) minimalist and maximalist view of citizenship, describe two models of citizenship education. According to their approach, the minimalist model aims to provide information about society and to socialize young people into a given and taken for granted social order. It stresses duties and responsibilities and has little to do with developing pupils' critical thinking. On the other hand, the maximalist model has to do with empowerment and with the development of pupils' ability to take control over their own lives. Critical thinking, self-awareness and understanding on a wider global and societal level are among the goals to be achieved through this model of education for citizenship.

In their efforts to implement social change through education, feminist writers tend to consider education for citizenship as a useful context for the promotion of a more democratic model of schooling 'in which teachers and pupils could reflect critically and openly on the nature of the society in which they live' (Arnot et al. 1995: 11). Here, education for citizenship, instead of functioning as a 'male narrative' (Arnot et al. 1996: 5), could be used to introduce the concept of gender equality as an important element of social justice (Kelly 1993, Troyna and Vincent 1995).

How could the existing models of citizenship education be modified, broadened and enriched, in order to include this new dimension of democratic schooling? Arnot (1995) suggests a range of strategies and approaches. One perspective focuses on the concept of democracy in the family and emphasizes the importance of freedom in personal life. The promotion of human rights through education – as for instance women's right to live free of male violence and to control their own sexuality – could be the key-issue in this approach. A second strategy focuses on the re-conceptualization and promotion of democratic values. From this perspective, education for citizenship should be broadened to include not only male values of the public sphere, for instance competition, individualism, militarism and nationalism, but female ethics of caring, empathy, fusion, anti-élitism and harmony as well. Motherhood as a value and women's concern for social equality should be parts of this broader model of democratic citizenship education.

Trying to introduce change through education is not always possible and some would argue that it is in contradiction to the role of educational systems. During the last two decades feminist action research has been used in schools in order to introduce strategies and intervention practices to promote gender equality and equal opportunities for men and women in society. Their results have been ambivalent, sometimes limited, or even contradictory, but in general encouraging, since they succeeded in making gender relations a central topic in education and in involving teachers in the process of gender equality (Holland 1993). Today we are conscious that any reform in education, and, more specifically, any change concerning gender relations, is doomed to failure, if it does not include strategies focusing on teachers' education. In this sense, if education for citizenship must contain a critical dimension, especially in relation to gender issues, then, by implication, the professional training of teachers will need to be structured accordingly. As Arnot et al. (1995) point out,

> if the school system was to promote a form of democracy, in which women could more easily participate, then a profession of teachers would be needed, who could both reflect critically on the historical and contemporary position of women in society, as well as being trained and sufficiently skilled to create classrooms and learning opportunities that are equally and democratically open to both male and female students.   (p. 12)

Our project on 'Promoting equality awareness: women as citizens', aimed to promote a new perspective on education for citizenship, focusing on teachers' initial and in-service training. Before proceeding to the presentation of the results, let's see how the Greek educational system currently introduces the principles of citizenship education in the secondary curriculum and in teachers' education.

Education for citizenship in Greece

Citizenship education in Greek secondary schools can be introduced through a range of different courses: Ancient Greek Literature, Philosophy, Education for the Citizen. The Ministry of Education perceives, at least theoretically, that possibilities exist within such courses for the promotion of civic education, since in the teachers' guide for humanities courses in secondary schools it includes objectives that are clearly reminiscent of the aims of Education for Citizenship. According to these objectives, during the Ancient Greek courses, for instance, the pupils should acquire 'the right civic education and a sense of responsibility' and learn 'about the democratic ideology', in order to become 'active members of the social community' and to contribute 'to the construction of a free and democratic life'. In philosophy courses, pupils should follow 'the philosophical questions from the beginning'.

On the other hand, there are two special courses in the secondary curriculum entitled 'Education for the Citizen: the components of the democratic regime' and 'Education for the Citizen: principles of political science and the components of the democratic regime' taught to pupils aged 14 and 17 years old respectively. These courses aim to teach 'the rights, the responsibilities and all other kinds of relations that are included in social life' and 'to inform tomorrow's citizens about contemporary forms of government, its rules and ways of functioning'.

All these courses are usually taught by humanities teachers. Consequently, humanities teachers are dominant in schools, given the fact that in the first three years of secondary school, for instance, out of a total of 90 hours per week, 33 hours (over one-third) are taken up with humanities subjects. The same applies to the last three years of secondary school.

As to future teachers' initial training, secondary school teachers for language and humanities study in the Faculty of Philosophy, i.e. either in the Departments of Ancient and Modern Greek Language and Literature, or in the Department of History and Archaeology, or in the Department of Philosophy and Education. During their undergraduate studies they are obliged to study a great number of Ancient Greek texts and extracts. Many of these texts will be taught later in schools, either from translation or from the original. There are also many courses on ancient Greek and contemporary European Philosophy. Student teachers following other specializations are given the opportunity to attend some of these courses:

however their choices rarely cover more than a small number of these options as part of their degree.

Potentially, therefore, humanities teachers in Greece have the opportunity to consider many dimensions of citizenship, through ancient texts, discussions of civic education and democratic ideology. Most such courses, however, when taught in schools, emphasize the literary and linguistic elaboration of these texts rather than the philosophical and political thinking about democracy, which lies imbedded within. Consequently, experience suggests that, in practice, teachers often abandon the meanings of the ancient Greek texts, losing, thus, a unique opportunity to show the roots of contemporary social and political problems and to discuss in depth democratic values and ideology. It is evident that gender issues are not a matter of concern for the secondary curriculum.

The above discussion shows that before proposing any change in teachers' training programmes and in the secondary curriculum, we should become aware of future teachers' views on education for citizenship and gender issues. The questions that need to be answered could be formulated as follows:

1 What are future teachers' attitudes towards the promotion of values and change through education in general and education for the citizen in particular?
2 What is the notion of education for citizenship that they are working with? How important do they consider citizenship education for the democratic socialization of tomorrow's citizens? And what is the model of citizenship education they propose?
3 Do future teachers include gender equality issues in their analyses of education for citizenship?
4 How much do they see themselves involved in the process of promoting the values of democratic education in schools? What are their educational needs?
5 Are there any gender differences among future teachers, in the way they perceive citizenship education (including gender equality)?

The research presented below tries to give an answer to the above questions.

The research

Aims, research design, subjects and methodology

The central aim of the research project 'Promoting equality awareness: women as citizens'[1] was the development of training material which, by promoting equality awareness, would introduce the notion of democratic citizenship in initial and in-service training of secondary school teachers. The project was divided into three stages:

1 Equality awareness: investigation of student teachers' perception of women's position in society;
2 The development of teacher training material;
3 Evaluation and dissemination.

During the investigation stage, a survey was carried out in all four countries that participated in the project. The primary focus of this research was secondary student teachers at the end of their professional training course. Quantitative and qualitative data were gathered through semi-structured questionnaires and single-sex focus group discussions. The research aimed to investigate:

- student teachers' awareness, values and representations of women's position in private and public spheres and in paid work;
- their views of how schools could promote the values of democracy and equality;
- the discourses of citizenship they work with;
- their notion of education for citizenship in secondary schools;
- their educational and training needs, in order to become able to introduce education for democratic citizenship (including gender equality) in their teaching.

Participating in the research were 298 secondary school student teachers, who had followed a 3 month initial training stage in Teacher Training Institutions in three sites in Greece in October 1994. Among them, 110 were men, mostly (61.8 per cent) mathematic and science teachers, whereas 188 were women, mostly (70.7 per cent) humanities and language teachers.

The research combined two methodologies. First, a questionnaire was administered to the participants. The questions asked about knowledge, perceptions and representations of the roles and the position of men and women in three spheres: public

life, private and domestic life and paid work. Second, focus group interviews, lasting approximately 1 hour were carried out with student teachers in each of the three teacher training institutions.[2] Semi-structured questions asked about the nature of citizenship, rights and equality, gender equality in public and private life and in paid work, the importance of education in citizenship and gender equality, and the perception of the role of the teacher in educating the citizen. Two all-male and three all-female groups were conducted, and in each case the interviewer was a female researcher. Five persons participated in each group. Participants had all completed the questionnaire and had volunteered to discuss some of the issues raised in it. The discussions were audiotaped and later transcribed in full.

This chaper reports findings from (a) the part of the questionnaires relating to student teachers' views on the aims of education in general and of education for citizenship more specifically and (b) from the part of the focus group interviews related to education for citizenship.

Values in education and education for citizenship

Educational aims

When asked about the aims of education, the majority of student teachers recognized all the aims listed in the questionnaire as important or very important for schooling. On the whole, there was perceived to be a clear need to support social reform. The majority agreed, for example, that tackling class and gender for inequality was important. (See Table 21.1 for the questionnaire results.) Of Greek student teachers 89.3 per cent agreed that a primary aim of school should be breaking down social class inequalities. A smaller percentage (77.3 per cent) thought that equality among different ethnic groups was important.

Again, a very high proportion of student teachers in the sample felt that it was important for students to learn how to be critical of the image of men and women presented in the mass media. They thought that schools should promote respect for women's work within the family, and encourage girls' participation in public life.

Promotion of family stability was considered too by 83.9 per cent of the sample to be an important aim of education. But only 62.5 per cent of student teachers agreed that sexual morality should be promoted within the educational process of schooling. It seems as if family stability rather than sexual morality should be the goal of schooling for these new teachers.

Table 21.1 Educational aims considered *important* or *very important*

School should aim to	Student teachers (N = 298)
1 Break down social class inequalities	89.3%
2 Encourage students to question media representations of men and women	88.0%
3 Promote respect for women's work in the family	86.3%
4 Encourage girls to participate in public life	82.9%
5 Promote family stability	86.3%
6 Promote equality between different ethnic groups	77.3%
7 Improve men's involvement in domestic work	76.6%
8 Encourage boys to consider careers in the caring professions	67.2%
9 Promote sexual morality	62.5%
10 Encourage women into non-traditional occupations	60.9%
11 Promote men as the main breadwinners	6.4%

Even though student teachers appeared to be interested in changing women's role in society through school, a comparatively lower percentage of them agreed that it is important to change the traditional structures of men's and women's transition from school to the labour market. Only 67.2 per cent of the sample thought that it is important for schools to promote boys in caring professions, while only 60.9 per cent agreed that promoting girls in non-traditional occupations was an important aim.

The extent to which social reform is acceptable to the new generation of teachers in Greece can be seen in the fact that 93.6 per cent thought that schools should *not* promote the idea of men as the main breadwinners. However, only 76.6 per cent thought that schools should encourage men's participation in domestic work. These views represent in some ways the contradictory range of social forces currently at work in the family. While a large number of women are actually in the labour market, they are not relieved of their traditional duties within the family, since men do not participate adequately in domestic work.

On the whole, the sample of student teachers seemed enthusiastic about the promotion of equality and optimistic about the possibilities of intervention by schools. What we do not really know, however, is whether student teachers feel that this can be done within the limits of the Greek educational system, which most of them know very well. It is also not clear from the quantitative data whether they think of themselves as capable of achieving those aims.

When asked about the specific educational aims of education for citizenship, the Greek student teachers emphasized the importance of gaining a personal sense of responsibility and participating in decision-making. Looking at Table 21.2, we can see that over half of the student teachers agreed with the importance of the first two aims. A smaller proportion thought that education for citizenship was about teaching critical and analytical thinking and a very small proportion indeed (26.4 per cent and 20.1 per cent) thought that education for citizenship should involve issues to do with legal issues and financial, political and social structures.

The emphasis on the whole was on personal development in order to participate actively in society, rather than to inform students about the law, the economy and politics. Although a large percentage of student teachers supported the idea that schools should break down social class inequality,

Table 21.2 Aims of education for citizenship

	Whole sample (N = 298)	Male students (N = 110)	Female students (N = 188)
1 Encourage personal responsibility for a healthy society	58.8%	59.09%	58.5%
2 Encourage active participation in decision-making	53.5%	55.4%	52.1%
3 Teach critical and analytical thinking	41.8%	50.0%	36.7%
4 Inform about legal rights and responsibilities	26.4%	21.8%	29.2%
5 Teach about financial, political and social structures	20.1%	23.6%	18.08%
6 Promote harmony between different social groups	18.4%	14.5%	20.7%

they did not see the promotion of social harmony between different groups as a main aim of a course on citizenship.

Student teachers had seemed optimistic in their replies about the possibilities of effective school intervention in social problems, but they themselves were less confident about their ability to teach about various social issues. Only 4 out of 10 felt confident to teach about issues of social class and family and even fewer (3 out of 10) felt confident about teaching on working and public life. Their greatest insecurity seemed to come in relation to ethnic minorities (2 out of 10) and legal rights (only 1 out of 10 felt confident). Statistically significant differences occurred between male and female student teachers. A much smaller proportion of female student teachers felt confident to teach such topics, apart from family life and legal rights, where their answers reflected those of male student teachers.

What might be a problem for student teachers is their ignorance of Greek society. The majority of student teachers (88 per cent and 89 per cent of men and women respectively) had received no training on gender issues during their university education. Here is an interesting quote from one female student teacher:

> I have never been taught such topics, thus, I have never had a chance to elaborate on them or to study more and in depth. Consequently, I feel insecure in case I'll have to teach those issues and I won't be able to convince anybody.

Tables 21.1 and 21.2 present only a rough outline of student teachers' views on the most important aims of education and of education for citizenship and on the potential of the school to promote change. In addition, these quantitative findings give us some information about student teachers' lack of confidence in introducing these topics in their courses, offering, however limited possibilities for further analysis.

One of the aims of the qualitative part of the research was the in-depth investigation of the notion of education for citizenship that student teachers are working with.[3] More precisely, the goal of this investigation was to find out what education for citizenship means for student teachers, how they perceive this education in the context of the educational process and what they suggest for this education to become more efficient and useful. The following section of this chapter reports on the findings of the groups discussions that deal with the above issues.

Education for citizenship, gender equality and student teachers' educational needs

Student teachers of our sample in their majority had some work experience in secondary schools, which meant that they already had the chance to consider the Greek school system and education for citizenship. Consequently, what they discussed during the focus groups, is, in most cases, based not on abstract expectations or theoretical assumptions, but on first-hand experiences concerning school reality. This gave them the opportunity to develop realistic approaches, but eliminated the possibilities of constructing future visions that are so important in education.

1 Discussion arising from the second part of the focus group questionnaire has revealed how student teachers understand 'education for citizenship'. Once again gender differences between male and female teachers appear; interestingly, we could only gather answers concerning this topic from the female student teachers' groups, since male student teachers avoided expressing their view. According to female student teachers' answers, education for citizenship can be seen as:

A chance to inform young people about their rights and, especially, their responsibilities as citizens. With this aim, young people should learn about the content of the constitution and the law, and the functions of the administrative apparatus of the state, in order to become effective citizens, and to feel like members of society. The emphasis here is on the school's role as an agent of socialization:

> It is very important for everybody to learn the rights and the responsibilities of the citizen. (female student teacher)

> It is very important, we have to pay attention, which we haven't done, it is important for the citizens, for these children that will come into the society, to know, let's say, what rights and what responsibilities they have, it is very important for their life. (female student teacher)

> It is a very good opportunity, rather a motivation, . . . for pupils' integration in the society.   (female student teacher)

The child has to learn [in the context of lessons or discussion on citizenship] to feel as a part of a whole, that she/he is not just a unit.   (female student teacher)

2   A chance to sensitize young people in topics concerning racism, environmental issues, and women's issues, and to abolish stereotypes and prejudices:

and what we discuss now, we can discuss in different words with the children, we can discuss about environment and racism and socialization and we can even develop some other issues, like women's issues for instance.   (female student teacher)

We must do it. I have tried to discuss about these topics with my pupils and I have realized that male pupils reject gender equality . . . I was surprised . . . in our days . . .   (female student teacher)

Many times these young women who participated in the focus group discussions pointed out that they wouldn't like to separate issues on gender equality from equality in general. As one of them said:

By the way is it only gender that interests us? Because I think that what we want is a school that will be sensitive to the needs of different social groups or, in general, citizens' categories, that experience inequality. In the same way I would deal with racism, I would deal with gender inequality. The term [racism] is an umbrella that can cover a lot of other things.   (female student teacher)

In another case, women's position or roles are seen from a different perspective:

I think that we have to pass the message, not only about gender equivalence, because I don't agree totally with the term of equality, but in addition, the child has to learn to recognize women's contribution and work within the family. Because we are always talking about the working woman while the value of the housewife's work is underestimated. But this woman works a lot as well, she contributes to the upbringing of the children, which is very important.   (female student teacher)

3   For a group of female student teachers, however, education for citizenship is not relevant for such issues. For them 'education for citizenship' is an opportunity to give young people the possibility of challenging the dominant ideologies, to develop critical thinking and to become able to contest the social order. And, in some cases, to learn to resist the state, to protest and to claim their rights. This view can be in conflict with the traditional goal of education, which is to pass on to the new generation the attitudes, values and beliefs of the society. Student teachers are aware of this. What they mean is that, despite the aims of education, the teacher by herself should try to be radical and challenging.

But the notion of the good citizen, as it is determined by the course and the official curriculum, means the individual who follows the official attitudes of the society, the established order. The teacher, however, should be able to offer the children the opportunity to criticize and to challenge.

and then, these young people will know clearly in what cases they will have the right as citizens to prosecute the State in court, because for example there are not enough hospitals or good motorways etc.

This idea of the citizen that has to learn how to protect him or herself from the arbitrariness of the state, and how to criticize or to dispute the state is very common among Greek citizens, and arises more than once in this research. It comes out, for example, in the group discussion and interviews from the quotes of some of the student teachers and trainers who discussed the concept of the 'critical citizen' (Arnot et al. 1996). On the other hand, quantitative research data (Arnot at al. 1995, Deliyanni et al. 1997) show that despite the fact that men are seen to exercise a high level of control over political decision-making, they are not described as 'powerful' in public life. An explanation for this might be the fact that people in Greece feel in conflict with the state (the state is an enemy that they cannot control), and they have to find ways to gain from this conflict.

How important do student teachers think a course or discussions on citizenship in general and gender in particular is? How important do they think it is to pay attention to such topics in the school? Male and female student teachers have different points of view. Three different groups of answers arose from this question:

i   Answers that agree that it is very important for

the school to include in its content the above topics in any form (as a course or as opportunities for discussion). Only female student teachers expressed this point of view.

> Yes, without any doubt
> Yes, I think it is very important
> Yes, it is very important, I believe that there are so many things to discuss!

ii Answers that declare that the everyday school practice very often offers the opportunity for discussions in such topics, so there is no need to provide special courses or to organize discussions. It is enough that teachers show children that they see them as equals, and this is the best way to teach them about equality. Only male student teachers expressed this point of view.

> You always have the opportunity to discuss those things, in one way or in another.
> You pass the message with your behaviour.... You don't have to have a course for that.
> There is no need to organize discussions, the only thing we have to do is to show to the children that they all are equal, that we don't discriminate.

iii A third group of answers say that these topics are very important, but should not be discussed in a course. Both male and female student teachers used this argument. They are not in favour of a special course because

- they would not want such topics to be discussed in the formal atmosphere of a course,
- because they don't think that this is a matter of knowledge,
- because they don't know who would be able to teach such a course and
- they know that a course can work in a negative way for teachers and pupils.

Here are some of the student teachers' views:

> I don't agree with a course, I am afraid, because I don't know who will teach it and what he or she will pass to the children ... A course always creates attitudes. (female student teacher)

> It should not be a course, it is not a matter of knowledge, children see a course with suspicion. (female student teacher)

To force a child to learn these things would not work, a compulsory course would not work positively. A course with evaluation etc. would not have any effect. (male student teacher)

> We would experience a compulsory course as we experience all such courses. (male student teacher)

In many cases, student teachers see difficulties in any attempt to introduce discussions or courses on citizenship and gender equality in the school. From their quotes we could identify three groups of constraints:

1 The first group of constraints have to do with the reactions of families or the community that are extremely traditional, or the traditional attitudes of the pupils, especially males, who have been socialized by their families according to stereotyped patterns. This view has been expressed by student teachers living and working in rural areas or small towns.

> There are many difficulties, especially in small towns. Issues concerning gender equality or women's rights create reactions. (female student teacher)

> It is a matter of how the family of the child will react. This is the worse enemy. The child is at school for six hours and at home for the rest. (male student teacher)

> Last year ... we had to clean the class ... and who is going to clean? Girls will wash the floor. Boys did not want to clean or sweep. They were ready to leave everything to the girls. We started to discuss it in the class and then a boy stands up and spoke so impertinently! 'What!' he said, 'we men come here to clean the school? We don't do this work at home!' ... By the end the boy took the mop ... 'I don't know how to do it', he said. And I told a girl, 'give him, do I know, give him a private course of how to wash the floor' ... And by the end he cleaned. But I imagine that this child saw it as an obligation and I am sure that he went home and complained that 'they made us clean the classroom'. (female student teacher)

2 A second set of constraints have to do with the lack of knowledge. Student teachers complained that they are not specialized to teach or to discuss these topics, since they have never been

informed about national and European laws, constitutional rights, administration and so on:

> I personally don't know the constitution, and I know that I should not ignore such things. Why do we ignore it? Why has nobody told us that this or that is our right? We don't need to learn all the laws, it is enough to know that the information is there and we can get it whenever we need.   (female student teacher)

3 A third set of constraints have to do with the difficulties over the curriculum and with the fact that pupils in the last two years of the secondary school are much too absorbed by their university entrance examinations.

> As a mathematician I am hard pressed by the curriculum, by the fact that I have to finish a specific number of chapters.   (male student teachers)

> What can you say to the pupils, who are so anxious about their examination? 'Look here, because, if you don't, you will have problems as citizens in the future?   (female student teacher)

This attitude of the student teachers is very much related to the fact that the last three years of secondary school in Greece, the so-called 'Lyceum' has lost its independence and is influenced by the demands of university entrance examinations. During these three years teachers and pupils concentrate on the content of the examinations and are interested only in those courses in which pupils will be examined. Few care about the rest of the curriculum.

How then do student teachers think that education for citizenship (including gender issues) should be introduced in the curriculum? The majority of the student teachers who participated in the focus groups have no clear idea about this question, either because they have never thought about it, or because they find the issue so important that they don't want to waste time by discussing how to teach it. Their view is that in any case, the most important point is to introduce the topic, it does not matter how. Two different points of view have been developed.

i   There is a tendency to think that education for citizenship and gender equality should be diffused across the whole curriculum and discussed either in all, or in some courses.

> It is better if it [education for citizenship] can be discussed in all courses. I mean, if teachers of every specialization could try with similar interventions, instead of having a course on education of the citizen. As far as I know, the results are not so good.   (male student teacher)

> And why not interdisciplinary?   (female student teacher)

> We can pass the message through the courses of History, Modern Greek Literature, Ancient Greek, through everything.   (female student teacher)

ii   However some student teachers (who all happened to be female), think that, despite all difficulties, these issues need to be introduced from within a specific course, because, as one of them said,

> I think it is a good idea to have a specific course, because, for example, the mathematician, if he has to finish a number of chapters, he will not have enough time to think about those things, he will not do it.

Student teachers also expressed very interesting views concerning the teaching methodology of education for citizenship. The unanimous opinion was that traditional teaching methods are inappropriate for education for citizenship and gender issues. Discussions, debates, workshops and working groups were some of the methods student teachers proposed as the most efficient ways to introduce the topic and most agreed that examinations and grading do not match very well with the content.

Despite the fact that the vast majority proposed permeation of the ideas of citizenship and gender equality in all aspects of the educational process and across the whole curriculum, they don't see themselves as responsible for undertaking the task of teaching this issue. The majority of student teachers seem to be afraid of the idea and agreed that a 'specialist' should be solely responsible to deal with education for citizenship. This attitude promotes the answer to the question of whether student teachers think of themselves capable of achieving reform and intervention through education. The answer is that, despite their optimistic view about the possibilities for changing the society from within the school, student teachers don't see themselves involved in this procedure. On the contrary, they seem to be rather afraid of the idea:

> I believe that we need a specialist, a specialist we need for sure. When our programme is so demanding, and you ask me to do these things, I cannot waste my time. (male student teacher)

> This work can be accomplished only by sociologists, they only are aware of all this knowledge. They only can answer pupils' questions. I think that sociologists are the best suited to teach those issues. (male student teacher)

> The teacher who will teach all this must be a specialist. (female student teacher)

> The most suited teacher must be specialized. I would like a sociologist to come, for example, to give a talk and to analyse research on these topics. (female student teacher)

It is very characteristic that not even humanities teachers have realized how many opportunities they have in their courses to discuss with their pupils the notions of citizenship and of gender equality. The view that teaching about citizenship and equality is not their job, is probably the reason why the participants in the focus group discussions were not able to articulate any needs in relation to their initial and in-service training.

Conclusions

In summary, the results presented above show that student teachers work with different notions of education for citizenship, using either the minimalist or the maximalist model. Depending on which notion they work with, they think that educating citizens does not mean only informing them about the function of the state, but should, at the same time, teach them the ideology of equality (including gender equality) and/or a critical attitude towards the state and the law. For the majority of student teachers, however, gender and women's issues are not included *ipso jure* and as a matter of course in their perception of education for citizenship.

Student teachers in our sample don't see education for citizenship as a formal course, but rather as an opportunity and a reason for discussions spread throughout the whole curriculum. The teaching methods employed to approach the topic should be different from the formal ones and include discussion, debates and work in groups. Finally, despite the fact that they are optimistic about the role of the school in promoting social change, student teachers don't see themselves as the agents of this change, nor as the appropriate persons to approach the issue of citizenship in the classroom. Thus, they ask for experts to undertake this task, denying their own role as socializers and change producers. In this context they were not aware of any training needs.

In addition, this data showed once again major differences between male and female student teachers. We were able to see that female student teachers were more able to elaborate the meanings of citizenship, seemed to be much more involved and personally interested in the process, and could formulate discourses on gender, citizenship and education. They used personal accounts in their descriptions, presenting their experience of the everyday educational praxis. Male student teachers, on the other hand, appeared to be more distant about the topic. They showed that they did not feel that education for citizenship was a matter of great concern for them, since what primarily interested them seemed to be the content of their own specialisms.

As we have already pointed out, training needs *per se* did not emerge from qualitative data, since the participating student teachers avoided expressing their demands. However, we detected an important training need that concerns all future teachers, which is to help them realize that the notion of citizenship includes the problematic of women's position in society, gender equality and gender relations. In addition, what becomes evident from the group discussion on education for citizenship is the fact that student teachers, and more precisely the humanities teachers (those that will teach ancient and modern Greek, history, education of the citizen, philosophy), have not realized how close to the topic of citizenship their specialization is. From their discussion it is obvious that they have not understood that *they* are the specialists and the experts they ask for. An evident training need then, is to make these humanities teachers, who are mostly women, focus their attention on those aspects of their initial education that bring them closer to the issues and values of citizenship, and to provide them with the appropriate feminist perspectives that will give them the opportunity to approach the content of their courses and of the schoolbooks in a critical way in the classroom. In proposing new perspectives on initial and in-service teacher training, we should always have in mind the declaration of this young female student teacher below:

> Every teacher should be aware of these issues of equality and democracy at every moment and be able to discuss them with her pupils.

Acknowledgements

This project has been funded by the Task Force/ Human Resources Division of the European Commission (DG XXII) as one of the projects put forward by the Equal Opportunities Unit. We are grateful to the Equal Opportunities Unit and EC for their financial support.

Each national project team had a number of members who worked on coordinating or participating in the research design and data collection. I would like to thank in particular Roula Ziogou, Maria Dikaiou, Eleni Mavrogiorgou and Christina Athanassiadou.

In addition I would like to thank Professor Markoulis, who proposed that I write this chapter for this series.

Notes

1　This project has been financed by the Commission of the European Communities in four countries, England, Greece, Spain and Portugal.
2　For a more detailed presentation of the methodology of the research, description of the sample population and statistical analyses of the quantitative data, see Arnot et al. 1995.
3　For an analysis of student teachers' discourses of citizenship and their representations of masculinity and femininity see Arnot et al. 1996, Deliyanni-Kouimtzis and Athanassiadis (1997) and Deliyanni-Kouimtzis (1997).

References

Arnot, M. (1994) Feminism and democratic education. In J. Santome Tores (ed.) *Rethinking Education*. Madrid: Murata Press.

Arnot, M. (1995) Feminism and democracy. *Proceedings of the Conference Education and Equality of Opportunities*. Athens (translated into Greek). 302–5.

Arnot, M., Deliyanni, K. and Ziogou, R. (1995) *Promoting Equality Awareness: Women as Citizens*. Final Report, Brussels: EC.

Arnot, M., Araújo, H., Deliyanni, K., Rowe, G. and Tomé, A. (1996) Teachers, gender and the discourses of citizenship. *International Studies in Sociology of Education*, 6(1): 3–35.

Buck, M. and Inman, S. (1995) Citizenship education – more than a forgotten cross curricular theme? In S. Inmann and M. Buck (eds) *Adding Value? Schools Responsibility for Pupils' Personal Development*. London: Heinemann.

Deliyanni-Kouimtzis, K. (1997) 'It's our fault . . .': The discourses of gender relations in the frame of a discussion on citizenship. *Proceedings of the conference: Women, Power and Citizenship*, Athens, 8–9 February 1996. Athens: Delphini (in Greek).

Deliyanni-Kouimtzis, K. and Athanassiadis, C. (1997) Teachers' representations of gender. In K. Deliyanni and R. Ziogou (eds) *Fylo kai Scholiki Praxi*. Thessaloniki: Vanias (in Greek).

Deliyanni, V., Ziogou, S. and Athanassiadis, C. (1997) Promoting the democratization in teachers' education: gender and citizenship dimensions. *Abstracts of the Seventh International Conference of the Greek Educational Society: Educational Research, Tendencies and Perspectives*. Athens: Ellinika Grammata.

Dynneson, T. and Gross, R. (1991) The educational perspective. In R. Gross and T. Dynneson (eds) *Social Science Perspectives on Citizenship Education*. New York: Teachers College Press: 1–42.

Heater, D. (1990) *Citizenship*. London: Longman.

Holland, J. (1993) Studying youth: research on gender and youth in Britain. In K. Deliyanni and R. Ziogou (eds) *Ekpaidefsi kai Fylo*. Thessaloniki: Vanias (translated into Greek).

Kelly, E. (1993) Gender issues in education for citizenship. In K. Verma and P. Pumfrey (eds) *Cross Curricular Contexts: Themes and Dimensions in Secondary Schools*. London: Falmer Press: 144–59.

Lister, R. (1995) Whose citizenship? The gendering of social rights and obligations. Paper presented at the European Sociological Association Conference, European Societies: Fusion or Fission? Budapest, 30 August–2 September.

Marshall, T. H. (1950) *Citizenship and Social Class and Other Essays*. Cambridge: Cambridge University Press.

McLaughlin, T. (1992) Citizenship, diversity and education: a philosophical perspective. *Journal of Moral Education*, 21(3): 121–45

Pateman, C. (1989) *The Disorder of Women*. Cambridge: Blackwell.

Phillips, A. (1993) *Democracy and Difference*. London: Polity Press.

Troyna, B. and Vincent C. (1995) The discourses of social justice in education. *Discourse*, 16(2): 149–66.

22 The Aims of Civic Education in a Multi-cultural Democracy

JAN STEUTEL AND BEN SPIECKER

1 Formulation of the problem

Suppose we are living, like most people in the Western world, in a society that is both liberal, democratic and multi-cultural. Suppose, further, that we are deeply devoted to the basic values of our society. And suppose, finally, that we want the younger generation to grow up into adults that are as strongly committed to those fundamental values as we are. What, then, should be our central aims of civic education?

In this chapter we formulate an answer to this question which is, in our view, plausible and tenable, though also pretty sketchy and somewhat dogmatic. First, in Section 2, we clarify the meaning of the constituent terms, in particular 'civic education', 'liberal democracy' and 'multi-cultural'. Next, in Section 3, we will argue that the aims of civic education in a liberal-democratic and multi-cultural society involve a particular group of *moral* virtues. Conceptions of civic education that do not accept these virtues as aims, or regard these aims as appropriate only for a particular kind of multi-cultural democracy, are, in our opinion, underdemanding. As an important example of such a view, we discuss a recently published paper of Yael Tamir. Thereafter, in Section 4, we defend the view that civic education in a multi-cultural liberal democracy also implies the cultivation of *intellectual* virtues. However, conceptions of civic education that stretch these virtues to the private sphere, are, in our view overdemanding. Amy Gutmann's theory of democratic education will be introduced as a major example of such a conception. In the final section we shall summarize our view and rebut the objection that our answer to the central question does not take the diversity of a multi-cultural society seriously enough.

2 Preliminary clarifications

Civic education may be typified by the slogan '*by* and *for* the state'. By the state: if we are claiming that a certain part of moral education should be regarded as civic education, we are placing the supreme authority over that part in the hands of the state. Here the word 'state' refers to a complex set of institutions whose function it is to define and impose collectively binding decisions, in particular by making, applying, interpreting and enforcing the law. Claiming that the state has supreme authority over a specific part of education implies that such institutions are assigned the *right* to interfere, for instance by making laws that introduce compulsory subjects or by enforcing these laws with the help of Schools Inspectorate. What is more, the claim at issue implies that the institutions of the state are also regarded as *responsible* for the indicated part of moral education. The state is not only entitled to intervene, it is also obliged to do so, if necessary.

Civic education should also be conceived as education *for* the state. This part of the slogan can best be explained by introducing the concept of citizenship. Just like being a parent or a teacher, being a citizen is having a certain role or position. But unlike parenthood or teachership, having the role of citizen is not related to being a member of the family or the school, but to being a member of the state. In this context, however, the word 'state' has a slightly different meaning. In the preceding paragraph we used this term to refer to a composite set of public institutions. But if we say that citizenship is membership of the state, we are using the term more broadly. Then the term refers to a *political community*, that is to a society which is regulated by a state in the former, more narrow sense. Being a citizen, in other words, does not mean being a member of the institutional framework of rule (the parliament, the cabinet, the civil service, the police, etc.), but being a member of a community that is ruled by such a central framework. On the basis of this analysis, the characteristic aim of civic education can be typified as the good citizen. Civic education is that part of moral education in which the child is stimulated to grow into a well-functioning member of the state, in the broader sense of the word. This is roughly the meaning of 'for the state'.[1]

Every political community is constituted by certain core principles. Constitutive of a liberal-democratic state is the first and most important principle of justice, as articulated and defended by John Rawls. This principle, the so-called principle of greatest equal liberty, is summarized by Rawls in the following way: 'Each person has an equal claim to a fully adequate scheme of equal basic rights and liberties, which scheme is compatible with the same scheme for all' (1993: 5). The main tenor of this principle is to protect the freedom of all citizens as much as possible by assigning every adult member of society an optimal package of the same basic rights. The central components of this package are the well-known civic liberties (like freedom of thought and liberty of conscience), the political-democratic rights (like the right to vote and the right to run for public office), and also the fundamental rights that are covered by the so-called 'rule of law' (like the right of legal due process or the right to impartial treatment in court).

We regard the implementation of this package of basic individual rights and liberties as a *necessary* condition for calling a political community a liberal-democratic state. Consequently, a state that is organized in accordance with a typical classical liberal view, cannot be labelled a liberal democracy. In classical liberalism each member of the political community is accorded the same civic liberties. In this respect, there is no difference with Rawls' first principle of justice. However, representatives of classical liberalism claim that central political rights should be reserved for citizens with a certain economic status only, for example to landowners (Locke) or to persons who are self-supporting (Kant). This is the main difference from Rawls' principle of greatest equal liberty, according to which each citizen has the same political rights. To put it more broadly, contrary to what is characteristic of a liberal-democratic state, classical liberalism involves no commitment to the modern ideal of

representative democracy on the basis of direct and general elections.

Moreover, we also regard the implementation of the basic rights that are covered by the principle of greatest equal liberty as a *sufficient* condition for calling a state a liberal democracy. That implies that a liberal-democratic community is not necessarily a so-called welfare state. In such a state citizens do not only have typical active rights, in particular the civic and political ones, they also are accorded certain passive rights, especially welfare or social rights, like the right to medical care, the right to a minimum income or the right to work. These rights are not implied by the principle of greatest equal liberty, and though one could argue that introducing welfare rights contributes significantly to the broad-scale use of political rights and civic liberties, our definition of 'liberal democracy' does not refer to them.

The last term of our central question that needs some explanation is 'multi-cultural'. Most countries in the Western world are not only liberal democracies, they are multi-cultural states as well. They are political communities that accommodate different *cultural* communities. Will Kymlicka (1989: 166–9) makes an important distinction between two meanings of the word 'culture', which we could call the substantial and the structural meaning. If the word is used in the former sense, the distinctive features of a cultural community consist in its current norms, values, beliefs, and their attendant institutions. According to this substantial meaning, a cultural community would cease to exist if its norms or beliefs were to change significantly. If the word is used with the latter meaning, however, the identity of a cultural community is not located in its current normative views, but in its shared heritage, including its common language, history, collective experiences and narratives. Then, of course, changes in values and convictions would not amount to a loss of one's culture.

Following Kymlicka, we opt in favour of this structural meaning. From now on we will use the word 'cultural community' to denote a viable group of individuals with a shared heritage.[2] The problem is, however, that if we speak about a multi-cultural society, we normally have in mind cultural communities of a particular kind. For example, if we think of The Netherlands as a multi-cultural state, we do not have in mind an autochthonous community in a labour class district, nor the gay scene in Amsterdam or the Roman Catholic community in the southern provinces. Kymlicka (1995: 10–25) rightly points out that we normally use the term 'multi-cultural' to indicate that a state contains different ethnic groups and/or national minorities. Ethnic groups are cultural communities that are usually the result of individual and familial immigration. If cultural diversity within a state arises from immigration, one may speak of a multi-ethnic state. National minorities are mostly territorially concentrated and potentially self-governing cultural communities that are incorporated in an encompassing state. If cultural diversity is the result of colonization, conquest, or confederation of previously self-governing communities, the society may be called a multi-national state. Because there are no national minorities, The Netherlands cannot be regarded as a multi-cultural society in the sense of a multi-national state. There are, however, a lot of different ethnic groups, of which the biggest are the Surinam, Moroccan, Turkish and Moluccan communities. Because of this diversity, The Netherlands is clearly a multi-cultural society in the sense of a multi-ethnic state.

After having clarified the meaning of the constituent terms, we are better able to explain the tenor of our central question. The aim of civic education is the good citizen, that is, a member of a political community who performs his or her role well. Most Western societies are multi-cultural, liberal-democratic states, which means they are political communities that accommodate different ethnic groups or national minorities and are organized according to Rawls' principle of greatest equal liberty. Our question is: what should be the aims of civic education in such a society?

3 The moral virtues of the liberal citizen

There is an instrumental relationship between the good citizen and a flourishing political community. Every political community needs citizens with characteristics that are functional for its preservation and vitality. Such citizens are called 'good' and their characteristics are regarded as virtues, at least by advocates of the society concerned. The viability of a liberal democracy and its institutions, too, is dependent on citizens with certain qualities. Without citizens with sustaining attitudes, a liberal democratic polity cannot function properly and might perhaps even disintegrate. Such citizens are

normally called 'liberal' and their qualities are considered liberal virtues. These are the aims of civic education that we are looking for.

With reference to our definition of a liberal democracy, we can argue that the typical virtues of the liberal citizen are precisely those that correspond with the principle of greatest equal liberty. Because this principle is a principle of justice, the cardinal corresponding virtue could be labelled, as Rawls does, 'a sense of justice'. In fact this virtue incorporates all other moral virtues that are constitutive of liberal citizenship. Important examples of these other corresponding traits are tolerance towards different ways of life, the disposition to respect the equal rights of fellow citizens, a deeply rooted aversion towards discrimination, an intrinsic commitment to the rule of law, as well as democratic attitudes like the willingness to compromise, to vote, to accept majority decisions and to justify political claims in terms of public reasons. All these traits are instrumental to or functional for a flourishing political community that is organized according to the principle of greatest equal liberty. For the bearer of the corresponding virtues is by definition willing and able to support and uphold the liberal-democratic institutions.

Though the traits at issue are clear examples of moral virtues, Rawls normally designates them as *political*. His reason for doing this is to make clear that he is not talking about the virtuous person as such but only about the virtuous person in his role as a citizen (cf. Rawls 1993: 194–5). To put it differently, liberal virtues should not be regarded as *general*, that is, as traits of the good human being, but have to be conceived as *specific*, that is, as traits connected with a certain role or position, in this case with our political role as citizens. Moreover, the listed virtues are not characteristic of the good citizen as such, but, even more specifically, only of the good *liberal* citizen. Some authors make a distinction between virtues needed to sustain all political communities and those required by a liberal-democratic community (cf. Galston 1991: 221 ff.). Traits like soldier's courage, law-abidingness and loyalty to the core principles of one's society are regarded as examples of the former group. However important the sustaining function of these virtues may be, including for the sustenance of a liberal-democratic polity, we will confine ourselves to the virtues of the latter group: the distinguishing characteristics of the liberal citizen (cf. Spiecker and Steutel 1995: 390–1).[3]

We now have a first answer to our central question: the aims of civic education in a liberal democracy include the moral virtues of the liberal citizen. If we want our children to grow into citizens who perform their role well in a liberal-democratic political community, we should at least cultivate the moral virtues that correspond with the principle of greatest equal liberty. Some authors, however, would protest against this view. For example, in a recent paper Yael Tamir (1995) has defended a kind of liberalism that clearly is incompatible with our conception of civic education in a multi-cultural democracy. In her paper she makes an important and illuminating distinction between two kinds of multi-culturalism. The first one, which she calls *thin* multi-culturalism, is typical of political communities that accommodate different but liberal cultural communities. As an example of such a state she refers to Canada. It is true that the English- and French-speaking communities in this country are different in many respects. Nevertheless, they both are liberal communities in the sense that they share liberal beliefs and values. According to Tamir, such a liberal unity in cultural diversity makes 'a unified stratum of civic education' (p. 166) both possible and necessary. And the way she conceives of this 'thin layer of civic education' (p. 165) is more or less identical with our conception.

However, there are also political communities that are multi-cultural in a second sense, which she calls *thick* multi-culturalism. Such states encompass both liberal and illiberal cultural communities. Most political communities in the Western world are thick multi-cultural societies. For example, in The Netherlands the political and cultural scene is dominated by communities that endorse basic liberal principles. Nevertheless, there are also quite vital religious communities which are opposed and even hostile to liberal values and democratic institutions, in particular fundamentalist Calvinistic and Muslim groups. According to Tamir, the right liberal attitude towards such groups is to *respect* them, which implies that no action is taken to assimilate these minority cultures. On the contrary, respecting them involves that efforts are made to retain their ways of life (pp. 168, 169). It is obvious that judged from this liberal attitude our view on civic education in a multi-cultural democracy will be condemned. As stated before, civic education is education *by* the state. Consequently, claiming that liberal virtues are central aims of civic education implies that the state is given the right and responsibility to take the lead in shaping young people accordingly, including, and perhaps even in particular, the younger members of illiberal communities. From the perspective taken by Tamir, assigning the state the authority to promote the assimilation of illiberal cultures by these educational means should be dismissed as a form of *dis*respect.

One may wonder how it is possible that both Tamir and the present writers are champions of a liberal democracy and yet think so differently about civic education in a thick multi-cultural society. According to Tamir, decent illiberal communities should, as a matter of liberal principle, be tolerated, respected and protected. Consequently, the state is not allowed to pursue a policy of opposing their anti-liberal ideologies and attendant institutions. In accommodating illiberal communities, says Tamir, a liberal state should compromise, for principled reasons, its own principles (p. 170). We, on the other hand, think that such a state has the right to actively impose liberal beliefs on illiberal communities, in particular by creating optimal conditions for fostering liberal virtues in all its citizens. With regard to illiberal communities, we would say, the liberal state should in principle *not* compromise its own principles.

In our view, Tamir's claim that the right liberal attitude is one of principled respect towards illiberal communities is based on a defective line of reasoning. Central in her argument is the distinction between autonomy-based and rights-based liberalism (pp. 167–8). The former kind of liberalism, she argues, takes personal autonomy to be paramount. Hence it judges illiberal cultures to be inferior to liberal ones. The basic value of rights-based liberalism, however, is not personal autonomy but equal concern and respect for persons. Therefore, says Tamir, rights-based liberalism can express respect for illiberal communities. It is this latter form of liberalism that she wants to defend.

Just like Tamir, we have a preference for rights-based liberalism. Indeed, in the next section we will argue that personal autonomy should not be regarded as an aim of civic education in a liberal democracy. Also in accordance with Tamir, we think that autonomy-based liberalism is opposed to cultures that rights-based liberalism can tolerate and respect, namely cultures that disavow the ideal of personal autonomy. But from this it cannot be inferred that rights-based liberalism can also be respectful to communities which reject the very rights it stands for. Tamir makes, without doubt, a fine distinction between two kinds of liberalism. But strangely enough she confuses the corresponding forms of illiberalism. As a matter of principle, rights-based liberalism can and should respect cultures that are illiberal from the perspective of autonomy-based liberalism, that means, communities which oppose personal autonomy. This, however, does not in any sense imply that rights-based liberalism can or should be respectful to cultures that are illiberal *from its own point of view*, that means, communities which oppose the rights that are covered by the principle of greatest equal liberty. And it is *this* form of illiberalism that we are talking about.

Apart from Tamir's reasons for claiming that liberalism involves an attitude of respect towards illiberal communities, we have serious difficulties with accepting the claim itself. For endorsing this claim boils down to depriving the state of important possibilities of sustaining and preserving the liberal-democratic order of the political community. Most illiberal communities are eager to transmit and spread their beliefs, in particular by founding their own schools, setting up their own political parties, and funding newspapers and networks that are favourable towards their views. Accepting Tamir's claim would mean that the liberal state is not allowed to curb or counteract such tendencies. On the contrary, the state would be obliged to protect and support them. But is it not odd to demand of the liberal state to sustain activities that affect its own foundation?

One could object to our view by arguing that most illiberal communities in liberal democracies are relatively small and powerless. Why, then, try to assimilate them? Would tolerating such harmless minorities not be a better policy? Our answer to this objection is twofold. First, contrary to Tamir, we are claiming that the state, from the perspective of rights-based liberalism, has the right to undermine the viability of illiberal communities. Whether a liberal state should exercise that right by actively opposing such groups is a matter of strategy. Under certain circumstances, and on the basis of practical considerations, the state could decide to tolerate and even to sustain illiberal communities. Our principal point is that such forms of state tolerance should always be instrumental and never be principled. Second, there is an important reason for a liberal state to be constantly on the alert for illiberal communities. As Tamir rightly observes, such communities will accept liberal-democratic institutions not as a matter of principle, but only out of self-interest. It is exactly this instrumental or extrinsic motivation that makes illiberal communities unreliable and potentially dangerous factors in a liberal democracy, for if they were powerful enough, they would demolish the liberal order and impose their own values on the whole of society. In order to prevent such eventualities, the state should have the right to take corrective measures. One of these measures is to create favourable conditions for civic education in which those motivations of self-interest are transformed into intrinsic commitments to the principle of greatest equal liberty.

4 The intellectual virtues of the liberal citizen

Moral virtues like justice, tolerance and respect are not the only qualities of the liberal citizen. Also typical of such a person are traits of character which are often called *intellectual* virtues. Examples of these virtues are open-mindedness, respect for evidence, intellectual honesty, tolerance towards rival views, intellectual fairness, a concern for accuracy in observation and inference, clarity, thoroughness and intellectual modesty. A main characteristic of intellectual virtues is that they are composed of so-called rational passions. Such passions can be conceived as wants and aversions that constitute, as R. S. Peters once wrote, 'the passionate side of the life of reason' (1981: 68). For example, someone who is open-minded will have a deep aversion to prejudice, a repugnance towards ignoring relevant evidence and the want to seriously assess the force of counter-arguments. A person who is intellectually honest will be averse to covering up private doubts about one's views, will have a desire to admit frankly his or her own errors in reasoning, as well as a contempt for smuggling away unwelcome evidence. The bearer of the intellectual virtue of clarity is characterized by a heart-felt aversion towards woolly or obscure language and the want to express his thoughts as clear as possible. Cultivating these passions and stimulating intellectual virtuousness amount to the same thing.[4]

In the preceding section we argued that the virtue of justice is the cardinal one, in relation to the other moral virtues of the liberal citizen. The group of intellectual virtues is also based on and unified by a cardinal virtue, in this case the virtue of concern and respect for truth. If we claim that traits like open-mindedness, precision and a willingness to participate in rational discussions are intellectual virtues, we indicate that these qualities can be derived from, or are specifications of, the virtue of concern and respect for truth. The principal characteristic of this cardinal intellectual virtue is the intrinsic willingness to investigate as thoroughly as possible whether non-trivial beliefs are true or well-justified. If we consider a trait of character an intellectual virtue, we assume that practising such a trait will increase the chance of properly forming and assessing such beliefs. Indeed, intellectual virtues are precisely those qualities which put us in the best position for generating beliefs that are true or at least based on good reasons (cf. Steutel and Spiecker 1997).

But why should we regard these virtues as qualities of the good liberal citizen? Why does a citizen need intellectual virtues in order to perform his role well in a liberal democracy? The answer to these questions is that the cultivation of these virtues, just like the cultivation of the moral virtues that are constitutive of liberal citizenship, is necessary for a healthy and stable liberal democracy. Intellectual virtues are constitutive of being a critical thinker (cf. Siegel 1997: 55–71). And it is often rightly pointed out that a properly functioning democracy needs citizens who are critical in at least two related ways (cf. Galston 1991: 224–7, Kymlicka and Norman 1994: 365–6). First, they must have a questioning attitude towards political authority. Covered by the principle of greatest equal liberty is the political right of citizens to elect representatives who govern in their name. Realizing this ideal of representative democracy requires citizens who are willing and able to assess critically the performance of officials. Second, democratic citizens have the mental equipment to participate critically in public discourse. It is an essential characteristic of a liberal democracy that decisions of the government are made publicly, through free and open debate. Without citizens who are prepared and capable of participating in such critical debates on political matters, the democratic ideal of public discourse would be nothing but an idle idea. It goes without saying that these two related forms of being critical imply a whole range of intellectual virtues. To put it more strongly, showing one's critical capabilities in assessing both officials and public debates, is *ipso facto* showing one's intellectual virtuousness. Consequently, if these ways of being critical are neces-

sary for a vital and flourishing liberal democracy, the same must be true of intellectual virtues.

It is important to notice, however, that these intellectual virtues should not be regarded as general but as specific traits. Just like the moral virtues discussed in the preceding section, they are connected to the role of citizen. Because this role is a political one, the scope of the intellectual virtues at issue is limited to the political sphere. Of the citizen *qua* citizen we only expect that intellectual virtuousness is demonstrated with regard to political policy and legislation, or, more particularly, with respect to the decisions of officials and in the public debate concerning the arrangement of the political community. To put it differently, intellectual virtues as general traits are characteristic of the critical human being, whereas the intellectual virtues we are talking about are specific traits that are characteristic of the critical citizen. Furthermore, and again just like the moral virtues discussed above, the intellectual virtues referred to are not typical of the good citizen as such, but only of the good *liberal* citizen. Traits like open-mindedness, tolerance towards rival views and respect for evidence are regarded as virtues because they are functional for a flourishing liberal democracy. From the perspective of an anti-liberal political community, for example a dictatorship or a theocracy, such critical qualities would be considered dysfunctional and therefore be regarded as vices, or at least not as traits of the good citizen.

The central question of this chapter is: what should the aims of civic education in a liberal-democratic political community be? Our first answer was that these aims encompass the moral virtues of the liberal citizen. Now we can add that the intellectual virtues of the liberal citizen are also part of these aims. Preparing our children for their later role as citizens in a liberal democracy implies cultivating intellectual virtues with regard to the political sphere. The political philosopher Amy Gutmann, however, would not be satisfied with this second answer to our central question. In several publications (Gutmann 1987: 19–47, 1989, 1993) she argues that democratic education should not only foster critical thinking concerning political policy and legislation, but should also encourage rational deliberation about non-political matters, in particular about the arrangement of our personal lives. According to her, the virtues of democratic character include the willingness and ability to think critically about both one's society and one's life. This view of the aims of civic education goes far beyond the view we defend. Gutmann does not limit the field of application of the intellectual virtues to the political sphere, as we do, but extended to the private domain. The qualities of the critical thinker are not merely interpreted as specific virtues that are typical of the good citizen, but also conceived as general traits that characterize the good human being.[5]

The implications of Gutmann's view on intellectual virtues are far-reaching. Actually she is advocating a theory of civic education that is based on a determinate conception of the good life or on an ideal of human perfection. It is true that she repeatedly points out that democratic education should not initiate the child into a particular way of life but instead should provide the child the necessary equipment for choosing rationally between competing ways of life. Recommending this as an aim of civic education, however, clearly implies a plea for a certain way of life, namely, a self-governed life on the basis of critical self-reflection. True to the tradition of Kant and Mill, the good life is taken to be the *examined* life, or at least the examined life is regarded as having more value than the unexamined life (Gutmann 1989: 79). Moreover, by claiming that the self-reflexive life is an aim of civic education, the state is given the right and responsibility to take the lead in educating children accordingly. Consequently, the state is allowed to counteract forms of education that hamper the growth of critical thinking about the ideals of life. Think, for example, of forms of religious upbringing which instruct the child not to arrange its life according to its own reason (autonomy) but to obey the commanding will of an external Lawgiver (theonomy). Such religious communities, Gutmann argues, 'must be prevented from using education to stifle rational deliberation of competing conceptions of the good' (1993: 4).

What to think of this view of civic education? Is critical deliberation about ways of living or conceptions of the worthwhile life a central aim of civic education in a liberal democracy, as Gutmann maintains? In our view, the answer to this question must be in the negative. We argued that certain virtues have to be regarded as aims of civic education because their cultivation is required for a properly operating liberal-democratic polity. Gutmann, too, argues in terms of such an instrumental or functional relationship. We do not believe, however, that she succeeds in demonstrating that a flourish-ing democracy needs widespread cultivation of critical thinking on conceptions of the good life. In her view, the core value of democracy is *conscious social reproduction*. Implementing this value means roughly that every citizen is assigned the same right to participate in the collective process of deliberately shaping the future structure of society. Conscious social reproduction, Gutmann argues, is not only a political ideal, it is at the same time the primary ideal of democratic education. Civic education in a liberal democracy should cultivate precisely those qualities that are necessary for taking part in collective deliberations concerning the arrangement of society. According to her, these qualities involve the willingness and capacity for rational reflection, not only regarding the good society, but also with respect to the good life.

But is cultivating critical thinking on ideals of life and human perfection really necessary for conscious social reproduction? The subject of deliberation in conscious social reproduction is the structure of our *political* life, not the arrangement of our *personal* life. Why, then, regard critical reflection on personal ideals as an aim of liberal-democratic education?[6]

In fact the principle of greatest equal liberty gives us good reason for making a distinction between being a good citizen and leading a good life. Rawls' first principle incorporates civic liberties like freedom of thought and liberty of conscience, which give each citizen the right to lead his or her life from the inside, according to his or her own values and ideals. Though fundamental, this right is not absolute, that is to say, good reasons can be given for overriding it. Indeed, we ourselves defend this position when we argue that the state is allowed actively to oppose conceptions of the good that are clearly in conflict with the principle of greatest liberty, like fundamentalist or racist ideologies. However, these overriding reasons are only *negative*, that is, they only indicate which ways of life may be thwarted or, if necessary, forbidden by the state. They are never *positive*; they are not referring to determinate conceptions of the good that may be promoted or even enforced by the state. To put it differently, the right to live one's life from the inside must be protected by the state against conceptions of the good that threaten this fundamental liberty. The state itself would endanger the right to arrange one's life according to one's own views if it were to impose a particular conception of the good on its citizens.[7] But isn't this exactly what Gutmann is arguing for? A certain conception of the good – the examined life – is regarded as an aim of civic education, which gives the state the right to impress a certain way of life on its citizens. Assigning such a right to the state does not protect but jeopardizes basic freedoms that are implied by the principle of greatest equal liberty. Consequently, if we want to prevent this danger, we should not define the good liberal citizen in terms of a particular conception of the good life.

5 A summary and an objection

The combination of a multi-cultural society and liberal democracy is not at all necessary. There are many countries that incorporate large cultural minorities while their political structure is plainly dictatorial or theocratic. History shows that political communities can also be liberal-democratic without being multi-cultural. Such countries, however, are rare nowadays, mainly because of the reunification of families of former immigrant workers and the considerable influx of political refugees. In particular in the present Western world, the combination of multi-cultural societies and liberal democracy is standard.

Against this political-geographic background we raised the central question of our chapter: what should be the aims of civic education in a multi-cultural democracy? In our answer we made a distinction between two kinds of aims, namely, inculcating typical liberal moral virtues like tolerance, respect and a democratic attitude on the one hand, and encouraging so-called intellectual virtues, which are constitutive of being a critical thinker, on the other. However, insofar as these virtues figure as aims of civic education, they should be regarded as political. They are exclusively connected with our political role as citizens and, consequently, their range of application is limited to the political sphere. Both kinds of aims were selected and justified by claiming a relationship of functional necessity between the pursuit of these aims and a flourishing liberal democracy. Typical of a liberal-democratic society is that its basic structure is arranged according to Rawls' first principle of justice, the principle of greatest equal liberty. Our claim is that such a society would wither and perish, or at least not function properly, if the indicated virtues were not to be cultivated in civic education.

However, the very combination of liberal dem-ocracy and multi-cultural societies can be a reason for an important objection to our view. Previously, we only introduced 'multi-cultural' as a descriptive characteristic of political communities. But, as with the essentials of a liberal democracy, central elements of a multi-cultural society are also often presented as a *value* or an *ideal*, normally going by the name of 'multi-culturalism'. This ideal is often defined in such a way that the pursuit of it, in particular by means of multi-cultural education, can come into conflict with pursuing the ideal of a liberal democracy. Especially in relation to cultural communities that reject or are even hostile to liberal values and democratic institutions, like communities with sexist, racist or totalistic belief systems, such a conflict can become salient. We have argued that from a liberal-democratic perspective the state has the right to *assimilate* such illiberal communities, in particular by creating optimal conditions for the development of liberal virtues in all its citizens. Multi-culturalism, however, is often conceived as involving an attitude of respect towards all cultures other than one's own, including illiberal ones, as well as a disposition towards valuing and taking delight in cultural diversity itself, even if illiberal communities are part of it. From this perspective the state has a duty to accommodate illiberal communities by publicly affirming and recognizing their cultural identity. So, the objection goes, highlighting the ideal of a liberal democracy and the importance of liberal-democratic education is partisan and clearly at the expense of the ideal of multi-culturalism and multi-cultural education.

In this context, our rebuttal of this complex objection can only be brief. We do not deny that one can define multi-cultural education in such a way that conflicts with liberal-democratic education are inevitable. However, creating such an opposition, though not uncommon, is misleading and confusing (cf. Macedo 1995a, 1995b). Certainly, enforcing the principle of greatest equal liberty will be inconsistent with respecting and valuing cultural communities with anti-liberal ideologies. But it would be a serious mistake to deduce from this that pursuing and implementing liberal-democratic values can be a threat to a multi-cultural society. On the contrary, the best guarantee of cultural diversity is to arrange the political community according to civic liberties and democratic rights. If we want to sustain a flourishing multi-cultural society, we should not stimulate an indiscriminate acceptance of diversity and plurality, but cultivate the liberal virtues. Indeed, multi-cultural education, properly understood, is an integral part of liberal-democratic education.

Notes

1 One could also postulate a conceptual relationship between civic education and the government. Then, however, it is important to make a distinction between two senses of 'government'. Sometimes this word is used to refer to the central institutional framework of rule. In these cases, the meaning of 'government' is the same as the narrow sense of the word 'state'. In other uses, however, the word 'government' refers to a certain aspect of the institutional framework of rule, namely, the administration or the ministry. It is clear that civic education is conceptually related only to 'government' in the former sense. Moreover, given this meaning of the term, civic education can only be typified as education *by* the government.

2 However, the fact that a group of individuals has a shared heritage is not sufficient for calling such a group a cultural community in the structural sense of the word. As Kymlicka (1989: 179) rightly points out, a complete definition of 'cultural community' will not only refer to objective components (common history, shared language, and so on), but also to subjective factors (self-identification with the group, feelings of affiliation between the group members, vicarious shame, and so on).

3 In her essay on civic virtues, White (1996) discusses general virtues (hope, self-respect, decency, and so on) and their 'particular form in a democratic society' (*democratic* hope, *democratic* self-respect, *democratic* decency, and so on). Just like the moral virtues we described, these democratic specifications of general virtues are not characteristic of the good citizen as such, but only typical of the good liberal citizen. However, in relation to the democratic virtues White discusses, our group of liberal virtues is more fundamental; the value of traits like democratic hope and democratic decency is dependent on the value of traits like justice and respect.

4 According to the motivation theory of Brandt (1970, 1988), virtues and vices can be construed as specific kinds of wants and/or aversions (or as the absence of such wants and/or aversions). The wants/aversions that are identical with virtues and vices, Brandt argues, are intrinsic by nature, relatively permanent and stable, and come up to a minimum level of intensity. Though we do not think that all virtues can be (fully) construed according to Brandt's motivation theory, we do believe that wants and aversions of the indicated type are central components of the moral and intellectual virtues of the liberal citizen.

5 By limiting the scope of the virtues of critical thinking to the political domain, our view of the aims of civic education is also materially different from the 'standard' view of liberal education, as developed and defended by Peters and Hirst. According to the 'standard' view, the central aim of liberal education is personal autonomy, which is partly explained in terms of critical or rational deliberation (cf. Hirst and Peters 1970: 52–5). As far as liberal *moral* education is concerned, the autonomous person is conceived as someone who is willing and able to reflect critically on moral traditions and conceptions of the good life (cf. Peters 1981: 120–2, 152–5). In other words, according to both Gutmann and the 'standard' view of liberal education, teaching the child to tackle the question of how one should live critically and reflectively is regarded as a central educational aim.

6 One could object to our view that the distinction between critical thinking on political matters (the arrangement of society) and critical thinking on personal matters (the arrangement of our lives) is artificial. In actual practice, promoting critical deliberation on public policy will almost certainly have the effect of fostering critical thinking in general, including with respect to the intrinsic value of views on the good life (cf. Gutmann 1995: 563, 573–6). However, referring to this 'spill over' effect cannot be an objection to our view. According to modern liberalism, it is important to make a distinction between neutrality of *aim* and *outcome* neutrality. State policies should not aim to promote any controversial way of life or conception of the good over any other. Therefore, the examined life, as an ideal of human perfection, cannot be an aim of civic education. It is not required, however, that state policies should induce outcomes that are neutral with respect to controversial ideals of life. Consequently, civic education may have positive effects on the growth of critical thinking in general.

7 In addition to the requirement of neutrality of aim, modern liberalism also advocates the principle of *procedural* neutrality. In our view, this principle deserves support only if it means that the state should not justify its main policies (including the central aims of civic education) in terms of controversial conceptions of the good life or ideals of human perfection. Often, however, the principle of procedural neutrality is explained in a much more demanding way. According to this interpretation, the state should justify its main policies in terms of grounds or values that are acceptable to every reasonable citizen. As we have argued elsewhere (Steutel and Spiecker 1999), this interpretation makes the principle impracticable, for even a central aspect of liberal state policy, the enforcement of political liberal principles, cannot be justified as the principle dictates.

References

Brandt, R. B. (1970) Traits of character: a conceptual analysis. *American Philosophical Quarterly*, 7: 23–37.

Brandt, R. B. (1988) The structure of virtue. In P. A.

French, T. E. Uehling and H. K. Wettstein (eds) *Midwest Studies in Philosophy. Vol. XIII. Ethical Theory: Character and Virtue.* Notre Dame: University of Notre Dame Press.

Galston, W. A. (1991) *Liberal Purposes. Goods, Virtues, and Diversity in the Liberal State.* Cambridge: Cambridge University Press.

Gutmann, A. (1987) *Democratic Education.* Princeton: Princeton University Press.

Gutmann, A. (1989) Undemocratic education. In N. L. Rosenblum (ed.) *Liberalism and the Moral Life,* Cambridge, Mass.: Harvard University Press.

Gutmann, A. (1993) Democracy and democratic education. *Studies in Philosophy and Education,* **12**: 1–9.

Gutmann, A. (1995) Civic education and social diversity, *Ethics,* **105**: 557–79.

Hirst, P. H. and Peters, R. S. (1970) *The Logic of Education.* London: Routledge and Kegan Paul.

Kymlicka, W. (1989) *Liberalism, Community and Culture.* Oxford: Clarendon Press.

Kymlicka, W. (1995) *Multicultural Citizenship. A Liberal Theory of Minority Rights.* Oxford: Clarendon Press.

Kymlicka, W. and Norman, W. (1994) Return of the citizen: a survey of recent work on citizenship theory. *Ethics,* **104**: 352–81.

Macedo, S. (1995a) Liberal civic education and religious fundamentalism: The case of God v. John Rawls? *Ethics,* **105**: 468–96.

Macedo, S. (1995b) Multiculturalism for the religious right? Defending liberal civic education. *Journal of Philosophy of Education,* **29**: 223–38.

Peters, R. S. (1981) *Moral Development and Moral Education.* London: Allen and Unwin.

Rawls, J. (1993) *Political Liberalism.* New York: Columbia University Press.

Siegel, H. (1997) *Rationality Redeemed? Further Dialogues on an Educational Ideal.* New York/London: Routledge.

Spiecker, B. and Steutel, J. (1995) Political liberalism, civic education and the Dutch government. *Journal of Moral Education,* **24**: 383–94.

Steutel, J. and Spiecker, B. (1997) Rational passions and intellectual virtues. A conceptual analysis. *Studies in Philosophy and Education,* **16**: 59–71.

Steutel, J. and Spiecker, B. (1999) Family education, state intervention, and political liberalism. *Journal of Philosophy of Education,* **33**(3): 369–84.

Tamir, Y. (1995) Two concepts of multiculturalism. *Journal of Philosophy of Education,* **29**: 161–72.

White, P. (1996) *Civic Virtues and Public Schooling. Educating Citizens for a Democratic Society.* New York/London: Teachers College Press.

Index